MOVING BEYOND BORDERS
A History of Black Canadian and Caribbean Women in the Diaspora

Moving beyond Borders is the first book-length history of Black health care workers in Canada, delving into the experiences of thirty-five postwar-era nurses who were born in Canada or who immigrated from the Caribbean either through Britain or directly to Canada. Karen Flynn examines the shaping of these women's stories from their childhoods through to their roles as professionals and community activists.

Flynn interweaves oral histories with archival sources to show how these women's lives were shaped by their experiences of migration, professional training, and family life. Theoretical analyses from postcolonial, gender, and diasporic Black Studies serve to highlight the multiple subjectivities operating within these women's lives. By presenting a collective biography of identity formation, *Moving beyond Borders* reveals the extraordinary complexity of Black women's history.

(Studies in Gender and History)

KAREN FLYNN is an assistant professor in the Department of Gender and Women's Studies and the Department of African American Studies at the University of Illinois.

STUDIES IN GENDER AND HISTORY

General Editors: Franca Iacovetta and Karen Dubinsky

KAREN FLYNN

To: Agnes
Dr. Karen

Thanks so much!
I cannot say enough
about how awesome
you are!
xoxo

MOVING BEYOND BORDERS:

A History of Black Canadian and
Caribbean Women in the Diaspora

UNIVERSITY OF TORONTO PRESS
Toronto Buffalo London

© University of Toronto Press 2011
Toronto Buffalo London
www.utppublishing.com
Printed in Canada

ISBN 978-1-4426-4021-4 (cloth)
ISBN 978-1-4426-0995-2 (paper)

Printed on acid-free, 100% post-consumer recycled paper with vegetable-based inks.

Library and Archives Canada Cataloguing in Publication

Flynn, Karen C. (Karen Carole), 1968–
Moving beyond borders : a history of Black Canadian and Caribbean
women in the diaspora / Karen Flynn.

(Studies in gender and history series)
Includes bibliographical references and index.
ISBN 978-1-4426-4021-4 (bound).   ISBN 978-1-4426-0995-2 (pbk.)

1. Black Canadian women – Social conditions.   2. Caribbean Canadian
women – Social conditions.   3. Black Canadian women – History.
4. Caribbean Canadian women – History.   I. Title.   II. Series: Studies in
gender and history

FC106.B6F59 2011   305.48'896071   C2011-903040-3

University of Toronto Press acknowledges the financial assistance to its
publishing program of the Canada Council for the Arts and the Ontario Arts
Council.

University of Toronto Press acknowledges the financial support of the
Government of Canada through the Canada Book Fund for its publishing
activities.

 Canada Council   Conseil des Arts
for the Arts   du Canada

 ONTARIO ARTS COUNCIL
CONSEIL DES ARTS DE L'ONTARIO

This book has been published with the help of a grant from the Canadian
Federation for the Humanities and Social Sciences, through the Aid to
Scholarly Publications Program, using funds provided by the Social Sciences
and Humanities Research Council of Canada.

This book is dedicated to

My partner Will Mitchell and my son Marshal James Flynn-Mitchell; you both have brought such joy to my life

Viviene Dickson for being a supportive mom!

To the best siblings anyone could ask for: Chris (Donovan); Kirk (Marlon) Simone, Shawna Flynn, George Mitchell, and Dwayne Reynolds

My nieces Amanda Reynolds and Shaya Flynn-Thompson and nephew Jesse Flynn – wishing for you both a better tomorrow

Marjorie and Larry Gibson for embodying the principles of inclusivity

Kathryn McPherson for seeing the best in me

Contents

Acknowledgments

When I began this project a decade ago, I dreamed of this moment, but had a difficult time believing it would actually come to fruition. I could not have completed this project without the support of many people and institutions who, across geographical spaces, provided intellectual, spiritual, and emotional support. I first want to thank the Creator who sustains me daily and who has blessed me beyond my wildest dreams.

My 'first' friends who dared to dream with me and whose friendship and love I couldn't imagine living without: Debbie Miles-Senior, Andrea Peart-Williams, Jackie Porter, Jo-Ann Gibson, Phillip Cole, Delia Grenville, Silvano Figaro, Marlon Paul, and Duane Griffith. Along the journey, I met some of the most wonderful and supportive friends anyone could ask for: Geena Lee, Nevilla Stapleton-Street, Audrey Taylor, Erica Lawson, Pramila Javahari, Alijcia Gibson, Suzzette Rhoden, Monique James-Duncan, Dalia McKenzie, Neil Armstrong, Cindy Lou Henwood, Tameron Rogers-Cambridge, Janet Haughton-Quarshie, Ronell Matthews, Ann Phillips, Tanash Lawence-Reid, Nicoline Ambe, Avonie Brown-Reaves, Hess Auguste, Sharon McLeod, Flora Calderon-Steck, Toni McRae, Michael Banfield, and Andrew Smith.

My multi-purpose friends are not only brilliant in their own way, they understand the intricacies and demands of academic life. Your encouragement and unerring support means a lot. My thanks to the Canadian expatriates Dwaine Plaza, Terry-Ann Jones, Charmaine Crawford, and Amoaba Gooden. I am grateful for the friends I met at St Cloud State and the University of Illinois, Urbana-Champaign: Jessica Millward, Pamela Salela, Leslie Reagan, Ruth Nicole Brown, Christina Denilco, Brendesha Tynes, Erik McDuffie, Menah Pratt Clarke, Edna Viruell-Fuentes, Assata Zerai, Lisette Piedra, and Chamara Kwayke, who helped care for Marshall when I needed assistance. Also included in the multipurpose category are those who provided comments on various stages of the manuscript: Patricia D'Antonio read the entire manuscript and offered invaluable editing suggestions; Erica Lawson read multiple chapters and was instrumental in helping me refine my analysis, especially around Black women and paid work.

At the beginning stages of the book, Jayne Elliot helped to edit and organize the chapters. At the conclusion of the process, my colleagues in the Department of Gender and Women's Studies and History read individual chapters; I appreciate all their thoughtful comments. I especially want to thank: Terri Barnes, Siobhan Somerville, Sharra Vostral, Liz Pleck, Vicky Mahaffey, and Antoinette Burton; my friends Margaret Shkimba and Shannon Littleton who provided editing suggestions; Winston James who offered his expertise on the Black Diaspora in Britain and Doreen Grant-Wisdom who offered hers on growing up in the colonial Caribbean. To my colleagues in African-American Studies (especially those who are no longer at UIUC), thanks for the encouragement; I miss you all. Irene Moore Davis willingly shared information regarding Blacks in Windsor and the surrounding areas, and she also provided the names of some of the interviewees.

During the writing of this book, I've travelled back and forth to Canada to conduct archival research and have had to depend on the kindness of individuals. At critical junctures in my career, Kathryn McPherson has provided advice and support; I have, and continue to learn many valuable lessons from her. I am grateful to Ed Ratz, Pauline Taylor, and Marlah Walker (New York City) who always makes sure that I'm well fed and feel at home when I visit.

To those friends who have made living away from family more bearable, I'm grateful that biology alone does not define family: June Parrott for being so wise! Dr Tiffani Clarke Dillard, my church sista friend, and who safely delivered my most precious gift, Marshall! Carla Bloom for being consistently kind and dependable; Omege Rose and VJ for reinventing Jamaica in Springfield. It's been a pleasure having you all in my life. Denise White, your consistent encouragement and your desire to live in the moment is really appreciated. Josiah Khaleed, welcome back! Lauren Wheeler, your visits with your mother are truly appreciated. Damion Mitchell, thank you for your spiritual example.

It is difficult to survive the academy without a spiritual home, and I have been blessed with two wonderful congregations: the folks at Park Avenue SDA Church (my home church), it's been a wonderful seven years; my friends at Bible Chapel SDA Church (especially Paula Irby), who consistently kept my name on the prayer list until I completed the manuscript, your support is appreciated beyond words. To my mother-in-law Olah Robinson whose support is unwavering, and whose love I feel in the phone calls, I am truly grateful.

Stephanie Clemons was divinely placed in my life at the final stages of this project and provided a safe and nurturing environment for Marshall, I am very thankful. Pastor Omar Palmer and members of Meadowvale SDA Church supported and nurtured my father, the late Errol Flynn, during his struggle with cancer.

My parents (including the late Errol Flynn) Beverley Johnson, and Viviene Dickson have supported my efforts and the path that I have chosen. I have also been blessed with (an other mother) Hyacinth Grenville who has been unwavering in her support for me from the moment I decided to pursue a post-secondary education. I've also been fortunate to have Marjorie and Larry Gibson in my life; they acted in a parental capacity on so many levels, and words cannot express my gratitude to them. And to their daughter (my sister) Jo-Ann, thank you for being my very personal cheerleader from the moment I decided to write this book.

I wish to express my gratitude to: my brothers and sisters Simone, Shawna, Chris (Donovan), Kirk (Marlon), George, and Dwayne, I feel honoured to have such amazing and thoughtful siblings. My partner Will, for going beyond and above so that I could complete this manuscript; on a daily basis, you challenge those gender roles that suggest parenting and domestic responsibilities are primarily 'women's work.' My son Marshall, you are such an incredible joy. My nieces Amanda and Shaya and nephew Jesse, I wish for you a more equitable and just world. Even though we rarely see each other, my aunts Dawn McGregor-Johnson, Andrea Johnson, Althea Johnson, and Jacqueline Bruce, and cousin Carol Johnson have encouraged me over the years. My sisters-in-law Liz Washington and Jeannette Flynn, who I love having in my family, and Jadaya, Alicia, Tenisha, Kristie, it is my hope that you too will follow your dreams.

My childhood friends and family that I have reconnected with: Susan Palmer, Evris Shepherd, Betty Bailey, Hillary Allen, Rosemarie Ryder, and the Grove Primary School folks; Elizabeth Davis, Viola Davis-Hamilton, and Sharon Blake, I look forward to the future that lies ahead.

The librarians at the public library in Trinidad and Tobago and the archivist at the University of Windsor, thank you for your patience. Special thanks to Orchanian-Cheff, Toronto Western Hospital, and, in particular, Bob McCauley, George Brown College, and Harold Averill at the University of Toronto who always made sure that my trips to the archives were productive. Agatha Campbell and Sarah transcribed the majority of the interviews; I cannot thank you both enough.

Franca Iacovetta and Karen Dubinsky showed interest in the project from the very beginning and provided wonderful advice. To the editorial staff at the University of Toronto Press, Len Husband, you are absolutely the best editor a first author could ask for; Frances Mundy, for calming my fears at the conclusion of the process. My research assistant, Angela Glaros, for reading multiple drafts of the manuscript and remaining committed to the very end. Esther Okero, you are an angel in disguise. To all the wonderful scholars, especially Peggy Bristow and Hermi Hewitt who took time out of their busy schedules and responded to e-mail queries, thank you. I am grateful to the anonymous reviewers (especially reviewer 2) for paying such careful attention to the manuscript. I have presented aspects of this research over the years at various conferences including the Caribbean Studies Association and American Association for the History of Medicine, and at other talks. The feedback has been helpful.

It is important for me to recognize those teachers and professors who directly and indirectly influenced my career trajectory. In Jamaica, Monica Harris (Ms. Rose) my basic school teacher; Pat Bennett and Mrs Smith, my primary school teachers who made me feel as if I was the smartest girl in the world; Mrs Newell (then Richards) who was more than a history and social studies teacher at Papine Secondary School. I'm so happy we have reconnected. Mr Luft and Mrs Rosemary Evans, my history teachers at Brampton Centennial Secondary School (Canada) were there at a critical time in my life; I appreciate you both for believing that I was capable and not just another statistic. At the University of Windsor, I was fortunate to have been taught by Bruce Tucker and Christina Simmons (my MA supervisor) and at York University, Kathryn McPherson (my doctoral supervisor), and Bettina Bradbury who helped to shape the initial project. At the University of Illinois, Chris Mayo helped make my move to Gender and Women's Studies possible. My current chair, Chantal Nadeau, thank you for being amazing! And, if I forgotten anyone, please forgive me; it was not intentional.

This project would have not been completed without the financial support of the University of Illinois Research Board, and the Hewlette Foundation Travel Grant. During the doctoral stages of this project, I was fortunate to be awarded the Hannah Institute for the History of Medicine Doctoral Award and the Ramsey Cook Fellowship.

To the thirty-five women whose lives are at the centre of this book, without you this project would not have been possible; my deepest and heartfelt gratitude. Some of you may not agree with my interpretation and conclusions, but I do hope that you all recognize my sincere attempts to do justice to your lives.

Although I have been influenced by many scholars, all mistakes, omissions, and errors are mine.

MOVING BEYOND BORDERS
A History of Black Canadian and Caribbean Women in the Diaspora

Introduction: Locating and Conceptualizing Black Women's Narratives

Inez had walked with her Aunt Daisy down the corridors of Savvanna-La-Mar Hospital in the parish of Westmoreland in Jamaica ever since she could remember. At fifteen, she decided to follow in her aunt's footsteps and become a nurse. In 1955, nineteen-year-old Inez entered the nursing program at the University College Hospital of the West Indies (UCHWI),[1] where she completed the three years of training. Within months of completing it, she met Owen Mackenzie, who expressed a romantic interest in her. The two began dating, but the romance was cut short when Owen migrated to Canada to attend Toronto's Ryerson Polytechnic Institute, an educational opportunity unavailable to most of the island's inhabitants. Prior to his leaving Jamaica, the couple agreed they would correspond, and over time, according to Inez, 'we actually became serious, [writing] that we would get married.'[2] Marriage plans were placed on hold, however, as they focused on completing their studies in Jamaica and Canada.

In 1961, Inez also migrated to Canada, where she had no difficulty finding employment. In fact, Caribbean migrant nurses such as Inez proved instrumental in alleviating the post–Second World War nursing shortage in Canada. When Owen graduated in 1962, the couple married. Approximately one year later, they welcomed their first son into the family, and a second child was born in 1968, events which confirmed their desire to settle and make Ontario home. For almost fifty years Inez and Owen Mackenzie have lived in Ontario, working and raising their children, combining lessons they learned while growing up with new experiences gleaned from various sources to which they had access in Canada.

The lives of Caribbean- and Canadian-born Black professional women like Inez are the central focus of this research. Drawing on theoretical analyses culled from postcolonial, feminist, and diasporic Black studies, in conjunction with insights from labour and nursing history, I argue that Black women's[3] multiple subjectivities and identities were first forged within the context of childhood – in the family, church, and school – then shaped and reshaped by various transitions such as migration, professional training, and their roles as wives, mothers, single women, and community activists. Following Chris Weedon, I define *subjectivity* as the 'conscious and unconscious thoughts and emotions of the individual, her sense of herself and her ways of understanding her relation to the world.'[4] Identity, on the other hand, involves the internal, external, and the subjective. Always being reconstituted, identity is a socially recognized and fluid position.[5] At the heart of this book is a narrative that underscores Black women's multiple and contradictory subject positions as they have navigated the transition from childhood to adulthood. This narrative raises new and interdisciplinary questions about migration, education, work, activism, and family.

Intersectionality – the notion that race, gender, class, and sexuality operate as simultaneous and mutually constitutive forms of oppression and identity – is often the primary analytic tool used by scholars to theorize about Black women's lives. An intersectional analysis seeks to expose how power relations structure Black women's identity as racialized, classed, gendered, and sexualized beings. In this book, however, I argue that race, class, gender, and sexuality are not the only vectors that contribute to identity and subjectivity formation. From childhood to adulthood, the critical importance of other markers in forming and reforming subjectivity and identity is evident. More specifically, we see how family of origin, religion, cultural values, hard work, education, family commitments, activism, and migration have also shaped these women's identities and subjectivities.

Scholars interested in questions concerning childhood, family, migration, reproductive responsibilities, and labour force participation have often considered these elements of Black women's lives as discrete phenomena. In the Canadian context, the richest area of scholarly focus is on Black women as domestic workers. But this single focus can result in a compartmentalization of Black women's subjectivities without much consideration of these women as wholly embodied and active subjects. To avoid this shortcoming, I use a life-course paradigm in conjunction with oral interviews to compare and contrast the material subjectivities of Caribbean- and Black Canadian-born women. *Life course* 'refers to the age-graded life patterns that are embedded in social institutions and subject to historical change. These patterns are defined by *trajectories*, which extend across much of the life course, such as family and work, getting a full-time job, and marrying.'[6] Thus a life-course perspective, while attentive to social structures, allows us to see commonalities that the interviewees for this study share with women of other cultural and racial backgrounds. In tandem with an intersectional analysis, the life-course perspective allows a more nuanced and complicated portrait of Black women's lives by connecting over a lifetime common themes – such as work, family, and religion – that contribute to identity formation. In this vein, a life-course paradigm allows an exploration of themes critical to Black women's lives.

Postcolonial research into the formation of multilayered diasporic subjectivities tends to focus primarily on Black expressive culture. The implication is that texts such as literature, music, and theatre render the most complex and interesting constructions of identity formation and reformation.[7] I posit that cultural analyses alone do not adequately uncover the material lived reality of people's lives. Consequently, my research grounds the theoretical debates over Black diasporic identities in empirical investigation, particularly through the use of oral history as a methodology. I also depart from the male-centred thrust of these studies to focus on Black Canadian and Caribbean professional women who trained as nurses as a way to explore multiple identity formation.

Why nurses as opposed to another occupational group? Until the late 1940s, Black women were excluded from nurses' training in Canada. In addition, the Department of Citizenship and Immigration placed restrictions on the number of Caribbean migrant nurses allowed to enter Canada. Some hospitals in Great Britain also denied Caribbean migrant women employment and training. Hence, those interviewees who began nurses' training in the late 1940s and 1950s were pioneers. These women integrated not only nursing schools but also hospitals in Canada, Britain, and the United States. Despite the initial barriers to nursing education, nursing has remained a particularly important skilled occupation for Black women over the past four decades.[8] Indeed, the education, training, and credentials required of nurses engender questions around identity and professional status that are different from those pertaining to domestic workers. Unlike domestic workers, the experiences of Black female professionals remain an underexplored area in the Canadian literature. Although a substantial scholarly debate exists as to whether nursing and other white-collar occupations should be considered 'middle class,'[9] there is no doubt that within Black communities registered nurses (RNs) enjoyed economic stability and social respect and prestige that located them within the communities' elites. Nursing, then, serves as the entry point to explore Black women's lives in ways that complicate our knowledge of how class, race, sexuality, and gender intersect.

Spatially and geographically, Canada is critical to this study for several reasons. Canada is visibly absent in most Black Atlantic/diasporic studies. This is despite the migration since 1605[10] of fugitive slaves, free people, and loyalists, who sought to escape the brutality of slavery and Jim Crow in what became the United States. Moreover, Caribbean people migrated primarily as an important pool of labour during the post–Second World War era. My objective is not to re-centre Canada, but to interrogate how, in its construction of itself as a benevolent nation, it dismisses, marginalizes, and ultimately renders invisible the past and ongoing struggles of Black Canadians and Caribbean women to inhabit and claim a part of the nation space. By placing Canada on the Black Atlantic route, portraits, sometimes unfinished, reveal the multidimensionality of Black women's lives.

Black women, however, are not a monolithic group: they are differentiated on the basis of age, skin colour, religion, geographical location, and education, for example. Consequently, in recovering Black women's life histories, feminist analysis and theories from other geographical locations cannot be uncritically imported to bear on Black women's lives in Canada. Black women's relationship to Canada as a white settler colony means that their social experiences are neither the same as, nor yet completely different from, those of their Black female counterparts elsewhere.[11] To account for the specificity of Black women's experiences means paying attention to the historical, political, social, and economic contexts as mitigating factors in shaping subjectivity formation. To map, examine, and chart Black women's subjectivity and identity formation, the interlocking systems of race, class, gender, and sexuality, although socially constructed and embedded with power relations, are placed within three broad and interrelated frameworks of family, nation, and the political economy of work. The themes that are discussed below emerged as common threads in the women's testimonies.

Situating the Women's Oral Testimonies: Family, Church, and School

With varying degrees and levels of intensity, the family, church, and school operated as 'regimes of truth,'[12] especially during childhood. These institutions – through the process of interpellation – transmitted ideas about behaviour, roles, and attitudes, which influenced identity and subjectivity formation. To explain how Louis Althusser's concept of interpellation operates in practice, Chris Weedon explains that 'individual subjects internalize particular meanings and values and take up the identity offered to them by the institution[s] in question.'[13] Obviously, the process of transmission is neither smooth nor coherent as individuals do not always respond to, or internalize in the same way the agendas of the institutions under discussion. These institutions are not neutral sites. In different ways, their dynamics are influenced by the economic, social, cultural, and political contexts in which they function. How these institutions are situated at a particular historical moment helps to shape the values, expectations, and ideals that, imparted to children, constitute subjectivity and identity formation. I want to explore how the family, church, and school are imbricated in subjectivity and identity formation in ways that are both empowering and repressive.

Family

In re-examining traditional interpretations relating to the organization, structure, and function of Black heterosexual families, scholars point out how those family structures – whether female headed, nuclear, or extended kin networks,[14] which often included non-biological relations – are developed to meet the material and emotional needs of their members. Feminist scholars further elucidate how the unequal and exploitative social relationships endemic in the wider society subsequently affect women of the African diaspora, who are primarily responsible for their households. Instead of seeing sole-support female households as an aberration from the nuclear family, which is posited as the norm, Black women are presented as subjects who make pragmatic choices based on their social location.

Unlike some radical feminist scholars in North America who view the family as a source of women's subordination, Black and Caribbean feminist scholars highlight the family's resistive potential against colonial cultural, structural, and economic inequalities.[15] They further maintain that limited economic opportunities, and racial and gender discrimination, more so than unequal relations between the sexes, affect Black families. In fact, Black people's daily encounters with institutional and systemic forms of oppression result in the family being viewed as a respite against white supremacy.

I argue that it is insufficient to explore only the effects of external factors, such as racism or colonialism, on the family, for the internal dynamics remain equally significant. Thus, I am interested in the inner workings of the family – from the perspective of the women as girls and as adults – especially as they relate to how gender roles, class, and racial identity are shaped and reshaped across spatial and geographical locations over time. Families not only provide food, shelter, and clothing; they also instil moral guidance. They constitute the site where cultural meanings about gender roles are produced and reproduced, and where girls begin to learn to perform those acts that give the appearance of a fixed gender identity.[16] Thus, it is hardly surprising that for the interviewees informing this study the family also contributed to decisions about future career choices. Moreover, the family is the place where as girls they first confronted and learned the varied and sometimes conflicting messages regarding the politics of respectability, class, colour, and race.

Church

If the family lagged in passing on moral principles thought necessary to guide and prevent young women from going astray, religion and their church filled the gap. Across the African diaspora, religious beliefs and practices have been and continue to be instrumental in shaping Black people's way of life, thought, and culture.[17] How Black families lived their lives was dictated by the Christian and Catholic faiths, which influenced and shaped children's beliefs. Mandatory church/mass attendance, the worshipping of a Christian God, and a belief in the Holy Trinity (the Father, Son, and the Holy Spirit), repeating and memorizing novenas, praying to Saints, and paying tithes, are a few of the defining features of Christianity and Catholicism. The church's agenda was and remains multifarious. It serves both the spiritual and social needs of its members. It sets guidelines and regulates behaviour, and it provides an outlet for its members to organize activities. In Canada, the Black church has further functioned as a political entity mobilizing its members when necessary to respond to institutional and systemic forms of oppression. Like the family, the Black church in Canada can be viewed as a reprieve from white hostility.[18] Consequently, as a result of its role in Black life, the church participates in reinforcing a collective, even if imagined, identity.

With respect to the Caribbean diaspora, scholarly analyses overwhelmingly focus on either Rastafarianism or other African-influenced religions,[19] which working-class and poor Caribbean people supposedly practise. Negatively viewed as an 'opiate' from a Marxist perspective,

Protestantism and Catholicism are the 'Master's' (read: European) religions practised mostly by the lower-middle, middle, and upper classes.
Thus their redemptive proclivities, such as emphasizing a common
humanity, remain understudied. Religion also produces discrete racialized and gendered hierarchies, and it assigns individuals social identities
that position some members as outsiders.

Given the importance of the church in transmitting fundamental values that shape belief systems regarding gender, for example, I had to
think about how to analyse the church not only from the standpoint of
the women while they were growing up, but also as adults. The church
helps to create a positive self-identity by involving children in activities.
Conversely, the church also produced and reproduced common sense
knowledge about gender roles that was intricately linked to definitions
of what was considered 'natural' and 'normal.' Very little is known about
how children and young adults actually feel about the church's position
on appropriate gender roles, church attendance, sin, faith, and other
biblical beliefs.[20] All these factors influence identity and subjectivity formation. In addition, discussions about identity have yet to include Black
professional women and the role of religion in their lives.

Education

Education further socializes girls and boys into seemingly appropriate
subject positions. Education systems are generally constructed in many
ways to reinforce the status quo and to reproduce social, gender, socioeconomic, and racial inequalities. Although the initial creation of terti-
ary and secondary education in the Caribbean was established for whites
and other elites, eventually Black people, particularly those who could
afford the fees, sent their children to school. Education in the Anglo-
Caribbean up until independence was imbued with British-colonial ideologies and values mirroring the race, colour, gender, and class dynamics
of the society.[21] Consequently, scholars argued that the education system
was irrelevant to the majority of the people.[22] A similar analysis could
be extended to Canada as well. One interviewee attended a segregated
school, which was severely substandard and underfunded, but where
Black teachers valued them. In integrated schools, the curriculum privileged white subjectivity and identity, and like the Caribbean schools
reflected and reproduced the gender, class, and racial ideology of the
time. As a 'regime of truth,' I am concerned with how the education
system, on the one hand, produced and disseminated knowledge that

devalued its members and, on the other hand, held radical potential for the very same students it marginalized. The goal here is to examine how subjectivity and identity are forged in systems and institutions fractured by power relations based on colour, class, race, gender, and other social divisions in the Caribbean and in Canada.

Nurses' Education

Since education systems are far from being gender-, race- or class-neutral, they help to orient students towards certain occupations conducive to their social location. Thus, female students learn very quickly that they are particularly suited for certain kinds of 'caring' work, such as nursing. Nurses' education emphasizes certain gender traits as constitutive of a proper nurse. I apply Judith Butler's argument that 'gender is manufactured through a sustained set of acts, posited through the gendered stylization of the body'[23] to nurses' training. To create a nursing identity, practitioners in training, not only performed multiple repetitive acts with varying intensity, but also participated in specific rituals throughout the three years of their training.

Constructed on middle-class ideals of white womanhood, nursing remains a contested space for Black women. Postcolonial scholar Homi Bhabha's concept of mimicry – an '*ironic* compromise'[24] because colonial subjects can be 'almost the same, but not quite' like the colonizers[25] – helps to explain Black women's gender performances. Victor Turner's concept of liminality – that is, in-betweenness – is another useful concept to explore how Black women navigate nurses' training, and construct a professional identity.

Nation, Migration, Home, and Belonging

Migration became the means through which some of the interviewees were able to train as nurses. Whether forced, as with the transatlantic slave trade, or voluntary, as workers, students, members of their family, or visitors, migration is an important element in the lives of people of African descent. The migration of Caribbean people and African Americans to former colonial centres such as Great Britain or to white settler colonies such as Canada provides insights into how national identities are defined. Although imagined entities, nations are constructed as homogeneous communities of people with supposedly shared interests, language, and culture.[26] Consequently, the national narrative – the telling of stories – that constructs Canada's national and British identity is almost always exclusive. Attempts to reify narratives of nation and national identity are far from uniform, or unproblematic.

As British subjects who were educated in schools where British values and ideals were promulgated, Caribbean people have held an idealized vision of Britain.[27] However, when they arrived in the aftermath of the Second World War to the urban centres of the 'motherland,' they discovered that although they retained the legal right to settle and work, they were seldom welcomed.[28] As a transition, migration forced the young women to come to terms not only with a different social reality, but to make sense of a new social space. Whether they live in Canada or the United States, or visit the Caribbean, Black women have found ways to form affiliations, however uneasy with the space they call home.

As transnational actors who move between borders, I am interested in how Black women, who migrated alone in their early and late teens, as young women, and later as adults, have negotiated their identities. Relying on postcolonial theorizing and transnationalism – how individuals inscribe and construct their identities and relationships across borders – I focus on questions of identity, such as belonging, alienation, dislocation, liminality, and hybridity as imbricated in the women's subjectivity and identity formation. I also focus on how the dominant modalities of sexism, racism, and classism influence identity formation. Since paid and unpaid work offer Black women other forms of identity, I also explore these spheres.

The Political Economy of Health Care and Work

Anti-racist feminist scholarship has also proved useful in terms of understanding how work is both gendered and racialized, and socialist-feminist analyses of women and work have provided the theoretical framework to think about the contradictory power relations in an occupation such as nursing. In assessing how Caribbean women are absorbed into the labour force, scholars have paid significant attention to how the ideology of racism and sexism structures capitalist relations of production. Consequently, Black women's labour is viewed as expendable, exploitable, and cheap, and as a result, these women are often concentrated in poorly paid and the least skilled sectors of the economies of industrialized countries.[29] Discussions about nursing in Canada and Britain reveal similar findings.[30] While Black women tend to be located at the lowest end of the nursing hierarchy, coincidentally, the majority of the interviewees for this study do not fall into this category. Of the twenty-two Caribbean-born nurses interviewed for this study, all but one were registered nurses in the Canadian context – that is, they took the measures, such as writing the requisite registration exams, necessary for licensure. I move beyond the subordination paradigm[31] to explore how, in their attitudes and responses towards nurses' training and work, Black women made conscious decisions and choices about their work lives, albeit within the constraints of structural forces.

I am particularly interested in the discourses Black women evoked to construct a positive professional identity. I depart somewhat from the traditional definition of 'professional,' which is concerned with workplace autonomy, to focus on how issues of accreditation, gendered racism, training, skill, and education play a role in fostering professional subjectivity. Influenced by women's historians who insist on the relationship between the world of paid and unpaid work, I focus on the unpaid work Black women do for their family and communities, a theme which to date has not been fully explored by Canadian researchers. Attention to Black women as nurses, mothers, wives, single women, and community activists speaks to how identities are transitional and change over time. Certain forms of identities took precedence at particular moments, and appear fixed at others. Throughout this book, I pay special attention to the role of human agency underscoring the role of the interviewees as social actors in their own right.[32] Given the paucity of research available on Black professional women, oral interviews emerged as the primary evidentiary data.

Oral Interviews

The narratives that form the basis of this study were gleaned from thirty-five Black women, of whom thirteen were born in Canada and twenty-two were born in various islands in the English-speaking Caribbean, including Guyana. Twenty-five of the interviews, conducted between 1995 and 2001, were completed for graduate work. I identified interview participants through personal contacts, the Jamaican Canadian Association Centre (JCA), and the Ontario Black History Society. I made initial contact over the telephone, and once the women expressed interest in the project, we selected interview dates. On the day of the interview, which consisted of open-ended questions, I asked the nurses to sign a consent form. The interview process was also governed by the university research ethics protocol. The names and relevant biographical information of the participants are given in the appendix; six asked to remain anonymous, and consequently, pseudonyms are used throughout this book to identify them. There were also instances when some of the nurses asked not to be identified in relation to certain stories they told.

The eldest interviewee for this study was born in 1914, with the majority of the women born during the late 1920s and 1930s, and three in the mid- to late 1940s and 1950s. Of the Caribbean-born participants, ten were from Jamaica, three from Barbados, four from Trinidad, and two from Grenada. Individual nurses also hailed from Dominica, Antigua, and Guyana.[33] Most of the women were between the ages of eighteen and nineteen at migration; the youngest was fifteen and a half and the oldest was twenty-four when they left the Caribbean. Most left in the mid-1950s – the first went in 1949 on a scholarship and the last in 1968. Seventeen of the Caribbean interviewees trained in Britain in hospital apprenticeship programs. Four of the interviewees trained in Jamaica, one in Trinidad, and another in Canada throughout the late 1940s to the early 1970s. Of this cohort, three migrated to Canada during the 1960s before the implementation of the 1962 and 1967 immigration policies. Several of the Caribbean- and British-trained nurses chose to upgrade in response to how their qualifications were assessed by Canadian nursing authorities. Of the Black Canadian-born cohort, one trained in Britain during the 1970s, and the rest trained in Canada. Most trained in Ontario, and two in Halifax, Nova Scotia. The first interviewee entered nursing school in 1947 and the others throughout the 1950s and early 1960s.

Like their Caribbean-born counterparts, the Black Canadian-born women trained in hospital-based nursing schools, some of which were affiliated with religious denominations. Four members of this group at different times crossed the border into Detroit, Michigan, to seek additional training and work. One nurse eventually made the United States home. All of the Black Canadian-born women were married and had had children at various points in their lives. Four of the Caribbean-born interviewees remained unmarried, and four remained childless. Thus, most of the themes (family, career, retirement) that emerged from the interviews correspond with the life-course paradigm.

As a group, Black professional women remain underrepresented in a disparate range of scholarly literature. Consequently, the interview process for this study allowed the women to participate in knowledge production – to reflect on, interpret, and articulate the meaning of their experiences with a depth that positivist approaches to research neglect. In other words, oral history as a methodology challenges traditional approaches that situate women as observable objects. Oral history locates women as subjects, not objects, and as producers of knowledge and agents of social change embodied within the complexities and contradictions of different histories and cultures. Oral interviews thus invite women to view themselves as legitimate knowers, and to disrupt the barrier between the researcher, who is often viewed as dominant and legitimate, and the researched, as subordinate.[34]

Theorizing Memories: Or What We Choose to Remember

It is generally acknowledged that personal recollections do not provide an unadulterated access to the past, and that interviewers tend to shape the interview process through what such recollections reveal and what they conceal. Moreover, despite the rich data gleaned from interviews, oral historians have raised some concerns about the reliability of people's memories, the relationships between participants and interviewers, and the way narratives are interpreted once the interviews are completed.[35] The process of remembering and retelling stories is far from uncomplicated, as Michael Pressley and Wolfgang Schneider explain: 'Autobiographical memories simultaneously reflect elements of the original experience as well as interpretations of those events that occurred during dialogues and monologues. Even an event never talked about before is recalled in light of prior knowledge, so that memory of it involves reconstruction rather than a reading off of a memory trace exactly reflecting the event as it happened.'[36] In other words, the retelling of stories is not exactly literal, but is reinterpreted at the time of retrieval, and very much affected by the present life of the interviewee.

Of course, it is difficult to ignore the issue of time and its relationship to memory. Pamela Sugiman points out that 'the time at which the interview takes place, the time that passes over the course of the interview, the passage of time from the events discussed to memories conveyed are all significant in shaping the narrative.'[37] As with Sugiman's Japanese interviewees, some of my interviewees' recollections, especially about their childhood, 'have been filtered through the passage'[38] of many decades and all that unfolded during those years. While acknowledging exaggerations, silences, omissions, and gaps in memory, my objective is to focus on what Black women said about their experiences, and how these experiences influenced and shaped their subjectivities and identities over the life course. The larger goal is less about 'accuracy or otherwise of memory ... but in the documenting of neglected voices and how *they* remember their own experience.'[39]

While acknowledging the limitations of oral history, Franca Iacovetta reminds us that it 'hardly justifies dismissing [it], anymore than the fragmented and biased character of preserved written records should prompt us to abandon the archives.'[40] Furthermore, Gretchen Lemke-Santangelo proposes that we think about the limitations of oral interviews in a manner that is particularly constructive. As she explains, oral interviews 'provide a different way of examining history, one that shifts the focus from "what really happened" to how people use the past to produce individual or collective meaning and identity. Just as memory shapes identity, identity also shapes the meaning we draw from the past.'[41]

It was clear to me that the stories of the women I interviewed, when considered in tandem with other sources, help to illuminate central themes in this research. I further realized that these women prioritized their recollections, which sometimes contradicted the archival evidence, raising interesting questions about the limits of the archives and what counts as evidence.[42] When scholars rely on oral narratives as the primary source, they must incorporate other sources, not necessarily to verify the interviewees' version of truth or to privilege written and accessible sources against the oral testimonies. Rather, the goal is to place the interviews in a broader historical, cultural, and social context that the interviewees themselves might not necessarily recall.

Organization of the Book

This book is organized chronologically. Two interconnected themes run throughout chapters 1 and 2. The first is the family, church, and school as media of socialization that helped the interviewees for this study navigate the multiple sites they occupied while growing up as girls and then later when they were adults. The second is how these institutions maintain the status quo by producing and reinforcing certain ideologies that are often congruent with the hegemonic principles of the larger society that these institutions inhabit.

The second part of the book explores how the interviewees chose nursing as an occupation, migration, and the world of paid and unpaid work. In chapter 3, I emphasize how the labour shortages experienced by Canada and Great Britain after the Second World War led to mass migrations of people of colour to these locales and, I argue, highlighted the racist debates around the national identities of these two countries.

Chapters 4 and 5 focus on how Black women navigated training, education, and paid and unpaid work. I explore how the various groups of Black women represented here articulated their professional identities, through an emphasis on skill and professionalism, within the changing political economy of Canadian, British, and American health care systems. Chapter 6 examines the meaning of unpaid work, which includes housework and child care responsibilities performed for immediate and extended family, as well as the volunteer and activist-oriented activities that Black women engaged in. The penultimate chapter examines how these women negotiated and renegotiated notions and concepts of border, home, belonging, identity, and dislocation. The concluding chapter assesses the women's journeys, underscoring how their lives challenge a wide range of theoretical suppositions.

1

The Family as the Agent of Socialization

To understand and define the 'self' within the context of adulthood, the Caribbean- and Black Canadian-born women I interviewed for this study drew on their memories of growing up. As they navigated their way through various life stages and transitions, time and time again the interviewees evoked key lessons that they felt were crucial to their evolution. In these recollections, the women pointed to the family as the institution that not only provided their basic human needs but also was most responsible for their social and moral development. The family, however, does not exist in a vacuum. Rather, it has to be interrogated within the cultural, social, and economic contexts of the particular period. This chapter explores and compares the women's recollections about their childhood in the Caribbean and Canada by analysing the meanings they attributed to certain events and situations while growing up. These episodes and circumstances are a testament to how the family was critical to subjectivity and identity formation in ways that were both empowering and repressive. Gender and racial ideologies, culture, and socioeconomic status not only influenced the structure, organization, and dynamics of the family; they also shaped how the interviewees defined and saw themselves.

What We Choose to Remember: Childhood Memories

Oral memories of childhood, some scholars argue, tend to be relayed in fragments and are often contradictory because much is forgotten, obscured, or repressed. Moreover, stories are often filtered over time, and might become more or less important to individuals as time passes.[1] Despite the inconsistencies associated with memory adults can, and do, give voice to their childhood experiences which are rooted in the political, economic, cultural, familial, and social milieu of time and space. Asked to recall past memories that are mediated by the present, the interviewees selectively highlighted conditions and episodes. As they recalled, reflected on, and recounted stories about growing up, it was obvious that the things they remembered were not always conveyed exactly, but were still critical in shaping their subjectivities and identities.

The Canadian and Caribbean Context

Caribbean women born between 1915 and 1950 grew up under British colonial rule. For some, their parents were only a generation removed from slavery. The vestiges of race, social class, gender, and colour cleavages established during slavery were still visible throughout the English-speaking Caribbean. Referring to Barbados, Constance Sutton and Susan Makiesky-Barrow maintain that 'emancipation in 1838 interfered with neither sugar production nor colonial rule; not until 1966 did political independence and a measure of economic diversification produce significant departures from the patterns established by 350 years of sugar and colonialism.'[2] Class status in the pre-colonial Caribbean was connected to race and colour: that is, whites and some light-skinned people owned the means of production and subsequently controlled the political apparatus. Subordinated and marginalized, Black people had virtually no economic, political, or social power. In fact, most of the inhabitants were unemployed and impoverished, while the mostly white elites reaped the benefits of the islands' resources as they had done during slavery.

In a gesture of benevolence, or possibly through the fear of continued labour uprisings throughout the Caribbean, the Colonial Office in London organized a commission led by Lord Moyne during the late 1930s. The commission's objective was to investigate 'the social and economic conditions in Barbados, British Guyana, British Honduras, Jamaica, the Leeward Islands, Trinidad and Tobago, and the Windward Islands.'[3] The findings confirmed what the inhabitants already knew: 'illiteracy, malnutrition, unsanitary environments, poor housing, [and] exposure to contagious diseases and unsatisfactory maternal and child care'[4] were widespread. The Second World War did very little to transform the social conditions of the Caribbean in a manner that would benefit the majority of the people.

Not immune to the colonial and patriarchal ideologies imported from England but rather reconfigured to continue the oppression of the newly emancipated slaves and their descendants, English-speaking Caribbean societies (including Guyana) were organized in a hierarchical manner to benefit all men, albeit not equally. The careers of the interviewees' parents reflected a mix of skilled and unskilled labour. Fathers' occupations included electrician, teacher, tailor, and a supervisor for a government company. A number of fathers were farmers, and a few were factory workers, while others worked in the banana industry and on plantations. Women generally had high levels of participation in the labour force. Some of the women's mothers were housewives, but those who participated in the paid labour force worked at a variety of jobs. Teaching and sewing (as seamstresses) were the primary occupations for the mothers.[5] One owned a small grocery shop, and another worked in a nutmeg factory. One mother was a trained nurse, although her career was cut short due to migration.

Whether they worked or not, the expectation embedded in lower-middle- to middle-class Caribbean culture during the 1940s and 1950s and embraced by the women's parents was a belief in gendered modes of behaviour. Women, as wives and mothers, were responsible for home and hearth, and fathers were to provide for the financial welfare of the family. There were mothers, some working full-time, who were active in community organizations, a sure marker of middle-class status. Like other women, labour force participation and community work did not exempt them from performing reproductive labour, tasks 'defined as work that is necessary to ensure the daily maintenance and ongoing reproduction of the labor force.'[6]

Despite growing up in a society where the colonial configurations of a three-tier social system – based on being white, light-skinned, or Black – were deeply entrenched, the majority of interviewees for this study were in a relatively better economic position than the vast majority of the Caribbean islands' inhabitants. Some families were in a position to hire working-class women to help alleviate the strain of combining domestic work and child care. The women linked social class, usually based on an individual's location in the economy and tied to wealth and income, to their parents' accumulation of tangible items. To ascertain whether their parents belonged to the upper, middle, lower-middle, or working class, or were poor, the women measured their families' socioeconomic position against their counterparts who lived in the same districts, villages, and towns. For the poor, it was the absence of electricity, running water, outdoor toilets, the lack of clothing, and inadequate nutrition that indicated, from their point of view, their position at the bottom of the economic, and ultimately the social, ladder. Most of the women identified their families as lower-middle class to middle class, but not necessarily in terms of income generated by their father's occupation.

The symbol of being middle class was having a home, land, and sufficient food to feed the family; owning cattle, which could have been purchased or inherited; and being able to hire domestic and yard help. Wearing shoes and the appropriate uniform to school, and having clothes for a variety of occasions also served as an index of lower- to middle-class status for the Caribbean cohort. Indeed, as the Black experience in Canada illustrates, a family's location in the social structure of a society has a significant impact on how childhood is experienced and remembered.

Black Canadian Context

Black Canadian-born girls who were teenagers in the mid-1940s to late 1950s belonged to communities that were demarcated most notably along race, gender, and class lines. According to historian James Walker, Black Canadians' social class location can be traced back to slavery, even though the institution did not develop on a mass scale in Canada. Walker contends that 'traditions established in slavery' have 'resulted in a prescribed economic position for Blacks, which was reflected in their social status, and which fixed them at the lowest level of the social class hierarchy. Their colour was a label announcing their inferior position.'[7] Employment for Black men in Canada before the Second World War was often seasonal and casual. Virginia's father worked as a labourer at a woodworking company and as a night watchman; in addition, he also worked as a barber, cutting hair in his home.[8] Laura's father was self-employed as a chimney sweeper – a seasonal business – and he also worked in a quarry.[9]

Unlike the majority of Caribbean interviewees who considered their parents to be lower to middle or middle class, the Black Canadian interviewees, especially those born in the early 1930s, were more likely to describe themselves as 'struggling' or 'poor.' Food, when available, was in limited quantities, and hand-me-down clothes were common. Some of the women spent parts of their childhood with no running water, electricity, or indoor toilets. The Great Depression and the Second World War would intensify an already fragile economic position for these families. It should be pointed out, however, that Blacks in Toronto were better incorporated into society and fared better economically than their counterparts in smaller and less integrated cities such as Chatham and Windsor in Ontario, and in Nova Scotia in general.

The collective existence of Black Canadians was also abysmally affected by established legal ordinances, which prohibited them from owning land and buying homes.[10] Blacks faced discrimination in many areas of public life. They were prohibited from jury service, barred from places of worship, and refused service by some hospitals. Blacks and whites sat in separate sections at theatres. Motels, hotels, taverns, and restaurants consistently denied service to Blacks[11] to which a few of the interviewees attested.

For a nation that constructs its identity on benevolence and commitment to democratic principles, Canada denied the basic rights and privileges of citizenship to Black Canadians. Consequently, the majority of Black Canadian children were born into, and came of age in, communities struggling for social, political, and economic advancement. Scholars of childhood and family have virtually ignored the experiences of Black Canadians.[12] Autobiographical accounts and oral narratives, however, have not only filled the lacuna in the literature[13] but also help to determine the uniqueness, if any, of Black Canadian families.

Resilient and Resourceful Families

If, in the most ideal situation, the primary obligation of families is to provide the basic necessities of life, and transmit morals and values to their children, then Black Canadian-born and Caribbean families were not exceptional. When the impact of colonialism, patriarchy, sexism, and racism are taken into account, a more complex portrait of Black and Caribbean families emerges. What Black women who self-identified as poor recalled about their socioeconomic status demonstrates that social class was a key component of subjectivity and identity.

Remembering the past also involves the process of re-evaluation as the interviewees assessed the meaning of certain aspects of events that occurred during their childhood. Jamaican-born Dorette expressed some ambivalence in trying to determine her family's class status because, as she pointed out, 'in Jamaica I didn't know what class was.' Born in 1942, in a rural community, Dorette lived in an extended family comprised of her grandmother, uncles, and aunts. At the age of twelve, Dorette left the countryside to attend high school in Kingston. She would later migrate to Britain, where she completed high school. In addition to describing her childhood as 'strict but fun,' Dorette also recalled:

We never expected a lot. We never had the china dolls, but we always had food and we always had clothes to wear, we had shoes on our feet. So in a way I didn't see myself as poor. There were other people that were more well off than you are. I know some people had some big houses, but we were never lacking food or shelter, we never had money, but we were never hungry. We were still happy because you had shoes to wear to school.[14]

When Dorette admitted 'we never had money,' she was actually referring to her mother, who was a sole-support parent. Living with her extended family meant that Dorette's basic needs were met, hence the emphasis on being happy.[15] Whether she would have enjoyed playing with china dolls, Dorette failed to disclose. Instead, she and others presented their families as responsible and loving units that functioned to temper economic deprivation.

In contrast to Dorette, Trinidadian Ancilla, who was born in 1945, spoke candidly about her family's socioeconomic status. 'Poverty was at the forefront,'[16] and everyone who was old enough 'had to do odd jobs here and there to make ends meet,' she said. Even when Ancilla and her siblings worked, their contributions were barely enough, which was in keeping with the reality of the Caribbean at the time. Like the majority of the citizens, Ancilla's family was unable to enjoy some of the luxuries that her middle- and upper-class counterparts could afford. Some families struggled to fulfil their obligations due to economic deprivation caused by historical events.

Although economic vulnerability and rampant racial discrimination structured Black Canadian families' subject positions, the Depression and the Second World War held special significance for some. Scholarship on both these historical events and their impact on Blacks remains sparse. Some insights, however minimal, can be gleaned from general sources on the period. For example, Black Canadian researcher Peggy Bristow notes that 'with the Depression, the always-slim prospects for blacks narrowed further and those for working-class blacks, particularly women, shrank drastically.'[17] Katrina Srigley further reveals how race dictated the employment opportunities available to Black women during the Depression in Toronto.[18] With respect to the Second World War, scholarship generally focuses on segregation in the military and the fight to integrate. Articles in the *Dawn of Tomorrow* often bemoaned the contradictions of fighting in a war when Black people were treated as second class citizens at home. However, the Second World War also opened up opportunities for Black women.[19] As the interviewees for this study indicated, the loss of family members – coupled with the apparent monolithic impact of the Depression – forced their families to adopt creative measures to cope.

In her study of working-class women during the Depression in Montreal, Denyse Baillargeon argues that these women were the primary architects of the survival strategies that they adopted. This argument rings true for Black Canadian women as well.[20] For example, Frieda – born in 1929 to Alton C. and Evelyn Parker of Windsor, Ontario – identified herself as a 'crash baby.' Although her mother Evelyn had been a teacher by training, she took up parenting full-time once her daughter was born. As was typical in Windsor and other communities across Canada, Frieda's father faced insurmountable odds procuring full-time employment. Instead, he worked at various odd jobs to support his family, which he believed was his responsibility as a man and father. As Frieda insisted:

> We never accepted welfare. My father felt he should be able to support his family, so he worked repairing cars, whatever came along. That was one of the things he took pride in.[21]

Frieda's mother Evelyn, on the other hand, was 'a wonderful manager who managed whatever he [father] brought in, she made the best of it.'[22] According to Frieda, her mother concealed the severity of their economic situation by implementing 'little tricks.' For example, Frieda recalled that when she was growing up her favourite dish was potato and cream soup, which her mother cooked on a regular basis. At the time, Frieda was sure that the frequency with which her mother cooked the soup was because she enjoyed it. Later as an adult, her mother disclosed to Frieda that the main reason potato soup was a common staple in their home was because they were poor. Indeed, ingenuity remained a necessity for women such as Evelyn.

What also resonated for Frieda was her father's willingness to work in the most undesirable positions to take care of his family, her mother's ability to economize during a period of economic uncertainty, and that regardless of how poor they were, her parents, if they could, helped others.[23] These examples betray how racism and classism affected Black Canadian subjectivity. Amid the family's deprivation, however, from both parents Frieda learned survival techniques, the importance of sharing resources, and how gender roles operated in practice.

If the Parkers struggled with only one child, the situation was worse

for families with multiple children. Agnes was born two years into the
Depression in 1931 in Maidstone Township outside of Windsor, Ontario.
Obviously too young to remember the Depression itself, Agnes appropriated the stories passed down and then added her own interpretation
to what these events actually meant. Ever since Agnes could remember:
'we were very poor, we grew up on a farm, we were never hungry, but we
didn't have the best of nourishment.'[24] Agnes's mother died when she
was five years old. Left alone to take care of six children, Agnes's father
turned to his childless sister, who resided in Detroit, Michigan, to take
Agnes to live with her, while another family member took Agnes's seven-
year-old brother. Agnes disliked the arrangement, behaving badly until
her aunt brought her back home.

The family's economic position did not improve during Agnes's short
absence. Already poor, things got progressively worse. Scarcity, especially
of food, characterized Agnes's childhood. She told the following story:

> We had bread but we did not have any meat, butter, peanut butter, or jelly.
> So we took potatoes, sliced them and put them on our bread – my sister
> and me. At school, we opened our sandwich, and we noticed that we must
> have [had] the wrong lunch and we put the lunch back. So we waited with
> the other kids who got their lunch, and our lunch still sat there. So we said
> 'that must be our lunch' but the potatoes had turned black and we thought
> it was meat.[25]

Clearly, the Depression had a differential impact on Black Canadians, yet
Agnes refused to paint her family members as victims of their economic and social circumstances. Agnes, Frieda, and the other interviewees
emphasized their families' abilities to pool their resources in times of
crisis, and to maintain their respectability through such acts as refusing government support. In essence, they provide an alternative view of
Black families different from the pathological portraits the dominant
society might have held.

In some communities, the Depression and the Second World War
often submerged race and social class tensions as some community members faced similar economic conditions. Virginia described her family as
being poor even though both parents worked at multiple jobs. During
the war, the family's economic position was most precarious, yet Virginia
pointed out:

> We were not poor. Everyone was in the same position during that time

because of the war, except the industrialists and the people that owned their own businesses. So it was not a disgrace to be in that situation. We never starved. The importance was cleanliness, eating, and having a place to sleep, and attending school.[26]

With Blacks constituting at least 17 per cent of its population in 1949,[27] the town of Dresden, Ontario, was considered to be one of the most racially segregated towns in Canada, which obviously did not change because of the war. Historian Ross Lamberston notes that 'while many Canadians turned a blind eye to racial discrimination, often denying its existence, it was incontrovertibly present in Dresden.'[28] Yet, paradoxically, in Virginia's recollections, during the war, divisions were less about race, but between classes, despite organzing efforts by the Black community against racism.

Dignity, Virginia's parents and extended family members stressed, was to be found in the tangible and relevant things such as being clean, attending school, and being able to afford the essentials for daily survival. For a time, however fleeting, Virginia's family's position resembled that of their disadvantaged white neighbours. Surely, as a young Black girl, Virginia's own subjectivity and identity were being reshaped by these events as well.

The Depression and the Second World War were more than just historical episodes used as a reference for how dire things were for Black Canadian families. These events offer insights into social class and racial dynamics, familial, and other interpersonal relationships. How the women in this study narrated their recollections became a way not only to make sense of the past, but also to memorialize their families. In coping with difficult economic circumstances as well as the pain of losing family members to the war effort through both enlistment and death, parents imparted valuable lessons. These pivotal moments of their parents' strength in adversity helped to construct the women's own subjectivities.

Values and Social Class

Just as constraints caused by poverty shaped the women's sense of themselves growing up, identification as middle class or lower-middle class also moulded subjectivity and identity. Assets, access to provisions, and owning property and animals were indices of a family's position in the middle-class stratum. Daphne C, who was born in Jamaica in1930, lived with an extended family comprised of her parents, grandparents, aunt, and uncles. They 'had a lot of animals like goats, pigs, and cows,' which meant they 'could feed themselves,'[29] Daphne C explained. She continued, saying, 'they could go out and purchase clothes [and] didn't have to go out and beg.' While poorer children made toys from odds and ends, Daphne C's parents were able to buy her dolls, and provide her with materials to sew clothes for them. Although race and colour mattered – and was ever present – in the English-speaking Caribbean, socioeconomic status sometimes overrode other markers of difference. In other words, families such as Daphne C's could move up the socioeconomic ladder despite not being a part of the white and light-skinned elite class.

Distinctions between the various social classes went beyond home and cattle ownership, and toys. Values were believed to be class-specific. Daphne B acknowledged that she was raised with 'middle-class values' in an extended family. Her father was a farmer and her mother was a popular seamstress. According to Daphne B:

> My mom taught us quite a lot of things, like how to be ladies, how to use a knife and fork, how to speak. You weren't supposed to speak poor English.[30]

In addition to successfully moulding their children to replicate British manners, language, and modes of respectability, Gertrude and Henry Temple Bailey's children joined organizations such as the 4-H Club. Thus, Daphne B had the opportunity to 'travel around the island and attend dances.' The ability to participate as her parents did in clubs and organizations was another indicator of social class. Surely, children who were socially and economically disadvantaged were excluded from these activities.

The Baileys also taught their children the importance of civic responsibility. Gertrude was a member the Parent Teachers Association and the Women's Guild. At Christmas, she and the other members came together to sew, sending 'out little passes for people who were in the poorer conditions' to collect items. In addition, during annual missionary meetings, Daphne B explained: 'we brought these sweets that my mom would give us to take to people around the area that couldn't make it to church.'[31] Identities are relational, relative, and fluid. Whether the interviewees were poor, working or middle class, their status was predicated on each group's views of the other. This was evident in the mandate of certain middle-class women's organizations.

With a husband who worked as a supervisor for the Public Works Department, Zina Gilfilian, Inez's mother, did not work for pay nor was she primarily responsible for housework. Zina hired a maid so she and her six girls 'didn't have to do much housework,'[32] and so that she could dedicate some of her time to the Women's Federation in Peter's Field. This organization played a role in the Mass Marriage Movement that took place in Jamaica during the 1940s, encouraging consensually cohabitating couples to get married.[33] Here, Inez recounted her mom's role in the Women's Federation:

> One of the goals was to get these unwed couples married. I can remember one particular woman. She was my mother's schoolmate and I would look at her living standard as being poor. She had about, say four kids, and not married and living in a one-room house. And my mother was very active in making sure that woman got married. They married them in other words, bought the ring, the gown, and had the reception for them. And there goes the married couple, and believe me they turned out to be brilliant kids. In other words, they have come from rags to riches.[34]

Inez wholeheartedly endorsed her mother's plan to create a nuclear family for her classmate as a viable alternative to remaining single.

Zina Gilfilian and her daughter clearly believed in the ideological discourses regarding poor and working-class families that were prevalent in the English-speaking Caribbean society beginning in the 1930s and intensifying in the 1940s. For colonial social welfare workers, social scientists, and religious leaders, Caribbean families who deviated from the dominant construction of the patriarchal, heterosexual, and monogamous family were in a state of crisis. Encouraging these men and women to marry and adopt the nuclear family paradigm was seen to be the only way to prevent poverty and children being born out of wedlock.

The interviewees who grew up middle class expressed an air of confidence about their status, even if it was unconscious, which was absent in the narratives of their poorer counterparts. They had a keen awareness of the self and where they fit in economically and socially in the districts and towns in which they lived. This is but one example of how subjectivities are forged.

Lower-middle- to middle-class families conveyed to their own adolescent girls their own taken-for-granted values and norms regarding family, marriage, and children. The message invoked was patently clear: the nuclear family arrangement was the standard to which unmarried couples with 'illegitimate' children should aspire. Moreover, they implied that only within the confines of a patriarchal nuclear family could children aspire to be productive and successful citizens, despite Afro-Caribbean women's cynicism regarding the benefits of legal marriage.[35] There was also some recognition on the part of the women who identified as middle class that working-class people's own subjectivities and identities were circumscribed by material factors. Consequently, when some middle-class families intervened in the lives of their poorer or working-class counterparts, it was viewed more as a religious or community responsibility and not always about reinscribing class distinctions, or as an imposition of middle-class values.

Women at Work

An event that intensified social inequality and brought death and despair to some families also turned out to be a blessing for them as well. Even before the Second World War ended, Frieda's father, Alton Parker, had graduated from the Detroit Institute of Technology and joined Windsor's police force as its first uniformed Black officer.[36] James Richard, Dorothy R's father, and other Black men found full-time work in the automotive industry,[37] where they were paid relatively well and for the first time experienced job security.[38] Back in Toronto, Edna's father, Joe Bailey, eventually purchased a nine-room home that he rented out to 'West Indian women,'[39] who were mostly domestic workers, generating additional income for the family.

An improved standard of living was empowering in the sense that it changed a family's self-identity. Agnes summarizes the changes brought about by postwar prosperity:

> After the 40s came and in the 50s, things picked up and everybody had a very good life and work was available. My dad was making more, and they had a better life. We had a bathroom put in, because we had an outhouse for all those years.[40]

These gains did not translate into mothers' withdrawal from the workforce. Although mothers continued to contribute economically to their households, it was fathers' employment that warranted comment. This suggests that some Black men were able to solidify their role as breadwinners, a subject position that was denied to them due to racism.

Feminist scholars Cecilia Ridgeway and Shelley Correll insist that 'gender is not primarily an identity that is taught in childhood and enacted in family relations.'[41] Yet, at the particular historical juncture when the interviewees for this study were growing up, the family played the most critical role in the production and reproduction of gender identity. As the primary mechanism of socialization, it is the site where boys and girls learn, identify, internalize, and act out sex role differentiation; hence, interpellation in process. Gender was woven into the unpaid and paid work of family members and into the values transmitted to girls. Yet, girls did not uncritically take up the identity offered to them by their parents or other family members. They sometimes questioned normalized conceptions of gender categories defining their own subjectivities. Socialization was never a unilaterally imposed process but involved much negotiation.

Compared with their Canadian counterparts, at least until the war ushered in full-time employment, Caribbean interviewees' parents enjoyed more stable and consistent employment. Hence, the women generally discussed their mothers' work for remuneration as more of a right than an expectation, and not in any way unusual since most women worked for wages. Unlike some mothers of the Black Canadian interviewees, none of the Caribbean women's mothers worked as domestic workers. The value of employment was not lost on these women, who learned that their parents required money to run their households and to provide children with the essentials for survival.

Black Canadian mothers contradicted cultural expectations about femininity and women's roles, exposing the mutability of gender while challenging the middle-class ideology of separate spheres. In a culture where women's primary role was expected to be that of stay-at-home mother and wife taking care of the domestic realm, Black Canadian mothers found it necessary to work because of their poorer economic circumstances. Like some of the fathers of the Black Canadian group of interviewees, some of their mothers held multiple jobs, many of which were concentrated in service work. Eleanor's mother had never worked for pay, but when her husband died at the age of forty-seven, she had no choice but to find employment to take care of herself and her three children; she found work cleaning bathrooms at Smith's Department Store in Windsor.[42] Virginia's mother worked as a cook in a nursing home and in a school cafeteria, as well as in a candy factory.[43] These women's wages remained critical to their household economies, and in some instances meant the difference between going to bed with, or without, food.

With only a Grade 3 education, Marlene's mother, Christine Duncan, was employed by the Ministry of Education to teach pre-school children in a segregated Black school, and she occasionally worked as a domestic in the homes of white families.[44] When parents' combined earnings were not enough to alleviate the material hardships the family endured, some parents turned to their children for assistance.

Like their mothers, Black teenage girls and young women found limited opportunities for employment. Those who worked expressed no reservations. Whether it was picking fruit and vegetables, working as a janitor, or being self-employed, they felt pride in being able to assist themselves and their families. The ability to earn money, however minimal, was one way young women learned to become independent and responsible individuals. For Black Canadian mothers and children working in the late 1930s and 1940s, their wages could hardly be considered 'pin money'; they all contributed significantly to their family's economic survival. Moreover, as families practised the Protestant work ethic, they instilled the same values in their children.

Memories of the Gendered Division of Labour in Households

The economic and racial dynamics of Canadian society meant that some Black Canadian fathers took on domestic and child care duties while their wives worked. Virginia, for example, included 'homemaker' among the multiple jobs her father held while she was growing up.[45] Some Black Canadian fathers bathed their children and combed their hair, cooked, and assisted with homework. Although men's caregiving activities suggest that gender roles could be fluid, this did not mean that the gender ideology of the period did not prevail. Mothers were never exempted from their reproductive activities – which, according to sociologist Evelyn Nakano Glenn, are necessary to maintain the workforce. This involves 'feeding, clothing, and cleaning for the male worker or creat[ing] the next generation of workers (i.e., bearing, nurturing, and socializing children).'[46]

On one level, the gendered division of labour allows households to function smoothly. On another, the distribution of tasks on the basis of gender, whether done unconsciously or not, remains intricately connected to perceived ideas about 'normal' characteristics and behaviours. These ideas subsequently influence an individual's sense of self and subjectivity formation. In essence, children begin to believe that there are innate differences between the sexes, justifying the kinds of work for which women and men are responsible. To the interviewees for this study, while household duties were allocated primarily on the basis of gender, the age and number of children in the household were also determining factors. Overall, the women understood and generally accepted their family dynamics as natural and normal.

Born in Canada of Jamaican parents, Edna explained that she was raised in a 'typical West Indian' household. Edna and her two sisters attributed the peripheral role that their father assumed in the family, and his expectation that they cook and clean, as a mere reflection of generational as opposed to inherent differences. 'Some of the men in those days never even knew where the kitchen was,' Edna remarked. She often wondered how her father was able to secure a job as a chef working on the Panama Canal prior to migrating to Canada: 'He went and applied for the job and he got it. So whether the men lived or died, he was the chef and he never boiled water [before].'[47]

Even though Joe Bailey subsequently trained formally as a chef, he left the cooking in the home to his wife and daughters. Using the collective 'we' that demonstrates a recognition of, and identification with, the traditional roles of wife and mother, Edna remembered:

> We did everything, we did the washing, the cooking, the ironing, anything, so Mother would have an easier life. On Saturdays, Mother would go down to St Lawrence Market to get fresh fruit and vegetables, at six o'clock in the morning. And at eight o'clock, we'd go down and meet her, and help with the parcels.[48]

Edna and her sisters recognized that their mother was overtaxed, and they wanted to alleviate some of the burden. Indeed, in the Bailey household, gender roles were generally fixed, and the family accepted the arrangement. In other households, some girls found the gender division of labour unfair.

Some parents assigned duties based on sex, but their response to whether these duties were completed was often gendered. That is, they had different expectations for their sons and daughters. During the week, Marlene and her sister performed household chores, which included taking care of their younger siblings. As Marlene got older, she continued to do the same chores, but baking was added to the list. Until their household had free running water, Marlene's brother Ivan had only two tasks, and these were to make sure there was enough water in the house and enough wood for the fire. If he was unavailable and their parents were absent, Marlene and her sister Yvonne assumed responsibility for his duties. Marlene's brother was never expected to do housework, but the same principle did not apply to his sisters. Being girls did not spare them from doing what was considered 'boy's work.' Marlene summed up the gendered division of labour in her household during the late 1950s as follows:

> It was always Yvonne and me, and my brother Ivan; he was more or less allowed to run scot-free as far as that was concerned, he is a boy, and as far as managing children, it's a woman's responsibility.[49]

Even if they lacked the language at the time to describe their household arrangement, Black Canadian girls were hardly oblivious to the gendered division of labour in their households or how their parents supported gender differentiation. Even though the interviewees recognized the double standard and were sometimes bothered by how the rules were often inconsistently applied, they maintained that they adhered to the rules and dictates of their parents. The imperative to survive, and their parents' struggle to provide for their families in what was sometimes a hostile racial atmosphere, probably made the allotment of domestic responsibilities less of a concern. Maybe refusing to admit outright dissatisfaction with the social organization of their households was the interviewees' way of shaping how they wanted to be perceived in relation to their family.

Grooming Daughters for Domesticity

Although both groups of interviewees had little input in determining how duties were allocated in their households, Caribbean girls were more vocal about the differential treatment between them and their brothers. Jennette, who was born in Antigua in 1939, described at length how tasks were allocated in her household during the 1950s:

> Because all my brothers were older, except for the sixth one, we used to complain because we thought he got away with murder because he had sisters. So he didn't do anything and we'd complain. We [the girls] had to take turns doing the dishes, and we got fresh fish every day so we had to clean it. I still hate cleaning fish, and [he] didn't do this. We found it was unfair and we used to complain … And on Saturdays, we had to do our school uniforms; we had to wash them even though my mother had somebody washing my brothers' shirts, pants, and the sheets and so on … My mother made sure we knew how to iron and that sort of thing.[50]

Even though Jennette's parents had household help, daughters had to do their own laundry. The message was clear: domestic duties were the domain of women and girls, while boys were free to roam. Surely, girls and boys were also being prepared for the roles they would assume in the future.

The idea that 'the individual is always the site of conflicting subjectivity,'[51] is evident here. Jennette and her sister grew up in a culture where the hegemonic discourse that 'children should be seen and not heard' was pervasive. Children occupied a distinct subject position and any opposition could have been construed as disrespect. Jennette and her sisters, however, had a strong sense of the unfairness and chose to address it, which is noteworthy.

Parents' own desires, culture, the boy-to-girl ratio, and age were also factored into how household duties were allocated. Parents, especially mothers, wanted to ensure that their daughters learned certain domestic skills whether they married or remained single. In the former case, they would certainly make good wives and mothers, and in the latter possess a degree of self-sufficiency. Born in Guyana during the 1930s, Jean, the only girl among six children in the family, insisted that there were no gender-specific duties in her household. 'Everyone had to do everything,' which included making beds and helping around the yard.[52] The variability in gender role expectations in Jean's case could be attributed to the boy-to-girl ratio in her house or that parents were more concerned about the actual task being completed than the sex of the child responsible for the task.[53] Older girls were expected to care for younger siblings. Equally significant, assigning chores to children was one way to instil a sense of responsibility, a critical component of ongoing subjectivity formation.

Whether parents verbalized their beliefs about gender role differentiation, or simply performed according to the dictates of their sex, they, along with extended family members, left children with explicit ideas about masculinity and femininity. As girls, and as young women, the interviewees selectively chose what aspect of these lessons they would draw on to construct their own self-determining subjectivity. Since households are hierarchical, with parents and children occupying different subject positions and different conceptions of their place, tensions are inevitable.

'Don't Spare the Rod': Teaching Children Obedience and Sacrifice

Both groups of women interviewed for this study were taught to show deference to adults in authority and most declared that they responded accordingly. Fully cognizant of their children's capacity to misbehave, rebel, or disobey orders, parents developed an arsenal of strategies to prevent any such occurrences. Whether parents were staunch Christians or rarely attended church, the Bible was incorporated into their child-rearing practices. Special emphasis was placed on the biblical verse 'Children obey your parents' and the Commandment 'Honour thy father and mother,'[54] which were also integrated into sermons at church, of course. The message conveyed was that disobeying and dishonouring one's parents was by extension disobeying and dishonouring God. The consequences could be severe.

In the Canadian-born cohort, this was most evident in Naomi's household. With sixteen children to manage, Naomi's parents emphasized submission and self-sacrifice as a tool to maintain order in the home. Naomi credited the willingness of all the children to accept whatever tasks they were assigned by their parents to religious teachings:

> We had to be attuned to working. It was my job to get breakfast on Sunday morning, which was not considered a chore to me, because I never heard my parents complain about having a large family. We all contributed. We all helped to clean. The boys did the outside yard work. No one said this wasn't my job; we worked together as a family. I do not know if that was just because we were brought up in a Christian home … It was something we just understood.[55]

Naomi, Frieda, Marlene, and Caribbean-born Lillie and Carmencita all emphasized how their religious upbringing positively influenced their social interactions with their parents and others. Parents also used physical punishment as a form of discipline.

Purported to be the wisest man who ever lived, parents drew on King Solomon's admonition, often paraphrased as 'do not spare the rod and spoil the child.'[56] Although both parents were responsible for punishing their children, many of the women declared that their mothers executed most forms of discipline.[57] Fully aware of contemporary discussions that condemn physical punishment as abuse, the interviewees were quick to defend the punitive measures adopted by their mothers. Inez asserted:

> She gave you a whack whenever necessary, and that whack was very often … well, to be honest, it worked good, because today I can look back and

say with that discipline she has really placed us in this world and I'm quite comfortable. I wouldn't call it physical abuse.[58]

In addition to the birch switch, Marlene's mother also '[had] a strap for quick things that she had to [hit] you for.' Neither the birch switch, nor her mother's ability to reason with her children, apparently served as a deterrent; Marlene stated that they continued to misbehave. Still, she pointed out 'if you chose to go your way, you suffered the consequences,' thus legitimizing physical punishment as an acceptable form of discipline.[59]

June recalled being hit only once at home and at school.[60] In contrast, Carmencita described her father Archie as a 'martinet' compared with her mother, who was very calm and 'more the reasoning type.'[61] Despite her mother's insistence that Archie 'reason with the children,' he 'was more forceful, [and used] the strap' regularly. Carmencita remembered one incident where she ran into the sea to escape from her father's beatings. Archie's propensity to use the strap to control and discipline his children remained unabated even when they were young adults. A staunch authoritarian, Archie left his imprint on his children. Carmencita attributed her shyness to a strict upbringing and was happy to escape from her father by migrating to Britain at the age of twenty.[62]

In a culture that condoned the use of corporal punishment against children and demanded obedience to parents, it was hardly surprising that none of the Caribbean women verbally objected to being hit. Orphelia recapitulated the general reaction of those women whose parents used the strap: 'We never complained because we had the utmost respect for our parents.'[63] Indeed, the women stressed that any physical punishment they received was deserved and shaped their subjectivity as adults. Outside the confines of the family, attempts to forge one's own identity can be frustrating and painful, when racialized and gendered discourses mark some children and young women as substandard.

Ending with Racism and Colourism

Scholars Becky Thompson and Sangeeta Tyagi, in their discussion about the formation of racial subjectivity among children, explain that 'living through childhood amid ... contradictions [about race] is, in effect, how people *become* raced, since children's exposure to racial contradictions – and their strategies for dealing with them – has everything to do with racial formation.'[64] Growing up in racially semi-segregated and segregated towns, most Black Canadian girls were unable to escape discussions about or encounters with racism, both covert and subtle. Many of these women formed their consciousness of race and the development of a racial identity at an early age as they learned how to navigate this new awareness. Even if they were unable to explain the complexities of race and racism, it was within the family that children ultimately sought refuge. Concurrently, to protect their children from the painful experiences of racism, parents attempted to arm them with a variety of tools to help them cope with the inequalities they faced.

At age nine, Frieda and her family were denied service at a restaurant in Windsor, Ontario. Racism rendered her 'father helpless' as he was unable to protect his family from the humiliation. Racial prejudice also shattered Frieda's dream of playing the piano. Since the family was in a better position economically, Frieda's mother attempted to enrol her daughter at the Ursuline School of Music, which was operated by Catholic nuns. Evelyn had visited the school without her daughter to complete the paperwork, but when they returned together, the nun who greeted them was speechless. The nun had assumed Evelyn was white, because, according to Frieda, her mother was 'fairer than me and my father.' The Mother Superior informed them that no space was available for her daughter, her response not masking the fact that she was refusing admittance because Frieda was Black.[65]

Frieda's mother refused to acquiesce. Before leaving the premises, Frieda recalled: 'my mother took me and she told them about themselves, about their religious self. But she didn't lose her class; she was a very classy person.'[66] At a very young age, Frieda learned two valuable lessons from her mother: Christians, regardless of colour, ought to be at the forefront of combating discriminatory behaviour; and while it is important to confront racial discrimination, one must remain composed and dignified in the pursuit of social justice.

Discriminatory practices against Blacks were not unique to Windsor, Ontario. In communities across Canada, Blacks struggled to procure basic citizenship rights. Born in 1933, Laura describes Kentville, the town in Nova Scotia where she spent the early years of her life, as 'a really prejudiced town' with 'unfriendly people,' who 'restricted ... where they could go.'[67] While some public facilities excluded Blacks entirely, the movie theatre had separate sections for Blacks and whites.[68] Although Laura's father was conflicted about allowing his children to sit in a movie theatre where they would be reminded of their subordinate status, he would eventually relent. Laura's father did not want to disappoint his children because he knew they loved the theatre:

Dad would let us go to the theatre on Saturdays. We had to do our chores before we left. We had to walk 2.5 miles and we got twenty-five cents to spend however we wanted, plus ten cents for the theatre ... We didn't have a choice, we had to sit upstairs; we were not allowed to sit on the main floor. Blacks were just not allowed to sit on the main floor.[69]

Regardless of white Nova Scotians' investment in their subjugation of Blacks materially and psychically, Laura and her siblings proved otherwise. Hardly unconscious to the symbolic meaning behind separate seating arrangements at the theatre, they focused instead on the pleasure they derived from their weekend treat, which they privileged over where they were physically located in the theatre.

The cognitive, psychological, and emotional impact of racism sometimes confused Black Canadian children as they tried to make sense of the multiple and conflicting messages they received. They were denied access to some public places and treated differently at school, yet at home they were supported and loved. This contradictory message was especially confusing for Virginia, who articulated how hard it was to 'assess how you were treated as a child, when you [knew] there was a difference in how you were treated publicly'; parents attempted to protect their children from racial insensitivity, and according to Virginia, did not allow them to 'get ice cream where you were discouraged from eating inside.'[70] In Dresden, Ontario, white adults had no misgivings about refusing service to children. Indeed, a simple and popular summer pastime such as purchasing ice cream was experienced differently by Black children.[71]

Growing up, there were multiple ways to deal with the realities of race and the effects of racism, which ranged from ignoring its impact, to adaptation and acquiescence, all of which could occur simultaneously depending on an individual's temperament, location, and situation. Here Edna, who was born in 1915, explained how her siblings dealt with non-Black children:

We were taught we've got to live in this country, and the colour of your skin is seen, so they know you are Black, you know they are white. It didn't bother me whether they talked to me or not. We didn't know anything else;

we just grew up with the white children and the Jews ... We had to go to
school with them, and play with them and talk with them, and we adapted,
we just adapted.[72]

Certainly, the differential treatment meted out towards children
placed parents and other family members in a precarious position. They
were faced with the task of helping their children cope with these interactions and encounters, which embodied and reflected dominance and
subordination. Regardless of how much some parents tried to assist their
children to deal with inequality, ultimately, they had to come to terms
with dealing with their own racial identity and image.

The involvement of family members in anti-racist activities served as a
means of raising racial consciousness among some of the Black Canadian-born women, allowing them to understand and negotiate their own
relationship to the dominant culture. Frieda's mother and Eleanor were
members of the Hour-a-Day Study Club.[73] Frieda's mother was actually
one of the founding members. The Hour-a-Day Study Club was an informal group 'of mothers [who] banded together to create a better life for
their children and to encourage them to stay in school.'[74] The Hour-a-
Day Study Club not only helped women improve their parenting skills,
but also it reflected the principle of self-determination and promoted,
to a certain degree, the understanding that motherhood was not an
essential characteristic, even if it was not the group's intent. The women
invited speakers, read books, and took part in fund-raising. Over time,
the group became more formalized and political. According to Frieda,
they 'sent the first Black representative to our local council of women,
and through that they were able to make appeals' regarding a number
of social issues. The club wrote to the Ministry of Health protesting discriminatory practices of Canadian nursing schools against Black women
who wanted to train as nurses. Through direct involvement in anti-racist
initiatives, parents such as Evelyn and Eleanor, when they became parents, modelled the importance of activism to their children and the significance of a collective approach to dealing with structural inequalities.

Parents also protected their children by minimizing discussion about
racism or allowing their children to socialize only with other Blacks. Naomi Banks, who was born around 1930, pointed out:

we never talked about it [racism] in our home so were not aware of that,
and we associated mostly with Black people even though we had whites in
our neighbourhoods and white teachers.[75]

It is highly unlikely that Naomi's father was ignorant to the reality of racism given public discussions about racism coupled with the anti-racist initiatives occurring at the time. With a wife who was a popular and well-known singer, and children who were equally gifted and did well academically, Naomi's father did his best to shield his children by focusing on their collective and individual successes. Focusing on racism was a mere distraction to this family, who had an excellent reputation in and outside of Windsor, Ontario. Although racism operated to restrict and limit young Black Canadian identities and 'the modes of subjectivity that go with them,'[76] parents insisted otherwise. Black Canadian parents, on the whole, repeatedly reassured their children that they were valuable, emphasizing that they were equally as good as white children. In addition, many parents stressed the importance of speaking out against injustice regardless of its nature, advice that the women carried with them throughout their lives.

Colourism in the Caribbean

Although the vestiges of slavery and colonialism ensured that the Caribbean was demarcated along race, colour, and social class lines, only a few of the interviewees recalled being disadvantaged by a system in which whites and light-skinned people controlled the political, social, and economic apparatus. Despite the fact that racial categorizations in the English-speaking Caribbean were far more complicated than in, for example, Britain colourism was a reality. Given how colour conscious Caribbean societies were, it is highly probable that at some point in their youth, all of the Caribbean women either experienced or witnessed the dark-skinned, light-skinned differentiation.

Jennette did not discuss being discriminated against for being dark-skinned, but she did recall her father's experience as a police officer within a system controlled by whites that speaks to the intricacies of race, class, and power in Antigua. Jennette explained:

> the police system in Antigua and the whole Caribbean was run on military lines with a colonel and so on. In those days the colonel was usually English or a white local.[77]

Despite what he perceived to be a corrupt police system, Jennette's father never succumbed to unethical practices throughout his career and always managed to maintain his integrity. Jennette proudly insisted: 'He never took part in all the bribes and stuff that went on. He suffered for it, in that he never made sergeant, whereas all the people he trained did.'[78] She recognized that apart from her father's decision to remain honest, he was further disadvantaged because he was Black, and although he was penalized professionally, his ability to stand up to his white superiors earned him the respect of the Black people within the community. Jennette's relationship with her father was sometimes tense, yet her memories of him 'doing what's right' served as a principal lesson that influenced her own subjectivity and how she negotiated similar situations as an adult.[79]

Living in rural Manchester, Jamaica, Monica Mitchell was not exposed to discrimination based on skin colour. When she relocated to the burgeoning metropolis of Kingston, she immediately recognized demarcations along social class and colour lines. As a teenager, Monica remembered: 'people with lighter skins got better job opportunities than people with darker skins.'[80] Nepotism was also common, a practice that accorded some people access to certain privileges and jobs. Coming to the city from the countryside, Monica had no connections and no one to 'pull strings' for her. She had to work as a clerk in a clothing and dry goods store, work that was not commensurate with her education. Monica's experience illustrates how subjectivity and identity formation are shaped by discourses about inequality. As part of their recollections, these compelling stories about racism and skin colour preference were filled with pain, sadness, and confusion, and they shaped the women's sense of self, values, and ideas about work, as they themselves underwent their own life-course transitions.

Conclusion

In recounting their stories of growing up, both groups of women interviewed for this study vacillated tenuously between the past and the present. They made comparisons between a romanticized childhood of the past and understandings of childhood in the present. Memories that could possibly tarnish the family, if any, were suppressed, forgotten, or deliberately omitted. Although some of the Caribbean women, for example, hinted at conflicts in their families, they did not share stories of any real dysfunction. Consequently, extra-marital affairs, marital instability, possible conflicts resulting from blended families, trauma, and emotionally absent or abusive parents were generally downplayed. Instead, stories about the family as resourceful and as a safe haven during difficult periods took precedence. Indeed, Hazel Carby's argument that 'we need to recognize that during slavery, periods of colonialism and under the present authoritarian state the Black family has been a site of political and cultural resistance to racism'[81] holds true.

The interviewees remembered their childhood as a time devoid of many of the conflicts present in today's society. Both groups of women experienced their childhood with all its complications, contradictions, and uncertainties. Personal tragedies and loss, social and economic disparity, and for some a punitive and restrictive upbringing were a part of their repertoire of memories. How the women reacted in these various instances illustrates how subjectivity and identity formation remain continuous processes.

With little social power or social status, economic deprivation through the Depression and into the Second World War, and parental restrictions, the family emerged as the central force for preparing the women to make the transition to adulthood. As the women reconstructed their childhood through the eyes of the present, it was clear that family relationships left an indelible print on their psyche. They remembered parents who had struggled against oppression, had sacrificed much for their children, and disciplined them while teaching them to be proud. On a whole, the women interviewed for this study recalled parents who had attempted to provide them with a balanced view of life.

2

'I Wouldn't Be Where I Am Today': Creating Moral Citizens through School and Church

The women's recollections of the significance of education and religion in their youth underscore the notion that memories are indeed filtered, constructed, discriminately chosen, and influenced by the social conditions of the period. Foregrounding the women's narratives, I argue that despite the incongruities and the seeming disconnect from certain events of the past, the institutions of church and school profoundly shaped the women's subjectivities as children and as adults. On the one hand, the prescriptive messages articulated in churches and schools reflected and perpetuated particular social norms and practices of the period regarding work, education, heterosexual relationships, family, social class, race, colour, and gender. Equally important, however, these institutions represented critical sites where girls learned to negotiate their own agency and social position as they made the transition from girlhood to adolescence and, eventually, to young adulthood. Through interpellation, the mechanism by which 'ideologies or discourse constitute individuals as subjects,' schools and churches play a critical role in subjectivity formation.[1]

School

Education as a Social System

Secondary to the family, schools are instrumental in socializing students into becoming model adults. For some scholars, education not only encourages conformity, it maintains the status quo;[2] yet interpellation is never a straightforward process. Rather, it is synchronously fraught with acquiescence and resistance as students simultaneously accept and contest subjectivity formation. As this chapter argues, primary and secondary (high school) schools were more than domains where the women in this study sought education: they also afforded opportunities for personal development, friendships, and for considering career prospects. Equally important, school was the site where class, colour, race, and gender ideologies were repeatedly re-enacted and reinforced. Education also offered many interviewees the possibility to enter a social class beyond that which they had experienced while growing up.

The extent to which Caribbean- and Black Canadian-born parents valued education was tied to social inequality in both societies. Most of the Black Canadian-born interviewees were raised in families where, because of systemic and institutionalized racism, parents did not have the opportunity to obtain an education beyond primary school. Caribbean men and women were streamed into agricultural work and related occupations as a way to maintain the islands' race, colour, and class hierarchies.[3] Throughout the English-speaking Caribbean, 'secondary grammar schools[4] cater[ed] to the white, and later, brown elite until well into the twentieth century.'[5] Moreover, up until the 1960s, these schools were also fee-based, which excluded the majority of the population. Thus, a few of the interviewees' parents struggled to pay for their children's education. Whatever the obstacles, Black Canadian and Caribbean parents inculcated in their children the value of book learning, and alternately, children accepted and acknowledged that education was the anodyne against social inequality. This ideal was reflected in the fact that none of the interviewees opted to drop out of school to work full-time for remuneration.

Background: The Caribbean and Canada

As a result of changes brought about by the unrest of the 1930s throughout the Caribbean, there was improved school enrolment in the general population. Consequently, those with lower-middle to middle-class status wanted their children to capitalize on these transformations as a way to maintain their class status. For working-class people, their hope was to move upward on the social class ladder. This is not to suggest that the social divisions that existed in Caribbean societies were absent; they still persisted, and girls remained at a disadvantage. Throughout the Caribbean region, provision of education favoured males, regardless of colour, from the middle and upper classes.[6] In Canada enrolment was high; for example, 94 per cent of girls between ages ten and fourteen, and 37 per cent between fifteen and nineteen years of age attended school during 1941.[7] Historian Joan Sangster points out, however, that in the interwar years, at least according to the cultural outlook of working-class white families in Peterborough, Ontario, prolonged education – especially for girls – held limited value.[8] Sangster's subjects worked in Peterborough's factories and thus they were among the 21.5 per cent of Canadians aged fourteen to nineteen who were working in 1941, and, possibly among the 31.4 per cent working in 1951.[9] Clearly, the notion that education was inconsequential for girls was not a value shared by Black Canadian parents. Encouraging their daughters to stay in school might also have stemmed from the fact that racism made procuring employment difficult.

The school experiences of both groups of women interviewed for this study were inextricably shaped by the hierarchical structure and discourses that characterized Caribbean and Canadian society. This was manifested not only in the education system itself, but was also embedded in the attitudes of the citizenry. The organization of the English-speaking Caribbean education system remained invariably British in 'educational provisions and philosophy, curriculum, methodology, textbooks, and certification.'[10] According to scholar Olive Senior, 'the curricula of all schools, borrowed from England and subject to little reform, continued to be irrelevant, an irrelevance reinforced by imported books and alien imagery and concepts.'[11] Furthermore, she continues, 'until a few decades ago, female education was explicitly shaped by the ideology based on gender-role stereotyping which had its origins in Victorian England – that the female is a dependent being whose true locus is the home and whose vocation is that of wife and mother.'[12] Remnants of the aforementioned gender ideology, which varied depending on the school, permeated the curricula. None of this mattered; parents wanted their girls educated. If scholarships were unavailable, parents paid for their children's education, which translated into a certain amount of privilege. Two of the interviewees attended religious schools, most attended elite high schools, and a few enrolled in secondary schools with a vocational slant. None mentioned attending private schools.

Both Laura and Marlene were raised and educated in Nova Scotia, where Blacks lagged behind whites in terms of education, income, and employment at least until the 1960s.[13] Reverend W.P. Oliver, regional representative in the adult division of the Nova Scotia Department of Education, conducted a survey of 381 Halifax County fathers, which provides some insight into educational inequality in the province. Oliver found that of the fathers surveyed '50% had completed grade 6 or less; 17% had less than grade 4; 3% had gone beyond grade 12; the largest group had completed [only grades] 4–6.'[14] Laura's father completed high school, which was exceptional given the above statistics. His wife had only had a Grade 7 education. Marlene's mother completed only Grade 3, and she hypothesized that her father got only as far as Grade 5, explaining that 'to this day, [he] does not write well.'[15]

Still, parents held hopes and aspirations for their children. Laura described her mother as ambitious, although she was unable to pursue her own dream of becoming a nurse; instead, she cleaned white people's homes to earn a living. Although her own dreams were deferred, Laura's mother reasoned that at least her children could have a better life by being formally educated. Likewise, Marlene's mother expected that her children 'would grow up to be law-abiding, educated children, to be able to make [their] mark on the world, and [to] be responsible citizens.'[16] School attendance, then, was a major priority for both groups of women.

Marlene was the only Black Canadian-born interviewee to attend a segregated elementary school with Black teachers. Inadequate facilities and lack of provincial and municipal support due to anti-Black racism affected these schools.[17] Laura pointed out that she and her siblings were the only Blacks in her school. As in the Caribbean, the Canadian curriculum was also exclusive and, for the most part, immaterial to Black students' lived reality. Students also encountered teachers and students who discriminated against them on the basis of their race and colour.

Memories of School

What did Black Canadian and Caribbean girls remember about school? What can be surmised from these recollections in terms of their identities and subjectivities? Education historian Neil Sutherland maintained that for most of his white working- and middle-class interviewees, 'learning to read was inextricably entangled with such matters as the sort of teacher they had, how they got along with other children, and how their parents felt about schooling.'[18] Both groups of women interviewed for this study had similar recollections to those of Sutherland's subjects. Less attention was given to the curriculum, tests, and exams, while high school was the period most referenced. Overall, the interviewees highlighted distance to school, positive and negative encounters, and their academic success in high school. In their recollections of specific episodes and events, the interviewees framed their narratives in a way that underscored their will to persevere, to avoid failure at all costs, and to overcome the odds.

Walking the Distance: The One-Room School House

Four of the women interviewed attended one-room schools at the elementary level in Ontario and Halifax, Nova Scotia, a common experience in Canada in the 1930s, as 35 per cent of the country's students were educated in similar facilities at that time.[19] Laura and her four siblings attended school in Port Williams, two-and-a-half miles from their hometown of Kentville, Nova Scotia. 'Because we were just little kids, it was difficult going all that distance,'[20] she commented. Agnes, who lived in Maidstone Township in Ontario, also walked three miles every morning, to a one-room school that she attended until Grade 8 and where she and her brother served as janitors.

Connected to the memory of walking to school was the relationship between Black and white children. In addition to dealing with the long walk to school, Laura and her siblings were the only 'Blacks in a whole community of whites,' and she recalled that 'there was a lot of prejudice and it was pretty blatant, they called you nigger, and so forth. There were always some nasty kids around that would do that.'[21] Since Laura travelled with her siblings daily, they were able to defend each other against the unfriendliness they experienced at the hands of white children. 'We took up for one another,' Laura pointed out. Agnes also recalled the low numerical presence of Black children, noting that there were only five or six of them in the class. Unlike Laura, Agnes viewed encounters with white students as childish play devoid of any real meaning:

> We had little spats. When we'd come down the road, they'd call us names, and we'd call them names, and we'd fight all the way home. And then, the next day we'd be right there holding hands, going back to school again. We were raised that way.[22]

It is in these exchanges that Laura's and Agnes's subjectivities oscillated. There were moments when their subject positions as children and students were more salient, and other occasions, when certain incidents made race more salient. Certainly, the integrated one-room classrooms operated to temper some of the negative interactions between whites and Black students. As they evoked these narratives, Agnes and Laura situated themselves as subjects with a sense of agency.

Segregated and Integrated Elementary Schools

Despite overwhelming evidence of racial inequality in Nova Scotia, Marlene Watson reported that both Blacks and whites coexisted without much incident in Windsor Plains (sometimes coloquially referred to as 'White Plains'). She recalled memorable occasions when the children would get together:

> Winter time was great. At Christmas time, whites and blacks, we would get a long board and make hitches and go sledding on the hills. During the summer, we played together, we built brush homes, playing out and down in our fields.[23]

Such happy occasions were often marred, however, by the reality that the schools from Kindergarten to Grade 8 were segregated, which was incomprehensible to Marlene, especially when Black and white students had no difficulties getting along.

The segregated Five Mile Plains School obviously provided Marlene Watson with the intellectual tools to attend Windsor Academy, the nearby predominantly white high school, in the 1950s. Yet Marlene sighed in response to queries about the segregated school, moving on quickly to discuss how wonderful her high school experiences had been, especially her academic achievements.[24] If Marlene and the few other Black students had endured any form of racial discrimination at Windsor Academy, she neglected to say so. Instead, she eagerly highlighted the positive interactions between whites and herself in and outside the classroom. Thus, Marlene saw her election as the class valedictorian in Grade 12 as a confirmation of acceptance by her white peers.[25]

For Marlene and other Black Canadians, validation by their white peers was one of the multiple ways they defined success. Nevertheless, the interracial encounters in high school that Marlene referenced stood in stark contrast to the social reality and conditions of Black life in Nova Scotia. Blacks were systematically denied privileges accorded to most whites. Memories of high school at this critical period in developing her own subjectivity were easier for Marlene to recall than those from when she attended the 'black school.' Marlene's reluctance to divulge any information about her elementary school experience may be related to Jefferson A. Singer and Martin A. Conway's argument that 'in the individual, memory filters and selects by "forgetting" transitory impressions and encounters that are not crucial to ongoing goals, plans and life scripts that come to define the long-term self.'[26] By calling attention to her attendance at Windsor Academy, and how well she did academically, Marlene was assuming an intellectual subject position that the wider society often discounted.

Sometimes, however, those students who attended schools with a disproportionate number of Blacks, or who went to school with family members, faced fewer negative encounters than their counterparts who attended predominantly white schools. For example, Naomi attended the same schools in Windsor, Ontario, as some of her siblings in the 1950s, which contributed to her enjoyment of school: 'We knew everybody, and we walked to school together, and we were very good. We were at a mostly Black school, and we excelled in school.'[27] Part of Naomi's success rested undoubtedly in having a lot of friends, and being 'able to assimilate with people.' Consistent with her Christian upbringing, assimilation for Naomi meant having the propensity to coexist with and be accepted by other people, which was not necessarily a negation of her own individual identity.

Racism at School

For Virginia and Dorothy R, the harmful experiences at school during the 1940s left them conscious of how their racial identity was used to deny them certain pleasures that were available to their white peers. Virginia stated matter of factly:

> There were some negative experiences in public school and high school ...
> The teachers were often biased, and there were those times when I was not
> chosen to do certain things. For example, I knew for a school play, it was a
> racial issue.[28]

Although Virginia's parents had taught her at an early age to 'only associate with those who want to associate with you,' this advice did not erase the pain of being ignored, dismissed, and belittled by teachers and students alike. Her parents' advice proved fruitful as Virginia matured, and she was able to navigate her survival both in and outside of school more successfully, leading her to have 'friends from both races.'

Like Virginia, Dorothy R also found elementary school challenging. In spite of being a bi-racial child who could virtually pass for white, Dorothy R hardly felt privileged by her light skin or the other European phenotypical features that distinguished her from darker-skinned Blacks. In the first few grades of the elementary school she attended in Windsor,

Ontario, Dorothy R was not bi-racial; she was Black, and her classmates knew this. It was especially hard at recess. Dorothy R remembered white children saying, 'Don't play with her!' She described a typical recess period:

> Here it's recess and everybody is having a good time, if you went to play with them, whether it was playing ball or getting on a swing or whatever, everybody would walk away. Oh yeah, there used to be a lot of that. There might have been half a dozen Black kids, a few of us scattered throughout the whole school. And of course, everybody shied away from you.[29]

These exclusionary experiences affected the self-esteem of these girls as they wrestled with making sense of the treatment they experienced.

For Agnes, being called racially charged names by her peers was defensible and attributed to mere ignorance. She had different expectations of adults, however, especially her teachers. Given their position as educators, teachers were expected to avoid colluding in racist behaviour, but this was not necessarily true. In elementary school, Agnes recalled, there were 'teachers who would call us names which was reported to the school authorities, [but they] didn't do anything, we had to live with it.'[30] Still, Agnes maintained, 'We confronted it.' By reporting the incident, even if the school authorities were unresponsive, sent the message that speaking out against injustice was necessary. Through discriminatory practices and discourses of inferiority, schools contributed to the instability and shifting nature of Black students' subjectivities. Whether on the playground, in the classrooms, or during extracurricular activities, as children, the interviewees struggled with being accepted by their teachers and classmates.

Colour, Social Class, and Favouritism in Caribbean Schools

Some Caribbean interviewees' recollections of their schooling conjured up mixed memories and emotions, as well. In some instances, they reflected the findings of a survey on women who attended school from 1920 to 1970, which concluded that 'school is too often a memory associated with punishment and humiliation.'[31] As adolescents, and later as teenagers, some of the women had to stake out a sense of self in school environments that were not always accommodating.

As soon as Lillie was old enough, she moved from the rural community where she had spent her formative years to Kingston, where she enrolled in the prestigious Wolmers Girls School. Wolmers, according to Ula Y. Taylor, 'represented the essence of elite education.'[32] Lillie, who was most likely one of few dark-skinned students at Wolmers in the 1940s, either witnessed or was subjected to the pernicious effects of 'colourism' in Jamaica:

> Our teachers in public school were all right. In high school, some were nice and others were not. Some teachers were prejudice [sic]. In Jamaica at the time, some teachers were white, and some were brown-skinned, and there was a lot of favouritism. But, you know, you had a goal and that was to get that certificate.[33]

Lillie's hesitation to name discrimination at Wolmers is perhaps attributable to her belief that intolerance based on skin colour was more of a 'foreign' phenomenon. In that even though colourism was deeply embedded in the structure and organization of Caribbean society that peoples' identification and relationship with each was far more complex than in, for example, Britain. Another probable explanation is the common perception that social class, rather than race, organizes Caribbean society. Perhaps nationalistic feelings prohibited Lillie from criticizing Jamaica's racial politics. Finally, it is highly probable that Lillie deliberately chose not to divulge the experience of being shunned because of her colour, because it was simply too painful to convey.

Instead, Lillie resisted unequal treatment by focusing on accomplishing her educational goals. To be identified with a reputable school such as Wolmers had its benefits in societies where formal education was closely connected to social class. Certainly a Cambridge Certificate from Wolmers or other prestigious secondary schools offered some assurance regarding one's future.

Inez's experience with her primary school teacher serves as an example of how teachers bear upon and help to constitute their students' subjectivities. When Inez's mother consulted her teacher about which high school she should attend in 1948, the instructor suggested sending Inez to a vocational school instead. How Inez retold the story – with much verve – decades later speaks to the impact of the incident on her psyche. She explained:

> This particular teacher thought I wasn't smart enough to go to high school, so she told [mother] she should just send me to go and do domestic science. My younger sister was very bright, so she was encouraging my moth-

er to spend more money on this sister of mine, and just forget about me. ·
Thank God, I can remember hearing my mother telling her, 'I will give
every child of mine their equal share. I will not spend more on one and
less on the other.' And today, I can tell you I respect my mother for that.[34]

Inez was less concerned about the partiality expressed by the teacher
towards her sister; she was hurt that her own academic potential was
invisible. Coming from a middle-class family with a domestic helper,
she was offended that the teacher would recommend domestic science,
which involved 'laundering, dressmaking, basketry, millinery, and child
management,'[35] duties reserved for working-class girls. Fortunately for
Inez, her mother intervened on her behalf, which motivated her to
do well academically at Mannings High School, a reputable school in
Savanna-La-Mar.

For those students who enjoyed their schooling, some aspects of their
relationship with the teachers were based on favouritism, which placed
them in a privileged position vis-à-vis their peers. Attending school also
in the 1940s, Jamaican-born Daphne C explained:

> School was fun. I could not say I did not enjoy school, because I did. We
> always wanted to go to school because the teachers were lovely, and as long
> as you could understand your lessons, if you were on the brighter side, you
> don't have problems with the teachers, and you get your homework done.[36]

Daphne C implicitly provided some ideas into how her school was structured. As long as a student was on the 'brighter side,' was liked, and performed well academically, she had the support of teachers.

Only Antiguan-born Jennette was vocal about the exclusionary secondary school system in the island that 'up to a certain year never took
Black people,' and that '[brought] white teachers from England,' one
of whom she had in her last year of high school.[37] Howard A. Fergus
corroborates Jennette's criticisms in his discussion of education in the
Leeward Islands, including Antigua. These islands' education system
provided privileged access for the children of the large number of white,
wealthy families.[38] While Jennette might have recognized the racial disparity at the high school she attended as a teenager, her scathing critique
of the education system in Antigua was most likely framed from knowledge about colonialism and racism gained as an adult. In other words,
Jennette's memory of the past is not necessarily her own, but gleaned
from other sources. Thus, her intense dislike of Antigua's education

system did not translate into any outright opposition while she was a student. Like the other women, she did not withdraw, fail, challenge her teachers, or act inappropriately. That the girls conformed in this way to the expectations, rules, and roles of the education system and its teachers, attests to the powerful place of education in their lives. Equally significant is the education system's position in the interpellation of its students and 'inducing [for some] a sense of belonging and identity,'[39] however fraught the space with tensions.

Resistance and Survival

Both groups of women attended schools that, despite different manifestations, valorized white/European values, ideals, histories, and cultures. As racialized 'Others,' the interviewees often felt burdened by their subject positions. Yet they avoided the inclination to present themselves as victims. To circumvent and cope with inequalities, the interviewees for this study found ways to situate and claim a space for themselves at school. Resistance occurred in various forms. While they were discriminated against and treated unfairly in some cases, none of the interviewees engaged in any form of outright protest; indeed, any complaints could be construed as a devaluation of their parents' efforts. Not all of the Caribbean interviewees won scholarships to high school, consequently, parents had to pay for them, which posed a challenge for some families. In turn, some students earned excellent grades, and others rejected certain subject positions imposed on them by teachers.

June's retelling of her educational experiences from the late 1940s illustrated how subjectivities and identities were far from static and were constantly being remade. June was privileged on multiple levels. She was light-skinned and attended a primary school where her mother was the principal, which meant that she was rarely reprimanded for insolent behaviour. June admitted that she was hardly 'one of the best-behaved students because I talked too much.'[40] June's comments revealed how schools regulated their students' subject positions especially in relation to gendered expectations that girls should remain quiet. In response, June excelled academically to avoid disappointing either the teachers or her mother.

Once June entered high school, however, she was less disruptive and took a keen interest in learning by asking many questions about the subject material, which surprised many teachers. June demonstrated repeatedly that she was an active and not a passive student, deviating from a culture that teaches children 'to be seen and not heard.' In other words, June rejected the suppression of her voice. Laughing, she explained:

> When I went to high school the teachers who knew her [mother] expected me to be this little lady that I wasn't. I guess they figured that I would sit quietly in class and not open my mouth.[41]

June was expected to engage in the gender performance of 'being a lady,' which was reflected in her observation regarding the teachers' expectations. By remaining vocal throughout high school, June challenged in a very small way the dictates of Caribbean culture regarding gender norms, behaviour, and expectations that the education system reinforced.

As June illustrated, high school became a site whereby some of the interviewees became more self-assured in how they constructed their identities. Once Virginia and Dorothy R entered high school, both made a conscious decision to become involved in sports, which helped to ameliorate some of the tensions that existed between Black and white students. Dorothy ran track and won a few races, which 'helped because some of the white guys would talk to me, even if the white girls would not.'[42] Similarly, there was no sport that Virginia did not attempt: 'I did broad jump, running and high jump. I was also a cheerleader.' Virginia attributed her participation in athletics to 'a value system that told me if I wanted to achieve, I have to go beyond the racist name calling.'[43]

Some teachers reacted differently, perhaps out of their own initial preconceived notions about Black students. Virginia explained that, 'because of our participation in sports, our teachers became more accepting of us.' Although scholars tend to underscore the gendered, classed, and racial dynamics of competitive sports, with emphasis on how women and girls are marginalized, the picture is more complicated. Dorothy R's and Virginia's experiences revealed that their participation in organized sports benefited them. Sports such as ice hockey, baseball, softball, and track and field helped to forge alliances between students, as their love of athletic competition often undercut racial and gender differences.[44] Virginia found her teachers and peers more amicable, which made a positive impact on her learning experience and identity. Similarly, some of Dorothy R's peers recognized her athletic abilities. Instead of rejection, sports helped the women to gain acceptance among their white classmates and teachers.

Nevertheless, high school resulted in some anxieties, although the interviewees made it clear that academic failure had never been an option, and they worked hard to ensure that they excelled. Some of them pointed to parents who insisted that they were equally intelligent and as capable as their white counterparts, and teachers who expressed an interest in their well-being by contributing to their academic success. Others credited their own tenacity in helping them traverse an education system that was sometimes unwelcoming to their presence. Agnes had intended to continue her schooling after completing Grade 8, but because her house was six miles away from the school, transportation was unavailable. Once Agnes heard that a school bus would be provided, she did not hesitate. Agnes painted her decision as autonomous, without the input of her father or other family members:

> Nobody told me. I had a father [who] was out trying to find himself a wife and my sisters – some of them were getting married. And I found myself getting on that school bus, going to high school.[45]

For the four years that Agnes attended Essex High School, in south-western Ontario, she placed 'first and second' in her classes. She was also proud to be the first in her family to graduate from high school:

> Something in my spirit told me to keep going. And sometimes I didn't have soap to wash. I didn't have deodorant to put under my arms. But I went to school, and I was very good in school.[46]

This was not the case for the four Black students who enrolled with Agnes. It is more than likely they were unable to deal with the alienation they experienced, because they withdrew from classes: 'When I got to Grade 12 [in 1950], there was nobody but me graduating; I was the only Black graduating.'[47] Agnes's retelling of her educational experience reveals the role that individuals play in constructing their own subjectivities, but also how they utilize myths in the process. Agnes was her own motivation: in essence, she was the self-made teenager. In this way, she drew on a pre-established mythical framework, similar to what Jean Peneff identifies as the 'self-made man.'[48] Regardless of the structural and personal hurdles that she confronted, Agnes had a vision of a future that was different from that of her family members. She would succeed no matter what the cost. While the school was a site of competing and conflicting forms of subjectivity for the other Black female students, Agnes excelled academically. Of course, the myth of the 'self-made' teenager could also apply to Marlene and some of the other interviewees who, despite an education system that was designed to mark them as inferior, still managed to defy the odds.

Curriculum in Canada and the Caribbean

CANADA

Canadian historian Patrick J. Harrigan contends that 'it is true that school-boards, teachers, and textbooks presented graven images to children. Many of those sharply distinguished gender roles and contributed to a cultural reproduction of gender roles over generations.'[49] Harrigan further adds: 'But boys and girls were taught by the same teachers in the same classes received similar messages ... about religion, class, and politics.'[50] The question, then, becomes: whose religion, which classes, and whose politics were at the core of the curriculum? While scholars writing about education in the 1950s certainly acknowledge that the education system played a critical role in creating and legitimizing gender differences, these scholars ignore race, including whiteness, in their analyses.

The contested nature of Canadian education as it relates to Black people is reflected in several articles that appeared in the 1940s and 1950s in the *Dawn of Tomorrow*, a newspaper serving London, Ontario, and the surrounding area. Black Canadians faced a dilemma: how could they endorse education as the route to equality when the education system, in upholding white supremacy, contributed to the dehumanization and marginalization of Black students? Michael Apple argues: ' there is a very real set of relationships among those who have economic, political and cultural power in society on the one hand and the ways in which education is thought about, organized, and evaluated on the other.'[51] Hence, those who have virtually little or no power have little input in shaping the education system.

An article in the *Dawn of Tomorrow* confirms Agnes's earlier recollection of teachers calling her derogatory names in elementary school. Students complained of speakers referring to them as 'nigger in the woodpile,' or teachers who '[made] remarks that the Negro boy is lazy and good to step dance or strum to a banjo, and the girls [made] good mammies to English girls' babies.'[52] Such racist and sexist stereotypes were undoubtedly used, whether intentionally or not, as a way to remind Blacks of their place in Canadian society. Based on these sentiments, Black female students were not expected to want to aspire beyond their designated subject position as domestic workers. No doubt students who sat in those classrooms felt marginalized, disillusioned, and wounded by teachers' racist attitudes, just as Agnes had been during the late 1930s and early 1940s.

Students in elementary and high school read books such as *Little Black Sambo*, *The Adventures of Tom Sawyer*, or *Huckleberry Finn*. For the most part, teachers were hardly equipped to provide some context to these books. Black students had no choice but to sit quietly and hope no one identified them with the images in their pages.[53] Charged with educating future citizens, some teachers produced and reproduced – albeit with some resistance from students and parents – a discourse of inferiority aimed at Black children.[54]

The education system perpetuated the premise that every individual has her own place in the social order, reflected in the establishment of technical, industrial, and vocational schools. These institutions provided gender- and class-specific practical training for boys and girls who were considered unsuitable for the professions. An examination of education in the province of Nova Scotia, where Marlene and Laura grew up, reveals this bias. At the Halifax Industrial School, training was provided to 'truant and delinquent boys' in 'farming, shop, wood-working, general wooden construction repair, painting, and bricklaying'; girls could take 'training in the household arts, laundry work, and restaurant waiting.'[55] White males from working-class backgrounds were featured in the industrial school photographs, which suggested they were being trained for skilled trades. The lone Black male featured was in the woodworking class.

For educator Ruth Binnie, a founding member of the Nova Scotia Home Economics Association, 'a functional program in home economics [was] one which [would] reach and serve the home.'[56] Binnie, for example, noted that a 'Negro circuit' was established in Halifax County in 1945, with a second circuit in Digby and Yarmouth counties. In addition, a second 'Negro Teacher was appointed for the Halifax County Circuit.'[57] Regardless of race and social class, presumably heterosexual boys and girls were being instructed for their proper roles as fathers, husbands, wives, and mothers.

Only girls took domestic science (later called home economics) and dressmaking, while boys concentrated on 'manly' trades, such as those offered at the Halifax Industrial School. Indeed, when Edna made the decision to bake cakes for sale so she could earn extra money, it was in Miss McLuhen's domestic science class that she learned and mastered her baking skills. Some of these skills transferred easily to other careers, such as nursing. As a powerful determinant, the impact of gender upon the structure, organization, practices, and processes of the education system influenced students' feelings towards certain subjects and decisions about careers.

Marlene recalled that she loved Latin and French, and received a perfect grade of 100, in addition to scoring high on her geography, chemistry, and English tests. Yet, she recalled, 'I didn't study physics, they always said physics was a boy's subject, so I didn't want to do it.' In retrospect, she added: 'I didn't study in physics, but might as well have done physics because I used to work with the kids at lunch helping them work out their problems [sets].'[58] Neither group of women interviewed for this study recalled teachers encouraging them to excel in science or mathematics. In fact, most expressed an intense dislike for math. Indeed, individual taste can account for the unwillingness to tackle these subjects, but it is hard to discount how the education system and its agents influenced student preference.

CARIBBEAN

While the Caribbean education system also reinforced gender roles through the kinds of subjects taught to young girls, there was some variation throughout the islands. Ula Taylor notes that at the beginning of the twentieth century 'secondary education in Jamaica had a literary slant, including classes in Latin, English language and literature, and modern languages as well as bookkeeping and shorthand.'[59] She further points out that by excluding manual education in the curriculum, schools prepared students for only the 'Cambridge Local Examinations, the External Training College Examinations, and the Pupil Teachers' Examinations.'[60] These exams distinguished schools such as Wolmers from their less elite counterparts and were designed with the intent to maintain the status quo.

Wolmers Girls School and Mannings High, both in Jamaica, St Michael's High in Barbados, and Naparima Girls High School, which Ancilla boasted was 'one of the most prestigious high schools in Trinidad,'[61] all seemed to have had a similar curriculum. At Mannings High, Inez explained, domestic science was not included as part of the repertoire of subjects she had to take: 'But you had to do math, English literature, geography, history, health science, religious knowledge, and a foreign language, [and] you could either do Latin or Spanish.'[62] Thus, elite schools such as Wolmers, which Lillie attended, prepared students for the white-collar positions of nursing, teaching, and clerical work.

Besides providing these young women with the tools to embark on their future, Taylor notes that a school like Wolmers 'acculturated its students to adopt the essentialized values and lifestyle of the British,' adding that 'Wolmers provided a training ground not only for occupations but also for the social roles individuals were expected to play as adults.'[63] This assessment can be applied to other elite high schools throughout the Anglo-speaking Caribbean.

Daphne C and Dorette, however, attended comprehensive secondary schools in the 1940s and 1950s, respectively, whose curricula were geared towards subjects such as sewing and cooking. Daphne C articulated the gendered nature of the educational practices at the school she attended in Jamaica:

> When you were going to school you have to remember that Wednesdays used to be sewing class. The boys used to go to the gardening, and the girls used to go to the sewing class and home economics. The boys didn't come to cooking and things like that. They got to plant the stuff.[64]

Similarly, Dorette pointed out: 'I did go to sewing classes and home economics, and learnt a few things to practice at home.'[65] The women found out that traits and skills that were taught to be innate were not so. 'I was not good at sewing,' Daphne C eventually found out.[66]

Like their Canadian-born counterparts, the Caribbean-born interviewees focused less on the subjects they took, and more on the possibilities that lay ahead once they had completed their education. Inez summed up what most of the women felt: 'I knew that if I focused on what I wanted to do, I could achieve it. So I knew I had to study, and my mother used to insist that you [had] to study.'[67] Literacy, unavailable and unaffordable to the majority of Caribbean people, was welcomed by the few who were able to attain it.

The Role of Teachers

School was more than a place to gain knowledge and a range of social skills; it was a space where some of the women developed their confidence and felt validated. In this regard, teachers were helpful. Marlene credited herself and her teachers for her success:

> The teachers themselves were supportive of me. If I had been a lackey kind of person that just sort of got through her grades, it may have been another

scenario there. I strove very hard and it was always that way in school with me, I must be the best in class. I was always an honour student. And so, they [teachers] had nothing to fuss with me about. I was basically a quiet person by nature in class and stuff, and so the confrontations did not arise, partly because of my personality.[68]

Marlene's passivity, coupled with her commitment to academic excellence, and being among a small group of Blacks at Windsor Academy, meant that she might have stood out as the 'exception' in the eyes of white teachers and students.

While there is no evidence that white teachers or school administrators collectively challenged segregation or institutional racism as a group, other interviewees, like Marlene, recalled a few teachers who abhorred bigotry against Black children and treated them equally. The assistance that teachers offered at different stages of the interviewees' educational journeys went a long way in reassuring them of their value and self-worth. Laura noted that one of her high school teachers 'was obviously racist,' but found that overall they were 'very good.' Deserving special praise was her high school principal, Mr Giles, who was likely mindful of the racial climate in Port Williams, and who took a special interest in Laura and her siblings: 'He was excellent, and he was good to all of us, and helped us to excel in whatever we wanted to do.'[69] In addition to providing books for them to read, Giles made certain that Laura and her siblings were aware of educational opportunities to which they might not otherwise have had access. Even though Laura thought the larger community was racist, the schools proved to be the exception. The encouragement of Mr Giles and the other teachers helped to increase the self-esteem and confidence of Laura and her siblings, and no doubt helped them to create a positive identity.

By creating an environment where Black students could be viewed as competent, teachers provided a model of interracial cooperation not only to Laura and her siblings, but to the predominantly white student body at large, even if it meant ignoring or subverting an education system that reinforced white culture, values, and perspectives. That a few of the women could recall a teacher's name decades later is a testament to their power, influence, and impressions. In a society where the dominant racial script reinforced whiteness and white privilege, to encounter teachers willing to choose a different approach and support their Black students' social development clearly meant something.

Church

'We Did Everything in Our Church'

Families and schools were not the only institutions that shaped the women's subjectivities. The majority of the women interviewed for this study identified church and religion as an integral part of their growing up. Most were raised in Christian households belonging to various denominations and a few identified as Catholics. Varying degrees of intensity, however, were placed on actual religious practice. What the women recalled about church and religion was based on an individual religious frame of reference, connected first to parental expectations and, as they got older, to their own religious interpretations and relationship with God. As with their recollections about school, some of the Black Canadian-born women's memories about church and religious activities were linked to the history of racism within the larger society. Religious teachings provided moral and spiritual guidance, and participation in church-related activities provided a sense of community.

The centrality of religion in all its variety cannot be underestimated in the lives of people of African descent, whether from the more formal Protestantism and Catholicism, or the hybridized religions of pocomania and Rastafarianism in the Caribbean. In Canada, the Black church was committed to meeting the multiple and diverse needs of a population that was often dehumanized in Canadian society.[70] Excluded and marginalized in the larger community, the Black church provided members with resiliency against inequalities, developed and sustained racial pride and identity, and valued certain Black cultural norms, such as 'a preference for passionate sermons, hymn singing, and other expressions of spiritual religion.'[71]

The establishment of Black autonomous churches in Canada followed a pattern similar to the development of Black churches in the United States. For example, the African Methodist Episcopal (AME) Church – founded in Philadelphia in 1816, with Richard Allen as the first bishop – was also visible in Canada. Eventually, the congregation in Canada wanted to separate from the parent body in the United States to create the British Methodist Episcopal (BME) Church. Dorothy Shadd Shreve attributes this decision to political tensions between Canada and the United States and that the former fugitive slaves wanted to 'demonstrate their loyalty to British institutions which protected them from slavery.'[72]

Versed in the history of the Baptist church in Windsor, coupled with

her own recollections, Frieda explained the formation of the Amherstburg Baptist Association (later renamed the Amherstburg Regular Baptist Association) and the relevance of the BME and AME church to the
Black community when she was growing up:

> Our Association was organized in 1841. We were organized because of prej-
> udice, and we decided to move away. As long as racism is alive and well in
> our communities, we are better able to support each other in our commu-
> nities because we have a unique understanding of things. When I was a kid
> everyone went to AME/BME [church] if you were Black and that was the
> centre of our society. We did everything in our church.[73]

Frieda's parents were both active members of the First Baptist Church.
Her mother not only held a leadership role in women's activities, she
was also active in the local association of churches.[74] Her father served
as a deacon for many years, while being active on several church boards.
Their religious and civic commitments undoubtedly influenced their
daughter.

Both groups of women's early memories of church revolved around
their weekly attendance, Sunday school participation, and various social
activities. As Sunday school or Vacation Bible School (VBS) teachers,
ushers, choir leaders, and actors in the numerous theatrical performances, children and youth developed and honed their communication,
organizational, and performance skills. African American psychologist Wendy L. Haight explains that, in the Black church in the United
States, 'children are valued as resources, and opportunities are created
for increasing their participation. Every individual is treasured, everyone
has gifts, and everyone has a responsibility to use those gifts for the common good.'[75] Her analysis holds true for Canada and the Caribbean as
well.

During her teenage years, Frieda belonged to the Baptist Young People's Union, a religiously oriented social support outlet for young people
that also created a sense of community among its members. The group
met weekly, played games, and participated in various outings, but as
Frieda grew older, her responsibilities increased. In 1944, at age fifteen,
with the support of her parents and other members of her church, Frieda took a leadership training course at the Young Women's Christian
Association (YWCA). Once she completed the course Frieda 'then went
back and helped the church,' assisting with the annual Vacation Bible
School. Every summer until she left for nursing school, Frieda provided

an invaluable service: she organized classes, crafts, games, and activities for young VBS members. Frieda's confidence and capabilities were cultivated in her family and developed materially in practice at church.[76]

Frieda also recalled fondly the social activities organized by First Baptist Church: 'It was a lot of fun attending the church anniversary and the Silver Tea. This was a well-organized, fancy, and formal dinner, with fine china and the like, it was very well attended.'[77] Through such events, their church simultaneously met the spiritual and social needs of Black Canadians.

Their church alleviated the strain and uncertainties associated with life as Blacks in Canada both before and after the Second World War. Outside the confines of their church, in school and at work, for example, Blacks were often judged by Eurocentric standards, and on many occasions they felt unable to measure up. In their respective churches, everyone, including children, was affirmed, valued, and appreciated. Although social class, education, and other distinctions existed in Black communities, racism in the larger society operated in a manner that assuaged differences. That is, as racialized subjects, the wider Canadian society constituted Blacks in essentialist terms, and Blacks often responded in kind by using their racial identity to establish and sustain their churches.

As a catechist, Lillie's father not only participated in organizing mass marriages during the late 1940s for unmarried, working-class Jamaicans, but he also channelled some of his energies into coordinating church socials and other activities. His wife and children followed suit. Like Naomi, Lillie directed the choir, and planned concerts for special occasions as a young woman. At Sunday services, she and her mother took turns playing the organ.[78]

One interviewee made a conscious decision about her spiritual and social life when she found that her needs were not being met. Joan's family attended a Christian Mission Church in Barbados, but once she enrolled in high school, she joined the St Barnabas Anglican Church. Joan's rationale was that she wanted to be with her friends, even though some family members expressed their disapproval. After all, Joan's family members (including her extended family) all belonged to the Christian Mission, and her grandfather was a minister at one of the Christian Mission churches. Still, friendship was not the sole reason Joan joined St Barnabas, as she explained:

> I enjoyed St Barnabas because it had more things for the young people than

at the Christian Mission. At the Christian Mission it was all adult things, it was nothing for the kids, it wasn't geared towards children. At St Barnabas it was geared towards everyone. The kids were involved. And I think that is why I preferred St Barnabas.[79]

Joan chose to be involved in a church that paid attention to young people, and she felt a greater sense of purpose and belonging than she had experienced at her former church.

Families also sometimes established their own religious rituals outside of the church that included praying, reading Bible-related stories, singing religious songs, and memorizing Bible passages – all of which were meant to assist them in their spiritual walk. Prior to returning to school in Kingston after the holidays, Lillie and her siblings were expected to 'read a passage in the Bible and pray.' She added: 'We were made to realize that you have to trust God, and he protects you.'[80] Once they left the physical building of the church, parents had the responsibility to ensure that their children did not go astray, and often reminded them about the importance of biblical teachings. To contravene the lessons taught regarding love, respect, and obedience, they were told, was to disobey an omnipotent and all-knowing God.

Monitoring Girls' Behaviour

As one of the driving cultural forces in society, religion serves to regulate behaviour both within the physical space of the church and outside. Children and young people were exposed to a set of beliefs and practices that were codified in rituals, sermons, and doctrine. The women's narratives revealed certain commonalities rooted in the Judeo-Christian tradition, particularly in relation to questions surrounding women's conduct.

Naomi grew up in a strict household where life literally revolved around Mount Zion Church of God in Christ. Besides her musical talents and public speaking contribution to, and on behalf of, the church, she was selected to teach a 'purity class' for girls approaching adolescence. Naomi made it clear that girls were primarily responsible for virtuous behaviour and self-control:

I told them about boys and how to conduct themselves around [them]. I told them don't be aggressive; don't be up in their faces. I taught them something about personal hygiene. Make sure you're clean. Brush your teeth, and take care of your body and wear clean clothes. You don't have to have new clothes, but just make sure they are clean, and look presentable, and take care of yourself because you were representing Christ.[81]

The church was never alone in producing gendered identities; fellow members were implicated in the process.

Naomi was obviously viewed as a suitable candidate to help mould the minds of young girls, and in so doing, she engaged to some degree in promoting what historian Evelyn Brooks Higginbotham refers to as the 'politics of respectability.' Middle-class African American women promoted sexual restraint, cleanliness, politeness, and temperance to their working-class counterparts with a twofold objective: to change individual behaviour and to prove to whites that African Americans met the barometer of respectability.[82] Although a nineteenth-century phenomenon, these ideologies clearly resonated in the twentieth century. Since the political, social, and economic conditions of Black life operated to subsume social class differences in Canada, Naomi's directives were not aimed only at working-class girls. Moreover, Naomi's emphasis on appropriate behaviour around boys, personal hygiene, cleanliness, and appearance was intricately connected to how children represented Christ first and their peers second.

Related also to the 'politics of respectability' was the idea of sexual propriety, which meant 'we saved ourselves until the day we got married,' said Naomi.[83] The women seemed uncomfortable discussing sexuality during the interviews, but their responses about boys, marriage, and dating provided some insight. Scholarly analysis of Black women's sexuality in the Canadian context during the late 1950s, when Naomi Banks was approaching adulthood, remains rather sparse, yet an examination of Black women's sexuality in other diasporic locations is helpful. Kamala Kempadoo, while noting the absence of any overt focus on sexuality in Caribbean scholarly literature, contends that 'Black working-class women figured in such studies of the Caribbean as the trope of the sexually free and uninhibited, and hence most sexually accessible, woman.'[84] Although Black women's sexuality does not manifest itself in the same way in all diasporic spaces, the interviewees' reluctance could also stem from their desire to uphold a particular representation of themselves that deviated from the stereotype of the sexually free woman.

Scholars have repeatedly demonstrated how Black women since slavery have also struggled with racist views of their own sexuality. Referring to Black women in the United States, Darlene Clark Hine argues that Black women created a 'culture of dissemblance' or a 'culture of secrecy' to counteract negative stereotypes.[85] This might partly account for the interviewees' reluctance to discuss intimate details. Other factors, such as the church, family, comfort level, and the fact that they might not have divulged their sexual experiences with other individuals, are equally valid reasons for the women's silence.

Naomi's proclamation that 'we saved ourselves until marriage' resonated among the majority of both groups of interviewees, whether they attended church regularly or infrequently. Even if stereotypes of Black women's sexuality were less pervasive in Canada than in Caribbean discourses, none of the women escaped the messages, both subtle and explicit, regarding the ramifications of sexual impropriety from the church and family. Whichever diasporic space the women occupied as girls, one objective of the church when it came to girls was to create a specific type of subjectivity. Girls were expected to remain chaste virgins, and they were exposed to the accompanying message that premarital sex was a sin, with such disobedience incurring God's wrath. While all young people were expected to be sexually inactive, it was less apparent that the young women's brothers were regulated in the same manner as their sisters, reinforcing a double standard of morality.

Regardless of the constraints of growing up in Christian households, it is not enough to view religious teachings about sexuality merely as a form of social control. Religious guidance played a role in discouraging activities, sexual or otherwise, that could compromise the young women's personal, professional, and educational future. Thus, their religious beliefs served as a shield that protected them from acting irresponsibly or engaging in risky behaviours. In what can be deemed as rigid social practices enacted by the church, the young women developed strategies that allowed them to create alternative religious subjectivities.

Marlene, who grew up in the Pentecostal Church, made a decision to accept Jesus as her personal Saviour at twelve years of age and was subsequently baptized by immersion. She found that the church's philosophies on certain topics corroborated her mother's teachings at home, which made religion more palatable to her:

> It just sort of fermented those things in my mind. I knew there was a certain code of behaviour expected [of a] Christian person ... And so, God played a very, very important part in my life because in my heart I didn't want to do anything that would bring disgrace or discredit Christ's name.[86]

As she grew older, Marlene maintained that in addition to providing a spiritual foundation, 'religion kept me out of a lot of things,' suggesting there were things she refrained from doing because she was a Christian.

Marlene did not reveal what 'a lot of things' meant, but she was not cloistered, either. Her discussion of high school illustrated how young women negotiated their subjectivities as sexual beings. Some of the interviewees, including Marlene, conveniently disregarded the admonitions of religious teachings. They found ways to traverse the lines of acceptable female behaviour without blatantly contravening certain norms. The young women did not entirely suppress all of their sexual desires and emotions and found ways to explore aspects of their sexuality 'without going all the way.' Marlene unabashedly explained: 'in my days, I may neck, but you better rest assured, I'm not going to step beyond that. Oh, no, no, no, the Lord want you chaste, and chaste [He's going] to have me.'[87] Despite a dominant discourse dictating acceptable codes of behaviour, Marlene found a way to negotiate her gender, religious, and sexual subjectivity.

Clearly, not all of the subjects interviewed for this study internalized discourses regarding sexuality in the same way. Although Agnes was baptized at the age of fifteen in 1947 and regularly attended the First Baptist Church in Puce, Ontario, unlike some of the other women discussed thus far, she resisted the messages commonly told about boys. Agnes refused to believe that boys should be avoided at all costs and, and along with her three friends who named themselves the 'Chick Club,' she made attracting boys one of her pastimes. Living in the country, Agnes maintained that 'we were always looking for boys that had cars, so they could get us out of here.' While she further explained that 'I didn't experience true love until I met Doug,' she admitted to having boyfriends before she met him, adding that for the sake of expediency there were moments when she and her friends had multiple boyfriends. Whenever the young women planned parties or other social activities, they would invite their many boyfriends to balance out the sexes. Agnes exclaimed, extolling the 'Chick Club's' ingenuity:

> They wouldn't know we had two, but we'd say, 'I'll invite this one and I'll invite this one.' And when they'd get [here], then we had other girls that we'd invite too. Oh, we had a good time![88]

While Agnes and her friends did not adhere to the theological principles that Naomi imparted to young women in her purity class regarding interactions with boys, Agnes's avid interest in boys and dating cannot be viewed simply as an abdication of her religious upbringing, as she adhered to the general principles of Christianity advocated by the church and her family. She found a way to reconcile the body and mind dualism found in most religions that view sexual desires as sinful outside the confines of a monogamous relationship. Furthermore, living in a predominantly white community where '[young white men] would never give us the time of day,'[89] having boyfriends made Agnes and her friends feel desirable. Indeed, some of these teenagers' actions appear to fly in the face of religious teaching about sexuality. Yet, these women rationalized that as long they refrained from having sexual intercourse, they were still obedient to the values and principles of their individual churches. Agnes and others like her were undoubtedly aware of the consequences of unintended pregnancies and the church's reactions to them.

For some of the women, holding hands, kissing, possibly touching, and, for at least one woman, engaging in sexual intercourse, marked the beginning of their forays into discovering their own sexualities. Trinidadian-born Carmencita hinted at being sexually aroused by her next-door neighbour when she attended his birthday party. 'We were dancing really close and stuff like that,' she says.[90] Far from being passive recipients, these women found ways to circumvent religious teachings that stressed piety and virtue, even if they waited until marriage or migration to delve further into their sexuality. Most Black Canadian-born and Caribbean women embraced the politics of respectability, yet they interpreted this ideology to suit their circumstances and individual needs, revealing a certain amount of independence in thought. As long as they abstained from actual sexual intercourse, some of the women found kissing and other forms of sexual activities acceptable.

Defining Religion

It is clear that the messages from the pulpit were far from uniformly absorbed. Betty attended the local United Church 'every Sunday' with her mother and participated in the choir, which subsequently led to an active social life and the forging of friendships with girls her age. Betty's mother had a box of 'promises,' scriptural passages written on cards shaped like a loaf of bread. After meals, everyone at the table would take a card, read the scripture, and discuss the meanings behind the scriptures. Betty enjoyed this ritual, which she felt imparted valuable moral lessons, but over time she began to define her relationship with religion in a manner that benefited her. According to Betty,

my mom was very strong about her faith, and she really hoped that some of us would get saved and feel the same love of God that she did. It didn't really happen. We kind of held back from it, but we did fall into what was expected of us.[91]

For Betty, church was more a social site, a place where she met her girl-friends and rehashed the past week's events. In fact, she pointed out, 'I never really listened particularly to the sermons. That was not something I related to.' Betty accepted certain aspects of her religious upbringing, but remained resistant to the didactic messages of the sermons.

Jennette maintained that she, too, was raised and confirmed in the Anglican Church in Antigua and that her family always attended church on Sundays, but at age fifteen, she 'refused to go church anymore.' Or rather, Jennette confessed, '[I'd] go to church and hang out in the grave-yard until the people were coming home, and we'd all go home together. I just stopped, it just didn't make sense.'[92] Even as an adult, Jennette's position on religion remained the same, even though she admitted that the church did impart some indispensable lessons that she maintained 'were good rules to live by.' Whether from the pulpit or through their youth groups and organizations, the 'good rules' were similar. The wom-en were taught that human relationships were important and a measure of one's relationship with God.

Religion served an important function in the lives of the girls growing up. They absorbed the tenets and practices of love, faith, forgiveness, and obedience that are foundational to almost all religions. Yet, as they matured, some began to interpret and redefine religious meanings and teachings in a more flexible manner.

Religion as Restrictive

Parents often used religious teachings as a way to manage and discipline their children, even as teenagers. While Naomi respected her religious upbringing and enjoyed the prominent roles that she held at Mount Zion Church of God in Christ, she too wondered about the uncompro-mising position of her parents, who took St Paul's admonition literally that Christians, while they lived in the world, should refrain from partici-pating in secular (sinful) activities:

We did not indulge in worldly things, like going out with boys and riding in cars, and staying out late at night. At that time it seemed normal, [but] at other times stretched, because I wondered how I would get to know a young man, if I did not at least talk to him. I often thought some things were unreasonable being a youngster, but I never said it to my mother.[93]

That Naomi never complained to her parents about how they used religion to justify controlling her activities is certainly understandable, considering that a fundamental characteristic of being a Christian is obedience – first to God, and then in the case of children, to their parents and other adults in positions of authority.

None of the women openly rejected her parents' religious imposition on her life. Naomi, for example, chose deference to her parents, despite wanting to spend quality time alone with her 'soon-to-be husband' and wishing that her brother or another chaperone did not have to accompany them on dates. Perhaps Naomi's silence could also be interpreted as understanding that her overzealous parents were attempting to protect her.

Carmencita's father, Archie, was a devout Roman Catholic, a strict patriarch, and, like Naomi's parents, took the scriptures literally. Secular activities such as parties and movies were generally forbidden; instead, his daughters participated in Christian-related activities. Carmencita and one of her sisters were members of the Legion of Mary, an organization that was involved in community and religious work. The group primarily focused on weekly prayer meetings, visiting the sick, and witnessing to others about God. Carmencita's younger siblings belonged to the Catholic Children's Organization, and once they were old enough, they too joined the Legion. Archie's prohibition against secular activities was a way to protect his daughters from what he considered to be a depraved environment. Social scientists, religious leaders, and colonial officials were not the only individuals who expressed concern about the status of Caribbean families. Carmencita explained that her father worried about the 'multiple fathering of children' and the lack of a 'whole family unit.' Still, she wished that her father had been more lenient.[94]

Other Black Canadian women offered different experiences of the church and its place in their religious and social lives. Unlike a few women who attended Black churches, Laura's family attended weekly Sunday service at the predominantly white Baptist church in Kentville, Nova Scotia, because 'there was nowhere else to go.' Laura described members of the general congregation as cold and wretched, pointing out that 'they didn't like us ... They'd gather their clothes up around when you sat in the pew with them.'[95] The minister was 'nice,' however, and made attending church tolerable. The irony of how her family was treated was not lost on Laura, who recognized the contradictions between the members' actions and the scriptures that taught Christians to 'love thy neighbor as thyself.'[96] Laura's family's options were limited in Kentville, but once she completed nursing school and moved to Ontario, Laura joined a Black church and has been a member ever since.[97]

Differences in the Caribbean and Canada

Some minor differences existed between the two groups of women that were interviewed for this study with respect to religion and church. Church attendance was irregular for two of the Black Canadian-born interviewees, and one did not attend at all. All the Caribbean-born women mentioned attending church at some point while growing up, and several attended religious-based girls' schools. None of the Black Canadian-born interviewees attended schools that were religious affiliated.

Grenadian-born Dorothy Jones stated that 'growing up in the West Indies, religion was first and foremost in everything.' In some families, mandatory weekly church attendance, as well as prayer meetings or other services during the week, remained the norm. For some of the women, church attendance was merely a ritual, but for others, it was the foundation of their social and religious life. Dorothy J attended weekly Sunday school as well as a religious-based school, where religious instruction was included in the curriculum. 'You had to attend those things,' Dorothy J said of her religious involvement, highlighting the lack of choice that some girls had in determining how and when they participated in religious activities.[98]

Conclusion

Outside of autobiographical accounts, and a few available studies – and, in the case of Canada, Sylvia Hamilton's documentary film, *The Little Black School House* – the actual voices of children are virtually absent in scholarly examinations of the school and church. The women's testimonies fill this lacuna. Through the process of interpellation, both institutions were imbricated in subjectivity and identity formation in ways that were both empowering and repressive. Schools provided an avenue for both groups of women interviewed for this study to obtain an education, develop friendships, and learn valuable skills. Schools, through the curriculum, contributed to how as girls they constructed gendered selfhoods. Nevertheless, racism, colourism, and favouritism at the hands of teachers and fellow students alienated some of the women.

The church was a site where children and young people were nurtured and encouraged to be competent individuals, although it also reinforced gendered (and, in one instance, racialized) hierarchies. At the same time, some of the women found ways to assert their subjectivity by redefining the meaning of certain religious convictions. Overall, the women interviewed for this study learned important values that provided support and strength for the next transitions in their lives, changes that took some of them far from home and away from the networks of support within which they had been raised.

3

'The Sky Is the Limit': Migration to Britain

By the time the interviewees for this study had completed high school, all but two had decided to train as nurses. Some took aptitude tests, others were influenced by family members and associates, and a few made the decision independently of external influences. Questions about where to train loomed large for all of the interviewees as they entered this new transition in their lives. Because seventeen of the twenty-two Caribbean-born and one of the Black Canadian-born interviewees migrated to Britain to secure training as nurses, this chapter maps the nuances of their migratory journey.

Since life is never lived in a linear or seamless fashion, to simply discuss the interviewees only in nurses' training reinforces one aspect of their subjectivity, that of workers. Thus, this chapter explores how subjectivities are constituted and reconstituted due to migration operating on the premise that, as Mary Chamberlain argues, 'subjectivity and identity, like memory, are never static and are always in a process of creation and transformation.'[1] I highlight both the material and symbolic reasons the interviewees gave for migrating to Britain, including their initial reactions to British society. To elucidate how young Caribbean women negotiated and renegotiated their subjectivities and identities, I draw upon postcolonial tropes such as liminality, or in-between-ness, which refers to periods of ambivalence and uncertainty as one modality of migration experience. In addition, I explore meanings of home and belonging in the context of 'migration as a hybridizing force.'[2]

Migration to England – and, for one interviewee, Scotland – engendered new subjectivities, although these remained incomplete, and were always being constituted. Migration provided opportunities that were not limited to pursuing a career. The interviewees were able to escape

the constraints of Caribbean society at a critical time in their development, which enabled them to engage in the process of self-fashioning
or the 'shaping of one's identity.' Away from parents and other family
members, migration allowed young women to develop their own world
views and to make decisions and choices that sometimes contradicted
the norms and values they had learned while growing up.

Post–Second World War Britain and Caribbean Migration

The presence of Black people on British soil dates back to at least the
sixteenth century.[3] Caribbean people had also migrated to England in
small numbers in earlier decades of the twentieth century.[4] However,
it was the post–Second World War transformation in the economy that
culminated in an acute labour shortage that led to the mass migration of
Caribbean and other people of colour to Britain. Clive Harris cautions
against what he views as an oversimplified rationale of the labour shortage argument given how Caribbean migrant workers were systematically
channelled as a result of the state and organized labour into semi-skilled
and unskilled work.[5] Equally important, Harris also points out how reluctant the state was to use Caribbean workers to resolve Britain's labour
dilemma. Despite the urgent need for health care workers, the government funded recruitment drives, first in Britain and other European
countries, and then, when the need remained unmet, in the Caribbean.
The Working Party on the Employment in the United Kingdom of Sur-
plus Colonial Labour reported that that there were '54,000 vacancies for
nursing staff in Britain.'[6] In 1949, the ministries of Health and Labour,
together with the Colonial Office, the General Nursing Council, and
the Royal College of Nursing, began a deliberate policy of recruiting
from the Caribbean. By 1961, approximately 172,000 Caribbean people
migrated to England and Wales, and by the beginning of 1964 this figure
had risen to about 300,000.[7] By 1966, the migrant Caribbean population was about 330,000.[8] Included in this exodus were young Caribbean
women seeking careers, education, and adventure.

When they left their various islands in the English-speaking Caribbean, the majority of the Caribbean migrants interviewed for this study
were between the ages of eighteen and nineteen; the youngest was fifteen and a half and the oldest was twenty-four. Most of these women
left in the mid-1950s – the first went in 1949 on a scholarship and the
last in 1968. Five were from Jamaica, three from Barbados, three from
Trinidad, and two from Grenada. Individual nurses were also from

Dominica, Antigua, and Guyana (although the last country is situated geographically in South America, the Guyanese interviewee identified herself as West Indian). The choice to migrate was framed as either a spontaneous decision or as the logical sequence of events upon completion of high school. On closer examination, however, the underlying reasons varied among the interviewees. For the most part, they predicated their decisions on a number of other factors. Economics remained the primary motivation, as few employment opportunities existed in their home countries, but the women provided equally compelling and overlapping reasons, which included: 'seeking adventure,' wanting 'to make better of oneself,' and 'it was the thing to do.' They also stated that invitations and encouragement from family members and friends helped inform their choices.[9]

Of the seventeen Caribbean interviewees who migrated there, all except five had some family member who resided in Britain at the time of migration. Whether the young women were well acquainted with these relatives or not, the knowledge that a cousin, aunt, uncle, brother, or father was already there made the decision less taxing.[10] The Black Canadian-born interviewee who migrated to Britain had a distant relative already living there. For this group of women, the impetus for migration was more than *In Search of a Better Life*, as the title of one scholarly book on the subject indicates.[11]

Once Dorothy J completed high school and obtained her school leaving certificate, she had the opportunity to teach. Yet she points to the lack of economic prospects for her age group as the impetus behind emigrating from Grenada in 1961 at the age of seventeen. She succinctly captured how high school teenagers 'who wanted to make better of themselves'[12] turned the thought of migration into 'seeking adventure.' Thinking back over several decades, Dorothy J offered the following explanation:

> If you didn't have a teaching job, you wanted to make better of yourself. So you had the opportunity to go to England ... It was the excitement, it was like an adventure, something fun. We didn't know what lay ahead of us, we didn't know about snow, what the country was going to be like – well for me, we just wanted to go. It was an experience then for us.[13]

Dorothy J's rationale with an emphasis on adventure, fun, and the unfamiliar encapsulates the centrality of mobility in Caribbean people's definition of freedom.[14] Such explanations reposition young Caribbean migrant women in relation to traditional views on migration; namely, that it was motivated solely by economic considerations.

Similarly, Ancilla provided multiple reasons for leaving Trinidad for England at the age of eighteen in 1966:

> I wanted to go because I couldn't be a doctor, and I didn't have the opportunity to go to university when I finished high school. I decided I wanted to go to England to do nursing, because other people from around the area were going. So, I got an address and I applied. I got the information. They said 'yes.' All I had to do was get a ticket to go there.[15]

Constrained financially from entering medical school, Ancilla looked to migration as an attractive alternative. In addition, she also echoed a common response of the Caribbean interviewees expressed by Daphne C, who explained, 'We were motivated. Everybody was on the move. They were going to England or they were going to Ethiopia, wherever they were going. So, you got the fever that you wanted to go.'[16] Clearly, some of the women got caught up in the excitement of travelling not just to any country, but the Mother Country. That some of the interviewees like Ancilla wrote to hospitals and inquired about nurses' training show them as active agents in the migration process.

Another equally valid reason that has yet to be fully explored in the migration literature is that of working-class, sole-support mothers who wanted their daughters to leave the Caribbean as a preventive measure against teenage pregnancy. Dorette was the youngest of the migrants in this study. Dorette left Jamaica in 1957, at the age of fifteen and a half to live with her dad. She was the only interviewee to complete high school in Britain. In her interview, she explained that in addition to wanting a better life for their daughters:

> mothers ... didn't want you to get pregnant ... In those days in Jamaica, a lot of girls got pregnant, and they got pregnant out of naiveté – a lot of girls had babies and didn't know how they had babies.[17]

Ostensibly, parents hoped that the excitement of travelling to Britain, in conjunction with all of the career options that such a journey offered, would distract their teenage daughters. With few job prospects and spare time, parents were concerned that if daughters stayed in the Caribbean, they would have more time to explore their sexuality.

There is also the strong probability that Dorette's mother realized that they continued to live in a culture where 'girls [were] still borne along, as on a conveyor belt, into what is presented to them as the only possible fulfillment for a woman – marriage and/or child-bearing.'[18] Given that 'considerable peer-group and culture group pressure' still existed on a 'young girl to prove herself by having a baby,'[19] migration became a pre-emptive measure against early pregnancy. Essentially, Dorette's mother was implicated in her daughter's subjectivity formation. When Dorette's mother encouraged her to leave Jamaica for Britain, Dorette did not object; she, too, keenly sensed the ramifications of choosing to stay.[20]

Considering that a disproportionate number of the women admitted to being raised in strict – and, in some cases, strictly religious – homes, few parents expressed reservations that their daughters would run amok in England. It is more than likely that parents viewed migration as temporary and that their daughters would eventually return with whatever resources necessary to 'realize the hope and aspirations connected with life'[21] in the Caribbean. Most parents wholeheartedly supported their daughters' wishes to leave the Caribbean. Nevertheless, some parents remained cautious. For example, Carmencita had always wanted to be a radio announcer, a seemingly unrealistic choice once she evaluated the field of broadcasting. She then decided to try nursing, because it gave her the opportunity to migrate to Britain: 'I wanted to see how the other half lived; I wanted to become a nurse. It was a good passport to leave the Caribbean.'[22]

Although Carmencita was twenty years old, and by all indications an adult capable of making decisions, her father consulted a priest before granting his daughter permission to leave Trinidad. The priest assured Archie Gomez that sending his daughter to England was fitting, considering the economic conditions of the island and the lack of job prospects for young people in Trinidad. Worried that a young, single woman alone in London could easily be seduced into a life of wantonness, the priest recommended a Roman Catholic hospital in Lancashire that was run by nuns. Such a hospital would reinforce the ideas of respectability that Archie had implanted in his children, and nursing would reinforce the disciplinary measures he had used to raise Carmencita.[23]

Although most of the women tended to paint an idyllic portrait of growing up in the Caribbean, a few hinted at possible tensions within their families, which also influenced their decision to emigrate. Jennette, for example, left Antigua for England at the age of eighteen in 1957 to avoid an impending confrontation with her father: 'I figured if I lived here, I would have gotten into trouble … I don't like conflict.'[24]

Moreover, Jennette also gave the impression that Antigua, with its rampant nepotism, was not the ideal place for her to live. She had watched her father being passed over for promotions because he refused to participate in illegal activities as a police officer. Similarly, she knew that to gain entrance into a university, she had to obtain a scholarship. In Antigua, according to Jennette, scholarships were linked to the politics of the region and depended on 'who your parents were.' Her family did not support the ruling party, which meant that no scholarships would be available. As she pondered a career, Jennette decided that she would 'do nursing.' This decision, while appearing impulsive, in fact, required great contemplation on the part of Jennette and of those who supported her. In this case, migration offered an escape from impending familial conflicts and other frustrations associated with life in Antigua.

When Lillie announced that she planned on pursuing a nursing career, her father emphatically responded, 'over my dead body,' believing that 'nurses have too much of a hard time.'[25] A man who read the newspaper frequently, Lillie's father might have seen the challenges facing Jamaican – and, by extension, all Caribbean – nurses. At this time, Caribbean nurses in the English-speaking regions were embroiled in a struggle to obtain registration, and they protested the ongoing exploitation of their labour and inadequate remuneration. In addition, they had to endure the patriarchal attitudes of physicians and the government that reflected the racial, gender, and social class dynamics underpinning Jamaican society.[26] At the same time, Caribbean nurses were admired and respected by their patients and the wider society, which was one of the reasons Lillie gave for being attracted to the occupation. Despite her desire to 'do nursing and serve others,' Lillie respected her father's wishes and went to Shortwood Teachers College. She taught for some time, but in 1954, much to her father's disappointment, Lillie, the eldest of the interviewees to migrate, left Jamaica for Scotland – the only one to train in that location – to answer her calling to be a nurse.[27] In underscoring their roles in the decision to migrate, these young women claimed an autonomous subject position. They understood the benefits of migration and took advantage of it.

As part of the effort to improve nurses' education, many young women were recruited and given government scholarships to train abroad, with the expectation that upon completing their training in Britain or elsewhere, they would return to their respective islands and assume leadership roles as matrons and ward sisters.[28] Eileen and Joan from Barbados, and Vera from Trinidad, were recruited in this manner and received scholarships.[29] The ability to travel during this period was indeed a luxury; as M. Bryce-Boodoo points out for Trinidad in 1946, only 'a few who could have afforded it financially [referring to those seeking additional training overseas] followed to gain new knowledge.'[30] Clearly, these young women were in a unique position to leave the Caribbean, revealing a divergent rationale that extended beyond economic motivation.

On the surface, Caribbean migrants had reason to remain optimistic about the possibilities that Britain offered. Certainly, news of labour shortages circulated in the Caribbean. Some of the young women might have heard about the recruitment efforts of the London Transport, and of hospital administrators desperate to meet labour demands. As colonial and ex-colonial subjects, Caribbean people's perceptions of Britain were positive. The image of Britain circulating in the colonial Caribbean was that of a benign and benevolent nation codified in the image of a 'mother.' This fiction of the 'mother country,' Caribbean scholar Elizabeth Thomas-Hope argues, was 'assiduously fostered by colonial administrators, who had gone a long way to determine the relationship of British West Indians to Britain and thus the position of Britain in the images held by those people.'[31] That migration to Britain was uncomplicated for this group of Caribbean migrants, who as subjects of the British Commonwealth enjoyed unrestricted access to Britain 'irrespective of their race, colour, class or gender,' no doubt reinforced the mother-country image. In the minds of parents, children, other family members, and even friends, there was no question that migration to Britain was the right choice for these young colonials and ex-colonials

Depending on the circumstances of their arrival, migrants encountered a post–Second World War Britain either full of pessimism or sanguinity. Caribbean migrants who, like Vera, arrived in the late 1940s, the 1950s, and the early 1960s, encountered an economy still recovering from the war. By the time the majority of the interviewees had settled in Britain, food and coal rationing had ended (in 1957 and 1958, respectively). Yet there remained a level of optimism as people, especially those from the working class, benefited from 'the relatively short, but in many ways unprecedented, burst of prosperity'[32] during this period. Deborah Philips and Alan Tomlinson capture Conservative prime minister Harold Macmillan's 1957 statement that 'people never had it so good' by pointing out: 'Released from the austerity of the immediate post-war years, choosing between jobs available in the new and booming industries, encountering new types of domestic and leisure living, many at the time believed that here was the new Nirvana; full employment, lots of

credit, affluence all around and a more open morality.'[33] If these pro-
nouncements accurately characterized the dramatic changes occurring
in Britain, then the young Caribbean women were moving there at an
opportune time. Rosalind Cassidy explained how the contributions of
women during the Second World War led to a 'greater acceptance of
women as responsible human beings free to express their aptitudes and
interests where they may best do so.'[34] This climate, however contrived,
certainly accorded with the visions of the young women in this study of
'making a better life' for themselves.

People who left for Britain in the late 1940s and 1950s usually travelled
on ships, with voyages lasting anywhere from three to six weeks. The
young women in this study travelled independently and all were alone.
Outside of the few women who had already moved from their rural
households to urban areas for school, the majority of these interviewees
left families and friends for the first time, in anticipation of a new life in
the 'motherland.' The women had varied responses to the long journey
at sea and their arrival in Britain. Weeks into the voyage, some of them
experienced a degree of seasickness, others began to miss their families,
and some registered feelings of regret. 'You wanted to go back, but there
was no turning back,' Dorothy J explained.[35] The seeming finality of the
move was not lost on the young women.

Ships became the first space where strategies emerged to deal with
migration, and thus friendships were created on board. In 1952, Jamaican-born Daphne B and Eileen from Barbados met on board a ship and
developed a friendship that spanned decades. Alone and with time to
ponder the reality of leaving Barbados, Joan recalled questioning the
decision to become a nurse. Before long, she met five other young wom-
en, and collectively they decided to make the best of their trip. Consol-
ing and comforting each other, 'we said, we'll survive, and that's what we
did.'[36]

Individually and collectively, the women wondered about what lay
ahead in Britain, a country that had exerted such influence on the culture, language, economy, and education system of the homelands they
had left behind. They speculated on the accuracy of the nursery rhymes,
fairy tales, and other colonial literature that they had been exposed to as
children and students, all of which had informed their early notions of
Britain. Images of the British Empire that bordered on fantasies of the
royal family, excessive wealth, and commodities unavailable in the economically impoverished Caribbean colonies all informed the women's
collective memories.

Identity and Migration

Excited about their trip to England, the young women took great pains to make sure that they were prepared in every way imaginable. In readiness for their journey, they judiciously chose to wear their best attire, but on arrival some quickly found that their clothes and shoes were inappropriate for the weather. Arriving in England in the mid-1950s, Daphne C summarized her first night in London with a description that was commonly reiterated among Caribbean female migrants arriving in the colder months:

> We had to travel from London to Birmingham. That was the first time I had anything to do with ice. The night I got to England it was snowing, and I had on this beautiful dress. You should see that dress. It was gorgeous! But it was thin! My aunt sent me a coat, and I left the coat in Jamaica and said, 'What am I doing with this?' And I had on this square toe shoe, square toe was just coming in. Here I'm dressed up going to England. When I got to London, I was cold. I was so cold. When I got to the place that I was going to I got out of the van, barefoot, my shoe was left in the car, and I didn't know my shoe was left in the car. That's how cold my feet were.[37]

Daphne C's vignette revealed the extent to which Caribbean people approached migration to Britain. Analogous to anticipating a reunion with a long-lost relative, migration to the 'motherland' demanded the very best dress for the occasion. Daphne C and the other interviewees would soon discover that they were hardly England's daughters; they were more like stepchildren whose place in the family remained marginal.

Despite the dire need for workers, and the fact that they had been encouraged to migrate, responses to the Caribbean presence by the British government and people were a far cry from the perception and image of Britain as the 'motherland.' Once Caribbean people began to arrive in England on a large scale, they began to be perceived as a problem. Intense public and private debates took place within Parliament and in the media during the late 1940s, 1950s, and 1960s about the need to control Black immigration. Discussions of the impact of immigration on housing, the welfare state, crime, and other social problems were abundant, as were concerns about the effect that Caribbean migration might have on the racial character of the British people and on national identity.[38] As Chris Waters points out, 'the characteristics of Black migrants to Britain were mapped against those of white natives, serving to shore up definitions of essential Britishness.'[39] To alleviate white fears of the 'Other,' and to maintain the fiction of Britain as a homogeneous nation, legislation was introduced during the 1960s with the intent of curbing the migration of people of colour. Those already settled in Britain faced pervasive discriminatory treatment. In fact, until 1966, it was legal to use race as the basis for discrimination not only in relation to housing, but also in terms of skilled employment and church attendance.[40]

As these philosophical, moral, and ideological deliberations were occurring, British national identity, constructed 'through the narrative of the nation by which stories, images, symbols and ritual represent "shared" meanings of nationhood,'[41] was being denaturalized as migrant communities expanded in Britain. British identity – once assumed to be stable, coherent, and unified – was supposedly ruptured by the arrival of Black bodies. The recognition of a loss or questioning of self is what postcolonial scholars have identified as dislocation or the de-centring of the subject.

As the British nation and notions of 'Englishness' were being destabilized, young Caribbean women were confronting their own inner disruptions as they landed on British soil. Initial reactions to Britain spanned a spectrum of emotions that ranged from sheer excitement, disappointment, loneliness, surprise, shock, fear, relief, and disengagement. As with migrants generally, the interviewees for this study, too, experienced periods of liminality. They felt ambivalence associated with coming to the realization of occupying an unfamiliar space far removed from familiar faces and routines that characterized life in the Caribbean. Yet it was at these times when the resilience of the young women was most visible. They came to terms with their choice to migrate, and they began to develop new relationships and to take risks, all of which were critical to ongoing subjectivity formation. Of course, the process was far from immediate and was interspersed with feelings of dislocation and moments of sadness.

At the time of her interview in 2000, Nancy maintained that her first day in London remained forever one of the worst days of her life. This experience set the context of how she would subsequently experience the length of her stay. She recounted her arrival in 1965:

My uncle had to meet me there [at the train station] because the hospital did not arrange for someone to pick me up because it was a holiday. My uncle picked me up, and dropped me off at the hospital. I didn't know that uncle very well, and when he dropped me off, I dropped my bags and cried myself to sleep.[42]

An absence of familial or hospital support contributed to Nancy's sense of not belonging and loneliness, even if these feelings were momentary.

After twenty-one days at sea, Dorothy J, seventeen at the time, waited with anticipation for her brother to pick her up in Southampton. After appraising the surroundings, a sinking feeling settled in her stomach, which Dorothy J identified as disappointment:

> The first things I noticed were the houses. I thought that going to Eng-
> land would have been like the fairy tales, the nursery rhymes right from the
> books. I thought you'll see castles, and it wasn't like that. I know I wouldn't
> find the streets paved with gold, but the houses, well, my heart sank, and I
> thought, 'that's England.' It was also May or June but it was still cold, and I
> was cold, it wasn't what I expected.[43]

Jennette, too, was surprised by the physical landscape of Britain and also found the 'arrogance' of the British people revolting. Dorothy J's and Jennette's reactions to Britain were not atypical and were reiterated by other migrants. The magical and happy ending often associated with fairy tales and stories about the Empire was for the most part a myth.[44] Once they discovered new knowledge about Britain, the young women amended their previously held assumptions. These women's particular expectations and ideas about the 'mother country' and their place as British subjects complicated this process.

In addition to the attitudes of British people, the weather required one of the most difficult adjustments of all. 'It was cold. It was cold. Cold, cold, cold' was a common refrain. For some of the young migrants, however, Britain was more than physically cold. Until the migrants became accustomed to the habits and customs of the British people, Britain also felt psychologically cold. Whatever sense of identification some of the interviewees might have felt as colonial and ex-colonial subjects with their British counterparts was now being called into question.

As the young women prepared to settle into their new home, certain realities caught their attention. Some were surprised to find Caribbean families living in cramped and overcrowded dwellings, working primarily in British factories and railways. Others were shocked to find out that poor white people lived in Britain, outdoor toilets were common, and that English people wrapped bread and fish in newspaper. The nation was indeed an illusion. Prior to migrating, Ancilla had heard rumours that 'white people didn't bathe very often, and they always camouflaged the smell with powder and perfume.'[45] Upon arriving in Britain, Ancilla discovered that taking a bath after work and taking a shower every morning or even during the day was not a priority for some people.'[46] She proudly admitted to 'actually converting a few British people to using water.'

These observations challenged the popular myths of an affluent and pristine Britain that had disseminated in the Caribbean. Indeed, the young women's immediate reactions to Britain rupture those narratives of the nation and complicate the centre/periphery discourse that has long dominated migration scholarship. Englishness, or more generally, Britishness, came to define itself in opposition to its 'Others,' or its colonies. Thus, by being even slightly critical of aspects of British culture, the young women confirmed Homi Bhabha's argument that colonial relationships were simply more than the imposition of, for example, British culture over the subordinate Caribbean culture.

As the colonials arrived and observed the class dynamics, they interrogated commonly held notions of the authenticity, purity, and superiority of British society and, by extension, its citizens. The women's immediate reactions further decentred Britain as the master 'sovereign subject.'[47] From the vantage point of some of these women, compared with the various islands they emigrated from, Britain was hardly a 'warm' or inviting place. Still, they had a purpose in mind, which was the reason for leaving the Caribbean in the first place. As Joan predicted in 1954 on her way to Netherne Hospital, in Croyden, England, however difficult the transition and the ambiguous position of coming to terms with Blackness and nurses' training, they would find ways to cope.[48] Indeed, migration was about evaluating traditions, planning the present, and looking forward to the future.

It Was Freedom

Motifs of dislocation and alienation are central to studies that analyse and explain how migrants experience a new society. As evidenced by these young Caribbean women, however, focusing exclusively on these narratives does not do justice to the heterogeneity of migrants. To be sure, arrival in Britain simultaneously signalled disruption, negotiation, and adaptation as the women faced the task of navigating a new phase of their lives. This is not to suggest that the young women did not experience a different way of viewing the world and their place in it. Educated in some of the Caribbean's most prestigious schools, with the belief that education was the passport to a better future, this group of interviewees was ambitious, assertive, committed to achieving their goals, and driven to improve or maintain their socioeconomic status. They were active agents who drew on the various resources available to aid them in the process of settling in and adapting to life in the United Kingdom.

Had the women remained in the Caribbean, they would undoubtedly have undergone similar transitions, which included leaving school, pursing careers, developing intimate relationships, marriage, children, separation, divorce, remaining single, and the death of family members and friends. While these and other transitions occurred in the women's lives as they moved from one life phase to the next, migration to Britain served as a different kind of self-discovery. Removed from the constant gaze of parents, extended family, church, and community members, migration allowed young women not only to question previously held values, but also to unearth and explore aspects of their identity that they heretofore had not examined. Surely, this was part of the thrill, as Muriel pointed out, of 'going out in the world literally on my own.'[49] Within the various discursive fields that constitute for young migrant women 'the world,' their subjectivities continue to take on new meaning.

The majority of the Caribbean-born women grew up in households where parents drew on and reinforced certain gender ideologies. On occasions, families privileged the desires of sons and placed restrictions on girls. Carmencita, for example, was anxious to leave Trinidad, her dictatorial father, and the constraints he imposed on her. Twenty years old when she left the Caribbean in 1968, Carmencita felt that she had missed out on her teenage years – transition years that should have been devoted to her own self-actualization and where mistakes could be made but also, hopefully, lessons learned. In England, however, she could reinvent herself, leaving behind the image of the 'Gomez nun,' a nickname that had plagued her in her youth. Upon reflecting on her migration to Britain, Carmencita offered the following:

> I thought, here it is, Carmencita, the sky is the limit. You came from this home, you couldn't go to this, nothing but church, but now the sky is the limit. You start evaluating values. I went out. Oh, yeah, I partied ... I certainly had what I did not have in the Caribbean. I enjoyed it, there was nobody to lay the law down, you know. So I had my teenage years in England.[50]

As Carol Boyce Davies argues, 'the re-negotiating of identities is fundamental to migration.'[51] Being a teenager at the age of twenty became one of the many identities that Carmencita assumed. Because her father had prohibited secular activities, such as dancing and dating, it is hardly surprising that dancing became one of Carmencita's two favourite social activities. 'Oh, boy, I danced. I danced an awful lot. I love dancing.' On Tuesdays, 'It was nurses' night at a local hangout,' and although she was 'lowly paid,' Carmencita made sure that her leisure activities were integrated into her expenses. She admitted without regret the pleasures of living independently from her family, in particular her father.

A number of the women used the phrase 'it was freedom' to describe being in England, a place where, according to Joan, one was 'away from home [and] doing all the things that you liked to do.'[52] This is not to suggest that these women ignored the distinct Caribbean values taught to them; on the contrary, they integrated these values into their new experiences in Britain as they tested new identities. As they navigated the terrains of British society, these women negotiated new understandings of selfhood and identity. They articulated new and sometimes contradictory identities that were neither wholly Caribbean nor wholly British, but an amalgamation of both – a hybridized identity. This process was uncomplicated for some of the young women like Carmencita, but posed difficulties at times for others who were coming to terms with their new social space and their new lives, autonomous of family and friends back home.

Echoing Carmencita's reaction, Dorothy J encapsulated the joys and pitfalls of migrants in her age group:

> Remember I was a little girl when I left home. I didn't know anything about life. In the West Indies you're under your parents' thumb, you weren't exposed to anything. Some of us really made life when we moved to England, for the first time, like having a boyfriend, and being open and things like that. In the West Indies, you couldn't have those sort of things, not openly, and then at that age too. So you gained some experience there. Some of us went [to England] and we had nobody there, you had to find out everything the hard way on your own and so you matured before your time. You grew up faster then.[53]

Dorothy J astutely summarized how subjectivities shift and change with migration. Although she was seventeen at the time of migration, and could have been a pupil teacher had she remained in the Caribbean, living with her parents signified that Dorothy was 'still a little girl.' Having grown up in a particular cultural and religious context with certain constraints, migration provided alternative ways of constituting the self. Despite painful revelations about race, and other aspects of life in Britain, it is the space where Caribbean girls became women, and where subjectivities 'can become more flexible, alter or multiply.'[54]

Migration allowed the young women to get to know the self in a deep and meaningful way as they made the transition from adolescence to adulthood. Despite the demands of nurses' training, the women found time to date, to experience their first kiss, and for some, to have their first sexual experience. Others mentioned enjoying certain forms of entertainment such as live theatre and even the Ice Capades, which were unavailable in the Caribbean.

In acclimatizing themselves to living in Britain, some of the young women realized that the traditions they thought transcended national borders were actually specific to the Caribbean or to their own families. Cognizant of the gender division of labour in her household, Jennette assumed that it had similar configurations elsewhere. She was surprised to find out that scrubbing floors was viewed as 'women's work' in Britain, because, in her household, it was the responsibility of men or boys. Laughing, Jennette explained her first reaction when she discovered this was not the case in England: .

> Until I left home, I thought women did not scrub floors because we didn't do the floors, my brothers and father did that. I remembered going to England and being quite shocked that women scrubbed floors. My father also polished all the shoes. I never polished a shoe in all my life, and so I was taught in every household this is what happened, because in those days we really didn't visit other people's houses – never ate in anybody's house, so I didn't know what went on in other people's houses. I just thought that in their houses, their fathers scrubbed the floors, cleaned up the yard, and polished the shoes because in our house that's what happened.[55]

Lillie echoed the same sentiments as Jennette; she too found out that scrubbing floors and polishing shoes were not considered 'men's work.'[56] That they recognized and articulated these differences suggests that young Caribbean women were experiencing a shift in their consciousness about the malleability of gender roles.

Religion in Britain

In her study on Jamaican migrants in England, Nancy Foner found that women, more so than men, retained their religious practices, particularly in relation to church attendance.[57] 'It is interesting that more than twice as many working women attended church as non-working women,'[58] Foner submits. Yet this pattern of female church attendance was hardly replicated among the young women in this research. The church and religion remained critical; in Lillie's words, it 'was the stabilizing force … It helped build character.' However, the young women's religious identities became secondary upon migration, and especially so once they commenced nurses' training. Since some of the hospital-based nursing schools had a religious affiliation, most of the women were encouraged to attend church and were allowed to attend for an hour on Sundays. Dorothy J welcomed the opportunity to attend church for the hour that was allotted instead of working the entire shift.[59] Others chose to sleep in rather than attend church if their days off fell on Sundays.

Some of the women cited the weather as being a further deterrence against going to church, while others found social activities they enjoyed more to occupy their time. Having spent their formative years attending church or participating in related activities, choosing an alternative to sitting in a pew was part of the freedom the women enjoyed while living away from home. Of course, the future self was being defined less by parental or community expectations and relationships and more by the women themselves.

Stark differences between churches in the Caribbean and those they attended in England were another reason the women cited for limiting church attendance. Carmencita explained:

> In England, it was too much of a power thing, and in the Caribbean, it was more laid back. You go to Mass, and you socialize with community, with what you called the extended family. [In England], they were cold, you go to church and some of them just look at you, and I thought I'm not here for that.[60]

An incident where a priest rebuffed her during confession further convinced Carmencita that attending church was no longer worth the effort.[61]

For Carmencita and some of the other interviewees, missing church in the Caribbean would have been unacceptable, as religion was intrinsic to the identity of their families. Still, to forego attending church in England cannot be interpreted as merely discounting the religious foundation that the women grew up with. Coupled with being independent in a space where their subjectivities were constituted and reconstituted, the interviewees had been accustomed to attending churches where the rituals and practices unique to the Caribbean were observed, and many of them were unable to find a similar welcoming church environment in the United Kingdom.[62]

Surviving in Britain

For the most part, the young women devised their own mechanisms to ensure success in their new environment. Some drew on existing resources such as family and friends of family, and others relied on the friendships created during nurses' training. Caribbean migration scholarship is replete with examples of how family networks facilitate migration. Most common are children reuniting with parents, and one spouse joining another.[63] Although the majority of interviewees had relatives in England, they were not necessarily acquainted with them. Black Canadian-born Darlene had an aunt who lived in Reading, Berkshire, whom she met 'a couple of times, but didn't really know her.' Eventually the two became friends and spent a lot of time socializing. Darlene fondly recalled: 'She was a lot of fun. She had her own children, but I used to take her to parties with me. I told people she was my cousin.'[64] Darlene's experience was very different from, for example, Nancy's uncle, who felt his only responsibility was to pick her up at the train station and drive her to the hospital.

Then there were those who had neither family nor other support systems, and yet were strong enough to depend on themselves. When she decided to leave Jamaica in 1954, Lillie asked a couple of her friends to accompany her, but they all refused. Although she was older and more experienced than all the other migrants, Lillie's adjustment was no easier than that of her peers. She was the only one to go directly to Scotland, where there were few Caribbean people. When she arrived, Lillie initially felt out of place and lonely, but she had repeatedly told herself: 'If I want to go the end of the world and nobody's going with me, I'm still going.' Even though she desired companionship, she came to the realization that 'I have one life to live and I'm going to get on with it.' With no social networks to rely on and with only the desire to fulfil her dream of becoming a nurse, Lillie relied on a philosophical explanation as part of her coping mechanism.[65]

In contrast to Lillie, Dorothy J remained the exception, as her family served to ameliorate the 'strangeness' of England and provided some sense of normalcy and stability. Dorothy J's parents and extended family were still in living in Grenada, but her older brother Nick and his wife were in England, and they continued the family tradition of 'getting together' for dinner on the weekends. She explained:

> When my sisters and my brother Nick came for the weekend, everybody was together. So you forgot about the coldness and the climate and the houses and everything because it was like you were back home, meeting up with everybody, until the Monday morning when they left for work and you were left alone in the house by yourself, and you got up, and you don't know anything. You opened the door and it was cold, the sun was shining, but it was cold. And you are not used to having six–seven people living in one house and those sorts of things. It was an experience, but like my brother [said], 'this is England.'[66]

These social gatherings helped to circumvent, at least initially, the unfamiliarity of England for Dorothy J until she enrolled in nursing. In this scenario, families not only provided the impetus for migration, but also helped to sustain the migrants once they arrived.[67]

Dorothy J's account of her family as a viable support mechanism was unique; in contrast, other migrants depended on non-familial forms of support. Unlike her mother's close-knit family back in Dominica, where 'everybody was everyone's sister and brother,' Nancy was unacquainted with her father's family in England. The uncle who picked her up at the train station was a distant relative whom she never saw again. The lack of support from family or community in Britain left Nancy without a bulwark against the isolation and loneliness that she would subsequently experience. Feeling displaced, she yearned to go 'back home.'[68] Home for Nancy meant not just the familiar physical space that she shared with her mother and siblings; it also meant the geographical and cultural space of Dominica to which she was intricately connected and legitimized. The concept of home outside of its familial context is a recurring motif in the migration literature and is often inextricably tied to the concept of belonging. At the heart of this discussion is whether foreigners such as Nancy can integrate – that is, feel at home – in another country, particularly one whose identity, however imagined, is partially based on positioning itself as superior to the place and people Nancy called home and family.

As Nancy struggled with settling in, she met Jenny, a Jamaican student nurse who helped make the transition smoother. Nancy admitted to crying repeatedly, to which Jenny would jokingly respond, 'The next time you cry, I will give you something to cry for.' This common Caribbean saying that was often repeated to children meant that Nancy's crying was in fact unwarranted. The two young women became fast friends and whenever Nancy yearned to return to Dominica, Jenny insisted that she couldn't go. Returning home would symbolize failure, the inability to take advantage of the opportunities that the motherland, or the 'land of milk of honey,' had to offer. Furthermore, Nancy knew that her aunt and other family members would be disappointed if she did not complete her nurses' training. Nancy credited her friendship with Jenny as the reason she survived England: 'She would take me to her family, and we would have West Indian food. They were so good to me, and that really helped.'[69] The fact that these two women were Dominican and Jamaican respectively was not an issue.

Living in Britain resulted in the formation of a West Indian/Black identity that replaced, according to historian Winston James, island chauvinism. 'Indeed the whole experience of living in a white racist society helped to forge a Black identity where in many cases such an identity did not exist previously or was not consciously thought. The colour of your skin matters here.'[70]

Racism in England

Unlike Canadian-born women, whose racial identities were formed as girls, Caribbean women's awareness of a racialized Black identity primarily emerged with migration. Theorist Stuart Hall observed that until he left Jamaica in the 1950s, he had never heard anyone call themselves or refer to anyone else as Black. In the Caribbean, there were many different ways of identifying people, ranging from different shades of skin colour, quality of hair, the kind of family one came from, and even the street a person lived on. Hall stated it was not until the 1970s 'that Black people recognized themselves as Black. It was the most profound cultural revolution in the Caribbean, much greater than they ever had.'[71]

For the young women who migrated to Britain during late 1940s, 1950s, and 1960s, the cultural revolution that Hall mentions would not have been part of their experience; they would have missed the process of Black identification that took place after they left. However, as scholar Anima Mama contends, 'Black people growing up in Britain in the 1950s, 1960s, and 1970s soon learnt that whiteness [was] very often equated with Britishness, an equation which [put] them in an ambiguous and dislocated position.'[72] This position of liminality would be further intensified for young Caribbean migrants, who, with very little or no understanding of the racial dynamics in Britain, discovered and witnessed the result of the social and discursive meanings attached to Black skin. Certainly the 1958 race riots in Nottingham and Notting Hill[73] – the latter of which had more serious consequences – and the ensuing discourse in the media and British Parliament made it hard to ignore the public debates. Some of the women experienced racism in Britain first hand, especially when dealing with patients and other medical personnel, while others learned about it through their families and other people's experiences.

The realization of the significance of skin colour in England occurred at different moments and contexts for individual interviewees. In addition to being ignored by her peers once she vacated the school premises, Dorette dealt with the racism of individual teachers. The messages she received from them echoed that of the dominant society: only white people, not Black people, were intelligent. Coming from an environment where she was accustomed to supportive teachers, Dorette's teachers in England undermined her sense of her own capabilities as a student. This affected her sense of self and forced her to think about her racial identity, an issue to which she had not given much thought while living in Jamaica.[74] Psychologist Beverly Tatum argues that Black youths' preoccupation with racial identity is a result of how the rest of the world views them. She explains: 'Our self perceptions are shaped by the messages we receive from those around us, and when young Black men and women enter adolescence, the racial contents of those messages intensify.'[75] The following excerpt from Dorette's interview confirmed how some white teachers participated in diminishing immigrant and Black students' academic capabilities:

I got a good background in Jamaica; my English was good and I wrote very well. But when I look and saw the reports that I have, I can't believe some of the reports. Some of my reports from school and from college [state]: 'Oh, she lacks good command of the English language' and 'She's come along very well.' I was born speaking English. When I read them, I thought, my God, you know, like an imbecile. I always kept them, because, I can't believe what they wrote about me considering I had a good background in English.[76]

Even though the English-speaking Caribbean education system was based on the British system, Dorette maintained that some of her British teachers were ignorant and offered very little support and validation. It was in these and other encounters of being disavowed that Dorette and other Caribbean migrants became aware of their identification as Black.

Daphne C recalled that her first three months in Britain '[were] not really good' because she had no luck finding employment:

> I was trying to find a job for about three months, and I couldn't find a job. I remember one day I had this particular experience. We [her cousin] saw an ad in the newspaper, and at that time, it was a typing job. And the paper came out, and we got the paper, and when we got there, they said the job was taken. And we'd say, 'How could the job be taken when we just got the paper?' But then we didn't learn yet that it [was] because of the colour of your skin.[77]

Three months was barely enough time for Daphne C to learn and adjust to living in a society that viewed her and others who resembled her as inferior. Darlene recalled going to a restaurant and watching while white patrons were served ahead of her, or standing in line at the post office, when a white male entered the queue ahead of her. On both occasions, Darlene – whose father raised her to be vocal about racism – called attention to the injustice she experienced.[78]

Certainly, these liminal experiences required developing an understanding of the multifarious ways that racial meanings played out daily in British life. Thus, part of negotiating life in Britain for Daphne Cand the other women meant developing ways of coming to terms with a new-found racial identity. Notwithstanding its own legacy of racism, nursing not only facilitated the transition towards the development of a shared professional identity for these young women in Britain, but it also operated as a refuge for some.

Conclusion

Leaving high school for both groups of women interviewed for this study, and migrating for the Caribbean cohort, constituted the first major life transition that they faced. The migration of young Caribbean women to Britain challenged the metanarrative that people migrate primarily for socioeconomic reasons or that families are always instrumental in migration decisions. Instead, the women, mostly teenagers at the time, provided multiple explanations for why they left the Caribbean. While the majority of the women had some relatives in Britain, only a few were close to their respective family members. The absence of family made the task of navigating a new environment all the more difficult. All of the interviewees experienced periods of liminality, moments of ambivalence, and uncertainty. Occupying a liminal or in-between space was also liberating, as the migrants worked through what it meant to be young Caribbean women in Britain.

Away from the gaze of their parents, extended family, and community, migration afforded young Caribbean women an opportunity to explore the 'self' while coming to terms with the disparity between what they thought they knew about Britain and the reality that they faced. It was in Britain, and as the women entered nurses' training, that they also encountered the indeterminacy of identities, as they pursued another transition – the development of a professional identity.

4

Nurses' Training and Education

Regardless of geographical location, the young women who entered nursing throughout the late 1940s until the 1970s trained in a hospital apprenticeship system that was hierarchical, authoritative, and often exploitative. Obedience and the showing of respect to those in positions of power, the requisite characteristics to successfully navigate the transition into nurses' training, were instilled in the young women when they were growing up. Moreover, when Black students entered nurses' training, the division of labour and many of their familial social practices were produced and reproduced in the hospitals. That is, much of the work they did, at least in the initial stages of the interviewees' training, resembled the unpaid work they had done all along with their mothers at home. Thus, Canadian historian Bettina Bradbury's insistence that workers' identities are forged before they enter the workplace is applicable not only to factory workers, but to nurses as well.[1]

This chapter explores nurses' education and training and the constitution of a professional identity in Great Britain, Canada, and the Caribbean. Seventeen Caribbean-born and one Black Canadian-born interviewee trained in Britain; twelve Black Canadian women and one Caribbean woman trained in Canada, and the other five trained in the English-speaking Caribbean. The formation of Black women's professional identity in Canada and Britain has to be considered in tandem with the development of nursing as a profession for middle-class white women, which was inextricably linked to Victorian ideals of respectability and femininity. In constructing and defining itself on these particular axes, an occupational hierarchy based on gender, socioeconomic status, and racial difference was forged. Due to the way that nursing identity was constructed on gendered characteristics associated with respectable womanhood, I use Judith Butler's notion of 'gender as performance,' and extend this analysis to nursing. Nurses, then, are created 'through a sustained set of acts'[2] that begins in their years of training. I argue, however, that Black students in Britain and Canada, cognizant of their Black bodies, performed a particular version of femininity in response to, and as a way to mediate and manage, the contested terrain of nurses' training where ideas about whiteness, womanhood, and femininity underpinned its very core. In exploring this process Homi Bhaba's concept of mimicry – 'almost the same, *but not quite*'[3] – and scholarly discussions of whiteness are most useful.

To be sure, becoming a nurse was not only about economic gain, because the professional identity the women developed held a heightened personal meaning for them. At the end of the process, the students thought of themselves as *nurses*: they assumed a professional identity and had confirmation of that status through their qualifications. In a society where gender, race, and social class are often interconnected with occupational status, these women challenged theoretical arguments that Black women's labour was dispensable, exploitable, and inexpensive.[4] The chapter begins with a brief overview of the political economy of the British, Canadian, and Caribbean nursing systems, followed by an examination of the various facets of nurses' training, such as reactions to the physical work, racism from patients and staff, and interactions between students, nurses, nursing personnel, and physicians.

The Political Economy of British Nursing

The students who entered nurses' training in Britain during and after 1948 belonged to the newly formed National Health Service (NHS), which was conceived during the war years as a part of the creation of a welfare state in Britain. The intention of the NHS was to create 'some form of comprehensive health service that would cover all forms of curative and preventative treatment,'[5] and allow universal access to free health care. Its creation, Charles Webster maintained, 'constituted the single biggest organizational change and greatest improvement in health care ever experienced in the nation's history.'[6] Once the system was put into place, 'the government became caretaker of 2,688 hospitals – 1,143 voluntary hospitals providing some 90,000 beds, and 1,545 municipal hospitals with about 390,000 beds, of which 190,000 were in hospitals for the mentally ill.'[7] The reorganization of Britain's health care system further intensified a previously existing nursing shortage.

In 1949, the ministries of Health and Labour – together with the Colonial Office, the General Nursing Council, and the Royal College of Nursing – began a deliberate policy of recruiting from the Caribbean. Official recruitment schemes were established in 'Barbados, British Guiana (now Guyana), Jamaica, the Leeward Islands (Antigua, Montserrat, and St Kitts), Trinidad, Tobago, and the Windward Islands (Dominica, Grenada, St Lucia, and St Vincent).'[8] Ignoring the institutional and systemic racism faced by Caribbean medical personnel, Sir Ian Carruthers, NHS Acting Chief Executive of the Department of Health, pointed out that 'by making that long journey into the unknown on boats like the SS *Empire Windrush* all those years ago, Caribbean people were critical to the success of the NHS in its formative years but also created a lasting legacy of diversity in its employees.'[9] Scholars and other commentators on Caribbean female health care workers have a less positive view of the experience of female health care workers within the NHS.

Popular culture scholar Julia Hallam and others[10] render a less optimistic portrait when examining the entrance of Black women into British nursing. To Hallam, Caribbean women were recruited to occupy a specific place in the nursing hierarchy that would not challenge white women's hegemony. As matrons, sister tutors, nuns, and staff nurses, white women could continue to control and define nursing based on middle-class notions of femininity. The influx of Caribbean women led Hallam to suggest 'that the strongest challenge to the nursing image of middle-class white femininity came not from men but from the steady flow of Black women entering from the mid-1940s.'[11] Is it possible, Hallam further queries, 'that the nursing workforce saw increasing numbers of black nurses as a threat to the profession's public image?'[12]

To maintain existing power and hierarchical relationships, and to protect the occupation's image, a significant number of Caribbean migrants were channelled into auxiliary positions, working as state-enrolled nurses (SENs) or as maids, even though they had migrated with high hopes of training as state-registered nurses (SRNs).[13] Caribbean women's subordination was further reinforced by the very areas in which they predominated in nursing. Black women were concentrated in 'hospitals for the chronic sick, mental hospitals, and geriatric nursing,' where the shortage was most felt.[14] Black women thus not only occupied the lowest echelons of the occupation, they were also channelled into domains that were unpopular with white nurses, where there was barely any room for upward mobility. This meant that Black women were rarely supervisors or administrators – roles that required consistent interaction with a predominantly white nursing workforce.

The constraints that Caribbean nurses and nursing students faced, however, were not experienced by everyone in the same way. Of the seventeen Caribbean and Black Canadian interviewees who trained in Britain, only two conformed to this pattern of Black women's place in British nursing. Fourteen of the women did become state-registered nurses, and of this group, nine completed midwifery training and two completed only part one of the program. One woman trained as a registered mental nurse (RMN). Two of those with midwifery training also completed additional courses in neonatal and mental nursing. The Black Canadian cohort all graduated with diplomas and earned the status of registered nurse (RN). Still, in Britain and Canada, Black students had to confront white cultural hegemony and the norms embodied in the nursing occupation on multiple levels.

The Political Economy of Canadian Nursing

As was the case in Britain, the decades following the Second World War resulted in transformations in the Canadian health care system that also intensified the nursing shortage. Federal funding for hospital construction and the proliferation of state-funded hospital insurance programs increased the need for hospital staff nurses. At the same time, new employment opportunities for women drew many prospective recruits away from the occupation. Thus, throughout the postwar decades, nursing leaders and educators faced the daunting task of ensuring that there were enough nurses to meet the labour demand, while maintaining the standards of the occupation. Funds were allotted for bursaries to encourage high school girls to choose careers in nursing, and nursing organizations introduced short training courses for subsidiary workers who required less training and education. Nursing associations attempted to reduce the turnover rate, bring 25,000 'unemployed' nurses (such as those who had stopped working to marry or have children) back into the workforce, and decrease emigration and increase immigration, all to alleviate 'the manpower problem in nursing.'[15] In addition, like Britain, Canada also turned to immigrants to alleviate the labour shortage. Thus, nurses and nurses' aides from Greek, German, and other white ethnic groups were encouraged to migrate to Canada. However, the demand for nurses and the declaration prohibiting discrimination issued by the

Canadian Nursing Association in 1944 did not lead to heavy recruitment of Canadian-born Black women into nursing, nor were Black women from the Caribbean encouraged to migrate to Canada.

To understand the experiences of the students who entered Canadian nursing schools means focusing first on these initial exclusionary policies. Until the late 1940s, Black women were excluded from nurses' training in Canada because of the fear of medical doctors, nurses, and other staff members of Black hands on white bodies. In justifying why, for example, a Toronto resident was turned down by the Toronto General Hospital in 1940, Miss A. Mann, director of nurses' registration, offered the following explanation: 'The Superintendent of any general hospital must keep in mind the reaction of patients to nurses in training, and there would no doubt be many protests from patients and doctors if coloured nurses were introduced into the ward.'[16] The applicants that Mann mentioned, such as Bernice Carnegie Redmon, were encouraged to seek training in the United States.

Redmon graduated with her RN diploma and a graduate diploma in public health nursing in 1945 from St Philip Hospital School in Richmond, Virginia. Redmon returned to Canada hoping to find employment. Anti-racist scholar Agnes Calliste points out that, 'despite [Redmon's] qualifications, her registration with the RNAO [Registered Nurses Association of Ontario], and nursing shortages in Nova Scotia, she had difficulty obtaining employment in the province.'[17] It was only after Redmon sought legal advice that she was subsequently hired by the Nova Scotia Department of Health in Sydney. Redmon's eventual employment as a public health nurse, and the entrance of a few Black students at hospitals such as the Hôtel Dieu Hospital in Windsor, Ontario, and the Children's Hospital in Halifax, Nova Scotia, did not lead to an influx of Black women into the occupation. Many hospitals were still unwilling to accept Black women as students.

Although the town of Owen Sound, Ontario, had been touted as one of the more liberal areas for Blacks to reside, Marisse Scott was rejected when she applied in 1946 to the Owen Sound General Hospital. This hospital was her last alternative after all other applications had been refused elsewhere.[18] Scott, who had had childhood aspirations about wanting to 'help others through nursing,' was reportedly told, 'Sorry, we don't accept coloured girls.'[19] To a certain extent, nursing mirrored the larger Canadian society in which the women had grown up: 'Like most children [Scott] had encountered race prejudice in one or another of its many ugly forms throughout her school days at Owen Sound, but it was not until she sought to enrol as a student nurse at the hospital that she realized just how cruel that prejudice could be.'[20] Undeterred, Scott and her parents went on a relentless campaign to bring her plight to the press, government officials (including Ed Sargent, Owen Sound's mayor), church authorities, and union officials. Despite widespread public appeal and support 'throughout the Dominion ... no hospital official came forward and said: "we will accept you because of your colour."' Reverend J.A. O'Reilly of the Church of Our Lady in Guelph eventually approached the Mother Superior of St Joseph's Hospital in that city regarding Scott's case, and she was finally accepted by the nursing school. Obviously cognizant of her role as a trailblazer, Scott excelled as a student. St Joseph's Hospital authorities 'termed her one of the most willing – and able – student nurses in the history of the institution.'[21] Scott is heralded as the 'woman who, despite the prejudices of her day, paved the way for other young black women to become nurses.'[22]

Similarly, the *Toronto Daily Star* in 1947 had also reported on the inability of Ruth and Doris Bailey to gain admittance to Ontario nursing schools. The publicity given to Scott and the Bailey sisters' struggle and the government policies that prevented the migration of Caribbean nurses to Canada in the 1950s and 1960s led to the mobilization of people and organizations.[23] Organizations such as the Nova Scotia Association for the Advancement of Coloured People, and individuals such as Pearleen Oliver (who wanted to become a nurse and was rejected because she was Black) in Halifax, and Donald Moore, Director of the Negro Citizenship Association in Ontario, successfully challenged the racially motivated regulations, which eventually led to the migration of some Caribbean nurses and the admittance of a few Black Canadian women into nursing. However, employment of Black students did not necessarily mean immediate acceptance by whites.

Concerns about the entrance of Black women into nursing and the impact of their presence on the image of the profession extended well into the 1960s, reflected not only in immigration and nursing records[24] but also in *Chatelaine*, a popular woman's magazine read across Canada. In 1964, Sheila Mackay Russell published a short piece of fiction, 'The Glass Wall: A New Chapter in the Human Drama in a Hospital,' which described the imagined angst that administrators, staff, and students felt regarding hiring a Black nurse 'for a key post on the faculty of nursing' at the fictional Civic General Hospital. In discussing whether the heroine Lydia Sanford would fit in, one instructor summed up her feelings to a colleague: 'Being brilliant isn't enough for the job she'll be stepping into. You know how students tend to regard the senior employees of the faculty as the ultimate in the professional image. Well, I don't see how they can identify with Lydia Sanford. She just doesn't fit the image.'[25] This image, embedded in the consciousness of the students and faculty, was that of a white nurse.

Clearly, the formal eradication of racist barriers did not obliterate the structures of white privilege embedded in the occupation. Young Black women who entered nursing during the late 1940s and 1950s and the period thereafter trained in a largely homogeneous environment of white doctors, administrators, nurses, and patients. White Canadian nurses were not always as explicit as those in Britain in claiming their white-skin privilege, but they were just as complicit in linking nursing identity to whiteness, not only in fiction such as Russell's 'The Glass Wall,' but in the actual responses of nursing leaders. In refusing admission to Black students, administrators such as Miss Mann both privileged and reified whiteness as the norm, by using themselves as the standard to define and legitimize who was worthy of becoming a nurse.

Nursing leaders were joined by students who participated in their own popular forms of reinforcing white privilege through stereotyping Blacks, as exemplified in the 1966 issue of the *Torgen* (the yearbook of the Toronto General Hospital). White nurses from the graduating class of 1967 painted their faces black to perform in a minstrel variety show entitled 'Basin Street Comes North.'[26] This late nineteenth-century American form of racist entertainment was presented despite the presence of at least one Black student.[27] A perusal of the *Windsor Star* during the 1950s reveals that minstrel shows were popular forms of entertainment in a number of Canadian churches, much to the chagrin of community activists such as Stanley Grizzle, president of the Canadian Pacific Railway Division of the Brotherhood of Sleeping Car Porters.

While whites generally viewed performances such as 'Basin Street Comes North' merely as recreation,[28] Grizzle posited otherwise. Minstrel shows, he maintains, 'perpetuated the stereotypes cherished in the minds of many White people'[29] about Black people. The audiences, Grizzle added, 'have never suffered from prejudice and discrimination to understand the humiliation caused by childish forms of entertainment involving minority groups.'[30] As audiences sat inertly enthralled by blackface entertainment, they were being schooled about racial identity, including their own. Hallam argues that 'imaginary constructions have social implications; they are not only "fictions" of the material world;

they mediate dominant ideals and values, creating insecurity and doubt, and even fear.'[31]

Whether in churches or on a stage, these minstrel performances cannot be viewed as isolated or innocent occurrences, but must be understood within the context of nursing and of how Black people were viewed in the larger Canadian society. These examples about white privilege and whiteness illustrate the extent to which nursing leaders and students attempted to define nursing based on their own cultural values, beliefs, and practices. It is on this racialized terrain that Black Canadian students would subsequently enter nurses' training and employment. Before exploring actual nurses' training and education, an examination of the political economy of the Caribbean health care system also deserves some attention.

The Political Economy of Caribbean Nursing

During the same period, nursing leaders in the English-speaking Caribbean region were engaged in monumental nursing reforms with the goal of legitimizing nursing locally and internationally. A concern of Caribbean people in general was autonomy from Britain. Subordinated and neglected by the Empire, Caribbean people increasingly became dissatisfied with colonial rule and the corollary effects – 'economic decline, political decay, and social dislocation' – that culminated in the disturbances of the 1930s that began in Trinidad in 1934, spread throughout the region, and ended in Guyana in 1939.[32] Caribbean people hoped that their discontent would shepherd in a new postcolonial social order, where the needs of the majority were paramount.[33] This spirit was also extended to nursing.

In Barbados, 'nursing service was not a high profession, [but] was considered sufficiently prestigious to confer social respectability upon the white women who dominated its ranks.'[34] A similar pattern existed in other Caribbean islands. Black women wanted desperately to have autonomy and input into the development of nurses' education. Empowered by the spirit of hopefulness that was sweeping the Caribbean region in the aftermath of the riots, Caribbean Canadian nursing scholar Jocelyn Hezekiah points out that nurses began fighting 'for better working conditions, higher salaries and better standards of living.'[35] Yet changes occurred unevenly across the region, and nurses in some of the Caribbean islands continued to struggle for registration, accreditation, and increased salaries until the mid-1950s. The issue of salaries among other factors remains one of the primary reasons why nurses migrated.

While Barbados had a formal system in place for training practitioners and formed the Barbados Registered Nurses Association in 1936, it was unique compared with other countries in the Caribbean. In 1946, according to Caribbean nursing scholar Hermi Hyacinth Hewitt, 'there was no law governing registration of nursing education programmes, [nor were there] any qualified nursing tutors in the Jamaican public sector to teach basic nursing education.'[36] Consequently, nursing leaders set to out to formalize and raise the standard of nurses' education in the Caribbean.

In 1946, the Jamaica General Trained Nurses Association was formed, and state registration was granted in 1951. A standardized curriculum was put into place, and entrance requirements were solidified. Training in Jamaica was now concentrated primarily at the Kingston Public Hospital (KPH) and the University College Hospital of the West Indies (UCHWI). Potential students were no longer arbitrarily chosen but were selected by a nursing selection committee. To be admitted to nurses' training in the Caribbean, candidates had to have the Cambridge school certificate and pass either the selection education test of the nursing council for their area, or the test developed by hospital authorities. Nurses' training ranged anywhere from three to four years, and those wishing to pursue additional postgraduate work needed an additional nine to eighteen months.

For other specialized training, such as district nursing, public health nursing, and mental nursing, nurses continued their education six to twelve months longer.[37] In Trinidad, sister tutors appointed by the Colonial Office in 1945 had revised the nursing curriculum four years later, which meant that students were exposed to more classroom knowledge. As with some hospital-based nursing schools in Britain, a preliminary training system was introduced, which concentrated on the theoretical aspects of nurses' education. Considered one of the most influential women to impact nurses' education in the Caribbean, Nita Barrow was concerned that 'nursing education [ought] to be perceived as a discipline rather than as the accumulation of a set of skills,' and her vision was one shared by her contemporaries throughout the Caribbean region.[38] While some scholarly attention has been paid to notable individuals such as Barrow who were instrumental in the development of nurses' education in the English-speaking Caribbean,[39] the same cannot be said for the rank-and-file students who trained as general nurses, public health nurses, and nurse-midwives.

Caribbean nursing leaders strove to portray an image of 'respectability and professionalism,'[40] in the Caribbean and overseas, particularly in Britain. As they worked to transform the structure of nurses' training in the Caribbean, they did so with the General Nursing Council for England and Wales in mind. The objective was for Caribbean standards to be accepted by the national nursing body responsible for registration. For example, when the General Nursing Council came into effect in Jamaica in 1951, it immediately applied to the General Nursing Council for England and Wales for reciprocity for 'nurses registered by the examination,' and this was granted in 1952. Jamaica was not the only country that sought reciprocity with the General Council. As Hezekiah points out, eventually 'only training recognized by a body external to the region, namely, the General Council for England and Wales, was accepted by all the islands' authorities as equipping a nurse to practise her profession outside her home territory.'[41] This particular gesture is significant because it confirmed an interdependent relationship between the Empire and its colonies.

Once Caribbean nursing schools adapted a syllabus similar to the General Nursing Council for England and Wales, granting reciprocity to Caribbean nurses became more feasible. As long as the Caribbean training system was patterned on Britain's, the latter could depend on the former to help solve the nursing shortage. Reciprocity with the General Nursing Council for England and Wales, and other countries like Canada, contributed to the transnational character of nursing, but subsequently led to a nursing shortage in the Caribbean.[42] How Black women traversed the contested site of their nurses' training is the focus of the rest of the chapter.

Nurses' Education and Training

As with the category woman, there is nothing inherent or essential about the category nurse. The nurse is an invention, or a social creation, 'a role being played, not an essentialized nurturing identity being expressed.'[43] In the complex web of the medical hierarchy, practitioners in training, like actors, learn how to play their roles, not only by gaining the required skills, but also through learning mannerisms and behaviour that they are expected to display. As practitioners in training successfully enact their roles in tandem with the dictates of the occupation, there are those who fail to meet the ideal. Thus, Judith Butler's argument 'we regularly punish those who fail to do their gender right,'[44] is applicable to nursing. Students who perform nursing inappropriately or insist that there are multiple ways of 'doing one's [nursing] identity' risk censure and punishment.

Few empirical studies currently exist using Butler's ideas to illustrate how racialized women participate in the production of gender. Because nursing identity is constructed on specific gendered ideals coupled with its exclusionary practices, the occupation serves as an interesting site to investigate how Black women participated in gendered performances. To underscore Black women's structural location in nursing, the occupation has been likened to that of a colony, and the relationship between white and Black nurses has been characterized as that between the colonizer and the colonized.[45] In the Caribbean, this relationship was in fact a reality up until the late 1960s when most Caribbean islands gained their independence from Britain. At one point, white women from Britain and later Canada dominated in leadership and supervisory roles. The structure of nurses' training in the Caribbean was, for the most part, a replica of nurses' training in Britain.

According to Bhabha, 'colonial mimicry is the desire for a reformed, recognizable Other, *as a subject of difference that is almost the same, but not quite.*'[46] While colonial discourse aims 'to produce compliant subjects who reproduce [the colonizers'] assumptions, habits and values – that is, "mimic" the colonizer'[47] – this goal is unattainable. Bhabha further notes that 'the effect of mimicry on the authority of colonial discourse is profound and disturbing.'[48] The end result of the colonial project is the production of an ambivalent subject, whose 'mimicry is never very far from mockery, since it can appear to parody whatever it mimics.'[49] The reality is that 'the colonials never simply reproduce the colonizers' habits, values or worldview, but instead, produce a "blurred copy" of the colonizer that can be quite threatening.'[50] This blurred copy is not inferior, but a subversion of or resistance to the original, as the colonized finds ways to legitimize herself, constructing her own identity.

Bhabha's theoretical concepts and frameworks are not unproblematic. In addition to 'reducing colonial dynamics to a linguistic exchange,'[51] his colonial subjects tend to be a homogeneous group, with very little attention to gender, social class, geographical region, or religion. These limitations notwithstanding, his concept of mimicry is valuable for my analysis precisely because of the ways in which British, Canadian, and to a lesser extent, Caribbean nursing was structured. As 'almost the same, but not quite,' non-white women's entrance into nursing in Britain and Canada was a potential threat to the occupation's image. If the image of the professional nurse, however fluid, contested, and historically specific, was constituted in the bodies of middle-class white women, how then did Black women carve out a distinct space for themselves in an occupation that often resembled a colonial space?

Nursing cannot be viewed simply as a colony based only on its organization and structure. The military-style training, rituals, and occupational and behavioural directives to which practitioners and trainees were exposed should also be included. In the social world of nursing, conventions and practices were acted and re-enacted through the bodies of practitioners, with the intent to make them appear to be natural aspects of the profession. The goal of matrons, nursing sisters, nuns, and instructors was to create a body of obedient apprentices who imitated those in positions of authority and then reproduced themselves via new recruits. By reading the oral narratives of the women in this study through the lens of performance and the concept of mimicry, it is possible to see how, as racialized and gendered subjects, Black women's overall success in Canadian and British nursing was contingent on particular performances of femininity. These acts involved acquiescence and accommodation, but also some resistance, which simultaneously conformed to – and unsettled – the traditional image of the nurse. Black women's performance in nursing was predicated upon both awareness and denial of their blackness, a belief in and acceptance of the gendered ideals promoted by the occupation, and an emphasis on skills as intrinsic to their professional identity.

Remembering Nurses' Training

Nurses' training, with some distinctions, shared certain similarities across the three geographical locations. Utilized as inexpensive labour for hospitals, student nurses often worked twelve-hour shifts of onerous and in some cases, monotonous and repetitive work. On the wards, uniforms served to differentiate the status of individual practitioners. They began as probationers, or 'probies,' then progressed to juniors, and finally to graduates. The majority of the women lived in dormitory residences, where they were subjected to constant surveillance regarding appropriate female behaviour and often penalized for any form of perceived insubordination. Student trainees had to mimic what they were being taught as proof that they were absorbing their lessons. While a few of the Caribbean and Black Canadian women were critical of their training, the more common response was, 'It was hard work [but] it was fun.'

Orphelia, who was born in 1914 and was thus the eldest of the Caribbean interviewees, grew up very poor but she was academically inclined. Separated from her cheating husband, and with two children to care for, Orphelia applied to nursing school at the Kingston Public Hospital in Jamaica in the early 1940s. Despite the hardship associated with purchasing her own uniforms, and her understanding that nursing students furnished hospitals with cheap labour, Orphelia recalled:

> The training was wonderful. You don't get a penny year one. You have to buy material and get your uniform ready and made. And you had to wear a cape and apron at that time and you had to pay for that.[52]

Orphelia was especially proud of the fact that her class was at the time 'the largest set of nurses in the history of Jamaica.' They were referred to as the '109 batch'[53] and were so happy to be there that they began planning their graduation a year in advance. Even though 'food was difficult to get' during the Second World War, and while 'some [students] got married and some failed,' those still enrolled continued to make plans to celebrate the completion of three years of training. Despite the decrease in their numbers, Orphelia declared that 'they still couldn't fit us all in one photo.' For her, the fact that the 109 batch 'made history' was the memorable aspect of her nurses' training.

Having come of age in homes and societies where to gain the approval of peers, family members, and societal institutions, young women generally performed to the dictates of their gender, nursing was simply another site where this performance continued. The interviewees for this study had this reaction once they understood the route involved to become nurses. They struggled with certain aspects of nursing work including long shifts. Jennette trained in the block system in Britain, which meant 'that formal teaching [did] not interfere directly with ward work.'[54] Six to eight weeks was spent in pre-training, where, 'you get the basics – anatomy, physiology, and [basic] nursing.' Following pre-training, students then had an opportunity to experience working on the hospital ward. In first year, Jennette explained:

> We did basic things like making beds, and I remember you would have to learn how to test urine for sugar. Now you just use a dipstick. But then you had the Bunsen burner and the solution and it turned blue. We did these things so we can get used to the patients.[55]

The 'basic things' that Jennette talked about constituted what the authors of the Nuffield Report referred to as basic nursing, or 'care required in the interests of the comfort and well-being of the patient for the maintenance of health and the prevention of infection, *irrespective of the disease from which [s]he is suffering.*'[56]

During pre-training, students had very little physical contact with patients, although patients' comfort and needs remained their prime concern. Dorothy J, who also trained in the block system, stated: 'You were still on the floor working, mostly in the sluice emptying bedpans, cleaning cupboards, putting out the patients' clothes, and those sorts of things.'[57] Indeed, many of the interviewees were unaccustomed to some of the demeaning work that constituted nurses' training. The reality of nursing stood in stark contrast to what what Dorothy J referred to as the 'glorified [image] on television.' She pointed out: 'You had to clean patients up, you had to bathe them, you had to clean their vomit and all those sort of things.'[58] Even with all these difficulties, once the practitioners reflected on the reason they left the Caribbean, they dismissed any thought of quitting.

In addition to the physical work, the interviewees were astutely aware of the organization of the hospital, and their roles within it. Jennette's recollection that 'student nurses [did] all the work ... We had to work long hours, and the work was difficult'[59] was reiterated by the majority of the nurses. Instead of viewing the relationship between the hospitals and themselves as exploitative, a few nurses, such as Jamaican-born Monica, underscored the reciprocal relationship between the practitioner in training and the hospital. Monica trained at University College Hospital of the West Indies (UCHWI) in the mid-1950s, and she offered the following analysis:

I was trained on what was called until the '60s the apprenticeship system. In the hospital, you were given an education for free. You were paid a very small stipend while receiving that education and you gave your services to the hospital. But it wasn't entirely giving your services because while giving your services, you would also develop skills and gain knowledge.[60]

Arguably, 'the giving of services' to gain knowledge and skills was hardly a mutual exchange given the limited monetary compensation, but nurses such as Monica felt otherwise. She felt that nursing not only allowed students the opportunity to develop skills and knowledge, and subsequently to sell their labour power for a wage, but also provided them with the tools to navigate the inner world of nursing as well as the world outside. 'Our training prepared us for life. We became very responsible citizens,' Monica added.

Nurses' training involved not only the development of a professional identity but also contributed to ongoing subjectivity formation. Nursing instructors and leaders impressed upon the pupils that the identity they assumed as practitioners went beyond the confines of the hospital walls, especially if their uniforms were worn in public. The nurse's uniform produced meaning and was considered a sign. As Hallam points out, 'the way these young women look, both on and off duty, is taken axiomatically to signify their attitude to their work and profession.'[61]

By no means did the work become easier, but as the students successfully completed each segment of their training, they were allowed to enter the next phase. British nursing historian Ann Bradshaw's discussion of Florence Nightingale's influence on nurses' training is especially relevant. Bradshaw argued that 'precision, infinite, carefulness was the basis for nurse training. It was for every ward sister to show every new probationer how to do her work, not only how it should be done, but also to guard against how it should not be done.'[62] Muriel, from Barbados, illustrated this in the following analysis:

At every stage of your training, there was proficiency. When you got from A to B, then you knew it; you didn't just walk through from A to B. You knew that before you got into B, you had well covered A. And it went through every stage like that. Even if you live to be a hundred, you could still remember the things that you were taught at stage A.[63]

Thus, the nurse is created and partly perfected in the regime and by the various nursing administrators that Bradshaw identified. As Butler contends, 'One does not "do" one's gender [or nursing] alone, one is always "doing" with or for another, even if the other is only imaginary.'[64]

As students moved into their second year, a new set of apprentices was now responsible for 'all the dirty work.' The notion of mimicry in practice became evident as upper-level students began to reproduce their own nurses' training with the probies. Senior practitioners were now equipped to take on more 'practical things,' such as 'doing medicines and giving injections' and 'all the tasks that are concerned with the treatment of the disease from which the patient is suffering.'[65] Technical tasks, which differed from ward to ward, included taking temperature, pulse, and respiration; administering drugs; and bandaging wounds. Also included were 'those medical procedures performed by the nurse when specifically required, procedures performed by either the nurse or the doctor (according to hospital policy),' and 'the collection and examination of specimens.'[66]

Whether they trained in the Caribbean, Britain, or Canada, all of the women maintained that they did 'more hands-on things for the patients.' Consequently, a core aspect of these women's nursing identities was linked to how they cared for the patients. Even though students learned through ongoing repetition, there was still an underlying sense that the ability to care was a natural attribute. On another level, however, the actual physical work that students' had to undertake meant assuming duties similar to a domestic worker or servant, suggesting the ambiguity in an occupation that constructed itself as being fit for white, middle-class women.

The ward, more so than the classroom, symbolized a theatrical stage, where nursing students regardless of their level of training were mainly actors. A senior staff nurse or nun played the role of director, and along with patients, the student nurses also constituted the audience. It is through the bodies of students that the entire nursing curriculum was enacted. Thus, performance was judged on how well, according to Muriel, one 'mastered certain things' – which referred not only to the skills one acquired but just as significantly, how one followed orders. Complex relationships on the wards, however, both reinforced and contested racial, gendered, and social class hierarchies.

Relationships on the Wards and in Classes

Interactions between doctors and nurses, especially student nurses, were pervasively gendered. Trinidadian-born Ancilla recalled that in England during the 1960s:

> You had to stand at attention when the doctors came in, and as a lowly student, you couldn't even speak to them. [When] you had to address them, you never called them by their names [but] as Mr So-and-so or Dr So-and-so.[67]

Similarly, at the Hôtel Dieu Hospital in Windsor, Ontario, students in the 1950s quickly learned the configuration of the hospital hierarchy. Agnes explained:

> The doctors were king, and the nursing directors were queens. They ran
> the hospital. The nuns were nurses also. They kind of put them [nuns] on
> a pedestal and when the priest came into town he was put on a pedestal.[68]

There was no confusion about how and by what means the medical hierarchy was constituted and legitimated.

Based on their supposed superior scientific knowledge, socioeconomic status, whiteness, and maleness, there was no doubt that the physicians embodied patriarchal authority. Consequently, the relationship between nurses, doctors, and patients was often viewed in a familial context. Ema Garminkov, for example, has argued that the nurse-doctor relationship reflected the archetypal nuclear family (read, white families) with the doctor as father, the nurse as mother, and patients as children. She not only presumed that all families reflected this model, but most importantly, she excluded the nurses' relationships with each other.[69] Matrons, ward sisters, nuns, and staff nurses wielded enormous power over student nurses, as the examples of Black Canadian-born Laura and Virginia demonstrate.

In general, Laura found her instructors at the Halifax Children's Hospital to be fair, and she 'didn't have any problems with any one of the teachers.' The head nurses, however, could make life as a student unbearable: 'They were very, very severe, and if you did something wrong, or [what] they considered wrong, they were very severe in the way they chastised you over it.'[70] Her most unpleasant moment during her entire three years of training occurred when:

> I was scrubbing for an amputation. This child was having a toe removed,
> and they used a product call gentian violet to mark where the limb comes
> off, and it's very staining. [The head nurse] was hurrying me out to make
> the operating room [ready] for the orthopaedic surgeon that she loved
> dearly. She shoved me and the Mayo stand that was holding the instruments
> with the little glass of gentian violet fell over, and it went all over her white
> marble floor.[71]

Embarrassed and terrified, yet following the code that 'you never talk back,' to your superiors, Laura immediately left the operating room (OR), but not before the head nurse told her: 'You will never get a job in the province of Nova Scotia in the OR, and in fact, the whole of Canada.'[72]

In the larger social and hierarchical context of nursing, Laura's experience was hardly atypical. For Laura, however, the intensity of the outburst, coupled with the threat, led her to conclude that the head nurse's reaction was racially motivated. To the white head nurse, Laura's blackness was the reason for her incompetence.

Butler maintains that 'even when gender seems to congeal into the most reified forms, the "congealing" is itself an insistent and insidious practice, sustained and regulated by various social means.'[73] The performance of the professional rituals of nursing is contingent on a 'stylized repetition of acts' subjected to approval or critique. A poor nursing performance can subject students to punishment, humiliation, as Laura illustrates, and in rare cases, expulsion. As a result of their race and gender, some Black students were subjected to injurious speech acts.[74]

Black Canadian-born women went into nursing with the burden of their race on their shoulders. Eleven of the women I interviewed entered nursing fully cognizant of two things: the occupation's exclusionary history and their subject position as trailblazers. Virginia Travis entered nurses' training at Chatham General Hospital, Chatham, Ontario, in 1954, and explained: 'my predecessor [who] couldn't enter nursing influenced [me].'[75] Virginia, like some of the other Black Canadian trainees, was always conscious of how her body was being read by white medical personnel, peers, and patients. 'I basically did whatever I was told,' she explained, until it was time to move to the next level in training. Virginia relayed the following incident:

> You had to meet the director of nursing, who told you whether [you had done well enough] academically ... to receive your cap and whether you were going to move on into the last half of the first year.[76]

During the interview, the nursing director expressed reservations about Virginia proceeding to the next level. She, on the other hand, was confident that she had fulfilled the requirements for the capping ceremony. Virginia saw no reason why her progress should be impeded and spoke up in her own defence. The nursing director then told Virginia that 'I would get my cap, but I was to stop acting like a monkey.' Stunned at the nursing director's blatant act of racism, Virginia left the meeting speechless and distraught: 'I was offended by that because the inference was definitely there. So, in [my] first year, at eighteen years of age, I knew that I had to be very careful.'[77] The nursing director's statement was a way of marking Virginia as different from herself and the mostly white medical personnel, and also illustrates 'how responses to subordinate groups are socially organized to sustain existing power arrangements.'[78]

Virginia's and Laura's experience further elucidates the consequence of being 'the same, but not quite.' Discovering that she was the subject of gendered racism at the onset of nurses' training, the stage was set for Virginia's negotiation of the rest of her training and career. Although she had no regrets about challenging the nursing director, Virginia became preoccupied with her demeanour and the perceptions of the predominantly white medical staff. To a certain extent, she began to police her own performance. Worried about the long-term consequences of crossing the boundaries of acceptable behaviour, she made a concerted effort to outperform her peers: 'I had to do better. I had to achieve rather than being mediocre. So, I strove to do that throughout my career.'[79] For Virginia, this meant also performing a version of femininity that conformed to the appropriate nursing identity as an act of resistance.

As an outsider to nursing theatrical performance, and ever mindful of the authoritative gaze of nuns and head nurses, Dorothy R also developed a strategy similar to Virginia's. Of her training at Windsor's Hôtel Dieu Hospital, in 1950, Dorothy R stated:

> I know I was nervous many times because all your patients are white. I was very conscientious to always make sure I did everything right, did it on time. If [patients] asked me for something a half a dozen times, I never refused. You wanted to be perfect. I wasn't gonna give anyone any outs.[80]

This act of self-regulation and passivity has to be interpreted against institutional practices that rendered Black women as naturally unfit to nurse, placing them in the position of having to constantly prove their proficiency to the medical establishment.

Training in an environment that privileged whiteness meant that students' performances could be deemed as unauthentic when racial categorizations were used to judge their actions. Feelings of in-between-ness, a consequence of the encounters between the colonizers and those colonized, cannot be discussed only in relation to how migrants were integrated into the broader society. The various institutions – in this case, in the medical arena – also produced and reproduced feelings of Otherness. Despite growing up in the colonial Caribbean, the interviewees' consciousness of a racial identity became pronounced once they migrated to Britain, unlike the Canadian-born women, whose racial identity was formed at a young age. It was in Britain that young Caribbean women truly discovered the social meanings attached to their skin colour.

The Caribbean students in this study who migrated during the mid-1950s trained and lived in a critical moment in British society. Certainly, they had heard of or knew about the 1958 race riots and the intense public debates both in the media and the British Parliament painting Blacks as the problem. If any of them had picked up an issue of *Nursing Times*, they would have been privy to the 'expert' opinion of E. Lees, Deputy Superintendent Health Visitor for Nottingham, that the Caribbean family '[varies] so greatly from our own.'[81] Lees drew upon the racist and gendered stereotypes depicting Black women as reasonably good parents and caretakers who refused, however, to embrace the health visitors' prescriptions. In addition to pointing out high illegitimacy rates among Caribbean women, their opposition to marriage, and the tendency for them to be on National Assistance, Lees further explained that 'they are difficult to teach; pleasant and smiling, they will reply "Yes, please" to any instruction given. Then they cheerfully exclude all fresh air from the room and live in an atmosphere suited more to the growing of tomatoes than the development of children.'[82] The message here is patently obvious: Caribbean women are unable to assimilate, and evidently do not embody middle-class notions of femininity.

In the same issue of *Nursing Times*, a public health administrator wrote that her friend, who was 'a TB visitor' presumably at one of the health centres, asked why 'in heaven's name … don't [sic] the Government do something to stop these people coming in such droves? Why don't they insist on chest X-rays instead of increasing the load on our sanatoria, with families on National Assistance?'[83] Encouraged to migrate albeit as a last resort in order to alleviate the labour shortage, Caribbean migrants were then viewed as intruders creating disorder in Britain's national character and way of life.

If the students had happened to miss these letters written in response to the Nottingham and Notting Hill riots, they still quickly learned how biological markers were assigned to them because of race. Some experienced racism firsthand from their patients, while others learned about it through their families and other people's experiences.

While Caribbean women did not collectively feel that they 'had to blaze a trail' for other Black women, as their Canadian counterparts had done, they soon recognized the particularities of living blackness in Britain. A determined group who were committed to achieving their goals, these women demanded much of themselves in training, initially as a result of their own ambition, but eventually because of their race.

As part of colonial discourse, ambivalence was created when white medical personnel drew on essentialist categorizations whereby skin colour was linked to intelligence. In practice, however, students contradicted these views. Having experienced racism as she tried to find employment and housing, Jamaican-born Daphne C did not assume that the nursing instructors were any different from the employers who refused to hire her, or from the rental owners who told her repeatedly that there was 'no vacancy available.' To be successful in nursing, Daphne C learned quickly that she had to outperform her white colleagues:

> You really had to study, but it was good. I used to be one of the ones that got the nursing award [chuckle]. When you are in a class of ten, and you are the one Black one in there, you have to study ten times as hard to get your A, as they have to study to get their B. They said, 'We don't study. We don't study.' But then, you have to be smart enough to know that that wasn't the truth.[84]

As the only Black student, Daphne C recognized her subject position in relation to her classmates. She and others excelled academically and in so doing they contested any perception on the part of white students about their intelligence.

Similarly, Muriel pointed out: 'I excelled in anatomy and physiology and I remember getting a certificate, [which you received] if you did well.'[85] Trinidadian-born Carmencita also did exceptionally well and attributed her academic performance as the primary reason she was able to be employed at Great Ormond Street Hospital in London. Disavowing any prescription of racial inferiority, she proudly declared: 'You didn't get into that hospital unless you had really good marks and passed your exams. I was a really good student.'[86]

Facing Racism

Racist ideologies could further disrupt Black women's performance, as patients, peers, kitchen staff, and cleaners alike questioned their presence and competency. In Britain, Jamaican-born Elaine recalled that during her training 'people would say they didn't want any Black hands to touch [them],'[87] an experience to which both Caribbean migrants and Black Canadian-born nurses could relate. Grenadian-born Dorothy J remembered being asked on the floor whether Black people lived in

Daphne Bailey. (Courtesy of Daphne Bailey)

Agnes E. Ellsworth, 1953. (Courtesy of Agnes Ellsworth)

Agnes E. Ellsworth, 2004. (Courtesy of Agnes Ellsworth)

Sheila Raymond, 1968. (Courtesy of Sheila Raymond)

Graduation photo of Laura Bush in Halifax, 1955.
(Courtesy of Laura Bush Tynes)

Contemporary photo of Laura Bush Tynes in Port Credit.
(Courtesy of Laura Bush Tynes)

Beverley Salmon. (Courtesy of Beverley Salmon)

E. Marlene Watson with her sisters Yvonne (right) and Donna (left) on graduation day. (Courtesy of E. Marlene Watson)

E. Marlene Watson (centre) with the unit staff at Brandon General Hospital, 1962. (Courtesy of E. Marlene Watson)

Ward Christmas party, 1963, at Humber Memorial Hospital – E. Marlene Watson far right. (Courtesy of E. Marlene Watson)

Second reunion of the graduation class of E. Marlene Watson. (third from left) (Courtesy of E. Marlene Watson)

trees and finding out that British people believed that 'we were mon-keys.'[88] The association of Black women with apes harkens back to the nineteenth century as a way to rationalize their dehumanization at the hands of Europeans. Clearly, these racist sentiments, albeit reconfig-ured, persisted into the following century.

Undoubtedly, the reactions, questions, and probing experienced by some Caribbean practitioners was uncomfortable, awkward, and often painful. For Dorothy J, however, these experiences served to confirm how ignorant white British people were:

> I used to say [that] these white people come to the West Indies and preach Christianity and all sorts of things to us, and when you go to their country, you find out that they are the stupid ones because of the things they would ask and what they could come up with. You'd wonder how these people could think about some things you wouldn't think about.[89]

Dorothy J's judicious indictment of British people's ignorance is another example of the decentring of Britain and the supposed superiority of its citizens. Caribbean students had responses to the negativity meted out by some health personnel. Only two of the interviewees for this study mentioned speaking out against unequal treatment. The majority either refused to comment or ignored discriminatory treatment, which is understandable given the reason the interviewees migrated, but also their having to deal for the first time in their lives with racism's deadly venom.

One purpose of nurses' training was to encourage students to obey rather than transgress or violate the cultural norms and practices of nursing. But this did not always work. As Ancilla illustrated:

> I was the senior student on the unit and at [one particular] time I was the only person there. And one of the doctors came to make rounds, and he looked right at me, and he said, 'Is there anybody here?' And I looked around, and I said 'nope.' So he said, 'What do you mean?' I said, 'Well, if you're looking at me and you're asking me if there's anybody here, then I guess I'm nobody, so I guess there's no one here.' 'Well, who's going to make rounds with me?' I said, 'You're on your own.' So, I never did.[90]

In the contested crucible of the medical field, a physician's place in the period after the Second World War was almost certain. Female health care workers, regardless of their position, were expected to defer to the physicians, and act in the capacity of 'helpmeet.' To overstep this clearly demarcated boundary, or to respond to medical doctors with anything but deference could have serious consequences. Certainly Ancilla insubordination could have led to her being expelled.

Surprised at Ancilla's assertiveness, the physician wasted no time in reporting her to the matron, who immediately summoned Ancilla to her office and interrogated her about the incident. According to Ancilla: 'I repeated my story, asking how could he be so rude as to assume that I'm nobody?'[91] Ancilla refused to yield to medical authority. She simply responded in a manner that reflected both an inversion of mimicry and subversion of the familial trope, which in the case of nursing, is modelled on the heterosexual marital relationship, which requires submission to the husband/doctor. In effect, Ancilla acted the part of a bad wife/helpmeet.

While the physician in Ancilla's case refused to acknowledge her presence, Guyanese-born Jean recalled that there were some physicians who, if 'they want to make rounds and if they see it's a Black nurses in charge, they would change their minds, and say they would come back to do the rounds.'[92]

In her final year of training, Lillie's encounter with a white supervisor was further evidence of how Black women's performances can be labelled as inauthentic. This subsequently isolates and marginalizes the actor, and maintains both real and symbolic relationships of power. Although she was not assigned any duties, each night, according to Lillie: 'the night duty charge nurse would tell me off proper that I wasn't doing anything.'[93] Eventually Lillie's colleagues discovered that she was being chastised by the night duty nurse and reported her to the matron. In response, the matron removed Lillie from the floor, which was a common practice of supervisors dealing with the discriminatory practices of white nurses. Refusing to hold the night duty nurse accountable for her actions maintained white privilege and treated racism as an individual problem.

During the entire ordeal, however, for fear of being misunderstood or have her complaints distorted, Lillie neither defended herself nor complained about how she was treated. She chose to acquiesce quietly, a quality that was expected and valued in younger recruits. Nonetheless, she packed her trunk with the intent to return to Jamaica, when a friend eventually persuaded her to stay. For Lillie, leaving was a way of coping:

I preferred it that way. Once you get someone acting like that (and I was very uncomfortable), the best thing is for me to move. I don't need to prove to anyone that I'm a human being. It's not my blackness that is important. I'm a good nurse. But what she was trying to say was that I wasn't a good nurse. I was in my third year, just before my finals – it was better for me.[94]

Lillie's comment encapsulates how Black women in general responded when their race was used to judge their nursing performance. Just like white women, Black women too had ideas about what it meant to be a nurse, ideas influenced by their culture, religion, and early socialization. They, too, believed in those seemingly universal womanly characteristics and apparently innate abilities to care for people and help them heal. The gendered ideals of the occupation, which both groups of women believed in and adhered to, allowed for a subversion of their racial identity. Despite living in a society that consistently marked her as 'Other,' Lillie insisted that blackness was not her only defining feature. She emphasized instead that she was a human being and desired to be treated as such.

Drawing on a discourse of professionalism, in which skills and training, rather than appearance and image, were indicators of a 'good nurse,' Lillie inadvertently supported the idea that nursing was indeed a performance. Subsequently, being a 'good nurse,' was not related to blackness, a point that was echoed by other nurses who responded to the multiple forms of gendered racism that they encountered, as trainees and later as workers. Black nurses' belief in their ability to nurse, whether in the classroom or on the ward, was a primary ingredient in their construction of a professional identity. In so doing, they resisted the perception that nursing was really a white women's enclave.

Some British expatriate sisters and matrons teaching in the Caribbean carried with them their air of racial superiority, which influenced how they interacted with Caribbean students. Having been rebuffed by her high school teacher, who questioned her intellectual capabilities, Inez was particularly sensitive to similar insinuations as a probationer:

We had an English or Scottish teacher. I'm not even sure why she taught in Jamaica because this woman was prejudiced. She was very mean [and] very rude. I remember one day she asked me a question, [and] I didn't know the answer or I must have answered something ridiculous and she said under her breath, 'I don't know what the hell you are doing here.' And I just [said] to myself, okay, I will soon tell you what I am doing here, and when the exam came, I came second in the whole bunch. I shocked the lady out of this world.[95]

The need to disabuse white people of the notion of Black inferiority was a diasporic resistive strategy that was also deployed in the Caribbean. Black women such as Inez, whether as students or actual nurses, refused to absorb negative stereotypes about their aptitude, but used negativity as a tool to empower and construct their professional identity.

The scholarship that currently exists on Caribbean nursing after the Second World War rarely mentions relationships between nurses in leadership positions and students. As with nurses' training elsewhere, there were serious implications if students chose to behave in a manner that deviated from established nursing norms and practices. To write and pass the examination set by the Council for Nursing in Jamaica in the 1950s, for example, and to gain the status of registered general nurse required adhering to a regulatory system that defined how the practitioners in training were required to act. If their superiors ever called their actions into question, the trainees were censured. Because 'discipline was rigid and important to survival,'[96] even if students had legitimate complaints, they 'often forfeited their rights in conflicting situations' for fear of disciplinary measures or even dismissal. Regardless of location, nursing as performance is contingent on similar criteria, such as acquiescence.

Nursing and Physical Appearance

Because white femininity as an ideological construct is intricately tied to the image of nursing and its identity,[97] Black women can be subjected to ridicule when they refuse to perform or otherwise challenge this representation. One area where Black women can face particular censure relates to their bodies. As anti-racist nursing scholar and activist Carol Baxter contends, Black nurses can get into trouble through an 'assertion of cultural identity through hairstyle, such as wearing plaits, even if they are worn away from the face and correspond with hospital regulations.'[98] Darlene, the only Black Canadian-born interviewee to train outside of Canada, left for Britain in 1971, where she met with disapproval about her choice of hairstyle. While she admitted to never being a 'Black Power person,' she was certainly influenced by the movement's aesthetic discourse of 'Black is beautiful,' which was reflected in her wearing of an afro. The hairstyle disturbed some of her white peers, especially the nursing sister in charge:

> I had this big, big afro, and one of the things that used to really bug them
> was that they could never see my nursing cap on my head because I'd have

it right on the back of my head where you couldn't see it. And you know I had to be cute when I was on the floor, and I also wore these earrings, which were prisms so you could see different colours, and it just seemed to really annoy them.[99]

Black women faced opposition when they failed to perform the role of the 'proper student nurse,' which was expressed not only in behaviours, attitudes, and mannerisms, but also in dress, which had serious implications. These 'historical prescriptions (issues of hair, color, facial characteristics, physical features, and even clothing), are identified and immediately linked to competence, status, and recognition.'[100] Still, trainees found ways to circumvent the rules, as the example of Darlene illustrates.

Constant surveillance by the ward sister hardly made a difference to Darlene. She made no effort to change her hairstyle and continued to place her nursing cap far back on her head and to wear her earrings, despite being interrogated every day: 'It [didn't] matter what unit I was on ... she would come on the unit to see if I had my nursing cap on.'[101] Black female bodies such as Darlene's, with their afros, plaits, braids, and other accessories deemed inappropriate, inadvertently subverted the supposedly unspoiled image of the nursing occupation that was legitimized in the normative bodies of white nurses in both Great Britain and Canada. However intent nursing leaders were on maintaining an image of nursing that was reminiscent of Victorian notions of femininity, the exigencies of labour helped to fracture the long-standing close connection of nursing with whiteness, both in Britain and in Canada.

Completing the Performance

The recurring social practices and processes required to become a full-fledged nurse must be viewed in dialectical terms. On the one hand, an emphasis is placed on ignoring markers of racial difference by emphasizing the gendered characteristics universally ascribed to nurses and nursing. On the other hand, whiteness and all that it embodies, though unacknowledged, is upheld and sustained as the norm.

To create the impression that nursing was natural for women, nursing leaders emphasized a set of essential traits, such as caring. Gendered performance, according to Betsy Lucal, is acceptable if the actor relies on 'culturally established sets of behaviors, appearances, mannerisms and other cues that we have learned to associate with members of a particular gender.'[102] Nursing, as a performance about gender, is contingent on signs perceived to be universal to all nurses, regardless of their sexuality, culture, racial, and socioeconomic background. These signs, some of which are based on gendered characteristics, operated to subsume social differences and motivated Black women to identify first as nurses.

The University of Toronto School of Nursing's Public Health Nursing Program attracted students from across the globe. The student records of the number of Black postgraduate nurses from Canada, the Caribbean, and the United States who attended during and after the Second World War are instructive. The postgraduate students were identified by their nationality, a few by religion, and a few by race for those who were viewed as not white. For example, nurses were identified as Black American or American Negro, Canadian Japanese, Canadian (Negro), and British (Negro), which referred to the colonial Caribbean. Because those racialized as whites do not generally have to name whiteness, they appeared simply as Canadian, Greek, Portuguese, English, and Norwegian, to name just a few of the nationalities mentioned in the records. Some instructors did acknowledge that a language barrier could affect a student's ability to complete the certificate.

Instructors subjectively appraised postgraduate performances on superficial, yet real, characteristics. All practitioners were assessed on their ability, interest, personality, independence, leadership, knowledge of objectives, planning, and teaching ability.[103] Emphasis was placed, however, on the women's personalities, interest, and how they responded to supervision. The assessment of the students' personality illustrated how important descriptors most often associated with women were to the instructors. Their descriptions of students' personalities included 'youthful,' 'pleasing, with a rather retiring manner,' 'pleasing, but somewhat lacking in force,' 'attractive,' 'good, but not impressive,' 'strong but repressed,' or 'quiet but forceful.'[104] The instructors were especially pleased with nurses who were confident, enthusiastic, cheerful, cooperative, conscientious, sincere, cheerful, and outgoing.[105] Nursing instructors valued the skilful performance of feminine characteristics at the expense of the scientific, technical, and theoretical aspects of nurses' training and education.

Because these women were being groomed to assume supervisory roles upon graduating, instructors evaluated them on their leadership ability. The students were viewed favourably when they complied with and behaved according to the rules and dictates of the public health program. If the women did not act according to the subjective set of criteria developed by the administrative body, they could be subjected to disapproval. Some of the students apparently lacked the requisite attributes, and students who failed to properly mimic their instructors were subjected to increased supervision. Students who were introverted could, with 'encouraging supervision ... develop into ... able public health nurse[s].' Those who had personalities that were lacking in force, 'with encouraging supervision should make satisfactory staff member[s].' One nurse was described as 'temperamental and hypercritical at times, and for this reason did not always adjust well,' but according to the instructor, she 'should develop satisfactorily under good guidance.' If a practitioner had difficulty with routines, then 'thoughtful supervision might help her overcome her difficulties in adjustment.'[106]

In two separate records, the student's race and socioeconomic status became part of the assessment. The instructor noted that one Black Canadian nurse 'should become a satisfactory community worker. Understanding supervision should help her make the necessary adjustment of a coloured person to the public health field.'[107] Not until the student learned and performed the appropriate skills would the condition of her blackness become secondary. One Japanese Canadian student, an instructor wrote, 'carried a heavy financial responsibility all through the course which probably affected her actual grades. She should prove capable of independent work. The fact that her parents are Japanese had made life difficult for her since 1939, but she has been popular with [the] class and very acceptable in the field.'[108] It is noteworthy that the instructor chose to point out how 'popular' the Japanese student was with her peers. Similar language was used to describe Marisse Scott, the Black Canadian student who was admitted to St Joseph's Hospital in Guelph after a public campaign. Being 'popular' for a nurse of colour was a sign that she performed well and was accepted even if she is *almost the same, but not quite.*

The idea that the Black women in this study had about nursing was already nurtured by the gendered ideals, both symbolic and real, that were propagated by their communities, popular culture, and churches, as well as by the occupation once they entered it. Although there is nothing inherent about being a nurse, the interviewees for this study believed otherwise. They believed that nurses had a special calling around the art of healing, caring, and curing. Many appeared to embrace the core principles of nursing along the lines of those explicated in the 1967 Atkinson School of Nursing yearbook, the *Pulse*: 'She is judged not by her race or religion, or social standards, she is measured by her professional yardstick that measures her ability to make a bed, apply a bandage, or sacrifice her time to ease the pain of a patient simply for the satisfaction of a job well done. She is a hardworking, determined young girl doing her best for her school and hospital.'[109] The classroom and the wards were not the only spaces where practitioners were able to forge an identity based on their subject position as students, in the process of becoming fully trained registered nurses. The nursing residence attached to the hospital also served a similar purpose.

'We Were All in the Same Boat': Living in Residence

Canadian nurses' residences, according to historian Dianne Dodd, 'provided a place for thousands of nurses to live, socialize, train, and form gender and professional loyalties.'[110] All students, regardless of their colour, social class, age, or sexual orientation, had to follow a similar route as nurses in the making. Thus, all the women were undergoing the shared experience of fashioning a professional identity through the transition from student to graduate. The women used their time in residence as an opportunity to bond with others over dealing with the difficulties of their training.

Prior to entering nurses' training at Wellesley Hospital in Toronto in 1950, Beverly had never considered smoking as a form of recreation. She soon discovered that smoking was a common practice among the cohort she trained with, and she too began smoking. Beverly rationalized her actions in the following way: 'We were all in the same boat, which was great. We'd come off shift and we'd sit and have our one-a-day cigarette. It was a camaraderie thing.'[111] Beverly and her classmates were engaging in an activity that was defined as male, but it was one of the many recreational pursuits they participated in that contributed to the imagined cohesiveness of nurses' training.

The residence did not have the same meaning for some Black Canadian-born nurses who recalled the unfortunate reality of segregated residences. Some nursing schools had an unspoken policy of admitting two Black students as a way to prevent interracial rooming. Laura explained: 'There were only two Black nurses that went into training before my cousin and I went. You had to have another Black person to room with you.'[112] Some claimed that this was a deliberate choice on the part of nursing administrators, who feared that Black students might be isolated and shunned by their white counterparts.[113] Agnes felt, however, that white administrators were more concerned with protecting their white students: 'They put us together, and we stayed in the dormitory. If there were any Blacks, they would put them by themselves. I could have lived with whites, but they couldn't have lived with me.'[114] Cathy also corroborated the 'two girls' admittance policy.' Her roommate was Doris White, another Black student. According to Cathy, 'They [the nursing administrators] had gotten a little smarter,'[115] as a result of anti-racist activities in Chatham, which meant that the practice was eventually eliminated.[116]

The practice of Blacks rooming together appeared to be short-lived and specific to certain nursing schools. Of the nurses who trained in the late 1940s and 1950s, Betty and Beverly, who trained in Toronto-based nursing schools, reported having white roommates. Compared with cities such as Windsor and Halifax, Toronto was deemed more progressive and had more interracial mixing.

Nurses' residences also served as an arena where cultural and racial misconceptions were explored and challenged. Thus, friendships developed, which might have been impossible in other circumstances. Those who forged interracial friendships often expressed pride in being able to look beyond skin colour and culture. Jamaican-born Daphne B described her experience in Britain:

> Living in residence was lots of fun. You met people from different places, Ireland and Europe. When I went I was the only Black in my group. There was one Jamaican, but she was already trained in Jamaica. I still got along. So to me colour doesn't matter.[117]

As in the classroom and on the hospital floor, life in a nurses' residence submerged racial and other differences. In this space, Daphne B took up the subject position of just another nurse in training.

As did Daphne B, so Joan, from Barbados, also mentioned the relationships she cultivated with non-Black students:

> Most of the girls that were in [residence] were Irish girls, and I went to Ireland twice, and then I went to Glasgow also with one of the nurses. I went to her home, and I always had a wonderful time.[118]

American nursing historian Barbara Melosh pointed out that 'the hospital was school, workplace and home combined,' and in this venue students developed a work culture based on their shared experience of living in residences and working as apprentices.[119] Residences could operate to cement the notion of sameness by ignoring or subsuming racial/ethnic difference. For the white, Black, and other students of colour who were living in close proximity with others from various racial and cultural backgrounds for the first time, the nurses' residences were a foray into acknowledging and learning about differences.

In many ways, the same guiding principles that governed the young women's lives at home were similar to those established by the nursing administrators responsible for the well-being of the trainees. As in their own households, these young women were expected to adhere to strict regulations, and to avoid incriminating behaviours that would embarrass themselves or the profession. Students were incessantly monitored, and, depending on the violation, were punished if caught breaking any of the rules.

However intent nursing leaders were on creating docile students, students found multiple ways to resist. Residence life helped to bolster the idea of a shared experience, and students banded together to support others who contravened the rules. Too afraid to sneak out at night, Cathy was often appointed to be the person who opened the fire escape door for her roommates who 'would sneak out and go up town and to St Catharines'[120] in Ontario. She and some of the others sometimes 'got caught,' and for punishment, 'You'd have to go and work some more in the hospital.' Cathy was not deterred, however, and she continued to volunteer to open the door when her dorm mates returned from their nightly escapades. Eleanor who also trained at Hôtel Dieu, in Windsor, Ontario, pointed out how students rarely complained if they were penalized for an infraction caused by others, which reinforced a sense of a homogeneous nursing identity:

> Mrs Richard, the housemother, lived [in residence] and had an office. If she heard a bunch of noise some place, the whole floor would be grounded and we had to be in, say, like eight o'clock or something like that. It took a little getting used to. It was a great big sort of community.[121]

Although living in the nurses' residence subjected the women to similar forms of surveillance that they had endured at home, their collective experience made it much easier to resist authority. When one white nursing sister acted unpleasantly towards Inez and her classmates, they discussed turn[ing] over [her] small car that had three wheels – one to the front and two to the back. Laughing, Inez explained how 'one day they put a stone behind the front wheel' of her vehicle, so that the instructor was unable to move the car.[122] Placing the stone behind the wheel of the car was a way for the students to exercise some power, however minimal, in response to the older nurse's treatment.

Regardless of how nursing administrators tried to regulate and control the behaviour of trainees, they were never fully successful. Students, aware of their own agency, devised oppositional strategies to counteract the seemingly total power of those in charge. Some of this resistance was covert. Even though she was only eighteen years old at the time, Ancilla exhibited a strong self-confidence. She had no problems obeying the rules of the dormitory, but, like many other nursing students, did not like the food. She organized a protest at the Warneford School of Nursing soon after she migrated, which was supported by most of the students. According to Ancilla, the objective of the 'sit-in on the lawn' was

> [to get the] menu changed and ... the place redecorated. It hadn't been done in years. I think those were army barracks that they turned into a residence. So, needless to say, the floor was horrible looking and the walls were awful.[123]

Ancilla, unlike many nursing students, realized that students had some power in the hospital training structure and she used it to get the matron's attention, explaining: 'The matron wasn't too happy, but she realized that they needed to take care of us.'[124] With the input of the residents, the dorms were eventually redecorated, and a new refrigerator in the recreational room and new menus were added. This provocative move to address the material environment in which Ancilla and her peers lived would manifest itself repeatedly throughout her career.

Conclusion

In the Caribbean, Britain, and Canada, the socialization and education of the Black women interviewed for this study helped to facilitate the successful navigation of their education and training. Raised primarily in authoritarian, and in most cases, religious households, which reinforced hegemonic ideas about gender, most Black students accepted how nursing was structured and the hierarchical social relationships that were endemic to the occupation. As they had learned in their households growing up, the women generally respected the nursing sisters, matrons, and others in positions of authority. The women also accepted the gendered ideals promoted by the occupation as to what constituted a good nurse.

Still, nursing continued to construct its identity on the ideals of middle-class white women, who were thought to possess the necessary qualities and characteristics of nurses. Thus, Black Canadian-born and Caribbean women entered an occupation where they were initially excluded, and where the Victorian legacy of femininity and whiteness underpinned the image of an ideal nurse. In response, they were forced to perform a complicated calculus of when to submit through mimicry to rules and regulations, and when to resist. Despite the routine and ritualistic nature of nurses' training – which was meant to subvert forms of identity, whether religious, racial, economic, or sexual – doctors, patients, and other nurses continued to focus on race, and often questioned the validity of Black women performing nursing.

Because of the precarious position of Black nursing students, any acts of resistance through transgression of the rules and regulations in nursing schools remained all the more remarkable.

5

'I've always Wanted to Work':
Black Women and Professionalism

Upon completing three years of gruelling and exploitative training – and, for some, additional education in midwifery or other areas of specialty – with diplomas and certificates in hand, the women interviewed for this study were more than poised to embark on their next transition, a nursing career. Accustomed to seeing their mothers or other women work for remuneration, and coupled with their own aspirations, the interviewees understood entry into paid work as normal. This was despite the remnants of cultural norms suggesting that paid work was an anomaly, especially for married women. The demand for health care personnel in Great Britain, Canada, and the United States meant employment prospects were more than favourable.

Some of the Caribbean-born women who trained in Britain worked there until they migrated to Ontario during the 1960s and 1970s. Of this group, two returned to the Caribbean to honour their scholarship agreement and, with their British education, readily procured employment. Jennette also returned to Antigua, because she did not like living in England. Having been away for at least three years, these women discovered that they had 'outgrown' the Caribbean and subsequently made the sojourn to Canada. Among the Caribbean group that migrated directly to Canada, five were already qualified nurses, and one would later train as a nurse a couple of years after her arrival. Of the Black Canadian-born cohort, four worked in Detroit, two until they retired, while the other two returned permanently to Canada. Throughout their careers, individual nurses would journey to other geographical locations for short periods to work, but ultimately Canada was home for most.

Whether in Canada, Britain, or the United States, two interrelated themes emerge in post–Second World War scholarship on Black wom-

en's labour. The first is Black women's overrepresentation as paid workers,[1] and the second, according to sociologist Patricia Hill Collins, is
their 'labor market victimization as "mules."'[2] Like mules, Black women
workers, even in nursing, 'are living machines that can be dehumanized,
objectified, and easily exploited.'[3] Yet the reality of Black women's subjectivities as workers is far more complicated. Even though the majority
of interviewees in this study were registered nurses,[4] they are far from
a homogeneous group. Time of migration, skills, training, age, experience, and education as configured in the marketplace over time are
critical factors. Furthermore, when additional factors such the ones out-
lined above are incorporated, a more nuanced portrait of Black nurses'
experience emerges. As a disproportionately female occupation, nursing
is not only affected by its relationship to the medical profession and the
state, comprised largely of white males, but also by its own internal and
structural configurations. To assess, explain, and analyse Black nurses'
subjectivities, these factors must be taken into account in tandem with
intersectionality and other feminist theoretical frameworks. Equally significant is exploring the multiple resistance strategies that Black nurses
employ daily while working.

This chapter focuses on the paid work of Black nurses within the
changing political economy of health care, primarily in Canada and to a
lesser extent Britain and the United States. It also draws on the concept
of liminality – that space of 'betwixt and between'[5] – to explore Black
women's professional subjectivity. Black nurses (the majority of whom
were RNs) articulated a professional identity based on education, training, and skills, a willingness to challenge inequality, and the ability to
overlook credentials when necessary. Thus, the aforementioned characteristics of professional identity (with lessons gleaned from childhood)
were integrally connected to patient care. At the same time, the women's
professional subjectivities were often impacted by structures of domination, power relations, and discriminatory practices that were manifested
within the occupation.

Since a disproportionate number of the nurses were involved in a
'transnational migratory circuit,' this chapter explores how migration
temporarily fractured some of the women's professional identity and
for others validated their sense of themselves as qualified professionals.[6]
Of special interest is how Black nurses defined their experiences with
the work process. Regardless of the manifestations of whiteness, or the
racist practices they encountered, the interviewees generally responded
in 'professional' or occupational terms, in relation to their identity as

nurses, rather than as 'Black nurses.' This chapter also highlights the transnational character of nursing. It begins with the women's recollections about work in the United States and Britain, and then moving onto Canada. In the latter, I emphasize the challenges surrounding accreditation. The final section of the chapter addresses the everyday nature of work and how Black women (regardless of geographical location) navigated the changing social space of the workplace. It considers restructuring and the impact these transformations have on nurses' work and their relationships with each other.

Black Canadians in the United States

The transition from student nurse to registered nurse certainly had its own challenges, which were further exacerbated for those who entered health care systems that were unlike where they trained and, in some cases, where they worked. In these spaces, Black Canadian and Caribbean RNs occupy a liminal position, based on the privileges associated with being trained elsewhere. The interviewees' reactions to new (and sometimes first) places of employment illuminate key facets of professionalism, which is tied to professional identity.

The summer before they graduated from Hôtel Dieu in Windsor, Eleanor and her friend Helen were approached by a physician about working at Sidney A. Sumby Memorial Hospital, a Black-owned and -operated hospital in Detroit, Michigan. In explaining the development of hospitals such as Sumby, Darlene Clark Hine points out that 'no single philosophical rationale impelled those who founded the early Black hospitals and nursing schools ... [but] even the most dispassionate observers felt something had to be done to improve the system of health care delivery for Blacks.'[7] The survival of Black hospitals depended on philanthropic, government, and community support, which was not always consistent. As a result, facilities such as the Sumby Hospital struggled to maintain efficient standards for their Black clientele, which often impeded patient care. There were 'things we weren't used to ... but you go along with the program,'[8] Eleanor explained. Growing up with a sole-support mother who struggled to make ends meet, Eleanor was more than familiar with 'going along with the program.' As a result, the precarious position of Sumby was not lost on Eleanor who worked within the constraints of the hospital system. She also accepted without judgment the idiosyncrasies of the African American patients, such as their incessant use of hair products, which 'left stains on the pillows.' Treating people with dignity regardless of difference was a key component of Black women's professional identity.

When she graduated as the first Black nurse from Wellesley Hospital, in Toronto, in 1953, Beverly joined the Victoria Order of Nurses (VON), where she worked until she met her future husband Doug. When the couple moved to Detroit, so that Doug could complete his residency as a medical doctor, Beverly found employment with the Visiting Nurse Association (VNA), which had a similar mandate to the VON. Like Eleanor, Beverly, too, had to make adjustments in dealing with clients whose social backgrounds were different from what she had been accustomed to. Along with a Polish and white working-class neighbourhood, Beverly's assignment included 'the Black industrial area, which was extremely poor.'[9] Still, Beverly was hardly oblivious to how racial and economic inequalities impacted disenfranchised people's lives and was sensitive to this reality when she visited the various homes. Her objective was to provide optimal service to those with whom she came in contact and to refrain from criticizing their behaviours and lifestyle. This aspect of Beverly's professional identity was exemplified in a discovery she made several weeks into working as a VNA nurse.

Beverly noticed that the other 'nurses [were] working a full day.' As a VON nurse in Toronto, her daily patient load was twelve to thirteen patients, whereas in Detroit she had a maximum of five patients. In Toronto, Beverly walked or used public transportation, but in Detroit she had access to a car. With a smaller caseload, she completed all home visits by noon. Instead of simply being content with a reduced workload and the free time she had available, Beverly made some inquiries and 'learned that they [VNA] were more into health teaching.' Instead of limiting her visit to the families, Beverly joined the health team, where she worked with health care personnel with expertise in various areas to assist the families. Beverly's genuine interest in the well-being of the families that she visited daily led her to abandon her own method, adopting the more inclusive approach of the VNA. She also found the experience to be 'way more satisfying.'[10]

Reflected in Black women's professional identity was their willingness to lead, take risks, and act as visionaries, always with their patients' interest in mind. Both Agnes and Dorothy R felt that if they truly wanted to accomplish certain career goals and receive professional recognition their only alternative was to leave Windsor and find employment in Detroit. Long before she graduated from Hôtel Dieu in 1953, Agnes felt that as far as Black nurses were concerned 'over here [Windsor] we are nobody, we were not recognized.'[11] Equally important, nursing salaries were better in Detroit. The decision to work in the United States proved to be fruitful, as Agnes found much needed affirmation at Mercy General, Detroit's first African-American hospital:[12]

> When I got to the Black hospital, I was definitely respected. I was considered superior because I was educated differently than any of the American Black nurses, and they put me in charge and I took it. I took care of that operating room. It was just in my spirit to do that. I was in charge. I didn't get that opportunity in a white hospital and this was a Black-owned hospital.'[13]

Working among other Blacks meant forgoing a 'fissuring process,'[14] especially since Black women exist in spaces where often they are not taken them seriously, or believed to be competent.[15] There was no uncertainty about Agnes's credentials, ability, or skills when she was appointed as a supervisor. Indeed, it was a pleasurable experience for Agnes working among African American nurses who, she pointed out, 'were highly respected and motivated, which in turn motivated me.'

When Mercy Hospital closed in 1974, Agnes found employment at Sumby, as the director of anesthesia, until the hospital closed in the late 1980s. Employment at various Black hospitals in Detroit provided Agnes with benefits, both material and psychological. Ironically, Agnes found validation and employment in a country where her ancestors were unable to, and in hospitals that were created because of white racism.

Trying to procure employment in white hospitals was much harder for Dorothy. But after repeated rejections, she eventually found employment in 1954 at Mount Carmel Mercy Hospital in Detroit, Michigan, in the obstetrics department. Catering mainly to white patients, for several years the only Black people Dorothy R saw in the hospital were those employed in the laundry room and kitchen. In many ways, Mount Carmel Mercy reminded Dorothy R of Hôtel Dieu: it was the 'same old prejudice stuff, not only with patients but also with nursing staff as well.'[16] With diploma in hand, and plans to further her nursing education, Dorothy R was much more secure and confident in her abilities. Gone was the nervous young woman who, while in training at Hôtel Dieu, wanted to be perfect because she 'wasn't gonna give anyone any outs' and who went beyond what was expected of her as a student. Dorothy R joined the Mount Carmel Mercy staff a secure RN who, like her father, was willing to question discriminatory policies and procedures without fear of reprisals.

As the lone Black RN at Mount Carmel Mercy 'for quite a number of years,' Dorothy R occupied a liminal space, first as a relatively new employee, but also as a Black Canadian. She understood the manifestations of systemic racism, which was deeply entrenched at Mount Carmel Mercy. Throughout the duration of her employment, Dorothy R engaged in a number of resistive actions, both subtle and direct. One example was to give a Black 'expectant mother medication, so she couldn't be transferred out,' a practice that was common regardless of the stage of labour the patient was in. Keenly aware of her position as a Black woman and the repercussions that would ensue if her subversive act were discovered, Dorothy R admitted, 'I had to be cagey about it.' Several years later, she was promoted to supervisor of the obstetrics department, and in this capacity she became more vocal about segregation and the treatment of Black infants and their mothers at Mount Carmel Mercy.[17]

When Dorothy R attempted to discourage the practice of segregating newborn babies, she met with resistance. White nurses at Mount Carmel were socialized to accept the status quo as normal, choosing silence in the face of discrimination.[18] Dorothy R finally took a stand when she discovered that a premature Black baby was left alone, unattended. She met first with the nurses on the floor, where she insisted that all babies must be placed in the same room and given equal attention. She then proceeded to speak with the hospital attorney, using a legal as opposed to a medical argument to get his attention. The conversation went as follows:

> I said, 'You know, you're going to have a big lawsuit here.' And he asked me why. I said 'they're segregating the babies and the premature [babies]. And I said, 'You know, these premature [babies] can't get out of the isolates to contaminate anybody or do anything. If something happens to them, you're going to have big, multimillion dollar lawsuits going on. Are you aware of what is going on?' He said, 'No.' So, I guess he met periodically with the hospital staff hierarchy, when they had their monthly meetings. He brought up at the meetings the problem in the nursery and that they really needed to look at that, or 'we're gonna have a lot of lawsuits here.' And so, the administration said, 'Wherever the babies are needed to go, you put them in there, and no segregation.' So, it ended.[19]

Dorothy R credited herself for single-handedly integrating the nursery at Mount Carmel Mercy Hospital in Detroit, as well as the 'postpartum areas, the delivery areas, and the labour rooms, all of which fell in under obstetrics.'[20]

As the only Black woman in a position of power, Dorothy R could have easily enjoyed the privilege of her supervisory role, by accepting the racial arrangement of the hospital. Certainly, it would have been most expedient to remain silent at this juncture of her career. Instead of complying with and sustaining the practices of white supremacy, Dorothy chose to challenge segregation.[21] In essence, Dorothy R's professional identity included a spirit of activism, an ethics of care that translated into a belief in Black patients' inherent right to equality and justice.

Working in Britain

Three years of training and living in the nurses' residence helped to forge a professional identity among nurses regardless of their area of specialization. But the true test was how these practitioners applied their education and training as they made the transition from students to health care workers. This was especially true for Caribbean practitioners who sought additional training as nurse-midwives. That is, they acquired skills through medical training rather than practical experience. In the real world, midwives delivering babies for the first time often found the initial experience daunting. Anxiety, inclement weather, and ambivalence regarding their role vis-à-vis physicians were initial concerns. Still, the midwives utilized a discourse of efficiency with a focus on mother and child as they carried out their responsibilities.

Up until the beginning of the twentieth century, British midwives were subjected to intense government examination and regulation. Midwives, on the other hand, waged a protracted battle to gain legitimacy in the larger medical arena.[22] However, nursing historian Monica Baly, noted that 'by 1957, 64 percent of all births were taking place in hospitals, but the percentage varied widely between regions, with those in the greatest need getting the poorest service.'[23] Lowered rates in home births were attributed to several factors including but not limited to improved maternity services and changes in how fertility, childbirth, and pregnancy were perceived.[24] These transformations proportionally meant a reduction in patient load for domiciliary midwives who[25] perform home births. That new graduates might have had fewer patients than normal was hardly reassuring as they came to terms with their new role. Virtually on their own, Caribbean nurse-midwives were no longer subjected to the commanding gaze of matrons or nursing sisters.

In the contested, hierarchical, and dynamic terrain of medicine, the development of a professional subjectivity is far from static and involves continuous definition and redefinition. In the case of nurse-midwives, this begins with reconciling the knowledge and skills gleaned through training with their own individual principles and personalities. After four years in England, Daphne C had never grown accustomed to the weather, and was terrified at the prospect of delivering 'babies in the night due to the cold and fog.'[26] As she began her foray into a career that fulfilled childhood inquiries about the birthing process, Daphne C's fears were allayed over time.

While delivering babies and providing pre- and post-partum instruction is considered the primary province of midwives, other factors can affect the process and practice of delivering babies. Thus, flexibility is critical when birthing babies in certain environments that are not always conducive for doing so. For working-class families adequate space was often a concern. Daphne C did not find these limitations an inconvenience; the ultimate goal was to deliver a healthy infant. She surmised:

> You cannot afford to mess up anywhere. One little area, one bed, and you have to deliver that baby, make sure that baby is alive, that the baby is healthy when you finish, and come out crying, and there is a little life in your hands.[27]

The ability to be accommodating in less than desirous situations, successful deliveries, and practical postnatal care not only legitimize midwives' competency within the larger medical field but also help to ground their own individual professional identity.

In the realm of employment, for example, Caribbean people in Britain generally occupied certain niches that reflected their marginal status in the wider society. In summarizing the plight of Caribbean people, Winston James contends: 'Because of the pervasive racism they encountered in the labour market, post-war Black migrants secured openings primarily in the most vulnerable and undesirable sectors of the British economy.'[28] This was not the reality of the health care professionals interviewed for this study who were employed during the late 1950s to the mid-1970s. Hired by the Oxfordshire County Council as the first Black domiciliary (one who visits patients at home) midwife, Lillie boasted: 'I did such an excellent job. I loved it.'[29] Similar to many Black Canadian-born nurses, Lillie was not oblivious to the historical significance of her hire. She had managed to enter an arena that had traditionally been the purview of white women. Her summation of working as a midwife in the United Kingdom testified to this:

It was a beautiful experience. Being a midwife, I had my own district, pupil midwives, and resident doctors who came out and did practical midwifery with me. That is, delivering babies, and knowing how to take care of mothers in labour. I enjoyed working with the mothers because they did appreciate you. It was your responsibility to assess normal cases for delivery and make a correct midwife assessment for mothers who should not be in my care. That means I refer them back to the doctor just before or during delivery.[30]

Even as she delineated the professional boundaries between her role and that of the physician, Lillie articulated this relationship not as one of subservience, but as one of authority.

As a nurse who received additional training as a midwife, Lillie occupied multiple subject positions, as the above vignette reflects. She positioned herself as a knowledgeable and skilled midwife and nurse, who enjoyed an interdependent relationship with doctors and students. In some cases, Lillie's authority superseded male students and physicians as she instructed them on birthing and delivery.

As they disrupted the homogeneity of the medical hierarchy, Black midwives simultaneously encountered situations that reproduced social inequalities. As a key component of their professional identity, Black health care workers preferred to highlight their professional identity focusing on their proficiency, skills, and knowledge. Still, they were often reminded of their racial identity and the meanings attached to it, sometimes in subtle and on occasion more overt ways. On a ward, a patient could actually request another nurse – meaning a white nurse, upon discovering that the caregiver was Black. It was much harder to make a similar request when midwives often worked autonomously.

As with their counterparts working in the hospitals, Black midwives experienced white patients' fear of their touch, and questions about their abilities to adequately perform their duties. Daphne C graduated with her diploma as a state-registered nurse (SRN), and with a certificate in midwifery (SCM) and neonatal training in 1958. This formal training and education was viewed as inconsequential, as some prospective patients were more concerned with her blackness. Daphne C reported: Some of the parents didn't want to have Black nurses coming into their homes to deliver [their babies].' This was the case when she arrived at the home of a police officer who called the hospital requesting another midwife:

They told him they didn't have anybody else. But my supervisor came out, and she was there when the baby was delivered. But she didn't do anything; she'd just stand by. The man thought, I was a Black nurse and maybe I couldn't deliver his child; he was uptight.[31]

Since whiteness operated as an unmarked identifier, the police officer did not need to say 'send a white midwife'; the department automatically knew what he meant. The organization of nursing and the concomitant power relations operated to privilege white nurses' identity and knowledge. Subsequently, it was only under the careful watch of the white supervisor that the police officer felt comfortable enough to allow his baby to be delivered by a Black midwife. In other words, whiteness operated to validate Daphne C's presence and expertise.

Working within one set of power relations – sometimes ambiguous and other times clearly defined – midwives, regardless of their social location, often found themselves in situations where their knowledge was called into question. In these instances, midwives engaged in careful gender performance in order to avoid giving the impression that they were usurping the physician's place in the medical hierarchy, while at the same time trying to ensure that their own competence was valued. According to protocol, midwives were expected to summon a doctor when a mother is experiencing complications, or, in other words, an 'abnormal' delivery. This, according to nursing historian Anne Thompson, was another calculated move by the medical profession 'which involved constructing ... elaborate distinctions between "normal" and "abnormal" childbirth, which, when accepted, resulted in a progressive deskilling of the midwife, as responsibility shifted from her domain to that of the doctor.'[32] What happens when a practising midwife ascertains that a delivery is atypical? Is she contributing to her own deskilling? Or, does she recognize her structural position as a Black midwife in a male-dominated health care system and choose the best action for herself and her patient?

Lillie's account of her experience with a physician during a difficult delivery revealed one way in which gender informs and organizes the medical hierarchy, and subsequently the relationship between midwives and physicians. During one of her deliveries, Lillie determined that the case was abnormal and summoned the obstetrician. According to Lillie, when the physician arrived he disagreed with her prognosis and insisted that she perform the delivery. As his subordinate, the physician expected Lillie to comply with his orders.

Feeling undermined and aware of both the legal ramifications and medical risks associated with the delivery, Lillie quickly and cautiously assessed the situation:

> I had to exercise good judgment in my assessment, so I did not fall into any problems. I had to make sure that I was good, assessing my patient well. He wasn't an exceptional obstetrician, so there were a lot of things that he wasn't seeing ... I had to cover myself slightly by pointing out stuff to him. To say 'I'm not supposed to carry out this case as midwife, this is your case.' You see, in England, there is a midwife code, and you must abide by it or else they could haul you up in court for not doing what you should as a midwife.[33]

Drawing on her expertise, knowledge, and confidence while 'keeping in mind the principles of the medical profession,' Lillie successfully delivered the baby. Emphatically, she made clear:

> I had to call on everything I had learned to cope in an emergency, with your doctor standing by and not doing anything. This is one of the things as a midwife you must know how to handle.[34]

Upon migrating to Canada between 1955 (Orphelia) and 1975 (Carmencita), Lillie and other Caribbean-trained practitioners discovered a health care system that was different from the Caribbean and the United Kingdom. The women discovered that their ability, knowledge, and dedication to patients' well-being, which constituted the essence of their professional identity, were being reconfigured due to the inability of nursing bodies to interpret foreign qualifications in the Canadian context, prohibition against midwifery practice, and divergences in nursing practice. Before migrating to Canada, three of the women returned to the Caribbean, where two (Muriel and Jennette) worked for a year and one (Vera) worked for five years before migrating to Canada.

Back to the Caribbean

British-trained nurses who returned to the Caribbean quickly reacquainted themselves with a medical system in which the number of patients per doctor or nurse was significantly higher compared with the United Kingdom. Overcrowding in hospitals and scarcity of resources were commonplace, and salaries were far from ideal. Working conditions were for the most part less than desirable. Another complaint was the slower pace with which daily routine activities were done in the hospitals and the wider society. These women's reactions to working in the Caribbean were reminiscent of the experiences of Eleanor and Beverly in Detroit.

Vera (1955), Muriel (1962), and Jennette (1963), who returned to their respective islands to work, admitted that it was 'pretty hard' adjusting to the systems and conditions they encountered. Regardless, there was a determined effort on the part of these returning migrants to work within the structural constraints. Although Barbados General Hospital was technologically deficient, it was committed to providing the best patient care which, for Muriel, was a critical component of her professional identity.

Muriel was more than willing to share her British knowledge and skills. This transfer of knowledge across borders is what sociologist Peggy Levitt refers to as social remittances. This includes 'ideas, behaviors, identities, and social capital that flow from receiving to sending countries.'[35] Muriel described her two years of working at Barbados General in the casualty (emergency) department:

> It was not automated, but the care was good. I had a lot to offer, and that's what made it. And a lot of people appreciated what little things you did. Like the person from the country who had to wait all day to see a doctor, and then, had to wait to get the medication. I would say, 'Leave the prescription with me. I would get the pharmacist to fill it for you, and I'll get it to you.'[36]

Although Muriel knew that her British education placed her in an advantageous position, she did not allow this to be a barrier between her fellow medical personnel and patients. Muriel immediately adapted to the hospital environment and was sympathetic to her patients, especially those from rural areas. As a newly trained nurse, who was in the process of honing her professional identity, Muriel found her confidence buttressed by how the patients and doctors appreciated her.

To satisfy the stipulation of the government scholarship, Vera returned to Trinidad in 1955. Like Muriel, her British training and midwifery certificate were assets and made finding employment relatively easy. Vera worked for five years at the San Fernando General Hospital as a staff nurse. She too was sensitive to the problems facing the health care system in her country of origin for the time she stayed. She too willingly overlooked certain shortcomings as long as patients' needs were prioritized.[37] The centrality of patient care as a marker of professional identity would be scrutinized once these women and others migrated to Canada. Jennette, on the other hand, found that at Hamilton Hospital in Antigua the 'pay was bad'[38] and the working conditions substandard. To make the situation more unbearable, Jennette also found there 'was a lot of resentment.' Apparently some of the women she had gone to school with who were employed at the hospital behaved atrociously towards her and so she decided to leave. According to Jennette, 'I decided I'm not coming here to fight with a soul, not for this pay and the working conditions, I'm not doing it. I was twenty-three years old and I didn't need that.' Jennette subsequently migrated to Canada where the process of having her qualifications assessed was one of many hurdles she and others faced as they sought employment in Canada,

Migration and Deskilling in Canada

Upon migration to Canada, between 1955 and 1975, British- and Caribbean-trained migrants grappled with what it meant to be a nurse or a nurse-midwife. In other words, they occupied a liminal subject position as result of the accreditation process, how patient care was administered, and the inability to practise midwifery. This disruption, however temporary for some migrants, resulted in feelings of disillusionment and insecurity, with a profound impact on the self. While there were registered nurses who were graduates of a three-year program either in the Caribbean or Great Britain, and who met the provincial licensing standards as registered nurses, which included education in obstetrical nursing, this group was the exception rather than the norm.

The majority of the Caribbean-born nurses interviewed for this study, in order to obtain their RN status, had to upgrade because the 'British system' (on which Caribbean nurses' education and licensing was based) defined obstetrical and pediatric training as separate qualifications not included in the regular SRN (Britain)/RN stream. Thus, these nurses lacked this crucial component necessary for Canadian licensure as RNs. In this group were those whose credentials were not accepted at all, and they had to complete a full registered nurse or registered nursing assistant (RNA) program or remain working in 'unprofessional' categories of nursing work, such as nurses' aides or health care aides. For example, Britain's state-enrolled nurses (SEN) had no equivalent in Canada, or any other country for that matter. Equally significant, trained midwives could not practise in Canada. To ground and defend their professional identity, superior skills and training became the trope that Caribbean nurses utilized to make sense of their initial marginality in Canadian nursing.

The entrance of British- and Caribbean-trained practitioners into Canadian nursing clearly affected 'the construction of worker subjectivities and identity.'[39] 'Degrading,' 'demoralizing,' 'non-educational,' or lacking in theoretical support' were terminologies used by those practitioners whose qualifications were not immediately accepted upon migration, and who were forced to work in menial positions. Although she worked as a staff nurse in England, in Canada, Dorothy J found herself working as an RNA, a position that was not compatible with her experience:

> I found things were different. You couldn't do certain dressings; taking out sutures and clips, things you did automatically [in England], suctioning and all those sorts of things … I found at the time that it was degrading for me. I was just like a second class; I was more like an assistant to the RN. I just grin and bear it, did what I had to do. As time went on, they started giving you little things like doing the G-feeds, and you were able to turn on the oxygen, and all these sorts of things that was nothing for me.[40]

Already 'twice diasporized'[41] as a consequence of multiple migrations, the work experiences of some migrant nurses further compounded the disruption. Occupying positions of responsibility and the efficacy to which they responded to routines and certain tasks was how these nurses partially defined their professional identity. Dorothy J characterized this liminal space, described by Victor Turner as a disconnection from a previous position or status,[42] as that of a second-class citizen.

British- and Caribbean-trained nurses were caught in the rapid and complex changes within the world of nursing, changes that had begun much earlier but intensified in the 1950s and 1960s. These changes, some of which included an increase in nursing duties, improved education, and the introduction of ancillary workers, resulted in a hierarchy of 'professional' nurses and 'non-professional' subsidiary workers.[43] Thus, duties that had been the responsibilities of doctors were now allocated to RNs, enhancing their scope of practice and culminating in white and some Black RNs vacating bedside nursing to take on more leadership roles. Consequently, some Caribbean-trained practitioners, such as the state-enrolled nurses, were relegated to assume repetitious and monotonous domestic care tasks, and they became subject primarily to the authority of the predominantly white nurse-managers and supervisors.

Commenting on the introduction of subsidiary workers in nursing and the impact of this on the division of labour, Kathryn McPherson makes clear that 'the ideological and formal divestment of those tasks that had bordered on the domestic and personal constituted a crucial line of demarcation between "professional" graduate nurses and "non-professional" subsidiary workers.'[44] The experiences of practitioners such Dorothy J showed the extent to which the accreditation process undermined their professional identity. Nurses who upgraded and met the requisite licensing requirements to become registered nurses occupied a different subject position than, for example, Dorothy J, but they too experienced a form of deskilling.

'They Just Call the Doctor'

The professional elite welcomed the expansion of nursing responsibilities as improving nurses' status, yet none of the British- and Caribbean-trained nurses who became RNs mentioned these tasks among their repertoire of duties. Instead, they consistently maintained that in Canada the duties were still primarily in the hands of doctors, thus limiting their own and Canadian nurses' roles.

It is patently obvious based on the interviewees' response to the Canadian system that they had not investigated the Canadian system prior to migrating. Perhaps they assumed that the Canadian system would be similar to Britain's, but they found out otherwise. During this transition of being integrated within a different structure and a more legalistic context, the interviewees' professional subjectivity and identity became increasingly contested. Thus, how the women saw themselves, particularly in relation to their expertise, skills, and qualifications, did not coalesce with how they were situated within Canada's health care system. Monica trained at the University of the West Indies College Hospital, and later as a midwife at the Jubilee Hospital, both in Kingston, Jamaica. Before migrating to Canada in 1961, she worked in Jamaica and Grand Cayman, and upon her arrival in Ontario worked as a graduate nurse at the Hamilton Civic Hospital until she wrote the required examinations.

Monica was confounded by how limited the scope of practice was for Canadian nurses, compared with the situation in the Caribbean, where she likened her role in Jamaica to that of a nurse practitioner:

In Jamaica, we were like nurse practitioners. If the doctor wasn't there, we diagnosed and initiated treatment. When I arrived in Canada, I realized

I couldn't give an enema without a doctor's order. Everything had to be prescribed by the doctor – that was a major change – you couldn't give an aspirin without a doctor's order, you couldn't take a patient out of the bed without the doctor's order.[45]

Perhaps, Monica later surmised, 'there are far more litigations in the medical community' in Canada than, for example, in Jamaica where 'you rarely hear of anyone suing the doctor.' According to Monica, the fear of lawsuits accounted for doctors' hegemony over procedures and practices, making them unwilling to forgo some of their responsibilities to nurses.

The reality, however, is that in many ways the medical arena reflects the larger society, reproducing ideas about gender, sexuality, age, and race, including whiteness, which are embedded in its organizational structure. Meaning is then attached to the work that men and women do – in this case, physicians and nurses, the former primarily white and male, and the latter, mostly white women – who are positioned in a hierarchy differentiated by race, training, age, and education. Thus, care (broadly conceived) provided by the physicians compared with that provided by nurses is often treated as more valuable.

Upon migration, Muriel, Monica, and other Caribbean- and British-trained nurses watched as doctors diagnosed patients, gave out prescriptions, checked patients' temperature, inserted nasogastric tubes, administered intravenoustherapy, catheters, anti-tetanus serum, and penicillin, all of which they recalled they were prohibited from doing in their respective hospitals upon migration to Canada. Muriel provides further evidence of how migrant nurses' subjectivities were mediated by the structure and organization of Canadian medicine:

We [nurses] had a lot of autonomy in England and the Caribbean. A lot of the skills weren't done by nurses at that time in Canada ... When I call the doctor [in England], I'm actually telling him, 'I think this person has a urinary tract infection.' And usually, nine out of ten, I was right, because I knew what symptoms they exhibited. I knew what they were like this morning. The doctor has not been there, so he's just going by what I say. And here, when I came, they [nurses] would just call the doctor.[46]

As part of a transnational movement of workers, these nurses compared and contrasted working in various geographical locations.

The ability to participate in and make decisions about a patient's well-being and to work interdependently with physicians are other ways that the nurses' defined their professional identity. The lack of continuity between nursing elsewhere and in Canada, and the absence of a more egalitarian relationship between doctors and nurses meant reconstructing one's professional identity to fit the new organizational structure.

Although nurses such as Monica and Muriel reacted to the differences in work practices with less intensity than their counterparts whose qualifications did not meet the licensing standards, they nonetheless experienced feelings of displacement in their new work environment. While the majority of nurses interviewed for this study felt that their skills and knowledge were negated, trained nurse-midwives were further disadvantaged when they discovered – much to their dismay and deep disappointment – that in Canada delivering babies was the domain of physicians.

Caribbean- and British-Trained Midwives in Canada

Just as some Caribbean nurses experienced deskilling because of how they were positioned in the nursing hierarchy, and others criticized the omnipresence of doctors in medicine, practising midwives were further deskilled because of the legal prohibition against midwifery generally in Canada. Many British- and Caribbean-trained midwives and nurses felt that this lack of crucial education placed their Canadian counterparts in a subordinate position vis-à-vis medical doctors who exercised authority in an area that they saw as women's rightful enclave. The near eradication of midwives is a part of the narrative that dominated nursing scholarship and was used as evidence to denote the unequal relationship that has existed between medical authorities and women.[47]

Writing about midwifery in the nineteenth and twentieth centuries, Canadian historian Diane Dodd asserted that the medicalization of childbirth, with the emphasis on 'physician-controlled and eventually hospital birthing,'[48] was part of the outcome of male practitioners' dominance over the traditional mothering role. Doctors' monopolization of the birthing process continued well into the twentieth century, with practising midwives being virtually eliminated in most provinces. By contrast, midwives continued to play a central role in the Caribbean and Britain. Pointing to Canadian nurses' lack of autonomy, particularly around childbirth, and vehemently emphasizing that this ought to be nurses' domain was a way for the women in this study to maintain their own carefully crafted professional identity.

Arguably, Caribbean- and British-trained nurse-midwives were the

group most deskilled.[49] It comes as no surprise that they were more able
to articulate an understanding of how patriarchal ideology positions
physicians as superior to nurses, including midwives. These migrants,
especially those who migrated before 1970, viewed doctors as often territorial and committed to maintaining their dominance. They asserted
that the physicians' maintenance of strict boundaries between their own
roles and that of nurses eroded the practitioners' professional identity.
According to Scottish-trained nurse (SRN) and midwife (SCM) Lillie,
who came to Canada in 1960:

> They give you no responsibility. The doctor has to order everything.
> Although it seems to be getting better, it seems all they [doctors] want is
> a 'handmaiden.' There are so many British-trained nurses who have their
> midwifery training, but none of them are accredited for it here.[50]

How Caribbean nurses constructed their professional identity was tied to
their self-worth – that is, to how they viewed themselves. For nurse-midwives, the inability to apply their midwifery knowledge, and the virtual
lack of recognition of their skills, were particularly painful.

What is clear throughout these various narratives is that Caribbean
nurses had a clear sense of their professional identity, which they elu-
cidated with confidence. And at the core of defining their professional
identity is patients' well-being. Even though the women's movement
helped to transform the 'handmaiden status' and power of nurses overall,
Caribbean nurses felt that remnants of this relationship still remained.
This was felt especially among nurse-midwives.

Daphne B trained and worked eight years in Britain before she migrated to Canada in 1960, where she found that 'the doctors were like little
gods, and the nurses seemed to be afraid of them.'[51] Below is Daphne B's
description of how as a midwife participating in a volatile ('abnormal')
birthing process, she traversed the professional boundaries, in the interests of the patient, without censure from the accompanying physician.
She added that an intervention of this kind in Canada would certainly
have been a cause for reprimand:

> I remember when I was midwife, this lady after she had her baby started this
> PPH, postpartum hemorrhaging, which can be deadly. By the time the doc-
> tor came I had it under control, and I was giving the doctor orders because
> it's an emergency. But she never said anything derogatory or negative. Here
> [referring to Canada] the doctors would probably say, 'Who do you think

you are, doing such a manoeuvre?' They should be doing it. I never worked in the case room delivering babies because I said I didn't want to be a glorified maid for any doctor, mopping up after they make the mess. In England, you delivered the babies and you were fine, but here the doctors delivered them.[52]

With their extensive obstetrical and neonatal training, licensed Caribbean midwives' knowledge of birthing procedures and experience with deliveries was ostensibly lost once they entered Canada. In response, the women found ways to deal with their fractured professional identity.

Professional identities are far from fixed, and they do undergo continuous revision, despite the circumstances that lead to their reconfiguration. As difficult as it was for them, several of the nurse-midwives in this study chose to work on the obstetrics ward, even if it meant being observers of a process that they were once connected with intimately. To avoid, as Daphne B aptly put it, being 'a glorified maid for any doctor,' she and Lillie enrolled in the University of Toronto, where they completed the requirements for a certificate in public health. To maintain some control over their work lives, the two found employment as public health nurses, where they enjoyed some autonomy comparable to what had been the case for them in Britain. Upgrading, pursuing equivalent studies, writing the registration exams, or refusing to upgrade was how Caribbean nurses (including midwives) dealt with the accreditation process and their experiences with deskilling. Simultaneously, a disproportionate number of the interviewees drew upon a discourse that emphasized their 'foreign' training, particularly in relation to patient care, as being superior to the training that their Canadian counterparts received.

The relationship with patients was a critical component of Black women's professional identity, which by no means was consistent. As RNs took on more leadership and administrative roles in lieu of personal care duties, which the Canadian nursing elite lauded as an indication of the occupation's improved professional status, some British- and Caribbean-trained migrant nurses felt that the fragmentation of work actually deskilled the job of caring. Some of them did make a distinction between functions central to patient care and other non-nursing duties. Daphne C, for example, decried having to wash the 'feeding bottles,' a task she had not done in England as a staff nurse.[53]

Similarly, Jennette recalled that when she began working at Humber Memorial Hospital, in Toronto, there were no orderlies, which meant that she 'had to go down to the kitchen, and get the cart with the cups and saucers.'[54] Jennette lasted approximately six months at Humber Memorial because as she explained, 'I didn't do nursing for this' in reference to tasks that were the RNA's responsibility. Interestingly enough, there was no opposition from Jennette to 'doing a bed bath' for a patient. Although they set up certain parameters regarding tasks that might be considered intrinsic to patient care, this did not detract from the nurses' overall commitment to their patients.

To deal with what appeared to be their professional identity under attack, Caribbean migrant nurses' boasted about their 'foreign' training. Whether they emphasized the practical aspect, or a combination of the practical with the theoretical, the consensus was generally the same. Although all the women trained in hospital-based training schools throughout the late 1940s until the early 1970s, those trained in the British system felt it to be superior to the Canadian system. Memories of any institutional and everyday forms of gendered racism during nurses' training were subverted in favour of a narrative that paints the British system as progressive. The women pointed to their bedside training and the preparation of prospective students as evidence. Daphne C asserted:

> When you're trained in England, you know 10 times more than what you learn in Canada. And that was one of the big snags, because I felt that the English-trained nurse knew a lot more than the Canadian nurses. Because we had the experience; we had the knowledge.[55]

Dorothy J further explained the difference between the two systems as follows:

> I knew I had the bedside training, I had [it] from scratch. They [Canadian-trained nurses] went to school into a college, and the only time they had the practical training was only two days a week ... But in England, when you're a nurse and in training you do those things, because you are the very person that is working on the floor with the patients.[56]

These interviewees' insights into nursing practice in Canada reflected an ongoing debate in nursing and became more pronounced once nurses' education was removed from hospitals into colleges and universities.

As writer Sarah Jane Growe argues, 'no single quality sets apart a profession more than the level of training and education necessary to gain access.'[57] This has led to the theoretical-practical schism with proponents on both sides. On the one hand, nursing leaders advocate a more scientific and technical education as a sure-fire way of preserving the occupation's place in the medical hierarchy. These nurses would most likely be university trained. Alternately, there are others, mostly practitioners – often hospital-trained – who uphold the notion that bedside care is crucial, and intrinsic to nurses' professional identity. In defining the sphere of nursing practice, much emphasis has been placed on formal education.

To be sure, Dorothy J was not opposed to college education. On the contrary, she eventually enrolled, attending school part-time initially and later full-time during the late 1980s. She eventually earned her diploma in 1991 from George Brown College, which qualified her as an RN. For Dorothy J, it was the limited bedside training student nurses received that was disconcerting.[58] Along with a piecemeal system of instruction, students were hardly prepared to work independently of instructors who, Jennette maintained, were complicit in the process. Laughing, she recalled:

> I remember being amused when the student would come on the floor with the instructor … They were always on the floor with an instructor molly coddling them. I remember June S., this English girl, and I had this big laugh. The instructor came and said the students were coming and they were going to take temperatures. So I said, 'Well, I think that's kind of weird. When I take somebody's temperature, I take their pulse.' So she [instructor] said, 'No, they're not taught that yet. They're just taking temperatures.' So we had to go around and take the patients' pulse and blood pressure. And when they did have the whole patient, they only had two patients.[59]

A minimum of three patients on an obstetrics ward, according to one instructor, gave students 'an opportunity to organize their work'[60] more efficiently, which was difficult for Caribbean migrant nurses to fathom. Pride in being trained in a more rigorous and thorough system and knowing Jennette added 'everything about the forty-five patients on the ward,'[61] was how the interviewees attempted to resolve the dilemma of their fractured professional identity.

No matter how much they underscored the advantages of the British system, and regardless of meeting the requisite requirement to obtain licensure in Canada, including additional training, all of the migrant nurses had to come to terms with the discontinuities associated with their migrant and professional positions. Many interviewees echoed – albeit with some modification – Monica's explanation of how she coped:

I accepted it and confined it to myself. When a migrant gets to the host country, I began to think, 'When in Rome, you do as the Romans do.' You've now left your family, you're pretty well alone here ... you have a strong need to be accepted and you don't want to do things that are not authorized or accepted by the host country ... and be threatened with alienation. You don't want that because you want to be a part of the whole thing as quickly as possible.[62]

Eventually, feelings of nostalgia for how nursing was practised in the Caribbean or the United Kingdom were replaced by the need to be accepted, to be incorporated into the Canadian system. This requires, as Monica fittingly remarked, 'doing as the Romans do.' This form of mimicry is really a strategy as Dorothy J eventually realized, 'as time goes by you learn to realize that this is the way they operate and you just went with the flow even though deep down inside you know how you were feeling.'[63]

This is not to suggest that the nurses rejected facets of their 'foreign training.' Along with their Black Canadian-born counterparts, they incorporated lessons from childhood in tandem with the new knowledge gained through upgrading, post-secondary education, leadership conferences, teaching, and workshops over the duration of their careers. Clearly, professional identities are far from immutable, impacted as they are by various social processes and other factors leading to their reconfiguration over time. Although the narratives are not generalizable, there are common principles that guide this group of nurses regardless of the positions they held in the occupation. A focus on the women at work during a critical period in Canadian nursing not only reveals specific commonalities, but also exposes how race as it intersects with gender continues to act as a mitigating force in the desire to construct a secure professional identity.

Working Daily

Sociologist Patricia Hill Collins has used the term 'controlling images' to denote racist stereotypes of African American women as a means to control and dehumanize them, making it difficult for them to articulate their self-identity. The 'controlling image' of Caribbean nurses as 'troublemakers,' while hardly as ubiquitous as the images of the welfare queen or Aunt Jemima in the contemporary United States, serves a similar purpose. When white administrators, medical personnel, and patients evoked this stereotype against Caribbean nurses who dared to challenge the various manifestations of gendered racism, the objective was to not only silence, but to maintain a racial and gendered hierarchy.

Disavowing Racist Stereotypes

A key aspect of nursing identity is the occupation's reliance upon and commitment to a hierarchical structure and organizational culture that reinforces subordination among various groups of nurses. This characteristic, coupled with how white privilege is sustained in its various configurations, meant that Black Canadian-born and Caribbean-born nurses worked in environments where '"race" and racism were vectors in the constitution and negotiation of relationships.'[64] As with other institutions in Canada, nursing is a site where, intentionally or not, the values of white supremacy are discursively and materially practised, expressed, upheld, and validated. In response, Black nurses continued to articulate a professional identity that remained integrally connected to patient care. Others, particularly those who held supervisory and leadership roles, emphasized their excellent communication, superior management skills, flexibility, and overall confidence in their abilities to perform their obligations as expected. The women interviewed for this study believed in their abilities to work efficiently, but they also remained conscious of what it meant to be Black women in positions of authority, exhibiting a willingness both to conform to, and disrupt, their performance of the 'proper nurse' when necessary.

How Black Canadian women functioned in nursing was also influenced by their acceptance of their role as trailblazers. Virginia's encounter with gendered racism during childhood and her first year of nurses' training at Chatham General Public Hospital served as a template for how she would navigate an impressive nursing career that spanned over four decades into the 1990s. In an environment where the medical hierarchy was dominated by whites, Virginia consistently monitored her presentation. 'I knew that I needed to be very careful about my demeanour' she offered, and further elaborated:

> I knew that I had to present a very professional persona in patient safety, patient care, and in nurse/doctor relationships. I had to be professional. When it was break time, I couldn't relax the same as anyone else. But I was very, very careful about what I would say, or if I saw a hint of any potential issues that I would not get angry.[65]

Virginia's vignette illustrates the liminal position that these Black women occupied. Working in an environment where white people's assessment of their behaviour tended to be coloured by racist and sexist stereotypes, even if Black women had legitimate reasons to be angry, they tended to suppress their own reactions. To be accepted and rewarded, Virginia presented herself as quiet and composed: 'I was the best I could possibly be ... It wasn't acceptable to just be minimum that was the philosophy that I stood by. I think that's why I received the promotions that I did.'[66]

In reference to any harmful stereotypes that whites might have had about Blacks, Cathy's father told her the following when she was growing up: 'If you do what you're told and do good work, you'll be all right. Prove them wrong.'[67] This advice proved instructive to Cathy, who worked at Mount Sinai, Sunnybrook, and St Joseph's hospitals in Toronto throughout her career, which she began in the 1950s. As with Virginia, Cathy's performance was often dictated by the perceptions that white people had of Black people.

As the first cohort of Black nurses to integrate Canadian nursing, they bore the responsibility of negating racist stereotypes, which to a certain extent denied them a sense of individuality. Both Cathy and Virginia concealed any negative emotions, and they worked instead to be extremely efficient to avoid the possibility of being labelled incompetent. Here Cathy summed up her relationship with her peers:

> They all seemed to like me because I'm sort of a happy person, and I'm willing to do my end of it. And then, when I got through doing the teaching and supervision – I did a lot of head nursing – and the people could see you're responsible.[68]

Due to 'white society's inability to move beyond stereotypical images of black women from slavery's past,'[69] Cathy evoked a happy subject position to avoid being negatively labelled. She further drew attention to those qualities that are intrinsic to her professional identity, which gained her the approval of her mainly white colleagues and patients. Dispelling stereotypes and proving to whites that they are capable of excellence was by no means unique to Black Canadians. As long as Black RNs acted in a manner that maintained the social order, they benefited, while those who overstepped the boundaries were likely to face disapproval if they performed nursing inappropriately.

Dorette knew that 'Jamaican nurses were being labelled as troublemakers because [they] stand up for what they believed in.'[70] Being Jamaican, Dorette took great pains to disassociate herself from this 'controlling image.' As the only Black nurse in the hemodialysis unit at Victoria Hospital in London, Ontario, in the early 1970s, Dorette's response was: 'my motto was to prove to them that they are wrong ... I'm going to do this job well.'[71] Eventually her peers recognized: 'You're a good nurse, and because I'm Black, I'm not stupid.'[72] Several interviewees for this study reported that some white nurses internalize the idea that Black people lack intelligence.

One nurse (who preferred that her name not be used in relation to this story) recalled how a white nurse administrator 'did everything possible,' such as extending the probation period, even though she met the requisite qualifications for the position. In response, the nurse relied on the knowledge that she was a 'hard worker' as well as her faith, with emphasis on the biblical scripture, 'I can do all things through Christ who strengthens me.'[73] She too worked to dispel any unfounded stereotype that the administrator held. At the conclusion of the probationary period, the administrator told the Black nurse, 'I was so wrong about you,' to which she replied, 'People tend to stereotype Black people and figure they are stupid.' The idea that race is socially constructed, arbitrary, and unstable does not necessarily reduce its impact, as it continues to influence social relationships resulting in a form of self-vigilance on the part of Black nurses, who often had to strive to convince their white colleagues of their capabilities.

To be sure, white nurses are far from a homogeneous group, and as auxiliary workers, some are subjected to the supervision of either Black, other women of colour or white RNs where their own skills and knowledge can be called into question. Alternatively, male physicians may discriminate against white nurses regardless of socioeconomic status, because their gender may appear more salient in a given situation. The difference, however, between white nurses and their Black female peers is that the former's racial identity is never the *basis* for their subordination.

Despite the burden of having to disavow notions of Black inferiority, the majority of nurses interviewed here refused to allow unfavourable constructions of blackness to affect them. Even though Monica readily admitted to feelings of insecurity, she still considered herself to be a self-assured individual. This disposition led her to apply for an instructor's position at Oshawa General Hospital School of Nursing, in Oshawa, Ontario, in 1964, according to Monica; other Black nurses were 'flabbergasted' at the thought of her going to 'teach in a white school,' but knew that she 'could do it.'[74] Like the fictional Lydia in 'In the Glass Wall,'[75] Monica got the position and was, of course, the only Black instructor on staff, until she was later joined by another Black Canadian-born nurse. Of her experience, Monica recalled: 'I don't know if I was a token Black, so to speak, but among the faculty I was treated very well.'[76] Conversely, a few of the students from the predominantly all-white student body gave Monica 'a very rough time.' Despite caricaturing her pictures in their yearbook, Monica's response to these incidences of racial insensitivity was 'I was quite bright, and I knew my stuff.' Monica's barometer for judging her performance was not always premised on her white students and faculty, but instead upon her belief in her own capabilities. Similarly, Brenda who was one of the first Black women in management at the College of Nurses found that 'it was lonely at first. I used to feel very intimidated to speak up. But then I overcame that and realized that I had a meaningful contribution to make, so I began contributing and adding suggestions.' Brenda's initial fear is but one manifestation of the psychic realities of racism in that despite being in a management role, she was still the other, that is, she was not a part of the cultural group that has dominated nursing.

Some nurses were less concerned about stereotypes and chose instead to speak out against gendered racism. They were more than willing to accept the consequences. It took some time, but Carmencita came to the following realization while working with some white nurses: 'I think sometimes the moment [they] find that you are outspoken, you are well read, and you can articulate well, you are seen as a threat.'[77] These behaviours are antithetical to the performance of the 'proper nurse.' Instead of being deterred by this conclusion from challenging the social order, Carmencita did the opposite, and she faced disapproval by several white supervisors throughout her career.

The fear of overstepping boundaries, and of being viewed as aggressive or intimidating, was a concern of June's throughout her career as a nurse instructor. June recalled occasions during the 1980s when suggestions offered by Black nurses were ignored, to be acknowledged only when a white colleague paraphrased or repeated their ideas. In these moments, Black women pondered whether this was a result of their status as Black women, or whether the words they uttered were merely incomprehensible. Referring to her own experience, June explained:

> You wonder whether you made the suggestion and it didn't go any further, whether it's because of me, or it was a useless suggestion. The one that used to bug the life out of me is when I make a suggestion and it comes back as somebody else's. I used to hate that.[78]

Over time, June realized that she 'had to be direct' in handling her invisibility during meetings. She also pointed to her personal growth, listening to other people's stories, and attending professional conferences, which 'helped in terms of how I perceive and handle racism.'[79] In addition to providing another example of how Black women dealt with their liminality in nursing, June's growth over time attests to the problem of reifying any form of identity.

Patient Racism

Still, Black nurses did not only experience gendered racism in the social relationships mentioned previously; they also had to contend with individual, everyday acts of racism on the ward. Frances Henry describes these as 'the many and sometimes small ways in which racism is experienced by people of color in their interactions with the dominant group. It expresses itself in glances, gestures, forms of speech, and physical movements.'[80] Philomena Essed further explains that 'everyday racism is also infused into familiar practices; it involves socialized attitudes and behavior.'[81] While some Black nurses encountered various manifestations of gendered racism, they felt most comfortable discussing the everyday racism experienced at the hands of patients[82] and less so from their peers and other medical personal. Some nurses claimed that due to their small numbers in the late 1950s and early 1960s, they rarely experienced racism from other practitioners. Given the specific gendered ideals on which nursing has been constructed, especially around caring, it is difficult to conclude that nurses who possess natural and innate qualities such as caring could simultaneously be racist.[83] Finally, it is possible that the ease with which Black nurses discussed their patients' racist attitudes was related to the fact that their behaviour could be rationalized. These interactions illustrate how childhood, including religious values, shaped Black nurses' professional identity.

Black nurses' responses to gendered racism from patients depended mainly on patients' age. They tended to dismiss or ignore racist statements made by elderly patients and children. Furthermore, for those who had trained and worked in Britain, the shock of disparaging comments from patients no longer had the same effect in Canada. Three frequent reactions that white patients expressed towards Black nurses were telling them to return to their homeland, name calling, and a refusal to receive care. Dorothy J, who is actually Grenadian-born, had this to say: 'They would call me "Black bastard," or they would say, "Go back to Jamaica or Africa."'[84] In response, she would retort: 'It's a good thing I came here to look after you.' She would then point to the number of nurses on the floor, while telling the patients that there were 'six staff on, and four were Black nurses, and two would be in charge, and the four [Black nurses] would be the ones doing the [rounds].'[85] On other occasions, Dorothy J stated: 'I would shrug it off [the racist remarks] because of their age. They were senile and they don't really know. They are old, so you forgive, they don't really know what they are saying.'[86]

Jean added: 'They would say they don't want a Black nurse to look after them. I would just smile and say, "I'm not going to force you."'[87] Black nurses refused to internalize the racism experienced at the hands of patients, which allowed them to respond compassionately and with forgiveness.

For Janet, racism from patients was indeed 'an everyday thing.' To illustrate, she provided this example:

> You could be washing someone, and they'll be saying, 'Take your Black hand off me, you nigger,' and they are full of mess and you are cleaning them up. Everyone knew me, and I didn't mind getting that kind or reaction from an older patient because I always feel that maybe if my grandmother has somebody else not of my skin colour, she might have been scared, too.[88]

Growing up in a culture where respect for the elderly was a fundamental value, the sensitivity with which Black nurses often responded to racist verbal abuse from patients is hardly surprising. The response of Janet and the other nurses reflects the biblical injunction 'Do unto others as you would have them do unto you,'[89] even though they used family members as examples. Indeed, cultural and spiritual values were significant tools in the daily domains of work, and were critical to Black nurses' professional identity. Deskilling as a result of migration and antagonistic and racist patients were not the only defining memories for the interviewees.

Working in Supportive Environments

Black nurses were supported by their white colleagues who acted as mentors. Rarely are these interracial relationships the subject of analysis. Too often Black women are presented as victims of white women's racism. After graduating from Victoria General Hospital in Halifax, in 1961, Marlene left Halifax for Ontario, where the prospects for full-time employment were better. She found a position at Toronto Western Hospital working in the recovery room.[90] One day Marlene received a call at home from Stephanie, a white colleague with whom she had worked at Toronto Western, asking her to consider applying for a charge position in the same city, at York Finch Hospital, in the intensive care unit. Marlene had serious reservations about considering the position because she 'had no direct hands-on experience in the intensive care other than working in the recovery room.' Marlene then asked Stephanie: 'Do you really feel deep in your heart that it's something I could carry off, and I could do efficiently?'[91] Stephanie replied, 'If I didn't think so, I wouldn't be on the phone.'

Clearly, Stephanie valued Marlene's expertise. Nancy Fraser defines this recognition as, constituting 'actors as peers, capable of participating on par with one another.'[92] In the institutional matrix of the nursing occupation, where race and gender intersect to shape Black women's career trajectory, Stephanie's endorsement of Marlene mattered.

Frieda also attributed her success partly to the support of one of the nursing sisters at the Hôtel Dieu Hospital, in Windsor, Ontario, who from the moment she commenced training took a special interest in her. When Frieda graduated in 1950, she remained undecided about her career direction, and it was the nursing sister who recommended that Frieda try teaching part-time at the nurses' training school. 'We had a wonderful relationship,' Frieda said of the sister, who appointed her to a position 'assist[ing] the director.' Frieda held the position until she left Hôtel Dieu to have her first child. Throughout Frieda's career, it was the same sister and other whites in leadership roles that appointed Frieda for the positions she held. Frieda proudly explained: 'I never applied for a job in all my years there. I never filled out an application for a job.'[93] Until she retired in the mid-1990s, Frieda was the only Black nurse in management at the Hôtel Dieu Hospital, a position that was created as a result of health care restructuring.

When she assessed her career of forty-plus years at Hôtel Dieu, Frieda's confidence even after the fact was still evident. Regardless of the responsibility, Frieda never doubted her capabilities. 'I accepted it. And I didn't waver from it,' she said.[94] Similar to some other Black nurses, Frieda emphasized the need to be excellent. No doubt this aspiration was mediated by the nursing ethos, and her view of her place in the occupation as a Black woman.

Conflicts, Cooperation, and Survival

Whether they worked in Britain, the United States, or Canada, this group of nurses bore witness to monumental changes within nursing. Some of these changes ranged from the profession's relationship to medicine, to the restructuring in health care, and the introduction of new technologies. Another component of Black nurses' professional identity relates to how they worked daily in spaces that were not only hierarchical, but involved working with people with a variety of backgrounds, personalities, and temperaments.

As nurses' work and skills are affected and shaped by modernization, reorganization of the hospital, and the introduction of technology, they have had to develop strategies to ensure the successful daily operation of the ward. While doctors' hegemony in medicine means that they have the ultimate decision-making authority with respect to patients' diagnoses, nurses remain crucial to this process. What became increasingly clear during their tenure is that nursing demands multitasking in order to effectively ensure that the wards operate smoothly and that all medical personnel cooperate fully.

Unlike other specialty areas, the intensive care unit, emergency room (ER), and surgical units are often high-pressure environments where time is of the essence. Nurses who worked in these areas were more inclined to stress the collaborative nature of their relationships with physicians, which ultimately helped patients. About working in the emergency room, Dorette said she found that the doctor relies on your knowledge and skills to help them along – we enhance each other.'[95] She also pointed out that as an ER nurse she had better knowledge of the patients than did the physicians, as it 'is the nurse that keeps the patient alive twenty-four hours a day.'[96] Dorette found tremendous satisfaction in being a part of a team and knowing that her knowledge and skills contributed significantly to patients' welfare. Nurses such as Dorette realized, if implicitly, that they played a role in how medical procedures are practised and implemented.

In her capacity as an ER nurse and a supervisor at the East Toronto General Hospital, Muriel positioned herself in a similar manner to Dorette. For Muriel, proficiency and intelligence were key aspects of her professional identity. It mattered to Muriel that her peers, patients, and the physicians she worked with daily took her seriously. She offered the following:

I felt I knew my job, and I think that's one of the things that helps you to relate with people, when you're very sure of what you're doing. And I could have a conversation about a patient and know as much perhaps as the doctor they have talked to. And I always felt like that. The other thing is they [doctors] would accept your input. But the worst thing you can do is to have a doctor talk to you and you don't have a clue of what he's talking about, and he knows. So I think in that way, I was always able to relate, because I think I knew my subject quite well. And if I didn't, I was always willing to find out more.[97]

As the only Black nurse in the ER for several years, Muriel worked hard, and found that her colleagues 'were the most supportive people.'[98] She also included patients in her assessment. In underscoring the mutual nature of their working relationship with physicians, nurses such as Dorette and Muriel moved beyond what nursing historian Julie Fairman refers to as 'the language of exclusion and victimization'[99] that both professions often use to talk about themselves.

That Muriel and other nurses consistently mentioned their own social location, and the absence of other Black nurses in various departments, could be interpreted in multiple ways. They could be implicitly acknowledging white privilege and dominance, or they could be intimating that their individual success came at a price.

In spite of the setting and circumstances, maintaining positive social interactions at work regardless of where an individual is situated in the medical hierarchy is another marker of professionalism. This belief was reflected in Black nurses' refusal to reinforce hierarchical relationships when this could compromise patients' welfare.

Overlooking Hierarchies in the United States

How practitioners conceptualize their nursing role is mediated by training, lessons appropriated from growing up, and one's own individual principles. At the same time, whatever ethos individual nurses bring to their respective work environments may be disrupted by factors sometimes beyond their control. Black nurses were unable to escape the restructuring of health care that was occurring in North America. But with the introduction of ancillary workers, some Black RNs were in supervisory positions, which meant that bedside care was no longer their domain. So that the patients' welfare remained a priority, Black supervisors often ignored existing divisions between themselves and subsidiary workers.

Following their short stint at Sumby in Detroit, in 1958 Eleanor and her friend Helen found employment at Art Center Hospital, also in Detroit, where Eleanor worked for a total of nine years, most of which were spent supervising the medical and surgical floors. Unlike Hôtel Dieu and other hospitals where she had worked, Eleanor noticed a lack of bonding between nurses and physicians. She also noticed how discrete the divisions were between RNs and the nurses' aides, most of whom were Black women. She described a typical ward routine:

> So, basically the nurses [RNs] seemed like they did the paperwork, they gave the medicines and if they had dressings to do – that was it. Well, we were so used to, if you're making a bed, we'd help in making a bed, and wash the patients. Just because you take care of the patient and give him his breakfast and change his bed, then that's not all you do. You go back and you straighten up their room or change the water.[100]

Because she was working with a number of Canadians, Eleanor was able to implement a system where the RNs assisted 'the aides who couldn't get over how much they [helped]' them.

What Eleanor articulated regarding the hierarchy between RNs and nurses' aides was a by-product of professionalization, with an emphasis on improving nurses' education, coupled with changes in the political economy of American and Canadian health care. These changes led to a reconfiguration of work and the workplace, simultaneously creating divisions and altering relations of power among rank-and-file nurses and nursing leaders, and also between hospital administrators and physicians.[101]

In the late 1980s and early 1990s, Canadian health care workers witnessed the effects of ongoing professionalization in conjunction with the effects of health care restructuring. This resulted in cutbacks, staff lay-offs, in some cases termination of nurses, and the centralization of departments.[102] Besides the impact of these changes on patient care, some of the women who were interviewed mentioned how structural changes led to the devaluation of their skills, while intensifying tensions between various nurses.

As a staff nurse who was often 'in charge' at the Queen Street Mental Health Centre in Toronto in the late 1970s, Brenda recognized tensions between, for example, registered practical nurses (RPNs) and RNs:

> Some nurses figure that they are way up there, and the others, such as the RPNs are down below, and never the twain shall meet. It puts a division between the RNs and the RPNs, and right now there is a lot of conflict. The RNs figure that they do x, y, z, and RPNs are down here and they should

only do x, y, z. Now the RPNs are saying that [they] have the skill and knowledge to do a little bit more, but it seems as though they have to get permission from the RNs to do that.[103]

Brenda refused to reproduce the schism described above in her daily encounters with RPNs. Having been employed as an auxiliary worker upon her migration to Canada, and as a Christian, Brenda remained sensitive to how she interacted with those over whom she clearly had power.

Another division identified by a number of nurses was between RNs with degrees (university/college educated) and those with diplomas (hospital/apprenticeship trained). Of course, these tensions also reflected generational differences. The majority of nurses took offence at what they felt was an assault on their professional training and expertise. Marlene, who has had extensive supervisory experience, had this to say:

There has been some thinking of the higher ups that unless you have a degree your nursing is missing something. Bedside nursing is bedside nursing, and that means that a nurse who has the experience far outweighs the nurse who walks in with her big fat degree and can sit behind the desk and do administrative work as well. I figure a degree helps you to improve your skills as far as leadership and things are concerned. But they certainly can never replace the work that the bedside nurse can do.[104]

Whether Black nurses had degrees or not, the idea that nurses' identity and skills are linked to their ability to provide bedside care for patients was critical to their professional identity.

Tensions among Black Nurses

Unlike nursing supervisors and administrators whose professionalization pursuits had been geared towards making the distinction between RNs and other subsidiary workers, Black nurses avoided such distinctions. RNs downplayed real differences based on education, experience, training, and skills. While she had had some unpleasant 'instances with [her] own people' Nancy concluded that overall 'it's been very good'[105] working with other Black nurses. About Baycrest Hospital in Toronto, where she worked since she migrated in the 1970s, Nancy had this to say:

We can talk with each other; we bond with each other rather than with oth-

er people. Some of them I didn't know at all, and we became good friends
and we support each other. The groups I work with, if you are an RN, health
care aide, we tend to bond with each other. If the health care aide doesn't
know something we help them. We have encouraged a lot of them. We'll tell
them 'You are doing a good job. Why don't you do the RPN and from there
you can go on further.'[106]

Surely, part of the reason that Caribbean-born nurses forged the bonds
they did was also based on shared migratory experiences, cultural affinity, and gendered racism. Thus, Caribbean RNs acted as mentors encouraging those in subsidiary positions to further their education, practising
a form of 'race uplift.' Professional identity was linked not only to the
ideals propagated by the occupation, but also to the individual and cultural values that nurses brought with them.

This bond or natural affinity identified by Nancy was seen by Black
nurses as essential to their survival. The fact there were so few Black
nurses in nursing could account for this 'imagined' solidarity. As a result,
expressions such as 'we have to solve these problems among ourselves,'
and the belief that nurses should avoid 'airing one's dirty laundry in public,' were often evoked during the interviews. The fear that whites might
use tensions among them as evidence that Blacks cannot get along pre-
cluded any real disclosure of conflicts. Still, Caribbean nurses' attempts
to forge cohesive bonds with each other were not always successful,
which reveals the fluidity of racial and professional identities.

Some Black nurses in positions of authority felt apprehensive when
supervising other Caribbean nurses. One RN (who preferred her name
not be used) in particular noted how difficult it was to supervise Caribbean auxiliary staff because they sometimes disregarded her role as a
supervisor due to a shared racial and cultural background. She maintained that outside of the routine responsibilities of being in a supervisory role, the non-professional staff brought external problems into the
workplace, often seeking her advice. The supervisor recalled how on one
occasion there was a disagreement between a Black and a white nurses'
aide. The Black aide told her husband about the dispute and he subsequently called the supervisor advising her to reprimand the nurse who
was 'bothering his wife.' The supervisor felt that had she been white,
the husband would not have felt as comfortable to call her on his wife's
behalf.[107]

Even though there were moments when she was clearly frustrated, the
supervisor tried to understand how these nurses were situated within the

health care field by focusing on their material and social realities as a way of understanding their behaviours. 'They were non-professional staffs, who were poorly paid, they were not well educated. It was hard work,' she contended.[108] That these Black women were also concentrated in long-term care with very little room for advancement was another issue to be considered. In the final analysis, the head nurse appreciated these subsidiary workers because, despite their low pay and limited room for upward mobility, they were excellent caregivers.

Reluctant to divulge any explicit details about what was clearly a contentious relationship, Cathy had this to say about the Black supervisor: 'We're hard on each other. She wants you to prove yourself that you are good or something.'[109] Paradoxically, the supervisor who was of Caribbean descent had similar expectations to those Cathy had of herself: the desire to prove to her white peers that she, too, was capable. However, in the intricate matrix of social relationships that is endemic to the medical field, Black nurses in positions of authority sometimes find themselves in a professional predicament. To be sure, the nurse Cathy referred to in her narrative shared a similar position with white nurses who occupied leadership positions. At the same time, the Black nurse was trying to disprove any suspicion in the eyes of her white colleagues that she, too, might be incompetent. Recognizing her own vulnerability as the only Black supervisor, the nurse in question could hardly afford to give the impression that she was allowing 'her own kind' to behave unprofessionally. That, according to Cathy, the '[nurse] seemed to expect more than what you can give'[110] speaks to how individuals who are similarly constituted as Other could also reproduce similar feelings among those who share a similar social location.

Resolving Conflicts

In any workplace, conflicts are inevitable, and nursing is no exception. Even though their attempts to work cooperatively were interrupted by the exigencies of nursing or by conflicts among nurses, Black Caribbean-born nurses accentuated how important it was for nurses to work cooperatively. Of course, this was not always the case. '[Nurses] don't always like one another,' Laura admitted.[111] Because of her propensity to resolve conflicts, Laura felt she was respected and admired by her colleagues. As a supervisor, she had her own strategy to deal with disagreements when they surfaced. Working at Toronto Western Hospital in the 1980s, Laura explained:

I would talk with that one and I would talk to the other one, and then talk to them together. I would say 'Look, we have a job to do here. We have people to look after, and I don't care what you do after you get off the ward. You are a team. You work together. If you can't do that, then you're going somewhere else.' It always worked. I have never lost a nurse over something like that.[112]

Similar to Laura, Jean had her own set of techniques that she mastered over the years for dealing with friction on the ward. If a conflict could not be resolved between nurses, Jean called one nurse for assistance, even if the assistance was not necessary, to remove the nurse from what could be a volatile situation. Another informal method was to give the nurses 'the eye,' a look that basically meant that the nurses had to immediately resolve whatever issue was taking place. Jean recalled a meeting at the Toronto East General before she retired in the early 1990s in which the nurses were asked to mark the characteristics that best described each other. She remarked: '80% of the nurses chose *peacemaker*. They say, "if anything goes wrong, [Jean] fixes it." They say, "[Jean] keeps us out of trouble."'[113] These skills earned her the respect of the doctors and her colleagues alike. Thus, Jean's longevity at the hospital and dedication to creating a peaceful work environment were reflected in the retirement party held in her honour in the early 1990s. She remembered:

It was a surprise party and the best retirement party at Toronto East General. It was beautiful. Everyone brought their different dishes, and everyone turned out. Three doctors closed their doors that day. The Chief Plastic Surgeon brought red roses, and the Chief of Thoracic Surgery spoke. Everyone was shocked, because he's a man of few words.[114]

Jean enjoyed a rewarding and fulfilling career as a nurse at Toronto East General, which influenced her decision to retire early. Certainly, the above nurses were not the exceptions when it came to dealing with disputes. There was genuine willingness on the part of nurses to avoid participating in any disruptive behaviours that could impact the provision of health care, and the nursing profession.

Conclusion

These varied experiences make it patently clear that there is no monolithic Black nurse experience. Black nurses were differentiated by their training, age, skills, education, and migratory experiences. At the same time, the interviewees for this study shared certain commonalities in relation to their professional identity. Throughout their careers, regardless of the geographical location, Black nurses drew on a discourse of excellence emphasizing their education, training, and skills, all of which were important aspects of their professional identity. How they defined their professional identity was also linked to their childhood and their race, in conjunction with the professional ideals of the occupation. Of course, time of the interview, age, and life experiences also helped to shape the interview process and what the nurses revealed. Nonetheless, this group of nurses believed in their innate ability to care, despite questions from patients and peers about their abilities. Thus, they articulated a professional identity as *nurses* rather than as *Black* nurses.

6

Combining Work, Family, and Community

At the age of nineteen, Daphne B discovered that she was pregnant. Although the young man was from a good family, there was no pressure for the two to get married. Indeed, Daphne B escaped any stigma associated with being a daughter of lower-middle-class parents and pregnancy out of wedlock. She had planned to migrate to England to become a nurse. Upon arrival there, Daphne B commenced training immediately, and took time off to give birth to her son. Under a picture of a toddler, featured in the *Nursing Times* of 12 February 1960, is the following caption: 'Born in London of West Indian parents, I stay with foster parents while my mother is nursing the sick at the German Hospital.'[1] The luxury of staying home with her son was not an option for Daphne B and other National Health Service employees. After her son was born, Daphne B returned immediately to the hospital and completed her nurses' training. With the assistance of a social worker, she put her son in a paid nursery, where, according to Daphne B, he was 'well looked after.'[2]

Daphne B carefully assessed her situation. Alone in England with no financial or familial support, and with the father of her child still living in Jamaica, she recognized that she needed paid work and fulfilled her dream to be a nurse. Black women's structural position in various locations in the African diaspora has resulted in higher labour force participation rates than other racial groups. As a result, much of the scholarship on Black women focuses on paid work, with little or no serious consideration given to their reproductive labour in families or to other unpaid work in which they engage. As sociologist Patricia Hill Collins notes, 'black women's unpaid labour within extended families remains less developed in Black Feminist Thought than does paid work.'[3]

The Black family, in all its many facets, has been viewed as a critical source of strength and protection, hardly a site of oppression. Historian

Mary Chamberlain's summary of her interviewees' oral narratives of their families is fitting here: 'It is a story of survival and resistance, of solidarity, and reciprocity. It is a story of emotional attachments and family support that extends vertically through lineages, horizontally through kinship networks, and transnationally across the oceans. Above all, it is a story of families that have evolved, against the odds of slavery and poverty.'[4]

How the interviewees negotiated their subjectivities (such as mothers or single women) and various life transitions such as marriage, divorce, and unpaid work in tandem with their nursing careers will be the central focus of this chapter. Unpaid work includes housework and child care responsibilities performed for immediate and extended family, as well as volunteer and activist-oriented activities. Both married and unmarried interviewees were influenced by the gender ideologies of their time, which informed their fertility, the social organization of their family life, and the distribution of their household labour. Alternately, Black women's volunteer and activist work was, for the most part, a direct result of recognizing the interrelated oppression of race, gender, and social class on the well-being of Black people.

Structural and historical impediments, systemic and institutionalized gendered racism, and other societal constraints contributed to Black women's extensive participation in the labour force.[5] The majority of women with children maintained that another reason they held paying jobs was to provide a better future for their children.[6] Still, like most working women, some of the interviewees confronted the challenges associated with combining paid work, family responsibilities, and volunteer and community work, together with all the surprises, disappointments, and pain of life.

When he was five years old, Daphne B sent her son 'back home to Jamaica,' where he lived with and was raised by his grandmother and an aunt who was a teacher.[7] She relied on a kinship system of support common in the Caribbean region and other areas of the Black diaspora since slavery, wherein relatives assumed parental responsibilities. Daphne B realized that as a single working woman in Britain, sending her son back to Jamaica was in his best interest. Black mothers devised strategies to, negotiate and navigate the terrain of both paid and unpaid reproductive work.

Married Women: Child Rearing and Work

At some point in their adult lives, at least twelve of the thirteen Black Canadian-born interviewees married, and they all had children. Only one of these women gave up nursing after she became a mother. With hardly any official allotted time for maternity leave, the others took anywhere from six weeks to six months off once their children were born, and then resumed working. During the 1950s, when many of these women began working, 'only one out of eight women who interrupted their paid work returned to paid work within two years.'[8] By 1967, only 21 per cent of all mothers worked outside the home.[9]

Of the Caribbean-born group, fifteen had children in a conjugal relationship, another had two children but never married, four remained childless and unmarried, and one married but did not have children. Unlike some Black Canadian-born nurses who had familial support when they had children, this option was unavailable to their Caribbean counterparts. The latter's families were mainly living in the Caribbean, Great Britain, or the United States. What the two groups shared, however, was the task of navigating their identities as single women, wives, workers, and mothers.

All interviewees exercised some degree of agency with respect to housework, child care, and other familial responsibilities. Yet such decisions were mitigated by the gendered and cultural ideologies of the time. The domestication and relegation of middle-class white women to the private sphere of the home, where their primary duty was to the family, was shared to a certain degree by Black women. Ironically, the belief that women possessed natural qualities that predisposed them to nursing was not expressed in the same way in relation to the family. That is, the essential characteristics that made them excellent nurses were not as salient in the women's discussion of mothering.

These women lived in a society where the lack of value placed on women's paid and unpaid work within the larger society generally impacted the distribution of wages, and, subsequently, the power dynamics within households. But these issues did not emerge as prominent concerns in the interviews. Black married women neither seemed constrained nor bothered by their multiple roles. In fact, some of them attempted to establish more egalitarian relationships with their partners. Overall, they understood that equality was in the family's best interest.

Finding Child Care

Black Canadian-born and British-trained Caribbean-born nurses who began working in the 1950s and 1960s were amazed that white women who had spent three years in nurses' training would abandon their nursing careers when they married. Even if their mothers had stayed at home when they were growing up, the majority of interviewees could not conceive of leaving the workforce permanently. Laura admitted: 'I couldn't imagine spending all those years to get through nursing and training and giving it up by not working.'[10]

Even though the workplace dramatically changed for married women during the Second World War, the discourse shifted after the war. Mothers were exhorted to return to the home for the sake of their children. Some Black Canadian women succumbed to these messages. Two years following graduation in 1953, Dorothy R married, and a year later she was pregnant with her first child. She had three more children about a year apart and maintained that with each birth she took 'at least a couple of months off.' Together, Dorothy R's husband's mother and sisters, who had no children of their own, helped with child care, an arrangement that pleased the couple. They felt secure knowing that their children were being cared for by family members who loved them.[11]

Like many employed mothers, Dorothy R felt guilty about whether she was neglecting her children:

> I'd always say what would happen if I'm home? But then, too, I would console myself by saying, well, even if I was home, they are in school until 4 o'clock, [and] so they didn't have me anyhow. So, where's the big problem? I adopted that kind of attitude with it, because yeah, at first I felt guilty [because] I'm not around. How are the kids going to make it? But they made it.[12]

She defended her decision to work, pointing to the futility of staying home while her children were at school. She also insisted that she planned carefully scheduled holidays so the family could spend quality time together. Women emphasized that their pay allowed their families to go on vacations and travel, and gave their children an opportunity to participate in extracurricular activities. They also saved money for their children's college education.

Agnes, exposed to societal ideas about motherhood, also justified her decision to work based on the particularities of Black women's lives. She got married in 1953 and worked for seven years before she started a family in 1960. She had four children, born about a year apart from one another. According to Agnes, 'I took four months off and then I was back to work.'[13] Like Dorothy R, Agnes and her husband Doug also relied on his mother and her stepmother for child care. Agnes explained that her children 'reacted to her working,' but that she did not 'feel sad,' because 'this was what I had to do. I had goals for my kids. I had to send them to school.' Still she sought the assistance of a psychiatrist to help her understand the eldest child:

> My oldest daughter would cry. She'd go all crazy. She was with Doug's mother. I went to a psychiatrist at work and asked him, 'Why would my daughter act like that?' I said, 'I'm treating her nice. I mean, she's under good care. Her grandma loves her to death.' He said, 'It's not about you. It's because she wants your attention, and she is trying to make you feel guilty. And you stop allowing her to do that.' When I realized that, we didn't have [any] more trouble with that. I let her know that I have to work, 'and you have got to behave.'[14]

All in all, Dorothy R and Agnes believed their jobs benefited their children.

When families were unavailable, most of the nurses in this study depended on babysitters to care for their children while they were at work. Eleanor lived in the countryside and was fortunate to find a reliable babysitter who watched her daughter while she commuted back and forth between Detroit and Windsor. Eleanor was left without child care because of an accident involving the babysitter's daughter. Nine years into her career, Eleanor had no alternative but to resign her position as a supervisor at the Art Center Hospital in Detroit. She then found employment in Windsor working part-time, but eventually had to stop altogether. That Eleanor had to give up her nursing career because of the unavailability of child care speaks to gender norms during the 1960s. Her husband's career as a certified public accountant took precedence, and his earning power and status as breadwinner clearly outweighed Eleanor's. Thus Eleanor, not her husband, made the sacrifice of procuring alternative employment, then gave up her career altogether to assume responsibility for their daughter.[15]

Beverly was the only interviewee who voluntarily quit her job in the early 1960s to devote herself to full-time mothering. Her husband Doug wanted her to remain at home, and Beverly agreed. Once she had her first child, Beverly realized how much she relished her role as a mother, 'I loved it!' she exclaimed. No doubt, Doug's position as a surgeon – coupled with the fact that he was making history as one of Toronto's first Black physicians – contributed to their child care arrangement. Beverly was solely responsible for finding child care, particularly in the early years. She explained: 'We had totally different nights. I wouldn't hear the phone, and he wouldn't hear the baby.'[16] Doug's position allowed him to acquire economic and social prestige. Beverly was not perturbed that he was rarely home. In return, she was able to able to hire a 'cleaning woman' on alternate Saturdays to assist with the housework, a luxury only two other interviewees enjoyed.

Unlike their Canadian-born counterparts, the Caribbean-born women did not express feelings of 'maternal guilt'[17] or self-reproach. Working outside the home was normal to them. 'I believe it's the quality time you put in the home with your family,' Janet pointed out, insisting: 'When I go out and work and I come in, I give them my quality time, and to me that is more important than staying at home all day and still haven't done much for them.'[18] Nevertheless, like most women, Janet faced the challenges associated with harmonizing her multiple roles.

Nancy Zukewich Ghalam, a Canadian statistics analyst, maintains that 'for much of the twentieth century, men earned an income working in the labour force, while women were responsible for the unpaid work of caring for the home and family.'[19] Clearly, this was not Black women's reality. If gender, race, and class had been incorporated into Ghalam's analysis, then the conclusion might have been different. Partly by design and partly by circumstance, Betty acted as breadwinner and caregiver for most of her married life. Two years after graduating from Toronto General Hospital School of Nursing in 1955, Betty met her future husband, a struggling writer. For many years it was Betty, not her husband, who worked outside the home. As with her Black Canadian-born counterparts, Betty exhibited the capacity to combine multiple roles. She explained:

I got married in 1957, and my husband was a student at that time. And he left school but didn't have a job, and I had a job. So, I was the one who started out working. And I got pregnant six months after I was married. So, even after I had the baby, I was the one who was working. He hadn't gotten a job for awhile, but for a lot of my marriage, I was the major breadwinner.[20]

Husbands, Child Care, and Domestic Work

To explain the dilemma that working mothers faced after they left the workplace and entered their households, Arlie Hochschild coined the term 'second shift.'[21] Negotiating the 'second shift' has long been a part of Black women's existence. On many levels, Black women are 'viewed as departing from established feminine roles.'[22]

While they were growing up, the women interviewed were exposed to alternative – albeit at times contradictory – visions of masculinity and femininity. Mothers worked and their wages were indispensable, and some fathers assisted with child care and domestic labour. Unlike the work of the interviewees' mothers, which for the most part was unskilled and sometimes sporadic, nursing required formal education, and was full-time and stable. Nursing helped to secure a future that most of the women's parents could only imagine.

With wives who rebuffed the idea of staying at home, or quitting work altogether, Black Canadian-born husbands were generally more willing to do their share of household and child rearing. Indeed, the nature of nursing, with shift work and long hours, also contributed to the malleability of gender roles. Of course, there were husbands (especially those from the Caribbean) who were far less enthusiastic about household work and child rearing, and there were also wives who believed they were better suited for cooking, laundry, and taking care of the children than their husbands were.

Women were primarily responsible for managing and ensuring the smooth functioning of their households. The distribution of labour varied over time, and depended on the number and ages of the children and the availability of parents and extended family members. Virginia admitted that she was responsible for most of the domestic work and child rearing when she was available, even though while she was at work her husband supervised the children, cooked dinner, and helped them with their homework. Once their daughters were in high school, the couple hired household help so Virginia could take classes, and remain active in the Baptist church.[23]

Some husbands were involved in infant care, such as Agnes's husband Doug: 'He would do the washing, fold the clothes, change the diapers, and bottle feed them. He took good care of the children.'[24] Married for over fifty years at the time of the interview, Agnes credited Doug's mother in particular for socializing her son to be more than a breadwinner, acknowledging with some pride: 'He was here all the time ... He was a good father and a very good husband.'[25] Men like Doug were raised to nurture and parent their children and to do domestic work as a reflection of their commitment to and investment in their families and marital relationships. Agnes's confidence in her husband's homemaking and child-rearing capabilities was especially important, given that the couple lived in Maidstone Township outside of Windsor, Ontario, and Agnes worked in Detroit, which was more than an hour away. Agnes was also able to take on additional part-time employment, which allowed the family to purchase a home over a ten-year period without taking out a loan.

Having left most of their families (especially parents) behind, Caribbean women did not have immediate access to familial or social networks.[26] Most of their male partners believed that child care, cooking, and cleaning were women's work while breadwinning was theirs. Convincing Caribbean men that their assistance with household labour and child care was necessary led to considerable tensions, indeed, often to separation and divorce.

June, as opposed to her husband, elected to assume the responsibility of parenting and socializing her two boys. This decision had more to do with June's capability and was not necessarily based on any biological explanation. June intimated that she had a different parenting style than her husband. For her, parenting exceeded discipline, and included helping children to acquire the social and intellectual skills that were critical for their development. Since she was the parent responsible for the children's welfare, June insisted that her husband assist with housework, but he rarely did so: 'I didn't come home to bed, I came home to housework, and if I'm just having the flu or whatsoever, sometimes [I] get up and make supper and go back to bed.'[27] June discussed her husband's lack of participation in household labour with him 'many times,' but he generally disregarded her requests. There were only a few occasions during their marriage when he 'did whatever had to be done around the house.' The frustration of continuing her nursing education, full-time work, and caring for two children caused tensions in June's marriage. Eventually she divorced.[28]

In Joan's case, her husband 'did all the things outdoors' such as cutting the grass, while she was responsible for the bulk of inside household work. What perturbed Joan was the lack of involvement by her husband in their children's lives. According to Joan, her husband's excuse was 'he was in real estate and he didn't have the time.'[29] She, however, disagreed, insisting that 'he could have made the time.' According to Joan, even with her nursing schedule, which was at times erratic, she accommodated her children. She offered the following example:

> I came from work and got them into swimming. And that was difficult in the early days. To register for swimming, I remember going at 6 o'clock in the morning in the middle of winter in the cold, and I had to register the boys for swimming, and I did that every year until they were able to register on their own.[30]

However, despite the scholarly supposition that work dominates Black women's lives, Joan and the rest of the interviewees confirmed that their identities as mothers remained just as important as their professional identities.

Since the Caribbean-born women received less assistance from their husbands, they often opted to rearrange their work schedules, especially when pre-school children were involved, or to rely on babysitters. A few husbands also helped out. Janet's situation was different from, for example, June's and Joan's. Janet explained: 'My husband did a lot of work, too. I don't have any problem with [having] to do most of the housework, we really work together.'[31] From the onset, there were women who knew that they would shoulder the burden of child rearing and domestic labour, and they planned accordingly. To perform and manage their household and child care duties, a disproportionate number of the nurses curtailed or arranged for more flexible work hours. They worked nights, permanent days, part-time, and although rare, avoided weekends altogether. Such strategies were but one indicator of how Caribbean women valued their parental identity.

Dorothy J's unfettered commitment to fostering her three children's growth on multiple levels led her to work nights up until the 1980s when her last child was born:

> I wanted to be here with them [children] and to go to parent-teacher's meetings, and all those sorts of things ... I always put myself out to go because I didn't want them to feel as if they were just going to school and you were just leaving them to the wilds. I went in and saw how they were doing, and got to know the teachers.[32]

Describing herself in terms of the responsibility associated with her household, Inez remarked: 'My gosh! Like a superwoman – wife, mother, working late and domestic work, everything you had to do. I mean today you call me a superwoman.'[33] With two children, Inez elected to work part-time permanently, during the early 1970s, which was 'almost like full-time' with weekends off for five years using a babysitter when necessary. According to Inez, 'when they were babies he [my husband] would know what to do and this type of thing, so we split it [referring to some child care duties], and it worked out well.'[34] Once the children were older, Inez explained that her husband picked them up from the day care and then school and fed them when necessary. Nurses with husbands who helped to co-parent, even if they did little or no housework, tended to be more satisfied with their marriages.

The majority of married migrants had children within two years of their arrival in Canada. This was especially difficult for Elaine, whose husband worked for the Canadian National Railway, which meant, 'he was out of town for three or more days.'[35] In essence, Elaine felt as if she was a sole parent. Once she left the hospital and picked up her son from the babysitter, they went home to an empty apartment. Tensions between Elaine and the landlady further compounded the situation. Since the house was furnished, she explained:

> The woman would cover the chesterfield [couch] with sheets [and] would come into my place [unannounced] ... I had a baby then and since we had to bathe in the mornings and evenings, she complained that I was using too much water.[36]

The landlady was Italian and the language barrier between the two women intensified a difficult situation.

Elaine found adjusting to life in Canada upon migration in 1969 painful. But she had had two friends from England, who, along with members of the Seventh Day Adventist church that she joined, 'became [her] second family.' The church became a space to find solace when Elaine divorced and was left on her own with two children.[37]

Carmencita, married with no children, found that she struggled with her identity as a wife in the context of living in North America. Attempts to organize a more egalitarian household felt out of sync, or unnatural to her. This was particularly difficult because it was unlike what she was accustomed to while growing up:

> I was brought up in the Caribbean where the mother – the matriarch is the head of the household; I changed to the Western way, where [husband's and wife's] responsibilities would be on par with each other, where the man is supposed to do everything. [38]

Carmencita reverted to maintaining what she described as a matriarchal household: 'After the first year of my marriage, I realize[d] there are things that are a part of one's make-up, beliefs, and cultural norms. I don't want society to predict my behaviour.'[39] Carmencita drew on biological and cultural explanations, coupled with her own sense of agency, to justify her role as wife.

Caribbean households and societies were not matriarchal. As historian Claire Robertson points out, there is 'no historical record anywhere of a matriarchal society in a sense equivalent to a patriarchal, that is, where women held most positions of power and authority and dominated the society's economic and ideological structure.'[40] Rather, mothers' position as nurturers, overall resourcefulness, and money and household management skills, conditioned by various societal factors, earned them the title of matriarch. In other words, the practices and activities of the interviewees' mothers were shaped and reshaped by cultural ideologies, economic status, and a host of other environmental factors. Although they did not refer to themselves as matriarchs, the interviewees drew on lessons from their own families in raising their children.

Raising Children

Most, if not all, mothers raised their children to be spiritually grounded, responsible, independent, and successful. The women (especially the Black Canadian-born cohort) revelled in their children's accomplishments. One measurement of achievement was the completion of a diploma or degree, followed by a successful career. Whatever discrimination or challenges the children suffered while growing up were submerged beneath narratives of adulation by some of the interviewees. Any resentment, ambivalence, or frustration the women experienced due to the demands of parenting were long forgotten.

Children's achievements are an index of how well parents, particularly mothers, do their job. After all, if children fail to live up to their potential, or are maladjusted, it is mothers as opposed to fathers who are scrutinized, and held responsible. Of course, ideas about race are implicated in mothering discourses. Thus, as some of these mothers spoke about their children, they were also testifying about continuity – breaking cycles of disenfranchisement – that are a consequence of racism, sexism, and poverty. Who and what the children became were partly a result of the instructions gleaned from the parents, which were passed on to the children:

> My dad always said if you do something that brings on a responsibility, then it's your responsibility to follow it through. I think I've done the same with my kids. I told them, 'You get married, you have a family, and then you need to provide a home. Hopefully you'll go and get a home rather than rent it. Own something. Getting a pay cheque, it's fine, but don't spend all of it on foolish things. Save. You don't know what tomorrow will bring.' My kids have done that. They pretty much did what I did, and they expect their kids to do that.[41]

The hope that these women had was that the wisdom and guidance passed on for generations would continue to be incorporated as a part of their legacy.

Virtually every parent dreams that her or his children will rise to their full potential, but such successes appear the more remarkable in the case of parents like Frieda, who raised six children single-handedly. Frieda recalled moving into a home after she separated from her husband where 'we didn't have anything but blinds on the windows, no rugs on the floor, just sparse furniture and the bare essentials.'[42] Still, she proudly admitted:

> Each of my six kids has graduated. They have at least their basic degree, and most of them have continued on. So, they have other certifications at least. People have told me, we're rather a unique family. We've done well. We've been truly blessed.[43]

'Motherwork,' according to Patricia Hill Collins, 'consists of a cluster of activities that encompass women's unpaid and paid reproductive labor within families, communities, kin networks, and informal and formal local economies.'[44] Both groups of women interviewed for this study participated in motherwork on multiple levels. One concrete example involved nurturing Black children in a society that, according to Caribbean-born Monica relied on a language of inferiority, which dehumanized Blackness. She explained: 'Everything about Black people is degrading, our hair is coarse, our skin is dark, our lip is thick.'[45] Because race is a significant organizing feature of society, an 'important aspect of socialization for Black children is racial socialization.'[46] This was defined as the attempt on the part of parents and other key people to prepare children for being Black.

Despite a multiracial background including white and Chinese ancestry – which, according to Monica is important to colour-conscious Jamaicans – this mother of one child refused to have her daughter evoke the non-Black aspects of her racial identity. Monica told her daughter:

> You are a total Black child. You don't want anybody go looking for your white ancestry because anytime the white children start to look for their Black ancestry that is the time you can start to look for your white one.[47]

Monica's assertion of her daughter's Black heritage can be read as an oppositional response to discourses that render multiracialness (particularly in women of lighter hues) as superior to blackness. Monica further deployed two other common strategies shared by some of the interviewees. She encouraged her daughter to revel in the fact she was Canadian-born and in the concomitant rights accruing to her. Monica also utilized a biblical explanation, one that acknowledges a God that is truly no respecter of the colour of people's skin,[48] loving all humans equally regardless of race or other differences.

When she considered becoming a parent in the late 1960s, June wanted to have only male children, much to her own mother's dismay. June remembered her mother asking, 'Was growing up so terrible for you why you don't want any daughters?' June told her mother: 'Life is too hard for women, it is too one-sided ... I didn't want to bring women into the world.'[49] June's failed marriage and her own childhood might have contributed to these views. Although she preferred to raise boys, June did not anticipate having to repeatedly counteract the racist stereotypes that the education system in particular reinforced about Black males. June was astutely aware that she needed to counter stereotypes about Black male inferiority. Indeed, June learned, that sometimes 'it makes no difference [raising boys or girls] anymore, your heartaches are still the same.'[50]

Brenda made every effort to instil in her Canadian-born children a sense of belonging and identification with Canada. Brenda repeatedly warned her children that they 'need to be prepared to make sure that if an opportunity presents itself [they] are ready to embrace it.'[51] Discriminatory experiences faced by her children, especially her son, prevented them from strongly attaching to Canada. In fact, Brenda used the term 'displaced' to describe how her son felt about negotiating what it means to be born Black and Canadian.[52]

Mothers were unable to protect their children from racism as they got older. Furthermore, although parents (specifically mothers, in many cases) did their best to ground their children's identity to their place of birth, they were not always successful, as the example of Brenda's son illustrates.

Beverly refused to replicate her mother's style of parenting. Indicating her mother's role in her own subjectivity formation, Beverly recalled how her mother had refused to take a trip 'because she couldn't leave us. And I was just determined that I was not going to be so 100% mom, that I couldn't, you know, be a wife.'[53] Yet, being an activist ranked highly as another aspect of Beverly's subjectivity. Once she had all her children, by the 1970s, Beverly 'started doing things like joining the little local neighbourhood bridge club.' From there, she began participating in community activities, specifically those surrounding Black heritage. Her rationale was as follows:

> I wanted the kids to know about their Black heritage, unlike how I grew up, not feeling proud. You know, like low self-esteem. And I really wanted them to have a real appreciation of Black heritage and a positive sense of self, a sense of identity. When my oldest was seven, I started getting them involved in Black heritage programs.[54]

Because some of these women had been raised in environments, such as the school, where they experienced blatant forms of racism, there was a sense that their children had it easier. Black Canadians extolled the privileges their children grew up experiencing. They emphasized benefits such as private lessons and school for some, as well as extra-curricular activities, summer vacations, birthday parties, and assistance with postsecondary education expenses. Of course, the above were not exclusive to Black Canadians, as Caribbean-born parents provided similar opportunities to their children.

Like their parents before them, these women taught their children about the importance of family, to be honest, kind, respectful, responsible, and obedient in the face of authority. Most importantly, they emphasized the Protestant work ethic as the route to success. Canada, as the aforementioned quote by Brenda demonstrated, provided multiple avenues for success, and if children failed some parent's reasoned, it was usually of their own doing.

Religious observance declined with migration. This was especially true for the Caribbean women, who upon migration virtually ceased going to church altogether or attended services only on special holidays. As with their Canadian-born counterparts, there were some mothers who, in wanting their children to have a strong spiritual foundation, made church attendance mandatory. But often their children did not continue to do so as adults.

Virginia, for example, wanted her two girls to be independent, responsible, and Christian: 'We raised them in the Christian ethic as far as attending church and Sunday school ... And [now] they're both involved in their churches.'[55]

Naomi's three children were also very involved in the church while they were growing up. Yet, there was a remarkable difference in how Naomi incorporated religion into her children's lives compared with how her own parents did. Naomi recalled that when she was growing up she 'would have liked to participate in sports more, and [to have] travelled with young people.'[56] Her children participated in secular activities as long they did not interfere with, affect, or take priority over Mount Zion Baptist Church and its related activities. Thus, Naomi found a way to balance her desire to carve out a strong religious identity for her children, while allowing them the opportunity to enjoy certain privileges and freedoms that she had been denied. Caribbean-born Brenda and Elaine were staunch Seventh Day Adventists, who raised their children in their faith. Both women attributed their children's professional success to their belief and faith in God. For these women, their lives were a testament to God. Brenda explained how she often reminded her children of the hardships and inequalities she suffered upon migration and insisted that she was able to survive because of her spiritual background, and 'knowing the power of prayer.' Similar to Naomi and Virginia, Elaine's children attend and are very active in their respective SDA church. However, most of the Caribbean-born women took their children to church only on special holidays or other special occasions. Some families attended church when their children were younger, but their attendance decreased as the children got older.

When Joan got married, she joined the Catholic Church, her husband's denomination. She attended Mass regularly with her two boys, and enrolled them in Catholic school, which they attended up until high school. Now in their mid- and late thirties, Joan maintained that 'I cannot get them into a church unless it's a special occasion.'[57] According to Joan, her sons, told her that 'they had enough religion in high school.' She further added: '[when] Dennis [her son] was getting married, they, he and his fiancée at the time, went to church for two years before they got married, and now I guess they don't go. Mother has to do it for them.'[58] The lack of church attendance at a specific juncture in the lives of these women cannot be construed to be an absence of religious belief, especially among Caribbean migrants. Moreover, had many of these women, especially those who migrated first to Britain, found places of worship that engendered feelings of belonging and support, their religious practices might have been different.

At the same time, the structure of nursing with its shift work and extended hours, coupled with the reality of their reproductive duties at home, prohibited regular church attendance. Betty explained the place of religion and church in her life at a specific moment, an explanation that captures the sentiments of many working mothers:

I was working full-time, and on Sundays I used to spend the time at home catching up on other things. They [children] did go to church when they were very little, and then, for many years I didn't go. And then they were more or less on their own. Not so much my older daughter, but my younger did when she moved to the United States, and was away from home.[59]

Even if their children were no longer involved in organized religion, all the women concurred that they provided their children with a spiritual foundation that helped them negotiate various contexts and social roles throughout their lives.

While most interviewees did not mention their children's flaws, Ancilla was less reticent to do so. She realized early that children would never exactly replicate their parents, as they developed their own value systems. Ancilla's only daughter had two children and never married. While her husband decried his daughter's choice, Ancilla disagreed:

I don't see that as a stigma. I see that as, okay, so if it is a mistake – and basically as a friend of mine said to me, 'Nothing is a mistake, 'cause you make a decision based on the facts that you have at the time.'[60]

It was important, Ancilla continued, to never 'divorce yourself from your children. You do not ignore them. You do not leave them alone. Because they are your kids, you're always going to be there for them.'[61]

Other interviewees had children who were in a similar position to Ancilla's daughter. A few had sons and daughters who were single, and two had sons living with them. These choices appeared not to be a concern to interviewees, since by all indications their children had reached their place on the barometer of success and were contributing to society in different ways.

When Life Takes Its Toll: Dealing with Sickness, Divorce, and Death

The various transitions the women underwent at different junctures afford glimpses into other spheres of their lives. Besides migration, parenthood, and job-related transitions, the interviewees also faced unexpected deaths, widowhood, illnesses, and divorces. Consequently, they had to deal with the concomitant emotional and psychological effects of these transitions, which necessitated adjusting, and in some cases, reorganizing their lives.

Because of the stereotype of the strong Black woman,[62] many women were uncomfortable exposing their vulnerabilities, fears, or weaknesses. Daphne C's discussion of her husband as a good man was interrupted by tears. She explained: 'It still hurts. That's why I don't like to talk about my family life. Whenever I talk about my family life, I go sit down and cry after, and I don't want to do that.'[63] Daphne C was at work in 1981 when her husband called to tell her he was not feeling well. Daphne C was on her way to tell the supervisor that she was about to leave for home, when the following took place:

> I heard they called a code blue in emergency. And I went to emergency, and they were working on him. And I stood there, and nobody realized that that was my husband. And I stood there throughout the whole thing. And finally, the monitor just gave a blank line, and the doctor said he was gone. It was like my mind went totally blank. I couldn't even remember my own phone number after that.[64]

Daphne C's husband died from cardiac arrest, and a few years later, one of her sons died.

As a result of these losses, Daphne C suffered from bouts of depression for many years. Her involvement in the Windsor community helped her to cope. For other women, a strong spiritual/religious foundation, family members and friends, or their own inner strength when other support systems were unavailable helped to buttress the pain and sadness of dealing with unanticipated life transitions.

When most calamities struck, the interviewees' children had already left home and had their own families. Extended family members were often living in other geographical regions, and for a number of Caribbean women, outside the country. In these situations, the interviewees had to depend on their faith and their friends to assist them through difficult times. No sooner had Virginia entered the University of Windsor's nursing program part-time to obtain her Bachelor of Science degree in the 1980s than her husband's ill health intensified. Still, she continued her education while working full-time and taking care of him, graduating in 1991 with an honours degree in Nursing. Around the same time, Virginia's sister passed away. Distraught and emotionally exhausted, Virginia was unable to function, and took a leave of absence from work.[65]

Like Virginia, Laura's career was interrupted by unexpected death and illness. After twenty-seven years of marriage, Laura's husband passed away in the mid-1980s, much sooner than she would have anticipated. She also had two sisters who died when she was a teenager. Visibly shaken at the memories of her sisters and husband, Laura tearfully explained how she has been personally marred by their passing:

> Yes, it has taken a heavy toll because there has been so much death in my family. Sadness has changed me because I'm basically a happy person, but you see me crying today over death. Yes, it has changed me, and it has had a negative effect on me in many ways.[66]

In the same discussion, Laura explained that marriage and having a child were critical junctures in her life, as these two transitions simultaneously matured and transformed her outlook.

As a dynamic process, mothering does not necessarily end when children leave home. For example, some years after the pain of her husband's death, in 1993 Laura faced the possibility that she could lose her only daughter. According to Laura, her daughter, who was single at the time, underwent a number of surgeries, one for a brain tumour and two for hip replacements. With all their extended family members residing in Nova Scotia, Laura's daughter moved in with her. For four years, Laura worked full-time and cared for her daughter until she was well enough to resume living independently. The church provided some spiritual and social support; but for the most part, Laura was forced to cope on her own.

Coping with Divorce

Of the thirty-five women interviewees, five Black Canadian-born women and four Caribbean women were divorced. Of the two groups, Black Canadian interviewees were more comfortable in sharing details about their divorce. Caribbean interviewees generally avoided the topic, but alluded to regret or a sense of personal liberation. Cathy identified her Caribbean-born husband as a traditionalist who expected her to stay home with their four children. Once the children were in school, Cathy returned to work part-time, much to her husband's displeasure. In 1967, she decided to get a divorce. She said: 'I just got annoyed, and I said, "I'm tired" because he was always out, never home.'[67] After working with three different lawyers, Betty finally was granted a divorce. Betty's former husband did provide some support for the children, but still she maintained, 'I really had to skimp along,' adding, 'I'm used to going without.'[68]

The women's insistence on continuing to work after marriage and children obviously benefited them in the event of divorce. A year after she graduated from Hôtel Dieu in 1950, Frieda got married. Seven months later she was pregnant with her first child. Eugene, Frieda's husband, expected that the home would be her domain, and he would be the breadwinner. Frieda, on the other hand, could not conceive of leaving nursing permanently: 'I told him, "Nursing is my love. I will have to work at something."'[69] They eventually came to a compromise whereby Frieda worked occasionally until 1960.

Frieda went back to nursing full-time in 1970. Having grown up in the segregated community of Buxton, where according to Frieda 'all the authority figures were Black,' her husband's interactions with whites were limited, and as a result, he did not experience overt racism until his relocation to Windsor. As the only Black male firefighter, Eugene Steele lacked the social power to challenge the institutionalized and systemic racism inherent in the policies and procedures of the fire department and that were designed to ensure that the fire department remain the purview of white males. The mistreatment and hostility Eugene Steele suffered at the hands of the people with whom he worked eventually took its toll. Clinically depressed, Eugene quit his job. Frieda had to pay the bills. One day, Frieda found that Eugene 'had kind of gotten rid of all of our stuff except the house,' and at that point she made an unconventional decision to separate. She explained: 'I got to the point where I realized if I don't do something … these kids are going have two ill parents.'[70]

Three years later, Frieda divorced Eugene, which she correctly pointed out 'was not a popular thing' at the time. As a sole-support parent, with six children, Frieda's income was no longer supplementary, but indispensable to her family's economic welfare. Frieda recalled bringing home her first paycheque after the separation and convening a family conference with her children. She said: 'I put it on the table and told them [the children] this is what we have to pay out: rent, water, [and] heat.'[71] Without the security of Eugene's wage, Frieda and her children worked out a budget, and the older kids worked part-time and helped care for their younger siblings.

Divorce also allowed room for self-reflection. June maintained that she grew tremendously as a result of the divorce. She asserted:

> I became much surer of myself. I became self-sufficient, it mattered less what or how people perceived me, not that it didn't matter; it just mattered less. I just went about what I had to do and did it.[72]

As in most divorce cases, June was awarded custody of her two children, and although she found it difficult at times to manage motherhood and paid work, she enjoyed raising her boys.

It took some time for divorced women to adjust to their new status. Frieda Steele recalled calling the Sears department store to make a purchase, only to be told that it had to be authorized by her husband. 'Those were the positions women were in,' she explained.[73]

Community Work

Blacks in Canada were cognizant of the Black Power, civil rights, and colonial independence movements occurring throughout the 1960s and 1970s in the United States, the Caribbean, and beyond. Black Canadian newspapers such as the *Dawn of Tomorrow* and the *Canadian Negro* provided their audiences with information about struggles against white supremacy. Occasionally, connections were made between the plights of Blacks in the United States and Canada. The 1942 editorial, 'Hopes Race Bylaw Is Enforced,' in the *Dawn of Tomorrow,* was but one example. The author argued for 'the Double V,' victory against enemies and victory against racism at home. The article noted: 'The great numbers of Coloured Canadians as well as Americans, who are among the invasion forces fighting, bleeding and dying to liberate those enslaved peoples, also know what it means to be oppressed.'[74]

By the 1950s Canadian women also empathized with the suffering of Black mothers in the United States. In 'The Woman's Window,' Jean Daniels appealed to women's collective identity as mothers. She wrote, 'We are all filled with grief and anger because of the [Emmett] Till boy, of Chicago, who was killed in Mississippi.'[75] Similarly, Stanley Grizzle, president of the Toronto CPR Division of Sleeping Car Porters, appropriated the discourse of the National Association for the Advancement of Colored People in the United States in its campaign against the *Amos 'n' Andy* television show in opposing minstrel performances in churches during the 1940s.[76] Through widespread coverage of religious functions, celebrations, commemorations, and other events, both newspapers helped maintain links between Blacks in Windsor and Detroit. Diasporic linkages were further reflected in Caribbean newspapers, such as *Contrast* and *Share.*[77]

The civil rights movement shaped the consciousness of some of the women especially those born in Canada. Frieda explained: 'I didn't make it any secret that I was an adult who was concerned for the condition of Blacks.[78] Frieda recalled how in support of Martin Luther King's march from Selma to Montgomery in 1965, the people of Windsor held a march in solidarity:

> I remember the march on Selma in the 1960s, and you know, that whole period just enflamed me so. And we decided to have a sympathy march here in the city [Windsor]. We conscripted everybody. My husband even talked to our milkman, who was white, into walking with us. The children wanted to march too. And the youngest one was the only one that didn't march. But all the others marched. We had to make a stand and say what we believed in.[79]

Some women were also shaped by late 1960s Black nationalism. In the wake of the Detroit riots in 1967, the New Detroit Committee was 'a citizens' coalition comprised of a cross-section of community leaders.'[80] The goal of the committee was to identify urban problems. In addition, 'New Detroit not only serves as a forum for identifying urban problems, but also, by providing financial and technical assistance to grass roots community development programs and to a multitude of New Detroit-initiated projects, promotes strategies to reduce them.'[81] Dorothy R, who joined the organization as a member of the health subcommittee, was motivated by her concern for the plight of ordinary Black Detroiters. She explained: 'I brought up a number of issues and things that were going on with various agencies and people in the city, that we needed to address because it did affect Black folks.'[82] The lackadaisical attitude of the board members led to Dorothy R's disillusionment and resignation from the committee. Her overall dissatisfaction with the lack of action by 'her own people' lingered in her recollection in 2007:

> They always use these kinds of excuses, just to prevent us from getting ahead … Many times there are things that we get involved with, and we don't do them to the best of our ability. I think Black folks, if they really wanted to go out there and make changes, they could.[83]

To cope with the accusation of patient negligence by a fellow nurse and the attendant psychological and emotional distress she faced, Daphne C decided to volunteer at Windsor Women Working with Immigrant Women, an organization dedicated to assisting immigrant women and their families. 'I try to help people that are in need of help, rather than sitting back and thinking about me,' was how Daphne C explained her initial involvement.[84]

Although volunteering with Windsor Women Working with Immigrant Women was rewarding, she found there was a critical component missing from the organization's mandate, and subsequently Daphne C founded the Immigrant Women's Centre. The centre's primary objective, as Daphne C explained, was to also support immigrant women, but with special emphasis on domestic workers. Because of their subordinate status as temporary workers, domestic workers enjoyed very little protection from their employers or the state. Daphne C provided her assessment of the situation at the time:

> All these domestic workers were coming in from Jamaica, and they were suffering because of the employer/employee situation. They had no one to take up for them, and if something was wrong, employers would go report them to Immigration, but Immigration would not take their sides. So, they had it really, really rough. And it was out of empathy and sympathy for these people that I started the organization. And it's still going.[85]

Instead of revelling in her own pain, Daphne C made a conscious choice to put her energies into empowering women, a number of whom shared a similar cultural heritage with her.

Sitting in the Montego Alkebulanian Enterprize Black History Book Shop that she currently owns, Daphne C spoke with pride about her legacy, and how others have built on what she started. More than two decades of activism in the Windsor community have not gone unnoticed, or unrecognized. Daphne C has been the recipient of numerous awards. Two of the most prestigious include the Golden Jubilee Medal, and the 125th Anniversary of Confederation Medal. Both are awarded to 'Canadians who have made outstanding and exemplary contributions to their communities or to Canada as a whole.'[86] Although Daphne C mourned deeply the loss of her husband and one of her children, and experienced incredible psychological distress at being named in a negligence case,[87] she did not allow these to paralyze her. Instead, these losses served as a catalyst for community involvement. Today, Daphne C not only manages her bookstore, she is also the vice-president of the Wyandotte Towne Centre Business Improvement Association, participates in city council activities, and remains an active member of other community-related organizations.

Unlike white mothers, who took for granted that their children would have access to educational resources that supported their intellectual growth, the same cannot be said for Black women. This recognition led Beverly to launch the Black Heritage Education Program during the mid-1970s. According to Beverly, the organization's mission was 'to get

Black curriculum taught in the schools and to deal with the racism going on in the schools'; consequently, education became a site of struggle for Beverly and three other mothers who 'used to absolutely drive the Northrop Board insane,' as they lobbied for a more inclusive curriculum.[88] Some women became more active when their children were older.

By the time her four children were in their early teens, Beverly had been president of the University Negro Alumni Club, and a member of the National Black Coalition. She was also involved with an organization in her neighbourhood, and in 1976, she ran for city council, but lost. For the next eight years, she served on the Ontario Status of Women's Council and the Human Rights Commission. In 1983, amid a rancorous campaign during which she experienced not only the impact of gendered racism but also allegations of anti-Semitism, Beverly, with the help of a number of prominent Jewish supporters, won the election and became the first Black member of the Northrop Council. During the same time, Beverly was also running for a position on the Metro Council, and was acclaimed as a process of the appointment. Until she retired in the mid-1980s, Beverly had served in various capacities on a total of twelve boards and organizations, as a tireless anti-racist advocate.[89]

Beverly's activism reflected the multiple subject positions she occupied as a Black woman, mother, nurse, and citizen. She credited her nurses' training and the time she spent as a public health nurse in Detroit with giving her the confidence to interact with people from various backgrounds. Alone, because of husband Doug's long hours at the hospital, Beverly became involved with a number of anti-racist initiatives, such as working with a community group of racially diverse people who were working to integrate areas of Detroit. 'I used to go to a lot of meetings about things like that,' she explained. Beverly recalled churches with Black and white members who 'were really making an effort to make things work' and attending events featuring speakers such as Thurgood Marshall and Martin Luther King. According to Beverly, 'I found that was really an inspirational period.' As with Dorothy R, being Black Canadian did not preclude identification with African Americans and their plight. Indeed, both women's involvement in various anti-racist activities was predicated on an acknowledgment of shared commonality with Blacks in Detroit. Beverly was able to draw on her myriad experiences as a public health nurse in Detroit when she entered the political sphere.[90]

Betty understood the importance of positive mentors for Black children. When her cousin, radio broadcaster Dwight Wiley, approached her in the early 1990s about taking part in a mentorship program, Betty did not hesitate. Together, the Black Business Professional Association, the

Toronto Board of Education, and the Bank of Montreal partnered to create the Leadership for Today Program. Betty explained the mentoring aspect of the program:

> There was an agreement where every week you would phone them [mentees] in their home and just get to know them and find out how things were going at school and if there was anything they wanted to talk to you about. I think it was once a month. We would meet with the teacher and the people who set up the program, and the mentors, in person ... We would try to build up a relationship to encourage the students.[91]

Students, parents, and teachers valued the time and effort that mentors like Betty put into the program. Betty volunteered until the government cut the program's funding. Being able to see tangible results from her involvement led Betty to conclude that of all the activities that she has been involved in, Leadership for Today was 'the most rewarding program.'[92]

These women became active retirees. For example, Virginia had always served as archivist and historian at her church, but since her retirement from nursing in 1991 she devoted a significant portion of her time trying to raise money to write and publish 'the history of the First Baptist Church in Chatham.' She is also a member of the Board of Directors for the Chatham-Kent Community Family Health team, where she continues to utilize her nursing knowledge.[93] Virginia has also served as volunteer chairperson for the Nurses Alumnae Association and has participated in fundraising efforts for the Chatham-Kent hospitals.

As they got older, many of the women interviewed for this study renewed their religious fatih. Churches, some of which were interracial, become an arena where formal and informal volunteering formed the locus of unpaid activities for a number of them. Outside of regular church attendance on Saturdays and Sundays, weekly prayer meetings, and Bible study groups, the women sat on a variety of committees, where they organized and planned numerous activities throughout the year.

Retirees such as Inez made an effort to visit and socialize, although not always exclusively with members of her church. This seems a way to connect with other women who have, for example, lost their spouse, or whose grown children no longer live in close vicinity. 'I go for a lot of lunches,' Inez adds.[94] Naomi is perhaps one of six interviewees whose involvement in church-related activities has been consistent throughout her lifetime. A product of Mount Zion Church of God in Christ as a child, as a wife, as a mother, and as a nurse, Naomi's commitment to Mount Zion never waned, and continues today.[95] For over a decade, Naomi was the musical director of 'Unique Ontario Chorale,' which, according to author Dorothy Shadd Shreve, was 'one of the most popular singing groups in the province.' In fact, Shreve writes, the choir 'was invited in 1966 to perform in the Voice of Many Nations concert, sponsored by the United Nations Association of Ontario, held in Windsor, and in 1967 it represented the city of Windsor at Expo '67 in Montreal.'[96] Three decades later, Naomi continues to direct the choir, and serves as a member of several committees.

Frieda was the first female deacon appointed by the British Methodist Episcopal church, although the congregation did not unanimously support her. Instead of being disturbed by patriarchal assumptions about her ability to assume the position of deacon, Frieda saw the role as 'an interesting challenge.' She also belonged to a committee with members from other churches who, she pointed out, were 'more accepting of me as a female deacon,' as opposed to 'the resistance I experienced from individuals from my church.' She continues to serve on several community committees in Windsor, including the publicity committee for the Hôtel Dieu class of 1950 Alumni Association. Despite intermittent periods of ill health, Frieda stated, 'I love retirement, and I enjoy volunteerism.'[97]

As the examples of these women illuminate, unpaid work can be just as rewarding as work for remuneration.

Conclusion

Regardless of societal norms that suggested that children were best raised by stay-at-home mothers, the women in these interviews defied those claims. They embraced their identities not only as workers, but also as mothers. Moreover, as I discussed in chapter 3, they enacted a 'politics of respectability,'[98] and endorsed social values usually attributed to the middle class, including the significance of hard work, education, and moral responsibility, and they passed these values on to their children. Whether single or married, many of the women believed they had a special obligation to support and 'uplift' Black/Caribbean communities. Whether their activities were formal or informal, a significant number of these women continued a legacy that emphasized social responsibility. As wives, mothers, workers, and community volunteers who have undergone numerous transitions in their lives, these interviewees challenge theoretical frameworks that pay attention only to the race, social class, and economic dimensions of Black women's lives.

7

Nation, Home, and Belonging

As they reflected back, re-remembered, and ruminated about the present, the Caribbean-born and Black Canadian-born women in this study articulated multiple meanings of community and home. Community, like the nation, is an imagined entity that draws meaning from the political, economic, and social processes in which individuals and groups participate. There is no one Black community: race, class, gender, sexuality, and a host of other factors divide Blacks. Yet these differences are often subsumed in favour of the idea of a monolithic Black community based on shared skin colour or any other phenotype that constructs a person as Black. More importantly, shared colonial histories and experiences also reinforce a unitary notion of a Black community. Therefore, meanings attached to home, community, and their links to blackness depend on the historical context. Furthermore, meanings (as with identities) often shift for individuals over the duration of a lifetime, a political struggle, or even from one day to the next. In many ways, the interviewees' explanations support the claims of identity theorists such as Stuart Hall. An examination of the women's narratives over the life course repeatedly shows how identities are dynamic, fluid, and constituted temporally and spatially.

As the oral histories of the nurses show, retirement offers an opportunity for deep reflection on the total life course. 'You have time to reflect back on your life and see what changes you have to make before you go to meet your maker.'[1] While Muriel, seventy-one at the time of the interview, referred to religion in this statement, her reflection is applicable to meanings of home and community as well. As the Black Canadian and Caribbean women assessed their life journeys and the multiple transitions they had experienced, they expressed a general satisfaction that, regardless of the many obstacles they had faced, life had generally treated them well. The interviewees also agreed that they had made significant contributions to the multiple communities with which they identified in Canadian society. This chapter explores how Black women negotiate and redefine diasporic identities within the context of living in Canada by considering how they articulated concepts of community, home, and belonging within a transnational framework.

Caribbean Migrants Find Community

Until more Blacks arrived in Canada during the late 1970s and 1980s, these single professional women found ways of settling into their new homes, building community, and forging friendships that were not exclusively with other Black people or based on island affiliation. For example, Vera provided a glimpse of what Toronto was like in the early 1960s:

> When I came to Toronto, the only other Blacks here were students at the University of Toronto, and there were some domestic people. I didn't see any Black families on the street. If you saw a Black person, you would be very curious.[2]

It was Caribbean people, especially domestic workers, rather than Black Canadians, whom Vera and most of the other newly arrived immigrants recollected as occupying Toronto's landscape. Vera recalled fond memories of the dances held by the Caribbean students enrolled at the University of Toronto. Unlike the domestic workers, nurses were invited to these functions. 'We'd get to see some Black faces among the students; not many, a few,' Vera explained.[3] At least for Vera there was a sense of an emerging Black community, however small, where she and other nurses were able to forge relationships with other Caribbean people.

At the same time, the social class divisions of the Caribbean were being re-enacted in Toronto, although in a more subtle form. Students at the University of Toronto clearly formed part of the Caribbean elite, and when they were growing up they most likely had their own servants and probably did not hold them in high regard. The domestic workers Vera identified most likely experienced more isolation, oppressive working conditions, and greater marginalization in this newly created Black community. In essence, Caribbean domestic workers remained 'outsiders' among the 'outsiders.' In contrast, nurses, who constituted a professional and respectable group, were invited to the activities organized by Caribbean students at the University of Toronto.

The social lives of Caribbean migrant nurses also transgressed race, gender, class, and sexual boundaries. Recruited by Canadian officials during the 1960s, Daphne B arrived in Canada the same year as Vera. She socialized mostly at the German Club 'because there were not any Black men then, we used to go out a lot with the fellows there.'[4] Similarly, Vera recalled the functions organized by the YWCA for immigrant women and men:

> It was very multicultural, they catered to everyone. I met a lot of men from Europe who came to work. They included Germans, Hungarians, Italians, and we dated some of these people. Some of my friends got married to some of these men.[5]

In the absence of people from their own communities, heterosexual Caribbean women and immigrant men disregarded taboos associated with interracial coupling, and formed both sexual and non-sexual relationships. In the process of redefining their own identity they also redefined notions of community.

Just as they did in Britain and as nurses, Daphne B and Vera reflected Black women's capacity to exist in multiple locations,[6] which are not always associated with geography. They expressed pride in their ability to defy racial, ethnic, cultural, sexual, and class boundaries, forging mutual and satisfying relationships. Over four decades later, however, Toronto has changed drastically. The city is now a transnational community, and the Caribbean presence is firmly established expressing itself in multiple ways through associations, community organizations, businesses, and media sources, and a decision by Parliament to officially recognize Black History Month.[7] The Black population now hovers at close to 2 per cent. 'There is not much community among ethnic and racial groups nowadays. Today, we tend to stick to our groups; I wonder what happened,' Vera queried.[8] This perception of people 'sticking together,' however, is merely a counter-reaction to racial oppression, which often precedes increased migration.

Part of the double-lap migration (Caribbean to Britain and then Canada), Eileen arrived in Brantford, Ontario, during the 1960s. Her experience illustrates how finding community, however contrived, is often a lonely endeavour. It was not the absence of other Caribbean or Black people in Brantford that contributed to Eileen's isolation and feelings of exclusion. It was the social scene, dictated by the prevailing gender ideology that reinforced heterosexual coupling and subsequent marriage that she found most incommodious. Eileen retrospectively compared belonging in Britain and Canada:

> It was much harder socially, over here [Canada] you need a partner, here everyone was getting married ... If at twenty-one they [women] were not married ... they thought it was the end of the world. Here it was a couple thing and you did not fit in if you didn't have a partner. [9]

Eileen further added: 'In England, the fire fighters would have a dance, and they would invite the nurses; I did not find that here.'[10] As time elapsed, Eileen was able to establish meaningful and lasting friendships. She eventually met and married a white man from Brantford – a predominantly homogeneous community – and became a parent. Eileen's sense of community was based on other factors, none of which included being Black or of Caribbean heritage.

Diasporic Black communities are far from fixed. They are, rather, 'imaginary and symbolic communities and political constructs'[11] that are materially and discursively constituted. As Colin A. Palmer points out, 'It is we who often call them into being.'[12] This is apparent in how some Caribbean nurses articulated their conceptions of community. As with nursing practices, and as illustrated by Eileen, memories of a more hospitable and tolerant Britain were sometimes used as a marker to evaluate the new home and the social relationships that emerged there. When, for example, Myrna immigrated to Canada in 1971, she immediately noticed the lack of cohesion within the Caribbean community because of the divisions along island lines, or what Winston James refer to as island chauvinism,[13] in relation to Britain. Myrna recounted:

> In Britain, we were more like a family; there were no distinctions between Jamaicans, Trinidadians, or Grenadians, we all moved as Caribbean. In Canada, however, Caribbean people seem to be going their separate ways ... People are no longer friendly, even when you say hello to them.[14]

Thus Myrna confirms James's argument that racism in Britain led to the formation of Caribbean identity. [15] Much to Myrna's disappointment, a 'new' attitude prevailed among Caribbean migrants in Canada, an attitude that she described as 'you stay in your corner, and I stay in mine.' Myrna further explains that Caribbean immigrants had adopted a 'cold and individualistic attitude' which had been absent in Britain.[16]

For Myrna, Caribbean identity was not necessarily based on race or territorial affiliation, but instead on the common inheritance of shared values. These values, a defining philosophical component of Caribbean-derived African tradition, underscore the significance of community and the collective. To disregard this meant that, as Myrna claimed, 'We have lost our identity.'[17] Rather than having been totally lost, however, I argue that Caribbean identity has been reconfigured, partly due to the syncretic merging of cultures that result from multiple migrations and resettlement.

And yet, however emphatically migrants like Myrna point to a common Caribbean identity, such an identity is much more complicated in reality. Stuart Hall explains: 'In the diaspora situation, identities become multiple. Alongside an associative connection with a particular island "home" there are other centripetal forces: there is the West-Indianness that they share with other West Indian migrants ... There are the similarities with other so-called ethnic minority populations ... the identification with the localities of settlement ... all jostling for place alongside, say, their "Barbadianness."'[18] Hall's theorizing on multiple identifications is reflected in, for example, how Vera and Daphne B articulated their relationship with Eastern Europeans upon their arrival to Canada. Others recalled how like Blacks, Jews, and Italians, they experienced discrimination, especially in procuring housing and employment. Even if Caribbean migrants identified strongly with the Caribbean and Black British diaspora that they left behind, they shared a similar 'outsider' position with other migrants upon their arrival in Canada.

Judging from the responses regarding the absence of Black people on Canadian soil, there is some indication that Caribbean migrants expected the opposite. Like other migrants, Jennette also commented on the non-existence of Blacks in London, Ontario, when she arrived in 1964. Seeing Black faces – even if only on weekends, when Blacks from Buxton and the surrounding areas came into the city – evoked feelings of familiarity, and some sense of belonging, however ephemeral. Jennette, who first worked at the Victoria Hospital, discovered a small but thriving Black Canadian community when Mrs Houston, her landlady and 'one of the leading Black people in town,' asked her to attend church because she played the organ. Unwilling, but out of respect for Mrs Houston, Jennette relented:

I had played the bloody organ, and there were all these Black people, and in talking to them, they were saying that they were glad that all these Black nurses were coming because their sons had had to go and marry all these white women ... I was amazed at all these Black people that you don't see in the city.[19]

In this social and local arena, Jennette and other nurses were welcomed. This further illustrates how diasporic identities are often configured through Blackness, despite its precariousness as a signifier.

In contrast to some of the other interviewees, Carmencita insisted on a more contingent and contextual way of thinking about community. Even though she maintained that one of the disadvantages of living in Canada, as opposed to Trinidad, was that she missed being around Black people, Carmencita said, 'I don't think I would join a group that promotes Blackness,' and then continued, 'I went to one West Indian group and left because it was a waste of time.'[20] Her position was buttressed when a male member of the group chastised Carmencita for not being 'Black enough.' In responding to their own marginalization, organizations such as the one Carmencita mentioned constructed essentialized notions of blackness that subsumed difference. For Carmencita, however, an imagined unified Black community was not politically constructive within a broader context of belonging in Canada. Instead, she would have 'prefer[red] to join an immigrant society, where people have more in common, where we could fight towards a common goal. We can all march to Parliament Hill.'[21] Carmencita is among a few of the Caribbean migrants and Black Canadians who recalled or had some knowledge regarding discrimination against, for example, Jews and Italians after the Second World War.

Clearly, there is recognition on the part of a number of the women that community is not limited to people of the same racial background or that Blacks are the only group that encounters discrimination. Frieda, for example, recalled how she 'observed a lot of prejudice against Jewish students,' which she knew 'was not right.'[22] Edna also pointed to the affinity between Blacks and Jews in Toronto which translated into the latter providing accommodation for the former when there was hardly any other alternative: 'A lot of Black people mixed with Jews in those days. We all got along, and Jewish people were the only ones taking Black people into their homes.'[23] Organizations such as the National Unity Association (an organization that Dresden resident Virginia mentioned in her interview) and the Canadian Jewish Labour Committee embodied this spirit of cooperation to which Edna alluded.

These varied responses to community – whether in the form of 'race uplift' activities that exemplify the principles of collectivism that Myrna identified as uniquely Caribbean, or the interracial connections espoused by others – reveal not only the fluidity of identity, but how ideas of belonging are not necessarily based on race or island affiliation. Eileen insisted that she had 'never joined a West Indian Club, [because] I don't see the need for it,' adding, however, that 'I can cook West Indian meals.'[24] Unlike other Caribbean migrants who viewed culturally and race-related organizations as serving multiple purposes beyond a buffer against discrimination, this was not the case for Eileen. Still, Eileen's latter statement signals some form of affinity with her Caribbean background, despite disavowing any involvement in Caribbean organizations. Similarly, Jennette adamantly shunned relationships with other Antiguans, saying: 'I stay away from Antiguans. I don't go to any official Antiguan things. I make sure I'm not on their mailing list.'[25] Migrants often respond to alienation or dislocation by viewing their communities as homogeneous and fixed, based on the assumption that members share similar values. In reality, however, communities remain contested terrains that are continuously transformed by their own members. Carmencita's, Eileen's, and Jennette's sense of identity was not necessarily connected to island, racial, or cultural affiliations; these women had other means to develop and sustain community.

Religious and Secular Organizations: Building Community

Despite levels of intensity, the majority of the interviewees for this study grew up in religious households. Although individual connection to a religious community waned for some of them, especially for young Caribbean women upon migration to Britain, the majority maintained some aspects of a Christian and Catholic identity. As they got older, however, some of the interviewees reconnected with their spiritual selves, deepening their connection to God. Beyond an individual's intimate relationship with the Divine, a core component of Christianity is the notion that all people are equal in the sight of God. Thus, the church, as discussed in chapter 3, serves to mediate against an oppressive society. Furthermore, Nicole Rodriguez Toulis's argument that where national citizenship is divisive and for some, at least, a way of challenging the position of Black people in Britain, in the church it is replaced with an inclusive spiritual 'citizenship with God'[26] can certainly apply to Canada. Consequently, in the confines of a religious community, one's religious identity is sometimes more salient than racial or cultural identity. As Edna explained, 'we are all children of God ... We are all one.'[27] The emphasis here is on the relationship with God and others as a human family, not as racialized, gendered, classed, and sexualized subjects.

Intrinsic to Lillie's and the other interviewees' Christian identity is 'to have belief and faith in God,'[28] even if this belief manifests itself in different ways. Ancilla summarized her relationship to religion and God, revealing how religious beliefs are often individually negotiated:

> I do believe that religion is just some institution, but I believe that you need your faith, you need God, you need something to hold onto, and He's been there for me throughout my life. If it wasn't for Him taking care of me and looking out for me, I would never have survived some of the challenges in my life.[29]

Indeed, an indomitable sense of faith sustained the women through the obstacles that accompanied their life transitions. Whether in the face of the lonely sojourn to Britain, the demands of nurses' training, gendered racism in employment, divorce, or illness, the interviewees trusted that their God would follow through on his promises to care for them.

One principle reiterated by the majority of the interviewees who identified as Christians was the Golden Rule, the notion that 'you do unto others as you would have them do unto you.' Virginia further elaborated on this ideal by explaining how important the Bible is in imparting knowledge, religious values, and philosophy regarding 'God's expectations of you as a Christian in this world,' especially in relation to how to 'resolve issues and how people treat each other.'[30] Thus, embracing a Christian identity went beyond adhering to Church doctrines, embodied in, for example, attending weekly services and paying tithes. The women believed that their actions and behaviour must reflect that, indeed, they were followers of Christ. Thus, a significant aspect of the Christian identity is a belief in a call to serve. In essence, a Christian identity meant taking seriously the biblical principles of being 'thy brother's [and sister's] keeper'[31] as a true embodiment of God's love.

At the time of her interview in 2007, Beverly belonged to a predominantly white Anglican congregation whose members were largely middle to upper class. She served as the deputy warden, and worked to help the church include people from diverse racial and class backgrounds. She explained how a young priest approached her one day, expressing his desire to run a ministry for a working-class, primarily Caribbean community. She recalled the conversation:

'What do you mean, run a ministry?' And he said, 'Well, you know, we want to get them involved.' And I said, 'Well, unless you and the congregation can accept them fully and openly as parishioners, don't bother.'[32]

As an anti-racist advocate, Beverly's fight for equality and fairness for Blacks clearly extended beyond the political realm. She immediately saw the futility of extending an invitation to Caribbean people if it was based on superficial rather than genuine acceptance. The priest heeded Beverly's caution. In addition to ensuring that the church welcomed and valued members of the Caribbean community, he also implemented several children's programs, including an annual camp for children, summer barbecues, and Christmas programs. Beverly has remained involved with these programs, and they have become institutionalized within her church.

Betty – retired and with her children grown and living on their own – sought involvement in a religious community, which she found at the Verity Centre for Better Living in Toronto. In addition to attending weekly worship services, Betty pointed out:

I've also gone away to some conferences with my church. I went to one in Mexico and one in Puerto Rico, and one in the [United] States. My church has become an important part of my life in later years, more so than the earlier years.[33]

Other interviewees expressed similar sentiments. Even when they attended church regularly, time constraints prevented full participation in extracurricular religious activities, such as attending conferences. As a result of retirement, some of the women's activities in the church increased, and they took on a variety of roles, such as deaconesses or Sabbath school teachers.

Faith communities are not the only spaces in which Black women are actively involved, however. To meet their social needs, and as a response to their marginalization in Canadian society, Caribbean people have created numerous island community organizations. These organizations, regardless of the circumstances of their founding, can be viewed as a way of cementing the previously fluid and unstable Caribbean communities' presence and identities in Canada. The involvement of the interviewees in various organizations should also be read as an acceptance of Canada as home, however problematic that home may have remained.

When she discontinued her involvement with the nurses' union, Ancilla became involved with the Burlington Caribbean Connection (BCC), which was founded in the mid-1990s. Unlike the Jamaican Canadian Association (JCA), which serves a much larger constituency in Ontario and other provinces, the BCC serves a primarily local purpose, and has a slightly different agenda. The BCC provides scholarships and also raises funds to support local charitable causes. Although she started out as a volunteer, Ancilla had become president of the BCC at the time of her interview. She highlighted the organization's function and role in Burlington, including how she had benefited:

> It's been a very rewarding time for me in being involved in this group and working in the community. I've gotten to know so many people and actually representing the Caribbean community in Burlington. You actually have a voice, to the point where if something is going on the mayor's office and they want a point of view, they'll call me. Or, if somebody is having a function and they want to know something about somebody who could play the steel band or whatever, they'll call me. They think I should know. And I work very closely with the Burlington police. And trying to change that stereotype that, you know, the police hate all Black people, which is not really true.[34]

Ancilla found it significant that 'the Caribbean people are getting together and doing stuff.' As her remarks indicate, these women see themselves as making their mark, leaving a legacy – however small – behind.

Monica, Lillie, and Daphne B together have over seventy years of combined experience in the Jamaican Canadian Association. Formed in 1962, the primary goal of JCA was to acclimate newly arrived Jamaicans to Canada. The organization later expanded its vision and scope to include people of African descent in the Canadian diaspora. Monica's reason for becoming a member was 'because the [JCA] is supportive of Jamaicans.'[35] Lillie and Daphne B also concurred, pointing out what a resource JCA has been to various communities over the years since they have been in Canada. A few other women were also members of island-specific nursing organizations, such as the Barbados Nursing Association, where they volunteered their time when they could.

Of the thirty-five interviewees, two women from each cohort left nursing and founded organizations dedicated, respectively, to the arts and politics (broadly conceived). Vera migrated to Canada in 1960 and worked for twelve years as a registered nurse. She eventually left nursing, attributing her decision to the stark distinctions between the British and Canadian systems. Upon her resignation, Vera enrolled at Ryerson to study broadcasting and to pursue acting. The same 'love for people' that led Vera to seek a career as a nurse, in tandem with the absence of venues for young Black people to nurture their creative expression, was the impetus behind Black Theatre Canada (BTC).

The purpose behind BTC, Vera maintained, was for her to work with young people to 'learn about our culture and express it in a professional way.'[36] As the longest-running Black theatre group to date, BTC staged a total of thirteen productions since its inception,[37] as well as touring schools and running workshops. While BTC closed its doors in 1988, Vera's legacy continues to live on. Vera was one of the few Caribbean migrants in this study who unequivocally stated that she remained unperturbed by 'thoughts of home.' She welcomed venturing into uncharted territory, and found incredible fulfilment in her adopted home, which left no room for musings about Trinidad.

The faith and secular communities to which the women belonged allowed for times when their racial identification was subverted in favour of either a Christian identity or their island identification. In living their everyday lives, however, the women were often 'called upon to prioritize one aspect of their compound identities.'[38] How some of the interviewees negotiated and constructed their self-identification reveals how complex and dynamic the process remains.

Self-Identification: Black, White, or Both

In the Black Canadian-born cohort, both Dorothy R and Beverly Salmon are bi-racial and could certainly 'pass' for white. On the other hand, Virginia, Frieda, Eleanor, and Cathy are very light-skinned, and might have been able to pass for white, Italian, or Latina. Most of the other interviewees were, to use their terminology, fair-skinned; there was only one darker-skinned interviewee. In contrast, the majority of the Caribbean-born women interviewed were dark-skinned. Despite an acknowledgment of their multiracial background, those born in Canada identified as Black, an identity forged in early childhood. Whether they grew up in segregated, semi-segregated, or integrated communities, the message most of the women received from the public while they were growing up was that blackness and all that it embodied held negative connotations. Although they lived multifaceted lives and were also defined by their gender, class, religion, and age, whites generally viewed Black Canadians in essentialist terms. While racist ideologies relating to 'blackness' have been used to justify racial oppression, 'blackness' has also been used to instil a sense of pride in people and communities of colour. As Evelyn Higginbotham and others have pointed out, race often operates as a 'double-voiced' discourse – fortifying both racial subordination and racial affirmation and liberation.[39] Consequently, Higginbotham contends that, 'racial meanings were never internalized by Blacks and Whites in an identical way.'[40]

As a child of a Jamaican immigrant, Beverly remembered identifying herself as Jamaican because 'by law, up until I guess it was into the 1940s probably, your nationality was your father's birthplace.'[41] Higginbotham's analysis of race operating as a 'double-voiced' discourse is most relevant here. In recounting childhood memories, both Beverly and Dorothy R explicitly recalled incidents of racism. While Dorothy R remembered being ignored by other children during her elementary years,[42] Beverly felt humiliated 'reading *Little Black Sambo* with monkey-like characters.'[43] Both of these women could have sublimated their blackness, exclusively performing whiteness, or adopted an alternative racial identity, but they chose otherwise. Beverly explained:

> Even though I had a lot of things that made me feel ashamed, I always wanted people to know who I am, and I never tried to hide that. I knew exactly – like how my mother thought she was Irish after x-generations, I knew I was Black. And I would make sure people know that.[44]

Certainly, in response to white domination, Beverly could have capitalized on her bi-racial identity, and passed for white, especially where there was no physical bodily evidence that she could not be the latter.

Alternatively, these women also could have adopted other racial identities, as they and others had been identified upon occasion as Latina or Italian. Identifying as Black, rather than as bi-racial or another racial category, demonstrates the fluidity or precariousness of race, calling into question essentialist categorizations. Despite painful memories of growing up and the various instances of gendered racism experienced as adults, denying one's Black heritage was out of the question. As an act of resistance that is expressed as pride, identification with blackness offers a counter-narrative, which can be further conveyed in other ways besides skin colour.

Marriages across races and cultures led Virginia to insist that while she had to move within a number of communities, and while others might identify her as 'fair-skinned,' she identified herself as Black. Similarly, Cathy explained that there are 'a lot of whites in my family,' and that

'even though I don't half the time look like it' – that is, phenotypically
Black – her family discouraged her and her siblings from trying to pass
for white on grounds of legitimacy. 'You can't fool people, and you're
only fooling yourself,[45] Cathy maintained. Still, Cathy also recalled identifying as Negro, using the terminology of the 1950s. At the time of her
interview, she identified as Black Canadian, but often felt frustrated when
people assumed she came from elsewhere, presumably the Caribbean.
When people who tried to displace her and her ancestors from the imagined Canadian nation – or others simply interested in origins – would
ask, 'Where are you from?' Cathy would assert, 'Southern Ontario; a big,
Black and successful community.'[46]

Being at Home in Canada

Discussions of identity, belonging, and home are bound up with the historical construction of the Canadian nation. While the nation is socially
constituted and owes its continued development to various social, economic, and political processes, it too is fictionalized. Benedict Anderson
cautions that nations 'are imagined as limited because even the largest of them ... has finite if elastic boundaries, beyond which lie other
nations.'[47] In using the language of 'imagining,' theorists like Anderson
also understand that the nation is a 'real and objective entity' that divides
people in real ways. Historically, being 'Canadian' has been synonymous
with being white,[48] and despite attempts to make the nation inclusive,
an 'us and them' mentality continues to pervade nationalist discourses.

In this context, Caribbean interviewees offered varying testimonies as
to where and what constituted 'home.' Some suggested the idea of multiple homes: 'here,' in Canada and 'there,' somewhere in the Caribbean.
How these migrants self-identified was connected to where they considered home to be. Others defied ongoing racism, staking their claims
by calling Canada home, and identified as hyphenated Canadians. Still,
some Caribbean women (even those who had lived in Canada longer
than in their country of birth) retained a nostalgic and sometimes contradictory longing for home. Black Canadians, in contrast, although
peripheral in hegemonic discourse regarding the Canadian nation
(as evinced by Cathy's earlier statement), grounded their narratives of
belonging and home in their ancestors' struggle for social justice, and in
their very presence in Canada.

In *Home Girls*, Barbara Smith calls for a home space for Black wom-
en where 'it is above all a place to be ourselves,'[49] because, she contin-

ues, 'in the end, there is nothing more important to us than home.'[50] In expounding upon Smith's analysis of home, Madeline Ang-Lygate suggests that 'the focus given to exploring the notion of "home" lies so much not in the "place," although this is pertinent, but more so in the ways in which the homes we think we have left shaped us.'[51] I build on Ang-Lygate's analysis, by demonstrating how new homes (in this case Canada, and, to a lesser extent, Britain) remain critical in shaping and reshaping diasporic subjectivities. Length of stay, citizenship status, and contributions to the social, economic, and political life of the nation influence how some Caribbean-born women felt about Canada as home. Others continued to live in a liminal mode, or in Brenda's words, as a transient. Rinaldo Walcott explains that this ambivalence or exile status is conditioned 'by the plethora of national narratives from the idea of the "two founding peoples," to multicultural practices, to immigration policies, to provincial and policing practices and so on.'[52] These factors present at different times in the public discourse make it difficult for Black women to lay claims to the Canadian nation space as home.

If the encounter between the nation and immigrant produces alienation or intolerance, the notion of Canada as 'home' is not a safe place for Black women to be. This in turn intensifies the desire for Caribbean migrants to return to an original home, especially since many of the immigrants had not planned to stay when they emigrated. When June came to Canada in 1967, she had intended only to obtain a degree from McGill University and then to return to Jamaica. Soon after, she met the man she would marry, who insisted that they stay in Canada. She was reluctant, but after extensive discussion they reached a compromise. Once she had children they would return home – an agreement that, as with most immigrants, never came to fruition.[53]

Unlike other migrants who have successfully or even partially recreated a home away from the original homeland, June appeared to be 'living in displacement:'[54]

> Somebody asked 'how do you enjoy living in Canada' and I've always said, I've adjusted to living in Canada. I don't know if I've been able to truthfully say I've totally enjoyed it. By the time you really start to see yourself as living here, I was becoming very much aware of racism.[55]

Physically returning home, even when the desire is present, is not always feasible. Hence, many migrants are forced to come to terms with a permanent home that in many ways may not resemble the imagined home they left behind. I do not know whether June eventually returned to Jamaica permanently. At the time of her interview, she had already taken early retirement, and she felt uncertain as to whether she could live comfortably in Jamaica on her pension.

The intensification of globalization, Internet access to news of home, inexpensive flights to the Caribbean, the presence of Caribbean communities in certain enclaves in North America and Britain, transnational practices, such as maintaining citizenship – all of these factors impact not only how identities are constituted, but also how home is configured in the migrants' imagination. The opportunity to make periodic trips to Trinidad, in conjunction with memories (however contrived) of the past, allowed Brenda to compare and contrast living in Canada with her putative homeland. As she contemplated the meaning of home, Brenda echoed the point made earlier by Black feminist scholar Barbara Smith:

> [It's] a place where you feel comfortable, at home and at ease. I feel comfortable here [Canada] to a certain point; when I go back home, I'm myself again; I think people accept me a little bit more. I feel comfortable when I'm home because that is where I was born and bred. I'm used to the people there, they are used to you, and I'm used to the culture. It's such a more relaxed feeling when I hit the ground back home.[56]

For Brenda, shared culture, acceptance, and the ability to feel comfortable and 'at ease' determined what home is and where it could be. As in June's case, Brenda's notions of home subsequently determined her relationship to the wider Canadian society.

Unlike Brenda, Inez wrestled less with the idea of Canada as home, but more with identifying as *Canadian*. She chose instead to identify as Jamaican, which is not all that unusual given that, for a number of Caribbean people, their respective islands remain critical to their self-definition:

> I can never change to be Canadian; I will always be a Jamaican. Although I have lived in this country all these years, I don't feel I am a part of this country. Maybe I had to be born here to give me that feeling of being Canadian. I am just a Canadian on paper. I live my life here; it has been a fantastic country. I work hard, they pay me. I have my kids, and I can educate them, I get involved in community, church, the homeless, and everything, but there is something about me that I don't feel I am a true Canadian. There is something about the culture.[57]

Inez fixed her identity as Jamaican as opposed to Jamaican Canadian, and had difficulty inscribing her presence on the Canadian landscape and feeling that she belonged.

Inez further acknowledged her contributions to Canadian society, pointing to her involvement in charitable work and social activism, which can be construed as symbolic of being a good Canadian citizen. Inez's and June's tentativeness and concern about being able to 'fit in' could be attributed to their search for '"rootedness" a sense of historical "belonging." This, in turn relates to their historical experience of social displacement and rootlessness grounded in the slave experience and colonization.'[58]

Inasmuch as Inez and others emphasized the rewards gained by living in Canada, they understood especially as they grew older that this relationship operated reciprocally. That is, Canada has benefited from their presence, and as result, some of these women identified as Canadians, even if they did so tentatively. Ancilla remarked: 'I've seen progress. I now can probably call myself a Canadian, because I am part of the society. And I can safely say I helped to mould some of that, you know, leave my mark behind.'[59] Interestingly, while Ancilla is Indo-Trinidadian, she identifies as Black or Caribbean. Here, she persuasively explained why:

> In this country, we're all Black. As long as your skin isn't white, you're Black. I refer to myself as Black because I am Black. I'm not white. I'm not Caucasian white. So, I'm Black. Because nobody on the street will differentiate between myself and you; we're walking down the road, and, it's 'Blackies.'[60]

Although identities are fluid, and although people occupy multiple locations that influence their identifications, this process remains highly mediated. In response to the politics of racialization in Canada, and to the inaccurate perception of the Caribbean as comprised primarily of people of African descent, Ancilla jettisoned certain aspects of her racial identity. With respect to her Indian roots, Ancilla pointed out 'I don't dwell on that.' When mistaken for being South Asian, which occurred on a regular basis, she would reply, 'I talk to them. I say, "No, I'm not from your part of the world. I'm from the Caribbean."'[61] Ancilla's ethnic identity was subsumed in favour of a pan-Caribbean one, as reflected in her work with the Burlington Caribbean Connection.

Since identities are always in process and constantly under construction, it is safe to say that the women in this study, in the course of everyday routines, did not always hold feelings of not belonging at the centre of their consciousness. Rather, such feelings came to the fore in specific situations. Like Vera, some other interviewees expressed little concern for their attachments to their respective homelands. Others constructed their identity in relation to their original homes or recreated communities as alternative home spaces. Some of the women's engagement in transnational practices also played a role in how their identities were constituted.

Claiming Canada as Home

Ongoing connections with their original homes, dual citizenship status, length of time in Canada, families and extended kin, all made the desire of a permanent return home less urgent for some of the Caribbean-born interviewees. Interviewees who had returned to their respective islands at the completion of their training back in the early 1960s found that they had outgrown home. Their travels to Britain and other parts of the United Kingdom made the small islands they migrated from appear much smaller, and more confining. Having trained, worked, and socialized with people from a variety of cultures, these women wanted a more expansive view of the world. Jennette's comment that 'migration has changed me, it has made me a bit more global and less insular,'[62] encapsulates the general response. These newly returned migrants had changed, grown up, or matured. During their sojourns overseas, they had also contributed, however minimally, to the hospitals where they were employed. Of their own volition, a few of these women uprooted and left their homes of origin a second time with virtually no consideration of potential loss, or feelings of not belonging.

Like Muriel, Vera too had returned to Trinidad from Britain and subsequently migrated to Canada. Having lived away from Trinidad for most of her adult life, she identified Canada as home:

> I have grown tremendously as a person and this country, it has been good to me. I've never let the thought of home disturb me. A lot of people say they just came to this country for five years, and they are going home. I never said that because I'm cool. I can hang out wherever I have to. I went into the arts, and then sold mutual funds successfully for five years.[63]

Eileen, Muriel, and Joan, all from Barbados, expressed a similar reaction to Vera about returning home permanently, albeit with varying rationales. Besides her own self-confidence, the fact that Vera refused to allow the 'thought of home' to unsettle her could be traced to other dynamics beyond her involvement with Black Theatre Canada.

These women successfully navigated the particularities of Canadian society, where at present the focus is on *here*, in reference to Canada, and less about *there*, the homes they left behind. Moreover, with increased Caribbean migration, these interviewees gained access to the Caribbean. Whether through other migrants, or the importation of cultural products such as food, religion, organizations, and businesses, migrants can experience the Caribbean in Canada, albeit in a fragmented form. Frequent visits to 'return home,' even if these visits are intermittent, constitute one of many examples of transnationalism, defined as 'the processes by which immigrants forge and sustain multi-stranded social relations that link together their societies of origin and settlement.'[64]

Eileen admitted that she had never really entertained thoughts of returning to Barbados permanently:

There are some things I like about Canada and there are some things I don't like, but I made a choice to live here. Canada is my first home; it's where my husband lives, where I work, all the things that make up home (with the exception of not having blood relatives) are here.[65]

Connecting identity to place remains an incomplete process, even when articulated as such. Diasporas require their inhabitants to engage in ongoing identity negotiations, which are both global and local. For example, depending on the context – or, as Muriel phrased it, 'who I'm talking to'[66] – the interviewees selectively chose their identifications, whether in their original island homeland or Canada. Both those who settle elsewhere and the people they leave behind simultaneously engage in identity construction. However much Caribbean migrants want to claim some form of legitimate identity in relation to the various islands from which they migrated, this is not always possible. Whether they come to the islands on vacation or as return migrants, those who have settled elsewhere are rarely viewed as 'authentic' inhabitants, and sometimes face envy and outright derision.

On the other hand, migrants such as Jennette expressed disdain for the people in the homeland (family exempted), but not to the extent that she refrained from visiting. Here is her justification:

I can't spend much time in Antigua these days. I get very irritated with the people. I can hang out with them for brief periods. Antigua has changed so much for the negative. They are too focused on people's business and who has what. They used to always look outwards. They used to listen to news from all over the world, there was no TV, just radio, but there was always this interest in what was happening elsewhere and a desire to be part of it and to get out and so on. I don't see that now in Antigua. It's just having a bigger house or better car, and this sort of thing. It's a very sad place.[67]

Diasporic relationships remain contested and complicated, and they manifest in a variety of ways. Jennette's unreserved critique of Antiguans could also be reciprocated by the very same people she criticized, who view migrants like her as mere 'foreigners,' people who left long ago and who no longer have a basis on which to identify with these places or to call them home.

The fluidity of cultural identities also becomes visible when Caribbean migrants attempt to reclaim their island identification at specific moments during visits back home. Muriel explained: 'When I get back to the airport in Barbados, or some person is trying to rip me off, they soon know that I'm as Barbardian as they are.'[68] Still, with children and grandchildren in Canada, with family members 'who come and go from Barbados,' and with her own regular visits, leaving Canada was not an option that Muriel entertained: 'I go there, and it's nice, I enjoy it while I'm there, but when the time comes, I need to get back home. It's here [Canada].'[69] Joan, on the other hand, stated that she was both 'Bajan [the colloquial term for Barbadian] and Canadian.' In the same breath, Joan added that her sisters often insisted she was more Canadian than 'Bajan.' After giving it some thought, Joan admitted that she concurred with her sisters.[70] This proclivity for Caribbean-born interviewees to identify as hyphenated Canadians could be a direct result of Canada's multicultural policy. According to Lloyd Wong and Vic Satzewich, 'there has been a greater emphasis on encouraging immigrants to engage in transnational social practices and to develop transnational identities.'[71] Regardless, discourses of displacement and liminality, coupled with nostalgic longing for 'back home' have rarely preoccupied Muriel, Vera, Eileen, Jennette, or Joan while living in the Black Canadian diaspora.

It is worth emphasizing that for the women mentioned above, feelings of belonging and the ability to claim Canada as home took time to solidify. Upon migration, all of them experienced some degree of dislocation, especially in reference to working in Canada, where questions around professional qualifications reinforced their outsider status. To truly belong, Eileen and others exercised their own agency by choosing to adapt to or reject certain values and ideas from their own individual islands and from Canada's multicultural society, according to their needs. They incorporated remnants of their Caribbean culture, such as food, into Canadian culture, creating a synthesis that was beneficial to them. Yet even for those women who continued to experience feelings of not belonging, such feelings are never consistent.

Indeed, these uncertainties about home, identity, and belonging reflect the complicated and contradictory nature of identity. As Jonathan Rutherford surmises, 'there are no ready-made identities or categories that we can unproblematically slip into.'[72] Since their arrival in Canada, these women have negotiated and continue to negotiate, at times living in the in-between in order to survive. Even so, other interviewees engaged in transnational practices, exemplified most notably by the dual citizenship status that some of these women maintained, their long distance relationships with relatives and extended kin, and their remittances of currency and other non-monetary goods.

Caribbean Interviewees and Transnational Practices

Despite an ongoing policy debate regarding remittances and whether this practice assists or impinges on Caribbean development, families, including extended kin, benefit tremendously from this practice. Kezia Page suggests that 'indeed the concept of the remittance, money sent by post and the act of sending money, and other nonmonetary transfers that engage this sender-receiver dynamic, may be part of what James Clifford terms diasporist discourse.'[73] According to Clifford, 'Diasporic discourses reflect the sense of being part of an ongoing transnational network that includes the homeland not as something simply left behind but as a place of attachment in a contrapuntal modernity.'[74] Most of the interviewees for this study had been the first (along with other siblings) in their families to migrate. Consequently, each woman left some family members behind. In addition to wanting to fulfil their own dreams of becoming professional women, they also wanted to succeed in order to assist family members back home. For instance, until her son migrated to Canada at the age of nineteen, Daphne B sent remittances on a regular basis, which included money to pay for his college education, pointing out proudly that 'he's done very well.'[75]

Like Daphne B, Jennette and Joan also provided crucial monetary support to sponsor various family members to migrate to Canada. Families (including parents), many of whom refused to migrate, have benefited from financial support and other goods. As a result of remittances, land has been bought and houses built, renovated, expanded, and furnished; vehicles purchased; children educated; medical assistance made available; and funeral expenses paid. Other interviewees contributed time and money to a variety of island-related organizations in Canada. For example, some of the women contributed to hurricane funds for their respective islands in the aftermath of devastation. The fact that they grew up in a culture where the collective remained important – and where sharing and helping were crucial – made it imperative to continue this legacy even though home was elsewhere.

Despite minimal salaries during their training, Caribbean migrants remained committed to sending money home to their parents. In Ancilla's case, her father had to repay the money he borrowed for her trip to England, which she contributed to. With full-time and steady jobs, the women sent money and gifts first to their parents, and later to nieces, nephews, and other family members.[76] As with the other interviewees, Carmencita continued to make regular trips to Trinidad. She confessed: 'Sometimes I miss having a lot of Black people with me and I miss my family, I miss my community.'[77] Despite these desires, Carmencita evaluated how her family had benefited from her living in an industrialized country, thus she refrained from dreaming about returning to Trinidad. 'You can't have it both ways; you take the best from everything,' she added. In addition to sending money home on a regular basis, Carmencita assisted one of her sisters who needed medical attention, by paying for a visit to Toronto and absorbing the expenses incurred.[78]

On many levels these transitional practices are not unique to Carmencita, or to the other women, but remain typical among Caribbean migrants who continue to identify with their homelands. In contrast, Black Canadians' identities remain deeply rooted in a sense of belonging to the Canadian nation state.

Community, Home, and Belonging for Black Canadians

Black Canadian-born interviewees recognized that, in some instances, they had been erased from the Canadian landscape, their presence having at times been replaced by that of Caribbean people. While some Caribbean nurses spoke of displacement, of not belonging, or of focusing on home in another place, Black Canadians experienced a symbolic form of displacement – that is, a lack of acknowledgment by the wider Canadian society of their contributions and presence. Naomi pointed out: 'I think there's so much that Black Canadians have done that hasn't been exposed. We've sort of been kept in the dark, in a corner.'[79] In contrast to official discourses that place Black Canadians outside of, or peripheral to, the nation, the women's own narratives positioned them as *inside*, and as critical to Canada's development. Indeed, Black Canadian-ness requires constant negotiation. This negotiation began with the women's ancestors, who came to the north as free Blacks, fugitives, and former slaves, and who made Canada home regardless of how unwelcome they may have felt.

In their attempts to situate themselves firmly within the Canadian nation, and to claim Canada as their home space, Black Canadians to a certain extent rely on what Jacqueline Nassy Brown also refers to as 'diasporic resources.' According to Brown, these 'may include not just cultural production, such as music, but people and places, as well as iconography, ideas and ideologies associated with them.'[80] In this case, the term refers to Black Canadians' abilities to trace their family genealogies, to identify people and places, and to recognize their ancestors' struggle for social justice. These diasporic resources are not necessarily generated from personal memories – that is, directly from the women's experience – but rather from external sources such as family members, historical documents (i.e., newspapers, letters), and even museums.

Growing up, Cathy recalled how proud she was made to feel of the 'big successful Black community' in Chatham, Ontario. 'We fought hard,' she continued. 'I tell some of the West Indians, they think it was a hop and a skip here; it hasn't been.' Cathy felt that Caribbean people should recognize and acknowledge Black Canadians and their resistance against injustice. In so doing, they would avoid being complicit with the myth that the Black Canadian diaspora began with their arrival.[81] Evoking Black communities means simultaneously bringing to the fore individuals and organizations that had proved critical to challenging racism. Virginia grew up in Dresden, Ontario, a town that was often referred to as the 'Dixie of the North' because of its similarity to the southern United States. Similar to at least four other interviewees, Virginia had family members who had enlisted in both world wars. These two conflicts, especially the Second World War, became the thrust behind Black Canadian involvement in organizing for social change, just as it did for their African American counterparts. Virginia underscored the blatant paradox of fighting for freedom abroad while being denied it at home:

My brother was in the Second World War. My father served overseas in

World War I, with the Number Two Construction Unit [Second Construction Battalion] in France, Germany and Belgium … There were people who just felt that if the veterans had served in both world wars and their children were going to receive appropriate public education, which was supposed to be available, and then there needed to be something done about public accommodations.[82]

Subsequently, Virginia's brother and father joined the National Unity Association of Dresden, an interracial antiracist organization, which joined with other organizations committed to social justice.

Other interviewees mentioned their family members' union involvement and political involvement in the Brotherhood of Sleeping Car Porters and the United Negro Improvement Association (UNIA). Betty's father served as an executive member of the Brotherhood of Sleeping Car Porters, and Darlene's father also maintained an active membership. Similarly, Edna's father, Joe Bailey, while he was not born in Canada, had once served as president of the UNIA. According to Edna, her father once wrote to Prime Minister Mackenzie King when his daughters, Ruth and Doris Bailey, had both been refused nurses' training in Ontario.[83] As they recounted their families' participation in these organizations, the interviewees repeatedly demonstrated how the core of their activism was informed simultaneously by their belief in equality and by their sense of belonging to the Canadian nation.

Along with the memories passed down though the generations, personal pictures, letters, newspaper articles, and other mementos served as additional diasporic resources that Black Canadian-born interviewees used to insert themselves within national histories. Dorothy R's father, inspired by Marcus Garvey (whom he once met), instilled in his children contempt for injustice, the value of activism, and the importance of valuing themselves regardless of how they were viewed by society.[84]

Similar to Virginia, Dorothy R's father, James, and two brothers served in both world wars. In fact, Dorothy lost both her brothers, one in combat and another from suicide related to his experience in the army.[85] James Richards often wrote letters to government bodies and newspapers, decrying Canadian racism and how it conditioned Black people's treatment. In a letter to the *Windsor Star*, written in the 1940s, he wrote: 'Sir, I fought in the last war to protect the so-called rights of democracy and today, 20 years later certain companies have the audacity to return my money for a month's rent after paying a deposit down just because they would not allow coloured people in their houses. I always understood Canada as a Christian country, and British country with liberty.'[86] As a father whose sons exemplified the ideals of good citizenship by putting their lives on the line for Canada, and based on his own membership in the Royal Navy Reserve, James Richards demanded the right to be treated with respect. Evoking his status as a Canadian citizen and British subject, Mr Richards based his definition of citizenship on who he was, where he belonged, where he came from, and how he understood himself in the world.[87] Dorothy R emulated her father's tenacity, sense of fairness, and commitment to equality when she worked at Mount Carmel Hospital in Detroit.

At the time of her interview, Dorothy R resided in Detroit, and had obtained dual citizenship, a marker of transnationalism in practice. Because she had lived in the United States for over four decades, Dorothy's grandchildren insisted that she revoke her Canadian citizenship. This is how she explained her dual citizenship status and her feelings of being more Canadian than American:

> I was born in one place. I like the place where I was born. But I live over here, and I like living over here, and I'm not an American, not really … because I was born in Canada. I'm more Canadian. I get a little more conservative than Americans. I think sometimes Americans push themselves out too much. [They] want to be seen, want to be known.[88]

Dorothy R's identification as Canadian was not only a result of how she constructed herself relative to Americans in general. As for her father, James Richards, for Dorothy R, too, Canada is home.

In referring to the Black community in Windsor, Frieda insisted that 'the community contributed to us, it influenced me.' Frieda's father, Alton C. Parker, held an influential position in this community. According to Frieda, her 'father had always been an activist,' and his activism spanned decades. A former president of the Central Citizens Association, later 'reconstituted as the Central Citizens Association for the Advancement of Coloured People,'[89] Mr Parker worked to transform the material, social, and political reality of Blacks in Windsor. Frieda recalled that one objective of the organization was to bring attention to the underrepresentation of Black civic employees in the city of Windsor by petitioning 'city fathers to end discriminatory hiring practices.'[90] As a result of his activism and community work, Parker received numerous awards and honours, including the Order of Canada, Harry Jerome Award, and an honourary Doctor of Jurisprudence from the University of Windsor.

Retirement did not suspend Parker's commitment to community. For twenty-five years, Frieda's father and his wife Evelyn organized 'Uncle Al's Annual Kids' Party' for children. In 1976, as a tribute to his civic and community activism, the Alton Parker Park was named in Frieda's father's honour. In Frieda's living room hangs the picture of the statue of her father (Alton Parker was Windsor's first Black police officer) standing in a park holding the hand of a child. The statue of Parker is inscribed with his own words: 'A lot of people talk about doing something for these kids. I don't just talk. I want to do it.'[91] The park, which is close to her parents' house, currently occupied by Frieda, is located near the 400 block of Broadhead Street in Windsor.

Outside of churches and some schools, iconographies (such as the Parker's statue) representing and memorializing Black Canada remain rare. Aspects of Black Canadian presence have been erased, through, for example, the demolition of Africville, and the renaming of Negro Creek Road, in Holland Township, Ontario.[92] Consequently, on one level Parker's statue indicates the solidification of Canada as home, for Frieda, her descendants, and other Black people. On another level, the statue may reflect an attempt to rewrite Windsor's – and, by extension, Canada's – history by acknowledging that, indeed, Black Canadians deserve a place in the nation's historical record.

Black Canadians' use of family patrimony – such as Frieda's current home, which has been inherited from earlier generations, knowledge of family genealogies, personal pictures, letters, and other mementos – cement Canada as home, while at the same time destabilizing Canada's national narratives. Agnes told the story of her great-grandfather, George Albert Scott, a slave who escaped from Raleigh, North Carolina, and came to Canada via the Underground Railroad. Versed in her family's genealogy in Maidstone Township, Ontario, with pictures to corroborate the story, Agnes summarized:

They came to Canada with one son; he was about a year old, John Scott. Ferbie Ann was a dark woman. George Albert was a fair man. A white woman came across, and they pretended the baby was her baby, and Ferbie Ann was the servant. They snuck across the border and got here into Maidstone Township, right down here. They lived there all their lives, and then they had 10 children ... My dad's family Henry Scott had 16 children, and at one point he had the largest family in Essex County.[93]

Agnes also lamented how little of Black Canadian history is available, even though times had changed since she began working in Detroit in the mid-1950s. Whenever she confronted questions about her presence in Canada, Agnes would recite the story of her family escaping via the Underground Railroad, emphasizing that 'we have been here a long time.' Generations later, Agnes, her children, and grandchildren children reside in Maidstone Township. This is not to suggest that there were moments when Black Canadians did not and still do continue to feel marginalized in ways that are similar to their Caribbean counterparts. Their sense of belonging, however, remains much stronger.

Conclusion

Historian Mary Chamberlain points out that 'on the ground, migrant lives are also quite prosaic, concerned with the daily round of work, home and family, as well as developing and adapting older cultural patterns and social formations, creating a new syncretic Caribbean culture abroad.'[94] The narratives of the women in this study provide a window into how diasporic identities and experiences remain multilayered and constituted within and by various institutions, as well as by larger political, social, and economic forces. These nurses' realities encompass a whole range of experiences that influenced not only how they saw themselves but also their families, their communities, and their place within Canadian society. The Caribbean- and Black Canadian-born nurses in this study shared similar diasporic experiences based on their identification as Black women. Even though the Black Canadian presence remains virtually absent from mainstream discourse, these women articulated a counter-narrative that placed them not on the margins but at the centre of Canadian history and development. Similarly, while Caribbean nurses struggled with belonging in Canada because of the hegemonic construction of Canada as white, they continued to build their own lives and to define themselves in ways that can be considered counter-hegemonic.

Conclusion

This book posits that Caribbean- and Black Canadian-born women's interpretations and explanations of their realities were fashioned over time from the residues of childhood, inescapable transitions, and the variegated forms of racialized, classed, and gendered oppression that they encountered as girls and women. Consequently, I employed the life-course paradigm (in conjunction with oral interviews), which underscores the transformations that occur in human lives over time. This approach allows for nuanced and varied articulations of subjectivity and identity formation. The subjectivities of these thirty-five Black women (most of whom are still living) have been and continue to be shaped most notably by their race, gender, socioeconomic status, sexuality, and age. Additionally, the women's upbringing, education, migration, and status as married or single, with or without children, must be considered in conjunction with the aforementioned markers. Equally pertinent are the interviewees' personal ambitions, predispositions, and goals in shaping who they became, and who they strive to be. Despite their heterogeneity, these women constructed narratives, however contradictory, that challenge, build on, and support feminist, Black diasporic, and postcolonial theoretical formulations.

Scholars often explore Black women's subjectivities and identities from the vantage point of adulthood and the women's concomitant victimization at the hands of dominating systems of oppression. In contrast, my decision to engage with the premise of 'Black women's subjectivity as a migratory subjectivity existing in multiple locations'[1] meant beginning with the interviewees' recollections of their childhood. Notwithstanding, the memories that the women described were essentially those of an *idealized* childhood, which for some of the interviewees is consistent with what Jean Peneff describes as the poor but happy childhood.[2] Caribbean interviewees generally discussed their childhood as carefree and fun, a period devoid of the social ills that plague contemporary families. Most of the Black Canadians even if they described their childhood as fun recognized early in childhood that their experiences were shaped by race and socioeconomic status. However, both groups bore similarities to each other in the futures that their parents imagined for their children and the steps they took to make those futures a reality.

In addition to imparting certain morals and values to guide their children, the parents stressed the pursuit of education as a sure-fire route to upward mobility or to maintain social and class status. An exploration of the particularities of growing up in the English-speaking Caribbean (including Guyana) and in Canada reveals how experiences, both constructive and harmful, within the family, church, and school subsequently helped the women to navigate the multiple spaces that they occupied as adults. Equally significantly, these contested sites – which do not function in a vacuum – often unintentionally or inadvertently contributed to producing adolescents, teenagers, and women who, over time, showed much self-determination, courage, and ambition.

As one of many transitions, migration often prompts a reconstitution of subjectivity and identity. The fact that the majority of the Caribbean interviewees migrated to Great Britain as teenagers – often alone, and sometimes without familial support or social networks – provides some clues into their personalities. There was no one monolithic account of how young Caribbean migrants experienced Britain. Some were excited, others were bewildered, but all experienced a level of homesickness and loneliness. Still, the latter reactions were momentary. In periods of uncertainty, young Caribbean women would refocus on their rationale for migrating. In conjunction with figuring out how to navigate their new environment, the young women explored and discovered facets of themselves which led to a reconstruction of their identities. In Britain, they went from being connected to and identified in relation to their families, social class, and a particular geographical location, to being West Indian or Black. In addition, their nurses' training provided another avenue to develop a professional identity.

Caribbean migrants were not the only interviewees to cross borders, or whose identities had been reconfigured as a result of multiple migrations. Black Canadians in and near Windsor, Ontario, often visited Detroit, Michigan, as children, either to see relatives or to participate in leisure activities. As a new graduate, however, Agnes chose to live in Maidstone Township, and to travel across the border at Detroit daily for over forty years, because of the lack of recognition of Black nurses in Windsor. In Detroit, working with African Americans, Agnes felt affirmed and validated. That she was Black Canadian meant little to her colleagues, a gesture that demonstrates the fluidity of identity. In fact, being trained in Canada gave Agnes an advantage over her African American counterparts who valued her 'foreign' training.

The majority of interviewees arrived in Ontario around 1960, when the Caribbean population was relatively small, and the Black Canadian population was scattered throughout southern Ontario. While specific legal and informal prohibitions forbade Blacks to own property, to eat in certain restaurants, or to use certain public facilities were; less flagrant, institutional and everyday forms of oppression also remained apparent. In the context of late 1950s and 1960s Canada, blackness for some white Canadians signified the inability to assimilate, despite the presence of Black Canadians on the nation's soil. Some of the interviewees for this study recalled having difficulties procuring rental accommodations, and Lillie mentioned being denied a car loan at a large Canadian bank. These racist encounters hardly came as a surprise to the Black Canadian-born interviewees, who often envisioned themselves as outside of the Canadian nation. Attuned to this invisibility, Black Canadians repeatedly asserted their ancestors' presence within Canada's genealogy by highlighting their participation in the struggle for equality. In essence, these interviewees declared that by virtue of their history, they had a right to claim Canada as home and to assert a Canadian identity, even one that had been diminished by racism. Moreover, this gesture of resurrecting their ancestors also worked to decentre the role of Caribbean migrants, who are often valorized as the voice of civil rights in Canada. Some interviewees voiced the opinion that Caribbean migrants participated in eliding the Black Canadian presence. To avoid this penchant for subjugating Black Canadian existence, I sought to include Black Canadian-born women's voices in this book.

Another aim of this book was to examine the experiences of the two groups of women with the hopes of deconstructing monolithic constructions of Black womanhood. The difference between Black Canadian-born and Caribbean-born women's experiences is particularly apparent in their responses to the sociohistorical specificity of race and racism in constructing their identity. Growing up, Black Canadians were shaped by first-hand experiences of racial subordination within public and institutional spaces such as schools and churches. The women's status as children did not always offer protection, and many spent their adolescence dealing with the psychological assault of racism. Beverly, Dorothy R, Cathy, and Virginia all discussed the manifold impact of racism as contributing to low self-esteem. Race and colour were embedded in the structure of the colonial Caribbean, yet only three interviewees acknowledged this manifestation, and only to a certain degree. It is upon migration to Britain and Canada that they encountered a gendered and racialized social structure where they were rarely seen as equals. That is, they bore witness to and experienced gendered and racialized subjugation in a manner that was linked to their presumed inferiority, something that they had not experienced while growing up in the Caribbean. As these examples demonstrate, attention to childhood memories, however fractured, helps to explain how the interviewees negotiated their *adult* lives.

These women's instantiations of gendered racism and its myriad effects point to the importance of race and gender and how they operate in various contexts. How race and gender interfaced to shape Caribbean interviewees' realities was not immediately self-evident. It took a while for some of the women to identify episodes of gendered racism, and even then they questioned whether their suppositions were accurate. Consequently, Black women deployed multiple strategies to deal with gendered racism.

Hoping to dispel any racist and sexist stereotypes, Black women, whether students or workers, often performed submissively while working hard. Except for one, all the Black Canadian-born interviewees entered nurses' training fully cognizant of Black nurses' exclusion from the occupation. Caribbean interviewees, on the other hand, learned over time how racism and sexism often operated to their detriment. Consequently, Black nurses insisted that they be objectively evaluated on their professional skills, education, and experience, as opposed to being subjectively judged on the basis of their gender and race. Insisting that supervisors, patients, and other medical personnel look beyond race, and focus instead on experience and skills, cannot be construed as a rejection of blackness, but rather as an act of subversion.

As health care workers, the interviewees resigned from hospitals, changed wards, pursued additional educational qualifications when necessary, spoke out against inequality, took legal measures, offered other explanations for racist/sexist behaviours, and forged alliances with non-Black nurses. The latter is especially relevant considering the lack of scholarly attention given to interracial relationships in nursing. The tendency has been to focus on affiliations that are fraught with tensions.

Indeed, Black health care workers could never escape the constraints imposed upon them because of their race and gender. Furthermore, white nurses, and the medical profession overall, remained invested in maintaining white privilege and dominance. In spite of this, Black nurses sometimes forged supportive and meaningful relationships with whites and other nurses of colour. If nothing else, the women generally shared the gendered ideals on which nursing was predicated.

The interviewees' sense of agency was not only visible in how they managed and negotiated their work lives, but also with respect to their personal lives. One example of this is the ingenuity demonstrated by some of the interviewees in their heterosexual relationships, especially those that eventually led to divorce. Choosing to legally separate was an unconventional option during the 1960s and early 1970s. Besides the stigma associated with divorce, the absence of a second income was a major concern, especially when children were involved. Still, Frieda and Cathy left their husbands, responding to the contingencies of their new-found freedom with creative strategies. In Cathy's case she recalled times in her childhood when her family was able to survive on very little, and she drew strength from that knowledge. These women had no intentions of reinforcing the image of the self-sacrificing Black woman who put her partner's needs above her own. Leaving unhealthy relationships was based partly on the need to protect mind, body, spirit, and children.

In a culture where heterosexual coupling is the norm, a few of the interviewees chose to remain single and childless, stressing familial connections as equally important than those of a long-term monogamous union. Although she had received marriage proposals, Lillie pointed out that 'by and large, men don't like their women to be independent.'[3] She eventually concluded that her strong-willed personality might have been a deterrent to a long-term conjugal partnership. None of these women expressed regret that they had remained unmarried and had no biological offspring of their own. From their viewpoint, family was not restricted to a nuclear form. For example, when asked about children of her own, Jennette mentioned her nieces and nephews, suggesting that she sometimes played the role of what scholars such as Patricia Hill Collins identify as 'othermother.' Others mentioned close connections with family and even friends. Indeed, Lillie and Jennette's reactions testify powerfully to another aspect of Black womanhood, in which one's identity is not linked to that of mother and wife.

Another objective of the book was to draw attention to the diversity and complexity of Black women's lives. It is clear that race, gender, socioeconomic status, religion, and age are imbricated in subjectivity formation. Yet, these operate in conjunction with other variables, such as marital or parenting status. Despite the differences that existed between some of the women, one commonality the majority shared was their activism, which included but was not limited to community work and volunteerism.

Whatever forms their activism took, the interviewees displayed an unwavering desire to look beyond the individual self and work to 'uplift' the Black community. This desire motivated Daphne C to establish the Immigrant Women's Centre, providing support to Caribbean domestic workers. Likewise, Betty acted as a mentor in the Leadership for Today Program for Black youth. The role of family and church in the politicization of some of the interviewees is also evident. Growing up, their parents modelled and instilled in their children the principle of the collective versus the individual. They were taught to empathize with those whose lives were encumbered by poverty and other social ills. Lillie explained: 'I come from a family that believes in teaching, and a family that believes in community. We believe that every person has a purpose here. We believe in giving, for in giving you get.'[4] To underscore the significance of the preceding explanation, Lillie asked:

> 'Who is thy neighbour?' to which she responded, 'Everybody.' Not only the person next door, but all people, that is not an easy thing to strive for. To love people and not be judgmental, and just because people are poor does not mean you can't talk to them.[5]

These biblical principles demonstrate the extent to which the oft-repeated admonition to 'Love thy neighbour as thyself' became embedded in the activism of the interviewees, and illustrates how their upbringing encouraged them to act in accordance with their Christian values.

Black women's activism is complicated and layered. Thus, the way the women defined their professional identities as nurses – particularly the priority they placed on their patients' well-being – represents one dimension of activism. For example, Dorothy R admitted to doing 'a little conniving work' as she recalled medicating Black women in labour to prevent them from being removed from Mount Carmel Mercy Hospital in Detroit. Dorothy R explained that she 'had to be cagey about it.' On the one hand, she safeguarded the lives of vulnerable women, but on the other hand, Dorothy R fought against the practice of segregation. As this example shows, Black women defied institutional restrictions when necessary, and sometimes suffered the consequences in the interest of their patients, or their own well-being.

Working in predominantly white spaces, Black women's race and gender, in conjunction with other factors, sometimes made it difficult for them to cross social class, race, and cultural lines. Yet, in their commitment to providing the best possible care for their patients, they also overlooked various boundaries. As midwives and public health nurses, Beverly and Daphne C reserved judgments about patients who sometimes lived in less than desirable conditions, focusing instead on the tasks that they were commissioned to do as nurses. In the case of their working-class counterparts relegated to the bottom of the hospital hierarchy, Black women in leadership positions offered encouragement, support, and assistance. As supervisors, Black women expressed pride in downplaying the discrete boundaries that divided health care practitioners according to education, experience, and skills. As registered nurses, it was not beneath the women to assume the tasks of nurses' assistants, for example. This principled refusal to take advantage of their higher status, which is tied to Black women's professional identity, could be easily overlooked by attention to other, more apparent, forms of activism.

At the core of theorizing about Black women's lives is the centrality of race, class, gender – and, to a lesser extent, sexuality – as interconnected and mutually reinforcing vectors shaping Black women's subjectivities. Throughout this book, however, it is clear that other markers such as religion, age, education, and migration also impacted the women's subjectivities as students, nurses, wives, mothers, and single women. For example, both groups of women embodied a religious ethos, with varying levels of intensity in terms of applicability and practice. Whether located in the Caribbean or in Canada, the church remained the mainstay of social and spiritual activities, although it also defined the role of women and girls, using religion as a tool of social control. Still, the church helped to shape the social world of the interviewees as they were growing up. It was in church that Black girls learned about a God who treated all human beings equally and about the importance of faith and love. Caribbean interviewees recalled participating in community-related activities for those who were less fortunate. Black Canadians, especially those who belonged to Black congregations, recalled how their church nurtured their talents. As adults, most of the interviewees continued to draw on these spiritual and religious traditions in all spheres of their lives. Religious principles underpinned and influenced how some of the women responded to gendered racism at work. Concern for the elderly, forgiveness, and treating others as one would like to be treated in turn, had been inculcated in the women while they were growing up, and these values continued to guide their activism as adults.

Moreover, religious and spiritual beliefs, in conjunction with the women's own tenacity and courage, proved helpful when they experienced life's imminent transitions, such as death, illnesses, and divorce. As they faced the pain associated with life transitions, some of the women found solace in their church, biblical scriptures, hymns, and songs. Indeed, some remembered the popular verse from Psalm 30: 'Weeping may endure for a night, but joy comes in the morning.'[6] Steeped in this tradition of finding strength, some of the interviewees could articulate the anguish that they experienced with various transitions; therefore, tears were not uncommon during some of the interviews. As Black women articulated, for example, the unbearable pain and depression that accompanied the loss of a loved one, they unknowingly revealed an aspect of Black womanhood rarely broached in the scholarly literature: vulnerability. Discourses of survival in the face of gendered racism tend to favour images of Black women who remain 'strong' in the face of adversity, rather than those in need of solace. As this book has illustrated, subjectivity and identity formation encompass other variables, such as religion in conjunction with race, gender, social class, and sexuality, to reveal the multiple dimensions of Black women's lives.

To be sure, most of the women interviewed for this study grew up in families where their parents were married, but a few grew up in sole-support households or with parents who were separated. Extended families were also quite common. Mothers in particular exerted a tremendous influence on daughters, especially in shaping their outlook on paid and unpaid work, and on heterosexual relationships. Nevertheless, the interviewees eschewed a uniform focus on family, with mothers always at the centre. Fathers, aunts, uncles, cousins, siblings, and children also played a critical role in shaping the interviewees' subjectivities. In contrast to the way such stories are told in much of the scholarly literature, however, some fathers also played critical roles in politicizing their daughters and shaping their world views.

Conservative politicians and religious leaders often consider women's participation in the labour force as contributing to the breakdown of the nuclear family. Mothers, it seems, do not spend enough 'quality time' with their families. Black sole-support mothers who work multiple jobs to support their children are further vilified, as they are assumed to be prioritizing work over family. These women, for the most part, have come to signify deviant Black womanhood. These negative views notwithstanding, motherhood and mothering remain critical to Black women's identities in North America, the English-speaking Caribbean, and Britain. The interviewees, on the other hand, rejected this as their *primary* identity, making no clear demarcation between women's supposed primary (mothering) and secondary roles (work). These Black women did not view work for remuneration and the unpaid work they performed for their families as mutually exclusive; rather, they valued both.

For many of the interviewees, nursing remained the quintessential 'caring' occupation, which spoke to their gendered sensibilities. It embodied all of the values with which they were raised. For Black Canadians, nursing was a far cry from the drudgery, alienation, and dehumanization associated with domestic work. Nursing brought personal fulfilment and economic stability. For most of the women who decided to have children, nursing appeared to be the perfect occupation, as it provided flexible working hours. Instead of choosing to remain childless or to leave the occupation permanently in order to have children, the interviewees viewed working as a necessity. Nursing allowed them to provide for their children's immediate and future needs. At no time did the interviewees report that working meant a lack of interest in their families' well-being. On the contrary, their families reaped the benefits of their paid labour. Significantly, childless Black women such as Lillie and Jennette, and those interviewees, both married and unmarried, who raised successful children while working full-time, remain absent from most contemporary discussions.

How much do the interviewees differ from other Black women and from women generally? The majority of these women worked for remuneration, married, had children, and experienced various life transitions, including marriage, divorce, death, widowhood, and illnesses. A few of the interviewees never married, and some remained childless. Certainly, on the surface, these interviewees' lives parallel those of other women, yet there are also dissimilarities. One objective of this book was to reflect on the interplay of race, gender, socioeconomic status, religion, age, migration, education, and other factors in shaping and reshaping the interviewees' subjectivity formation.

First, the majority of the interviewees share the distinction of being the first group of nurses to integrate British and Canadian nursing. Included are those who worked in Detroit and in integrated white hospitals along with their African American counterparts following the Second World War. At a time when the prevailing white middle-class gender norms insisted that mothering was a woman's primary identity, the interviewees chose to work for remuneration. Both groups of women, including those whose own mothers worked at home, scoffed at their white counterparts, who trained for three years and then gave up working after marriage to devote their lives to home and hearth. Arguably, Black people's socio-economic status required married women to work, as the family's survival depended on their income. In reality, however, half of these women could have opted to stay home, as in the case of Frieda and Beverly, but they chose to do otherwise. Nursing allowed the interviewees to forge a professional identity that was shaped in part by the values gleaned from childhood.

Second, these interviewees entered an occupation that, although deeply feminized, also possessed a history of exclusionary practices against women of colour. The exigencies of the labour market did little to alter the perception that Black women were suited to a particular place in the nursing hierarchy, which is reflected in the available scholarship on nursing and work in general. On the whole, a disproportionate number of the interviewees worked as registered nurses (RNs), even if upon migration, some worked in an auxiliary capacity until they upgraded. These women did not occupy the lower echelon of the nursing hierarchy, and although the social organization of nursing meant that they were unable to escape gendered racism, some occupied leadership and supervisory roles. I tell this story, then, not from the vantage point of Black women on the bottom, or even from the margins, but from those who were sometimes in the middle, or at the apex, despite the unequal power relationships that inhered in the medical field overall.

Often, an interviewee was the only Black woman working in her respective area (or at most one of only two Black women in that area) and that made her sharply aware of the meaning attached to her body. While the women told stories of racial/sexual subjugation (some occurrences of which took place outside of the workplace), they also told stories of redemption, forgiveness, hope, and excellence. Although they were unfairly victimized, it would do these Black women a disservice to call them 'victims.' Surely, I do not intend to diminish in any way the gendered racism that the interviewees faced, whether in the form of covert and insidious name-calling or in the institutionalized forms manifested, for example, in the assignment of patients. Still, some of these women could agree with Lillie, who said:

I managed to reach the highest I could in my profession – in that I was a nurse, midwife, I was a public health nurse consultant, and I was a Director of Nurses – I couldn't have gone any higher.[7]

This is especially pertinent for the Black Canadian-born group, despite their small numbers. They were able to fulfil aspirations that their mothers could only dream about. Their accomplishments and the recognition of their predecessors' struggle to transform Canadian society now makes it easier for Black Canadians to claim Canada as home and to affirm their citizenship status. In contrast, some Caribbean migrants underscored their volunteer and community activism, and raised successful children, as a way to situate themselves within the Canadian nation.

Third, these women built on a legacy that has long been established by Black women in the diaspora. Most striking is that some of these women continued involvement in community and religious organizations despite their age and accompanying illnesses. In addition, a number of these women were widowed – one of the final transitions in the life course paradigm – and living mostly by themselves. In Lilli's case, she had no relatives living in Canada, and often longed for more connected relationships. Absent, however, from these women's narratives were feelings of despair; on the contrary, they found meaning and value in their post-retirement activities. The lives of already retired women such as Frieda, Agnes, Lillie, Daphne B, Daphne C, and Ancilla, who was close to retirement at the time of her interview, reflect a counter-narrative to traditional understandings of retirement.

Furthermore, these interviews attest to the value of oral history as a methodology. The women provided insights into their lives that could not be gleaned from any other sources. They have left behind a solid legacy reflected in their individual lives, the inroads they made working as nurses in various geographical locations, the children they raised, and the community activism in which they have engaged. They drew on the values imparted to them by their families, churches, and their educational experiences, and despite structural constraints and gendered racism, they lived their lives with incredible determination. The narratives of these thirty-five women serve as a reminder of the omissions, silences, and gaps visible in the absence of Black Canada in studies on the African diaspora, women's studies, nursing history, and Canadian history generally. Indeed, their stories call us to sustain and support Black women's intellectual legacies.

Appendix: Biographical Details of the Women Interviewed

The first set of interviews was conducted with five Caribbean nurses who trained in Britain in 1995. The second set of interviews was conducted between 1999 and 2001 with an additional twenty nurses. This cohort included Canadian- and Caribbean-born nurses who trained in Canada, the English-speaking Caribbean (including Guyana–though that country is geographically outside of the Caribbean), and Britain. The third set of interviews was conducted in 2006–7 with ten more nurses who trained in Britain and Canada. In addition to questions focusing on migration and work experiences, the second and third set of interviews included questions about family, religion, and activism, among other themes. Since the interviews were completed in three stages, the interviewees were not asked and/or elected to not answer certain questions. The names and locations of the hospitals where they trained are given when known.

Abbreviations

DOB   date of birth
RMN   registered mental nurse
RN   registered nurse
SCM   state-certified midwife
SEN   state-enrolled nurse
SRN   state-registered nurse

Born in the Caribbean

1 Daphne Bailey
Age*: 63; DOB: 1932

---

* Age referes to age at the time of the interview.

Birthplace: Jamaica
Mother: dressmaker
Father: farmer
Migrated: to Britain in 1952; to Canada in 1960
Trained: as an SRN and SCM in Britain at Hallam Street Hospital, West
Bromwich, and Pembury Hospital, Kent; completed Public Health
Nurse certificate in 1971 at the University of Toronto
Marital status: single (never been married)
Children: 1
Employment status at the time of the interviews: retired
Interview date: 29 May 1995

2 Janet Barrett (pseudonym)
Age: 60+
Birthplace: Jamaica
Mother: postmistress
Father: Parish Council employee
Migrated: to Canada in 1968
Trained: at Humber College, 1970–74; earned a diploma (RN)
Marital status: married
Children: 3
Employment status at the time of the interview: employed full-time
Interview date: 5 June 2000

3 Orphelia Bennett (pseudonym)
Age: 86; DOB: August 1914
Birthplace: Jamaica
Mother: stay-at-home mother/wife
Father: farmer
Migrated: to Canada in 1955
Trained: as a general nurse/midwife (1946) at the Kingston Public
Hospital and at the Jubilee Hospital[a]
Marital status: widowed
Children: 2
Employment status at the time of the interview: retired
Interview date: 14 Oct. 2000

4 Myrna Blackman
Age: early 70s
Birthplace: Grenada

Mother: unknown
Father: unknown
Migrated: to Britain in the mid-1960s; to Canada in 1971
Trained: as an RMN in London, England
Marital status: married
Children: 2
Employment status at the time of the interview: retired
Interview date: 29 May 1995

5   Daphne Veronica Clarke
Age: 76; DOB: 1930
Birthplace: Jamaica
Mother: stay-at-home mother
Father: deceased at time of birth
Migrated: to Britain in 1959; to Canada in 1970
Trained: as an SRN and SCM in Britain (1959), at Dudley Road Hospital and Queen Elizabeth Hospital, Birmingham, and Huddersfield Royal Infirmary, Huddersfield
Marital status: widowed
Children: 3 (one deceased)
Employment status at the time of the interview: retired
Interview date: 27 April 2006

6   Vera Cudjoe
Age: 67; DOB: 1928
Birthplace: Trinidad
Mother: teacher
Father: cane farmer
Migrated: to Britain in 1949, returned to Trinidad in 1955; to Canada in 1960
Trained: as an SRN/SCM in Britain
Marital status: single (never been married)
Children: none
Employment status at the time of the interview: retired; changed career in 1962
Interview date: 5 Jan. 1995

7   Carmencita Gomez (pseudonym)
Age: 51; DOB: 1948
Birthplace: Trinidad

Mother: teacher/stay-at-home mother/wife
Father: electrician
Migrated: to Britain in 1968; to Canada in 1975
Trained: as an SRN in Britain, at Providence Hospital, St Helens, Lancashire
Marital status: married
Children: none
Employment status at the time of the interview: working full-time
Interview date: 14 Oct. 1999

8   Jean Harry
Age: late 60s; DOB: 1930s
Birthplace: Guyana
Mother: stay-at-home mother/wife
Father: farmer
Migrated: to Britain in 1958; to Canada in 1960
Trained: as an SRN in Britain, at the Royal Hospital and Home for Incurables, Wandsworth, London
Marital status: married
Children: 2
Employment status at the time of the interviews: retired
Interview date: 9 Aug. 2000

9   June Heaven
Age: 56; DOB: 1943
Birthplace: Jamaica
Mother: school principal
Father: banana industry employee
Migrated: to Canada in 1967
Trained: as a general nurse (1962) at the University College Hospital of the West Indies; earned a Bachelor of Science in Nursing (BScN) from the University of Ottawa in 1971
Marital status: divorced
Children: 2
Employment status at the time of the interview: retired
Interview date: 11 Nov. 1999

10   Ancilla Ho-Young
Age: 62; DOB: September 1944
Birthplace: Trinidad

Mother: assisted with farm work
Father: sugar cane farmer
Migrated: to England in 1966; to Canada in 1970
Trained: as an SRN in Britain at Warneford and Warwick School of
Nursing, Midlands; part 1 midwifery (Croydon)
Marital status: married
Children: 1
Employment status at the time of the interview: working full-time
Interview date: 15 Aug. 2007

11   Eileen Jacobson
Age: 63; DOB: 1932
Birthplace: Barbados
Mother: stay-at-home mother/wife
Father: plantation manager
Migrated: to Britain in 1952; to Canada in 1960
Trained: as an SRN/SCM in Britain
Marital status: married
Children: 2
Employment status at the time of interview: retired
Interview date: 6 Jan. 1995

12   Lillie Johnson
Age: 70; DOB: 1930
Birthplace: Jamaica
Mother: schoolteacher
Father: schoolteacher
Migrated: to Scotland in 1954; to Canada in 1960
Trained: as an SRN/SCM in Scotland; completed Public Health Nurse
certificate in 1961 at the University of Toronto
Marital status: single (never been married)
Children: none
Employment status at the time of the interviews: retired
Interview date: 9 Aug. 1999

13   Dorothy Jones (pseudonym)
Age: 67; DOB: 1943
Birthplace: Grenada
Mother: factory worker

Father: tailor
Migrated: to Britain in 1966; to Canada in 1971
Trained: as an SEN in Britain; earned a diploma (RN) in 1991 from
George Brown College
Marital status: married
Children: 3
Employment status at the time of the interview: retired
Interview date: 29 Feb. 2000

14   Muriel Knight
Age: 71; DOB: 1935
Birthplace: Barbados
Mother: stay-at-home mother/wife (seamstress)
Father: employed
Migrated: to England in 1955, returned to Barbados in 1962; to Canada
in 1963
Trained: as an SRN/SCM in Britain, at the Epsom Hospital, Surrey
Marital status: single (never been married)
Children: 1
Employment status at the time of the interviews: retired
Interview date: 12 Sept. 2006

15   Brenda Lewis
Age: 55; DOB: 1945
Birthplace: Trinidad
Mother: stay-at-home mother/wife
Father: labourer
Migrated: to Canada in 1971
Trained: as a nurse, specialized in psychiatry (1967), in Trinidad, at the
San Fernando Hospital
Marital status: married
Children: 3
Employment status at the time of interview: working in management
Interview date: 24 Feb. 2000

16   Inez Mackenzie
Age: 64; DOB: 1935
Birthplace: Jamaica
Mother: stay-at-home mother/wife
Father: supervisor, Public Works Department

Migrated: to Canada in 1960
Trained: as a general nurse/midwife (1955) at the University College of the West Indies and the Jubilee Hospital
Marital status: married
Children: 2
Employment status at the time of the interview: retired
Interview date: 13 Oct. 1999

17 · Elaine McLeod
Age: 64; DOB: February 1943
Birthplace: Jamaica
Mother: domestic/childcare worker
Father: hotel worker
Migrated: to Britain in 1966; to Canada in 1969
Trained: as an SEN in Britain
Marital status: divorced
Children: 2
Employment status at the time of the interview: working full-time
Interview date: 5 May 1995

18   Monica Mitchell
Age: mid-60s
Birthplace: Jamaica
Mother: stay-at-home mother/wife
Father: subcontractor
Migrated: to Canada in 1961
Trained: as a general nurse/midwife (1956) at the University College Hospital of the West Indies and the Jubilee Hospital
Marital status: divorced
Children: 1
Employment status at the time of the interview: working full-time
Interview date: 7 April 2000

19   Jennette Prince
Age: 60; DOB: 1939
Birthplace: Antigua
Mother: stay-at-home mother/wife (grocery store owner)
Father: police officer
Migrated: to Britain in 1957, returned to Antigua in 1963; to Canada in 1964

Trained: as an SRN/SCM in Britain at Leicester Hospital, London, and Kirkcaldy, Scotland
Marital status: single (never been married)
Children: none
Employment status at the time of the interview: retired
Interview date: 8 Oct. 1999

20   Dorette Thompson (pseudonym)
Age: 57; DOB: 1942
Birthplace: Jamaica
Mother: worked occasionally at a variety of odd jobs (Jamaica)
Stepmother: self-employed (Britain)
Father: employed (Britain)
Migrated: to Britain in 1957 (went to high school); to Canada in 1968
Trained: as an SRN/SCM (1962) in Britain
Marital status: single (never been married)
Children: none
Employment status at the time of the interview: working full-time
Interview date: 17 Aug. 1999

21   Joan Virtue
Age: 73; DOB: March 1933
Birthplace: Barbados
Mother: seamstress
Father: businessman
Migrated: to Britain in 1954; to Canada in 1962
Trained: as an RMN and SRN, with part 1 midwifery, at Netherne Hospital, Croydon, and Hackney General Hospital, London, England
Marital status: divorced
Children: 2
Employment status at the time of the interview: retired
Interview date: 12 Sept. 2006

22   Nancy Ward (pseudonym)
Age: 52; DOB: 1948
Birthplace: Dominica
Mother: stay-at-home mother/wife (occasional seamstress)
Father: grocery store owner
Migrated: to Britain in 1965; to Canada in 1970
Trained: as an SRN and SCM

Marital status: married
Children: 4
Employment status at the time of the interview: working full-time
Interview date: 5 Jan. 2000

Born in Canada

1   Naomi Banks
Age: mid-70s
Birthplace: Windsor, Ontario
Mother: professional singer
Father: worked in the automotive industry
Trained: as an RN at Windsor Western Hospital, Windsor, Ontario, 1960s
Marital status: married
Children: 3
Employment status at the time of the interview: retired
Interview date: 26 April 2006

2   Darlene Barnes
Age: 49
Birthplace: Winnipeg, Manitoba
·Mother: chef
Father: sky-cap
Migrated: to Britain in 1971; returned to Canada in 1975
Trained: as an SRN in Britain, later qualified as RN in Canada
Marital status: divorced
Children: 1
Employment status at the time of the interview: working full-time
Interview date: 22 Oct. 1999

3   Dorothy (Richards) Campbell
Age: 76; DOB: December 1930
Birthplace: Windsor, Ontario
Mother: stay-at-home mother/wife
Father: diver (held several jobs) until hired in the automotive industry
Migrated: to Detroit, Michigan, USA, in 1955
Trained: as an RN (1950) at Hôtel Dieu Hospital, Windsor, Ontario
Marital status: married
Children: 4

Employment status at the time of the interviews: retired
Interview date: 27 April 2006

4   Betty Clarke
Age: 77
Birthplace: Toronto, Ontario
Mother: housewife
Father: Canadian Pacific Railway
Trained: as an RN (1952) at the Toronto General Hospital School of
Nursing
Marital status: divorced
Children: 4
Employment status at the time of interviews: retired
Interview date: 19 Nov. 2007

5   Agnes (Scott) Ellesworth
Age: 70; DOB: 1931
Birthplace: Maidstone Township, Ontario
Stepmother: worked at various odd jobs
Father: worked at various odd jobs
Trained: as an RN (1950) at Hôtel Dieu Hospital, Windsor, Ontario;
worked in Detroit, Michigan, 1953–96; worked at Hotel Dieu for 3 years
Marital status: married
Children: 4
Employment status at the time of the interview: retired
Interview date: 5 June 2001

6   Beverly Salmon
Age: early 70s; DOB: early 1930s
Birthplace: Toronto, Ontario
Mother: worked for a while as a switchboard operator; stay at home
mother/wife
Father: business owner
Trained: as an RN (1950) at Wellesley Hospital, Toronto; completed
Public Health Nurse certificate in 1954 at the University of Toronto;
worked in Detroit, Michigan, 1956–60; returned to Toronto, worked
private duty for the summer
Marital status: widowed
Children: 4

Employment status at the time of the interview: retired; left nursing in 1966
Interview date: 8 Aug. 2007

7   Edna (Bailey) Black Searles
Age: 84; DOB: 1915
Birthplace: Toronto, Ontario
Mother: stay at home mother/wife
Father: chef
Trained: as RN
Marital status: divorced and then remarried
Children: 2
Employment status at the time of the interview: retired from nursing
early
Interview date: 4 Sept. 1999

8   Eleanor (Vincent) Shreve
Age: 73; DOB: December, 1933
Birthplace: Windsor, Ontario
Mother: stay at home mother/wife; worked at Smith's Department
Store
Father: automotive industry
Trained: as an RN (1953) at Hôtel Dieu Hospital, Windsor, Ontario;
worked in Detroit, Michigan, until 1966; worked part-time at Windsor
IOD (now Windsor Western) for a year
Marital status: married
Children: 1
Employment status at the time of the interview: retired; left nursing in
1966
Interview date: 29 April 2006

9   Frieda M. (Parker) Steele
Age: 72; DOB: 1929
Birthplace: Windsor, Ontario
Mother: trained as teacher, stay-at-home mother/wife
Father: worked at odd jobs, eventually became Windsor's first Black
uniform officer
Trained: as an RN (1947) at Hôtel Dieu Hospital, Windsor, Ontario
Marital status: divorced
Children: 6

Employment status at the time of the interview: retired
Interview date: 9 June 2001

10   Virginia Travis
Age: 64; DOB: 1937
Birthplace: Dresden, Ontario
Mother: cook in a nursing home and in a school cafeteria, as well as worker in a candy factory
Father: labourer, factory worker, and various odd jobs including homemaker
Trained: as an RN (1954) at the Public General Hospital,[b] Chatham, Ontario; obtained a BScN (honours) from the University of Windsor, 1991
Marital status: married
Children: 2
Employment status at the time of the interview: retired
Interview date: 5 June 2001

11   Laura Tynes
Age: 66; DOB: 1933
Birthplace: Kentville, Nova Scotia
Mother: stay at home mother/wife, domestic worker
Father: chimney sweeper and various odd jobs including quarry worker
Trained: as an RN (1951) at the Children's Hospital, Halifax, Nova Scotia
Marital status: widowed
Children: 2
Employment status at the time of the interview: retired
Interview date: 6 Dec. 1999

12   Marlene Watson
Age: 61
Birthplace: Nova Scotia
Mother: teacher, domestic worker
Father: farmer, quarry worker
Trained: as an RN (1957) at Victoria General Hospital, Halifax, Nova Scotia
Marital status: single (never been married)
Children: 1

Employment status at the time of the interview: working full-time
Interview date: 18 Jan. 2000

13   Cathy Williams

Age: mid-70s
Birthplace: Chatham, Ontario
Mother: stay at home mother/wife, helped on the farm
Father: farmer
Trained: as an RN (1953) at the Public General Hospital, Chatham
Marital status: divorced
Children: 4
Employment status at the time of the interview: retired
Interview date: 12 Aug. 2007

[a]Interviewees also used University of the West Indies (UWI) and University [College] Hospital of the West Indies (UCHWI).
[b]Interviewee also used Chatham General Hospital.

Notes

Introduction

1 Nursing scholars Jocelyn Hezekiah and Hyacinth Hermi Hewitt both use different acronymns when referring to what would later become the University of the West Indies (UWI). The former used UCHWI and the latter UCH. The interviewees used UWI.

2 Inez Mackenzie, interview, 13 Oct. 1999. See the Appendix for more details on the interviewees.

3 In this book, 'Black women' is used to discuss both groups of interviewees or Black women generally.

4 Chris Weedon, *Feminist Practice and Poststructuralist Theory* (Oxford: Basil Blackwell, 1989), 32.

5 Kath Woodward, ed., *Questioning Identity: Gender, Class, Ethnicity* (New York: Routledge, 2004), 7.

6 Glen H. Elder, Jr, John Modell, and Ross D. Parke, eds., *Children in Time and Place: Development and Historical Insights* (New York: Cambridge University Press, 1994), 4.

7 Rinaldo Walcott, *Black Like Who? Writing Black Canada* (Toronto: Insomniac Press, 1997).

8 This fact was brought to my attention initially by the disproportionate number of Caribbean nurses in the congregation at my place of worship in Toronto.

9 For two positions on the question of nurses' class see: Mary Kinnear, *In Subordination: Professional Women* (Montreal and Kingston, Jamaica: McGill-Queen's University Press, 1995), and Kathryn McPherson, *Bedside Matters: The Transformation of Canadian Nursing, 1900–1990* (Toronto: Oxford University Press, 1996).

10 George Ellliot Clarke, ed., *Eyeing the North Star: Directions in African-Canadian Literature* (Toronto: McClelland and Stewart, 1997).

11　Notisha Massaquoi and Njoki Nathani Wane, eds., *Theorizing Empowerment: Canadian Perspectives on Black Feminist Thought* (Toronto: Inanna, 2007), introduction.

12　Michel Foucault, *Power/Knowledge* (London: Macmillan, 1980), 131.

13　Chris Weedon, *Identity and Culture* (Maidenhead, England: Open University Press, 2004), 12. See also L. Althusser, 'Ideology and Ideological State Apparatuses,' in L. Althusser, *Lenin and Philosophy and Other Essays* (London: New Left Books, 1971), 121–76.

14　Peggy Bristow, 'Whatever You Raise in the Ground, You Can Sell It in Chatham,' in Peggy Bristow et al., *'We're Rooted Here and They Can't Pull Us Up': Essays in African Canadian Women's History* (Toronto: University of Toronto Press, 1994), 67–142.

15　Jean Besson, 'Reputation and Respectability Reconsidered: A New Perspective on Afro-Caribbean Peasant Women,' in Christine Barrow and Rhoda Reddock, eds., *Caribbean Sociology: Introductory Reading* (Kingston, Jamaica: Ian Randle, 2001), 350–70; Marietta Morrissey, 'Explaining the Caribbean Family,' in Christine Barrow, ed., *Caribbean Portraits: Essays on Gender Ideologies and Identities* (Kingston, Jamaica: Ian Randle, 1998), 79–90; Mary Chamberlain, *Family Love in the Diaspora: Migration and the Anglo-Caribbean Experience* (New Brunswick, NJ: Transaction Publishers, 2006); Hazel Carby, 'White Women Listen! Black Feminism and the Boundaries of Sisterhood,' in Heidi Safia Mirza, ed., *Black British Feminism: A Reader* (New York: Routledge, 1997, 45–53); originally published in *The Empire Strikes Back: Race and Racism in 70s Britain*, Centre for Contemporary Cultural Studies, eds, (London: Routledge, 1983), 212–35.

16　Judith Butler, *Gender Trouble: Feminism and the Subversion of Identity* (New York: Routledge, 1999).

17　Bridget Brereton, 'Society and Culture in the Caribbean, the British and French West Indies, 1870–1980,' in Franklin W. Knight and Colin A. Palmer, eds., *The Modern Caribbean* (Chapel Hill: University of North Carolina Press, 1989), 104.

18　Daniel G. Hill, 'Negroes in Toronto; A Sociological Study of a Minority Group,' doctoral dissertation, University of Toronto, 1960.

19　See, e.g., Noel Leo Erskine, *From Garvey to Marley: Rastafari Theology* (Gainesville: University Press of Florida, 2005); Nathaniel Samuel Murrell, William David Spencer, and Adrian Anthony McFarlane, eds., *Chanting Down Babylon: The Rastafaria Reader* (Philadelphia: Temple University Press, 1998); Barry Chevannes, *Rastafari: Roots and Ideology (Utopianism and Communitarianism)* (New York: Syracuse University Press, 1994). An alternative to the Rastafarianism scholarly focus is Diane J. Austin-Broos, *Jamaica Genesis:*

Religion and the Politics of Moral Orders (Chicago: University of Chicago Press, 1997). For African-derived religions in the Caribbean, see: Tracey E. Hucks and Dianne M. Stewart, 'Authenticity and Authority in the Shaping of the Trinidad Orisha Identity: Toward an African-Derived Religious Theory,' *Western Journal of Black Studies* 27 (2003): 176–85; Frances Henry, *Reclaiming African Religions in Trinidad: The Socio-Political Legitimation of the Orisha and Spiritual Baptist Faiths* (Trinidad and Tobago: University of the West Indies Press, 2003); Sharon Chambers-Gordon, '"Liberated in the Spirit": Telling the Lives of Jamaican Women in a Pentecostal/Revivalist Church,' *Women and Language* 24/2 (2001): 52–8. *In Canada, see* Carol B. Duncan, '"Dey Give Me a House to Gather in di Chil'ren": Mothers and Daughters in the Spiritual Baptist Church,' *Canadian Woman Studies* 18/2–3 (1998): 126–31.

20 In the African-American context, W.E.B. Dubois is credited as being one of the first scholars to explore children's religious beliefs. See Robert A. Wortham, 'W.E.B. Dubois, the Black Church and the Sociological Study of Religion,' *Sociological Spectrum* 29/2 (2009): 144–72.

21 See, e.g., Carl C. Campbell, *Endless Education: Main Currents in the Education System of Modern Trinidad and Tobago, 1939–1986* (Barbados: University of the West Indies Press, 1997).

22 Washington Archibald, *Reflections: On an Epic Journey* (Saddlers Village, St Kitts: G.W. Archibald, 1993), as quoted in Howard A. Fergus, *A History of Education in the British Leeward Islands, 1838–1945* (Kingston, Jamaica: University of the West Indies Press, 2003), 57.

23 Butler, *Gender Trouble*, xv.

24 Homi K. Bhabha, *The Location of Culture* (New York: Routledge, 1994), 86, original emphasis.

25 Ibid.

26 Benedict Anderson, *Imagined Communities: Reflections on the Origin and Spread of Nationalism*, rev. ed. (New York: Verso, 1991).

27 Mary Chamberlain, *Narratives of Exile and Return* (London: Macmillan, 1997).

28 John Solomos, *Race and Racism in Britain*, 2nd ed. (New York: St Martin's Press, 1993).

29 See e.g., Gail Lewis, 'Black Women's Employment and the British Economy,' in Winston James and Clive Harris, eds., *Inside Babylon: The Caribbean Diaspora in Britain* (New York: Verso, 1993), 73–96; Dionne Brand, 'Black Women and Work: The Impact of the Racially Constructed Roles on the Sexual Division of Labour,' in Enakshi Dua and Angela Robertson, eds., *Scratching the Surface: Canadian Anti-Racist Feminist Thought* (Toronto: Women's Press, 1999), 83–96.

30 Carol Baxter, *The Black Nurse: An Endangered Species – A Case for Equal*

Opportunities in Nursing (Cambridge: National Extension College, 1988), 16; Beverley Bryan, Stella Dadzie, and Suzanne Scafe, *The Heart of the Race: Black Women's Lives in Britain* (London: Virago, 1985); Agnes Calliste, 'Women of "Exceptional Merit": Immigration of Caribbean Nurses to Canada,' *Journal of Canadian Women and the Law* 6 (1993): 85–103.

31 Jeffrey Ferguson, 'Race and the Rhetoric of Resistance,' *Raritan* 28/1 (2008): 4–32. The topic of resistance is a major theme in Yvonne Bobb-Smith's, *I Know Who I am: A Caribbean Women's Identity in Canada* (Toronto: Women's Press, 2003).

32 Milton Vickerman, *Cross Currents: West Indian Immigrants and Race* (New York: Oxford University Press, 1999), 66.

33 Although Guyana is situated geographically in South America, this particular interviewee referred to herself as West Indian.

34 Karen M. Mason and Tanya Zanish-Belcher, 'Raising the Archival Consciousness: How Women's Archives Challenge Traditional Approaches to Collecting and Use, or What's in a Name?' *Library Trends* 56/2 (2007): 344–59.

35 For a discussion of this process, see, Sherna Berger Gluck, 'What's So Special about Women? Women's Oral History,' in Susan H. Armitage, Patricia Hart, and Karen Weathermon, eds., *Women's Oral History: The Frontiers Reader* (Lincoln: University of Nebraska Press, 2002), 3–20.

36 Michael Pressley and Wolfgang Schneider, *Memory Development between Two and Twenty* (Mahwah, NJ: Lawrence Erlbaum, 1997), 9. See also Martin A. Conway, *Autobiographical Memory: An Introduction* (Milton Keynes, UK Open University Press, 1990).

37 Pamela Sugiman, 'Passing Time, Moving Memories: Interpreting Wartime Narratives of Japanese Canadian Women,' *Histoire sociale/Social History* 36/73 (2004): 70.

38 Ibid.

39 Gemma Romain, *Connecting Histories: A Comparative Exploration of African-Caribbean and Jewish History and Memory in Modern Britain* (London: Kegan Paul, 2006), 32, original emphasis.

40 Franca Iacovetta, 'Manly Militants, Cohesive Communities, and Defiant Domestics: Writing about Immigrants in Canadian Historical Scholarship,' *Labour/Le Travail* 36 (1995): 227.

41 Gretchen Lemke-Santangelo, *Abiding Courage: African-American Women Migrants and the East Bay Community* (Chapel Hill: University of North Carolina Press, 1996), 8.

42 The contested nature of the archives is raised in Antoinette Burton, ed., *Archive Stories: Facts, Fictions, and the Writing of History* (Durham: Duke University of Press, 2005), introduction.

1 The Family as the Agent of Socialization

1 For different positions on the role of childhood memory, see: David
Kennedy, *The Well of Being: Childhood, Subjectivity, and Education* (New York:
State University of New York Press, 2006); Joan Sangster, *Earning Respect: The
Lives of Working Women in Small Town Ontario, 1920–1960* (Toronto: Univer-
sity of Toronto Press, 1995).

2 Constance Sutton and Susan Makiesky-Barrow, 'Social Inequality and Sexual
Status in Barbados,' in Christine Barrow and Rhoda Reddock, eds., *Caribbean Sociology: Introductory Readings* (Kingston, Jamaica: Ian Randle, 2001),
372.

3 West India Royal Commission Report. Cmd. 6607 (June 1945), xiii, as
quoted in Hermi Hyacinth Hewitt, *Trailblazers in Nursing Education: A Caribbean Perspective, 1946–1986* (Barbados: Canoe Press, 2002), 9.

4 Ibid.

5 Sutton and Makiesky-Barrow, 'Social Inequality and Sexual Status in Barbados,' 377.

6 Mignon Duffy, 'Reproducing Labor Inequalities: Challenges for Feminists
Conceptualizing Care at the Intersections of Gender, Race, and Class,' *Gender and Society* 19/1 (2005): 70.

7 James Walker, *Racial Discrimination in Canada: The Black Experience* (Ottawa:
Canadian Historical Association, 1985), as quoted in Ken Alexander and
Avis Glaze, *Towards Freedom: The African Canadian Experience* (Toronto:
Umbrella Press, 1996), 34.

8 Virginia Travis, interview, 5 June 2001.

9 Laura Tynes, interview, 6 Dec. 1999.

10 Sean Purdy, '"It Was Tough on Everybody": Low- Income Families and Housing Hardship in Post–World War II Toronto,' *Journal of Social History* 37/2
(2003): 459.

11 Windsor Interracial Council (WIC) Records, Council Meeting Minutes,
30 Jan.–21 June 1948, University of Windsor Archives, RG 05-002, Box 1,
File 1. The WIC was composed of a group of citizens involved in fighting discrimination in Windsor. Lyle Talbot, chairman of the council, was
instrumental in raising awareness about discrimination in Windsor, and he
and the WIC wrote letters to various provincial and local government officials, community members, and businesses. See also Constance Backhouse,
Colour-Coded: A Legal History of Racism in Canada, 1900–1950 (Toronto: University of Toronto Press, 1999), 351.

12 Norah L. Lewis, ed., *Freedom to Play: We Made Our Own Fun* (Waterloo: Wilfrid Laurier University Press, 2002).

13 For Canada, these autobiographical accounts are helpful: Karen Shadd-Eve-lyn, *I'd Rather Live in Buxton* (Toronto: Simone and Pierre, 1996); Carol Tal-bot, *Growing Up Black in Canada* (Toronto: Williams-Wallace, 1984); Stanley Grizzel, *My Name Is Not George: The Story of the Brotherhood of Sleeping Car Porters in Canada* (Toronto: Umbrella Press, 1998). See also Dionne Brand, *No Burden to Carry: Narratives of Black Working Women in Ontario, 1920s–1950s* (Toronto: Women's Press, 1991).

With respect to the Caribbean, a few studies offer some indication of how children were socialized in the 1940s and 1950s. See, e.g., Edith Clarke, *My Mother Who Fathered Me: A Study of the Families in Three Selected Communities in Jamaica* (Kingston, Jamaica: University of the West Indies Press, 1999); Raymond T. Smith, *The Negro Family in British Guiana: Family Structure and Social Status in the Villages* (London: Routledge and Kegan Paul, in associa-tion with the Institute of Social and Economic Research, University College of the West Indies, Jamaica, 1956); M.G. Smith, *West Indian Family Structure* (Seattle: University of Washington Press, 1962).

A few biographical and fictional accounts provide some insight into grow-ing up as girls in the Caribbean or outside the Caribbean diaspora, as chil-dren of Caribbean parents. For the former, see: Beverly Manley, *The Manley Memoirs* (Kingston, Jamaica: Ian Randle, 2008); Audre Lorde, *Zami: A New Spelling of My Name* (Watertown, PA: Persephone, 1982). For the latter, see Paule Marshall, *Brown Girl, Brownstones* (New York: Feminist Press, 1996); and Michelle Cliff, *Abeng* (New York: Penguin, 1984).

14 Dorette Thompson, interview, 17 Aug. 1999.

15 Carolyn Steedman, in *Past Tenses: Essays on Writing, Autobiography and History* (London: Rivers Osram Press, 1992), points out that the 'poor but happy' scenario is typical in working-class and Jewish autobiography.

16 Ancilla Ho-Young, interview, 15 Aug. 2007.

17 Peggy Bristow, 'A Duty to the Past, a Promise to the Future: Black Organ-izing in Windsor – The Depression, World War II, and the Post-War Years,' *New Dawn* 2/1 (2007):16.

18 Katrina Srigley, '"In Case You Hadn't Noticed!" Race, Ethnicity, and Wom-en's Wage-Earning in a Depression-Era City,' *Labour/LeTravail* 55 (2005): 69–105; 'Hotel London Discharges Colored Help and Replaces them with White Ex-Service Men,' *Dawn of Tomorrow* 6 (April 1934): 2.

19 Brand, *No Burden to Carry*; Ruth Roach Pierson, *They're Still Women after All: The Second World War and Canadian Womanhood* (Toronto: McClelland and Stewart, 1986); Peter J. Paris and Elmer G. Homrighausen, 'Native Born,' 2000, retrieved 10 Sept. 2009 from http://www.parl.ns.ca/nativeborn/wars. htm; Historica-Dominion Institute, 'Black History Canada,' retrieved

10 Sept. 2009 from http://blackhistorycanada.ca/timeline.php?id=1900.

20 Denyse Baillargeon, *Making Do: Women, Family, and Home in Montreal during the Great Depression*, trans. Yvonne Klein (Waterloo: Wilfrid Laurier University Press, 1999).

21 Frieda (Parker) Steele, interview, 9 June 2001.

22 Ibid.

23 See Brand, *No Burden to Carry*. Several of the interviewees discussed both the Great Depression and the Second World War.

24 Agnes (Scott) Ellesworth, interview, 5 June 2001.

25 Ibid.

26 Virginia Travis, interview, 5 June 2001.

27 Robin W. Winks, *The Blacks in Canada: A History*, 2nd ed. (Montreal and Kingston, Jamaica: McGill-Queen's University Press, 1997), 457.

28 Ross Lamberston, '"The Dresden Story": Racism, Human Rights and the Jewish Labour Committee of Canada,' *Labour/Le Travail* 47 (2001): 1–36.

29 Daphne Veronica Clarke, interview, 27 April 2006.

30 Daphne Bailey, interview, 5 May 1995.

31 Ibid.

32 Inez Mackenzie, interview, 13 Oct. 1999.

33 M.G. Smith, *West Indian Family Structure*, as quoted in Christine Barrow, ed., *Family in the Caribbean: Themes and Perspectives* (Kingston, Jamaica: Ian Randle, 1996), 10.

34 Inez Mackenzie, interview, 13 Oct. 1999.

35 Merle Hodge, 'We Kind of Family,' in Patricia Mohammed, ed., *Gendered Realities: Essays in Caribbean Feminist Thought* (Kingston, Jamaica: University of the West Indies Press, 2002), 474–85.

36 Frieda (Parker) Steele, interview, 9 June 2001.

37 Dorothy (Richards) Campbell, interview, 27 April 2006.

38 See, e.g., Pamela Sugiman, 'Privilege and Oppression: The Configuration of Race, Gender, and Class in Southern Ontario Auto Plants, 1939 to 1949,' *Labour/Le Travail*, 47/1 (2001): 83–114.

39 Edna (Bailey) Black Searles, interview, 4 Sept. 1999.

40 Agnes (Scott) Ellesworth, interview, 5 June 2001.

41 Cecilia L. Ridgeway and Shelley J. Correll, 'Unpacking the Gender System: A Theoretical Perspective on Gender Beliefs and Social Relations,' *Gender and Society* 18/4 (2004): 510.

42 Eleanor (Vincent) Shreve, interview, 29 April 2006.

43 Virginia Travis, interview, 5 June 2001.

44 Marlene Watson, interview, 18 Jan. 2000.

45 Virginia Travis, interview, 5 June 2001.
46 Evelyn Nakano Glenn, *Issei, Nisei, War Bride: Three Generations of Japanese American Women in Domestic Service* (Philadelphia: Temple University Press, 1986), 15.
47 Edna (Bailey) Black Searles, interview, 4 Sept. 1999.
48 Ibid.
49 Marlene Watson, interview, 18 Jan. 2000.
50 Jennette Prince, interview, 8 Oct. 1999.
51 Weedon, *Feminist Practice and Poststructuralist Theory*, 33.
52 Jean Harry, interview, 9 Aug. 2000.
53 Marie Ferguson Peters, 'Parenting of Young Black Children in Black Families: A Historical Note,' in Harriette Pipes McAdoo, ed., *Black Families*, 4th ed. (Twin Oaks, CA: Sage, 2007), 203–14.
54 Ephesians 6:1–3.
55 Naomi Banks, interview, 26 April 2006.
56 Proverbs 23:13–14.
57 Both Edith Clarke and M.G. Smith in their scholarship confirmed that mothers were primarily responsible for administering discipline, and in the case of harsher punishment in the form of beatings, the father would step in, which the interviewees further confirmed.
58 Inez Mackenzie, interview, 13 Oct. 1999.
59 Marlene Watson, interview, 18 Jan. 2000.
60 June Heaven, interview, 11 Nov. 1999.
61 Carmencita Gomez, interview, 14 Oct. 1999.
62 Ibid.
63 Orphelia Bennett, interview, 14 Oct. 2000.
64 Becky Thompson and Sangeeta Tyagi, *Names We Call Home: Autobiography on Racial Identity* (New York: Routledge, 1996), xii, original emphasis.
65 Frieda (Parker) Steele, interview, 9 June 2001.
66 Ibid.
67 Laura Tynes, interview, 6 Dec. 1999.
68 Viola Desmond, an entrepreneur and native of Nova Scotia, would bring national attention to the issue of segregation in Canada when she was ejected from New Glasgow's Roseland Theatre in 1946 for sitting in the section reserved for White patrons. See Backhouse, *Colour-Coded*, chapter 7.
69 Laura Tynes, interview, 6 Dec. 1999.
70 Virginia Travis, interview, 5 June 2001.
71 *Canadian Negro* 2/1 (1954): 1, reported that three children, aged five to seven, 'went to a restaurant for ice cream and the waiters not only refused to serve them, they just stood there looking at them.'
72 Edna (Bailey) Black Searles, interview, 4 Sept. 1999.

73 Frieda (Parker) Steele, interview, 9 June 2001; Eleanor Shreve, interview, 29 April 2006. See Peggy Bristow, 'The Hour-a-Day Study Club,' in Linda Carty, ed., *And Still We Rise: Feminist Political Mobilization in Contemporary Canada* (Toronto: Women's Press. 1993), 145–72. See also Windsor Mosaic, 'African-Canadian Community,' 2005, retrieved from http://www.windsor-communities.com/african-organ-studyclub.php.

74 Frieda (Parker) Steele, interview, 9 June 2001.

75 Naomi Banks, interview, 26 April 2006.

76 Weedon, *Identity and Culture*, 7.

77 Jennette Prince, interview, 8 Oct. 1999.

78 Ibid.

79 Ibid.

80 Monica Mitchell, interview, 7 April 2000.

81 Carby, 'White Woman Listen!, 46.

2 'I Wouldn't Be Where I Am Today': Creating Moral Citizens through School and Church

1 Chris Weedon, *Identity and Culture* (Maidenhead, England: Open University Press, 2004), 165.

2 David Kennedy, *The Well of Being: Childhood, Subjectivity, and Education* (New York: State University of New York Press, 2006), 154.

3 See, e.g., Carl C. Campbell, *Young Colonials: A Social History of Education in Trinidad and Tobago, 1834–1939* (Barbados: University of the West Indies Press, 1996).

4 Grammar school curriculum included classical languages (Latin and Greek), modern languages, such as Spanish and French in the case of Trinidad, as well as mathematics. 'The full grammar school curriculum was thought to be too strenuous for girls.' Carl C. Campbell, *Young Colonials*, 135.

5 Olive Senior, *Working Miracles: Women's Lives in the English-Speaking Caribbean* (Bloomington: Indiana University Press, 1991), 47.

6 Janice Mayers, 'Access to Secondary Education for Girls in Barbados, 1907–1943: A Preliminary Analysis,' in Verene Shepherd, Bridget Brereton, Barbara Bailey, eds., *Engendering History: Caribbean Women in Historical Perspective* (New York: St Martin's Press, 1995), 258–75.

7 Patrick J. Harrigan, 'The Schooling of Boys and Girls in Canada,' *Journal of Social History* 23/4 (1990): 803–16.

8 Sangster, *Earning Respect*, 26.

9 H.D. Woods and Sylvia Ostry, *Labour Policy and Labour Economics in Canada* (Toronto: Macmillan, 1962), 309.

10 Senior, *Working Miracles*, 46.

11 Ibid., 47.

12 Ibid.

13 Gwendolyn V. Shand, 'Adult Education among the Negroes in Nova Scotia,' *Journal of Education* 5/10 (1961): 11.

14 Reverend W.P. Oliver, 'The Negro in Nova Scotia,' *Journal of Education* 13 (Feb. 1964): 20.

15 Marlene Watson, interview, 18 Jan. 2000.

16 Ibid.

17 For a discussion of the history of Blacks and education in Canada during the time period under discussion, see Winks, *The Blacks in Canada*, Chapter 12, 'Source of Strength? The Schools.'

18 Neil Sutherland, *Growing Up: Childhood in English Canada from the Great War to the Age of Television* (Toronto: University of Toronto Press, 1997), viii.

19 Dominion Bureau of Statistics, Education Statistics Branch, Education Bulletin no. 3, 'The Size Factor in One-Room Schools' (Ottawa, 1938).

20 Laura Tynes, interview, 6 Dec. 1999.

21 Ibid.

22 Agnes (Scott) Ellesworth, interview, 5 June 2001.

23 Marlene Watson, interview, 18 Jan. 2000.

24 For a history of segregated schools, see Sylvia Hamilton, *The Little Black School House*, Maroon Films, 2007; H.W. Arthurs, 'Civil Liberties – Public Schools – Segregation of Negro Students.' *Canadian Bar Review* 41 (Sept. 1963): 453–7.

25 Marlene Watson, interview, 18 Jan. 2000.

26 Jefferson A. Singer and Martin A. Conway, 'Should We Forget Forgetting?' *Memory Studies* 1/3 (2008): 279.

27 Naomi Banks, interview, 26 April, 2006.

28 Virginia Travis, interview, 5 June 2001.

29 Dorothy (Richards) Campbell, interview, 27 April 2006.

30 Agnes Ellesworth, interview, 5 June 2001.

31 Senior, *Working Miracles*, 54.

32 Ula Y. Taylor, *The Veiled Garvey: The Life and Times of Amy Jacques Garvey* (Chapel Hill: University of North Carolina Press, 2002), 12.

33 Lillie Johnson, interview, 9 Aug. 1999.

34 Inez Mackenzie, interview, 13 Oct. 1999.

35 Olive Senior, *Working Miracles*, 49.

36 Daphne Veronica Clarke, interview, 27 April 2006.

37 Jennette Prince, interview, 8 Oct. 1999.

38 Fergus, *A History of Education in the British Leeward Islands*, 104.

39 Weedon, *Identity and Culture*, 26.

40 June Heaven, interview, 11 Nov. 1999.
41 Ibid.
42 Dorothy Campbell, interview, 27 April 2006.
43 Virginia Travis, interview, 5 June 2001.
44 Joanna Herbert, *Negotiating Boundaries in the City: Migration, Ethnicity, and Gender in Britain* (Aldershot, UK: Ashgate, 2008), 143. South Asian male interviewees expressed similar responses regarding the role of sports in bridging racial differences.
45 Agnes Ellesworth, interview, 5 June 2001.
46 Ibid.
47 Ibid.
48 Jean Peneff, 'Myths in Life Stories,' in Raphael Samuel and Paul Thompson, eds., *The Myths We Live By* (London: Routledge, 1990), 36–48.
49 Harrigan, 'The Schooling of Boys and Girls in Canada,' 5.
50 Ibid.
51 Michael W. Apple, *Ideology and Curriculum* (New York: Routledge, 2004), vii.
52 'And A Child Shall Lead Them,' *Dawn of Tomorrow* (Jan. 1947): 4.
53 Talbot, *Growing up Black in Canada*, 14.
54 Sheldon Taylor pointed out that community activist Daniel (Danny) Braithwaite single-handedly lobbied to have *Little Black Sambo* removed from Toronto schools. According to Taylor, Braithwaite 'was incensed that such racist stories, which had added sadness to his own childhood, were being used in the classroom of his son, Paul.' For Braithwaite, books such as *Little Black Sambo* 'could only encourage the perpetuation of Black stereotypes.' Braithwaite's efforts were eventually rewarded; in 1956 the book was finally removed from Toronto public school classrooms. Retrieved 9 May 2008 from http://www.sharenews.com/7-25-editor4.htm. While Braithwaite is usually credited for the removal of Little Black Sambo from Toronto Schools, Jean Daniels in her column 'The Woman's Window,' pointed out that the Open-Door-Club, a women's group organized around the *Canadian Negro* lobbied with Braithwaite 'and brought the issue to a successful conclusion.' Jean Daniels, 'The Woman's Window,' *Canadian Negro* 3/4 (1956): 3.
55 Nova Scotia, *Annual Report of the Superintendent of Education for Nova Scotia*, 1 July 1933, 176.
56 Ruth Binnie, 'Home Economics and Supervision, 1940–1956,' *Journal of Education* 6/1 (1956): 48.
57 Ibid., 52.
58 Marlene Watson, interview, 18 Jan. 2000.
59 Taylor, *The Veiled Garvey*, 12.
60 Ibid.

61 Ancilla Ho-Young, interview, 15 Aug. 2007.
62 Inez Mackenzie, interview, 13 Oct. 1999.
63 Taylor, *The Veiled Garvey*, 12.
64 Daphne Clarke, interview, 17 April 2006.
65 Dorette Thompson, interview, 17 Aug. 1999.
66 Daphne Clarke, interview, 17 April 2006.
67 Inez Mackenzie, interview, 13 Oct. 1999.
68 Marlene Watson, interview, 18 Jan. 2000.
69 Laura Tynes, interview, 6 Dec. 1999.
70 Dorothy Shadd Shreve, *The AfriCanadian Church: A Stabilizer* (Grand Rapids, MI: Paideia Books), 13; Lawrence Hill, *Trails and Triumphs of African-Canadians*, (Toronto: Umbrella Press, 1996); Bridglal Pachai and Henry Bishop, *Images of Our Past: Historic Black Nova Scotia* (Halifax: Nimbus, 2006), chapter 2. For an alternative view of the Black church see Winks, *The Blacks in Canada*, 360–1.
71 Shreve, *The AfriCanadian Church*, 42; D. Hill, *Negroes in Toronto*.
72 Shreve, *The AfriCanadian Church*, 81.
73 Frieda (Parker) Steele, interview, 9 June 2001. Carol Talbot, who also grew up in Windsor, recalled: 'First Baptist Church, or more probably the whole family of black churches, formed a physical link for me with the black community. There, as a young child … I experienced the dignity, authority, intelligence, creativity and goodness of our people. I saw that our people followed a spiritual pathway that transcended the burdens that daily lives steeped in a history of suffering and humiliation might bring.' See *Growing up Black in Canada*, 86–7.
74 In addition to underscoring the significance of Black churches to Black communities, filmmaker and historian Sylvia Hamilton also highlighted the prominent role of women. See Sylvia Hamilton, 'The Women at the Well: African Baptist Women Organize,' in Linda Carty, ed., *And Still We Rise: Feminist Political Mobilizing in Contemporary Canada* (Toronto: Women's Press, 1993), 189–203.
75 Wendy L. Haight, *African-American Children at Church: A Socio-Cultural Perspective* (Cambridge: Cambridge University Press, 2002), 19.
76 Frieda (Parker) Steele, interview, 9 June 2001.
77 Ibid.
78 Lillie Johnson, interview, 9 Aug. 1999; Naomi Banks, interview, 26 April 2006.
79 Joan Virtue, interview, 12 Sept. 2006.
80 Lillie Johnson, interview, 9 Aug. 1999.
81 Naomi Banks, interview, 26 April 2006.

82 Evelyn Brooks Higginbotham, *Righteous Discontent: The Women's Movement in the Black Baptist Church, 1880–1920* (Cambridge: Harvard University Press, 1993), 187.
83 Naomi Banks, interview, 26 April 2006.
84 Kamala Kempadoo, *Sexing the Caribbean: Gender, Race, and Sexual Labor* (New York: Routledge, 2004), 18.
85 Darlene Clark Hine, 'Rape and the Inner Lives of Black Women in the Middle West,' *Signs* 14 (Summer 1989): 912–20.
86 Marlene Watson, interview, 18 Jan. 2000.
87 Ibid.
88 Agnes Ellesworth, interview, 5 June 2001.
89 Ibid.
90 Carmencita Gomez, interview, 14 Oct. 1999.
91 Betty Clarke, interview, 11 Nov. 2007.
92 Jennette Prince, interview, 8 Oct. 1999.
93 Naomi Banks, interview, 26 April 2006.
94 Carmencita Gomez, interview, 14 Oct. 1999.
95 Laura Tynes, interview, 6 Dec. 1999.
96 Matthew 22:39.
97 Laura Tynes, interview, 6 Dec. 1999.
98 Dorothy Jones, interview, 29 Feb. 2000.

3 'The Sky Is the Limit': Migration to Britain

1 Mary Chamberlain, 'I Belong to Whoever Wants Me,' in B. Schwarz and P. Cohen, eds., '*Frontlines-Backyards*,' special issue *New Formations* 33 (1998): 47–58.
2 Sandra Ponzanesi and Daniela Merolla, eds., *Migrant Cartographies: New Cultural and Literary Spaces in Post Colonial Europe* (Lanham, MD: Lexington Books, 2005), 6.
3 See Peter Fryer, *Staying Power: Black People in Britain since 1504* (London: Pluto Press, 1984).
4 Caribbean migrants were recruited to serve in the British military during the Second World War. See, e.g., R.G. Spencer, *British Immigration Policy since 1939: The Making of Multi-Racial Britain* (New York: Routledge, 1997).
5 Clive Harris, 'Post War Migration and Industrial Reserve Army,' in Winston James and Clive Harris, eds., *Inside Babylon: The Caribbean Diaspora in Britain* (New York: Verso, 1993), 9–54.
6 Ann Kramer, *Many Rivers to Cross: The History of the Caribbean Contribution to the NHS* (London: Sugar Media, 2006), 15.

7 G.C.K. Peach, 'West Indian Migration to Britain,' *International Migration Review* 1/2 (1967): 34–45; and Peach, 'Factors Affecting the Distribution of West Indians in Great Britain,' *Transactions of the Institute of British Geographers* 38 (June 1966): 151–63.

8 See Ceri Peach's authoritative book in the subject, *West Indian Migration to Britain: A Social Geography* (London: Oxford University Press, 1968). These statistics must be used with caution. Peach pointed out that prior to the 1961 Census and the implementation of the Commonwealth Immigration Act of 1962, the only official statistics on migration were compiled by the Board of Trade. Included in these statistics were people who entered or left the country by boats on extended trips to or from non-European ports. Caribbean people who migrated between 1948 and 1955 used either Spanish or Italian vessels. When they landed at continental ports, the migrants had to find the channel ports, and from there they had to make their way, presumably on smaller boats, to Britain. They were excluded from the official count. For an analysis of these statistics see, E.J.B. Rose et al., *Colour and Citizenship: A Report on British Race Relations* (London: Oxford University Press, 1969), 96–119.

9 For the rationale surrounding Caribbean migration to Britain, see, e.g., Bryan et al., *The Heart of the Race*.

10 For an explanation on the role of the family in migration, see Mary Chamberlain, 'The Family as Model and Metaphor in Caribbean Migration to Britain,' *Journal of Ethnic and Migration Studies* 25/2 (1999): 251–66.

11 Ransford Palmer, ed., *In Search of a Better Life: Perspectives on Migration from the Caribbean* (New York: Praeger, 1990). For a critique of the traditional view of migration, see Elaine Bauer and Paul Thompson, '"She's Always the Person with a Very Global Vision": The Gender Dynamics of Migration, Narrative, Interpretation and the Case of Jamaican Transnational Families,' *Gender and History* 16/2 (2004): 334–75.

12 Dorothy Jones, interview, 29 Feb. 2000.

13 Ibid.

14 E.M. Hope, '"Island Systems and the Paradox of Freedom": Migration in the Post-Emancipation Leeward Islands,' in. K.F. Olwig, ed., *Small Islands, Large Questions: Society, Culture and Resistance in the Post-Emancipation Caribbean Society* (Ilford, UK: Frank Cass, 1995), 161–78.

15 Ancilla Ho-Young, interview, 15 Aug. 2007.

16 Daphne Veronica Clarke, interview, 27 Aug. 2006.

17 Dorette Thompson, interview, 17 Aug. 1999.

18 Merle Hodge, 'Young Women and the Development of a Stable Family Life in the Caribbean,' in L. Mathurin, ed., *Savacou* (Caribbean Women) 13:11 quoted in Olive Senior, *Working Miracles: Women's Lives in the English-Speaking Caribbean* (Bloomington: Indiana University Press, 1991), 68.

19 Senior, *Working Miracles*, 72.
20 Dorette Thompson, interview, 17 Aug. 1999.
21 K.F. Olwig, *Small Islands, Large Questions*, 6.
22 Carmencita Gomez, interview, 14 Oct. 1999.
23 Ibid.
24 Jennette Prince, interview, 8 Oct. 1999.
25 Lillie Johnson, interview, 9 Aug. 1999.
26 See, e.g., Pamella Elizabeth Hay Ho Sang, 'The Development of Nursing Education in Jamaica, 1900–1975,' Ed.D. Dissertation, Columbia University Teachers College, 1985; Joceyln Hezekiah, *Breaking the Glass Ceiling: The Stories of Three Caribbean Nurses* (Kingston, Jamaica: University of the West Indies Press, 2001).
27 Lillie Johnson, interview, 9 Aug. 1999.
28 John S. R. Golding, *Ascent to Mona as Illustrated by a Short History of Jamaican Medical Care with an Account of the Beginning of the Faculty of Medicine, University of the West Indies* (Kingston, Jamaica: University of the West Indies Press, 1994), 108.
29 Eileen Jacobson, interview, 6 Jan. 1995; Joan Virtue, interview, 12 Sept. 2006; Vera Cudjoe, interview, 5 Jan. 1995.
30 M. Bryce-Boodoo, 'A Fresh Look at Nursing Education in Trinidad and Tobago,' in *The Nursing Council of Trinidad and Tobago* (Port of Spain, 1976), 33.
31 Elizabeth Thomas-Hope, *Caribbean Migration* (Kingston, Jamaica: University of the West Indies Press, 2002), 6.
32 E. Ellis Cashmore, *United Kingdom? Class, Race and Gender since the War* (London: Unwin Hyman, 1989), 19.
33 Deborah Philips and Alan Tomlinson, 'Homeward-Bound Leisure, Popular Culture and Consumer Capitalism,' in Dominic Strinati and Stephen Wagg eds., *Come on Down: Popular Media Culture in Post-War Britain* (New York: Routledge, 1992), 12.
34 Rosalind Cassidy, 'Careers for Women,' *Journal of Educational Sociology* 17/8 (1944): 479.
35 Dorothy Jones, interview, 29 Feb. 2000.
36 Joan Virtue, interview, 12 Sept. 2006.
37 Daphne Veronica Clarke, interview, 26 April 2006.
38 For detailed examples of the impact and responses of Black migration to Britain, see Bob Carter, Clive Harris, and Shirley Joshi, 'The 1951–1955 Conservative Government and the Racialization of Black Migration,' in Winston James and Clive Harris, eds., *Inside Babylon: The Caribbean Diaspora in Britain* (New York: Verso, 1993), 55–72; Claudia Jones, 'The Caribbean Community in Britain,' in ibid., 49–57.

The experiences of Caribbean female migrants in Britain are also articulated in fiction. See, e.g., Andrea Levy, *Small Island* (London: Headline, 2004); Zadie Smith, *White Teeth* (New York: Random House, 2000).

39 Chris Waters, '"Dark Strangers" in Our Midst: Discourses of Race and Nation in Britain, 1947–1963,' *Journal of British Studies* 36 (April 1997): 207–38.

40 Andre Pilkington, *Racial Disadvantage and Ethnic Diversity in Britain* (Basingstoke: Palgrave Macmillan, 2003).

41 Chris Barker, *The Sage Dictionary of Cultural Studies* (London: Sage, 2004), 132.

42 Nancy Ward, interview, 17 Aug. 1999.

43 Margaret Shkimba and Karen Flynn, 'In England We Did Nursing: Caribbean and British Nurses in Great Britain and Canada, 1950–1970,' in Susan McGann and Barbara Mortimer, eds., *New Directions in Nursing History: International Perspectives* (New York: Routledge, 2004), 145.

44 These feelings were also revealed in oral accounts compiled by Wendy Webster that included Caribbean women who were well versed in colonial literature and fairy tales. Wendy Webster, *Imagining Home: Gender, Race and National Identity, 1945–64* (London: UCL Press, 1998).

45 Ancilla Ho-Young, interview, 15 Aug., 2007.

46 Ibid.

47 Ponzanesi and Merolla, *Migrant Cartographies*, 2.

48 Joan Virtue, interview, 12 Sept. 2006.

49 Muriel Knight, interview, 12 Sept. 2006.

50 Carmencita Gomez, interview, 14 Oct. 1999.

51 Carole Boyce Davies, *Black Women Writing and Identity: Migrations of the Subject* (New York: Routledge, 1994), 3.

52 Joan Virtue, interview, 12 Sept. 2006.

53 Dorothy Jones, interview, 29 Feb. 2000.

54 Pauline Leonard, 'Migrating Identities: Gender, Whiteness, and Britishness in Post-Colonial Hong Kong,' *Gender Place and Culture* 15/1 (2008): 47.

55 Jennette Prince, interview, 8 Oct. 1999.

56 Lillie Johnson, interview, 21 May 2000.

57 Nancy Foner, 'Male and Female: Jamaican Migrants in London,' *Anthropological Quarterly* 49/1, Women and Migration (Special Issue, 1976): 32–3.

58 Ibid.

59 Dorothy Jones, interview, 29 Feb. 2000.

60 Carmencita Gomez, interview, 14 Oct. 1999. See also, David G. Pearson, 'Race, Religiosity and Political Activism: Some Observations on West Indian Participation in Britain,' *British Journal of Sociology* 29/ 3 (1978), 340–57.

61 Ibid. Scholars strongly suggest that overall there was an overwhelming decline in Caribbean migrant church attendance. E.J.B. Rose cites similar reasons as the interviewees, such as climate, attitudes of white congregations, work habits, and mobility. See E.J.B. Rose et al., *Colour and Citizenship*, 370–80. For a short discussion on reasons for church decline, albeit among Caribbean men, see Anthony H. Richmond, *Colour Prejudice in Britain: A Study of West Indian Workers in Liverpool, 1941–1951* (London: Routledge and Kegan Paul, 1954).

62 See, e.g., Clifford Hill, *West Indian Migrants and the London Churches* (London: Oxford University Press, 1963). Caribbean migrants have also developed their own religious sects. See, e.g., Nicole Rodriguez Toulis, *Believing Identity: Pentecostalism and the Mediation of Jamaican Ethnicity and Gender in England* (Oxford: Berg, 1997). Toulis argues that 'Although the various denominational synods and more liberal clergy held favorable attitudes towards the newcomers, encouraging social integration premised upon the ideals of Christian universalism and brotherhood, lay members and many parochial clergy were reluctant to admit Blacks into their fellowship on equal terms' (26). Pentecostalism has been the focus of most studies given its 'visibility' as the primary Caribbean religion, but there are also other religious denominations. For a list of these religions, see Clifford Hill, 'From Church to Sect: West Indian Religious Sect Development in Britain,' *Journal for the Scientific Study of Religion* 10/2 (1971): 114–23. For Seventh Day Adventists specifically, see, e.g., Robin Theobald, 'The Politicization of a Religious Movement: British Adventism under the Impact of West Indian Immigration,' *British Journal of Sociology* 32/2 (1981): 202–23.

63 See, e.g., Bauer and Thompson, 'She's Always the Person with a Very Global Vision.'

64 Darlene Barnes, interview, 22 Oct. 1999.

65 Lillie Johnson, interview, 9 Aug. 1999.

66 Dorothy Jones, interview, 29 Feb. 2000.

67 For a discussion of how the family is involved in the migration process, see Chamberlain, *Family Love in the Diaspora*.

68 Nancy Ward, interview, 5 Jan. 2000.

69 Ibid.

70 Winston James, 'Migration, Racism and Identity Formation: The Caribbean Experience in Britain,' in Winston James and Clive Harris eds., *Inside Babylon: The Caribbean Diaspora in Britain* (New York: Verso, 1993), 243.

71 Stuart Hall, 'Old and New Identities, Old and New Ethnicities,' in Les Back and John Solomos, eds., *Theories of Race and Racism: A Reader* (New York: Routledge, 2000), 144–53. Also quoted in Karen Flynn, 'Experience and

Identity: Black Immigrant Nurses to Canada, 1950–1980,' in Marlene Epp, Franca Iacovetta, and Frances Swyripa, eds., *Sisters or Strangers: Immigrant, Ethnic, and Racialized Women in Canadian History* (Toronto: University of Toronto Press, 2004), 381–98.

72 Amina Mama, *Beyond Masks: Race, Gender and Subjectivity* (New York: Routledge, 1995), 112.

73 For a discussion of the Notting Hill riots, see, Edward Pilkington, *Beyond the Mother Country: West Indians and the Notting Hill White Riots* (London: I.B. Tauris, 1988).

74 Dorette Thompson, interview, 17 Aug. 1999.

75 Beverly Tatum, '*Why Are All the Black Kids Sitting Together in the Cafeteria?' and Other Conversations about Race* (New York: Basic Books, 1999), 54. While most of the studies on Caribbean students in the education system deal with the 1980s and 1990s and focus on Black boys, some of the studies allude to earlier decades. Unfortunately, the issues Dorette raised regarding her experience in the education system continue to persist for Black students in Britain today. See, e.g., D. Gillborn, 'Education Policy as an Act of White Supremacy: Whiteness, Critical Race Theory and Education,' 2005. Retrieved 4 Nov. 2010 from http://eprints.ioe.ac.uk/1654/1/gillborn2005education485text.pdf.

76 Dorette Thompson, interview, 17 Aug. 1999.

77 Daphne Veronica Clarke, interview, 27 April 2006.

78 Darlene Barnes, interview, 22 Oct. 1999.

4 Nurses' Training and Education

1 Bettina Bradbury, 'Women's History and Working-Class History,' *Labour/Le Travail* 19 (Spring 1987): 23–43.

2 Butler, *Gender Trouble*, xv.

3 Bhabha, *The Location of Culture*, 123, original emphasis.

4 See, e.g., Makeda Silvera, *Silenced: Talks with Working-Class Caribbean Women about Their Lives and Struggles as Domestic Workers in Canada* (Toronto: Sister Vision Press, 1983); Brand, 'Black Women and Work'; Linda Carty, 'African Canadian Women and the State: "Labour Only, Please,"' in Peggy Bristow et al., '*We're Rooted Here and They Can't Pull Us Up': Essays in African Canadian Women's History* (Toronto: University of Toronto Press, 1994), 193–229; Agnes Calliste, 'Women of "Exceptional Merit": Immigration of Caribbean Nurses to Canada,' *Canadian Journal of Women and the Law* 6/1 (1992): 87. For a discussion on Caribbean nurses in the occupation in the 1990s and later, see Rebecca Hagey et al., 'Immigrant Nurses' Experience of Racism,'

Journal of Nursing Scholarship 33/4 (2001): 389–494; Najja Nwofia Modibo, 'The Shattered Dreams of African-Canadian Nurses,' *Canadian Woman Studies* 23/2 (2004): 111–17; Tania Das Gupta, *Racism and Paid Work* (Toronto: Garamound Press, 1996).

5 Julia Hallam, *Nursing the Image: Media, Culture and Professional Identity* (London: Routledge, 2000), 90.

6 Charles Webster, *National Health Care Service: A Political History* (Oxford: Oxford University Press, 1997), 2.

7 Kramer, M*any Rivers to Cross*, 15.

8 Ibid., 17–19.

9 Ibid., 9.

10 See, e.g., Bryan et al., *The Heart of the Race*.

11 Hallam, *Nursing the Image*, 117.

12 Ibid., 120.

13 Ibid., 122. State-enrolled nurses (SENs) closest equivalent might be nurses' aides in North America.

14 Kramer, *Many Rivers to Cross*, 15.

15 Helen Mussaleem, 'Manpower Problem in Nursing,' *Canadian Nurse* (Aug. 1967): 26.

16 Kathryn McPherson, *Bedside Matters: The Transformation of Canadian Nursing, 1900–1990* (Toronto: Oxford University Press, 1996), 118–20; Karen Flynn, 'Beyond the Glass Wall: Black Canadian Nurses, 1940–1970,' *Nursing History Review* 17 (2009): 129–52.

17 Calliste, 'Women of "Exceptional Merit,"' 92.

18 'Negro Girl Popular Nurse, Guelph,' *Toronto Evening Telegram* (28 Feb. 1950): 10.

19 Clare McLean-Wilson, 'A Triumph of Will,' *Northern Terminus: The African Canadian History Journal* 3 (2006): 7.

20 'Owen Sound Negro Girl Leads Her Nursing Class,' PF 49, Owen Sound Historical Society Collection, Box 24: 'Izetta Fraser Collection, vol. 1, Black History,' 38.

21 'Owen Sound Negro Girl Leads Her Nursing Class.'

22 Roberta Avery, 'Rejection still Troubles Nurse,' *Toronto Star* (6 Aug. 2001).

23 Immigration officials also played a role in prohibiting the migration of Caribbean nurses. Her qualifications were approved by Mount Sinai Hospital, in Toronto, yet Jamaican-born Beatrice Massop was initially denied entry to Canada. See, e.g., Karen Flynn, 'Experience and Identity: Black Immigrant Nurses to Canada, 1950–1980,' in Marlene Epp, Franca Iacovetta, and Frances Swyripa, eds., *Sisters or Strangers: Immigrant, Ethnic, and Racialized Women in Canadian History* (Toronto: University of Toronto Press, 2004), 381–98.

24 Karen Flynn, "'I'm Glad that Someone Is Telling the Nursing Story": Writing Black Canadian Women's History,' *Journal of Black Canadian Studies* 38/3 (2008): 443–60.

25 Sheila Mackay Russell, "'The Glass Wall": A New Chapter in the Human Drama in a Hospital,' *Chatelaine* (Oct. 1964): 68; Flynn, 'Beyond the Glass Wall,' 133–4.

26 'Basin Street Comes North,' *Torgen: Toronto General Hospital, School of Nursing* (1966): 25. Students at Atkinson School of Nursing presented a similar performance entitled 'This Is Vaudeville,' *The Pulse: Atkinson School of Nursing Yearbook,* Toronto Western Hospital (1967): 18–19. See Flynn, 'Beyond the Glass Wall,' 133–4.

27 Miranda Whittaker, a Black student was a 1966 graduate.

28 'Churches Rapped!!! Grizzle, Moore Speak Out against Minstrel Shows,' *Canadian Negro* 4/1 (March 1956): 1.

29 Ibid.

30 Ibid.

31 Hallam, *Nursing the Image,* 25.

32 Carey Fraser, *Ambivalent Anti-Colonialism: The United States and the Genesis of West Indian Independence, 1940–1964* (Westport, CT: Greenwood, 1994), 37.

33 A. Lynn Bolles, *We Paid Our Dues: Women Trade Union Leaders of the Caribbean* (Washington, DC: Howard University Press, 1996), 46.

34 Hilary McD. Beckles, 'Nursing Colonial Wounds: Nita Barrow and Public Health Reform after the 1930s Workers' Revolution,' in Ruth Nita Barrow, Eudine Barriteau, and Alan Cobley, eds., *Stronger, Surer, Bolder: Social Change and International Development* (Kingston, Jamaica: University of the West Indies Press, 2001), 26–45.

35 Hezekiah, *Breaking the Glass Ceiling,* 9.

36 Hewitt, *Trailblazers in Nursing Education,* 16.

37 Ruby V. Grannum King, 'The Importance of Post Graduate Education for Graduate Nurses,' paper presented at the Caribbean Nurses Organisation Conference, Barbados, 1959, 11.

38 Margaret D. Gill, 'Nursing Politics and Social Change in the Caribbean: The Nita Barrow Years,' in Barrow, Barriteau, and Cobley, eds., *Stronger, Surer, Bolder,* 69.

39 See, e.g., Hezekiah, *Breaking the Glass Ceiling;* Hewitt, *Trailblazers in Nursing Education.*

40 Hewitt, *Trailblazers in Nursing Education,* 10.

41 Hezekiah, *Breaking the Glass Ceiling,* 42.

42 See, e.g., Catherine Cenzia Choy, *Empire of Care: Nursing and Migration in*

Filipino History (Durham: Duke University Press, 2003). Choy makes a similar argument regarding the role of the United States in shaping nurses' training in the Philippines.

43 Kathryn McPherson, '"The Case of the Kissing Nurse": Femininity, Sexuality, and Canadian Nursing, 1900–1970,' in Kathryn McPherson, Cecilia Morgan, and Nancy M. Forestell, eds., *Gendered Pasts: Historical Essays in Femininity and Masculinity in Canada* (Toronto: Oxford University Press, 1999), 181. McPherson recognizes that race and class are equally powerful influences on nursing performance, but she does not interrogate whiteness, and racially subordinated women are absent from her and Butler's discussion about gender and performance.

44 Butler, *Gender Trouble*, 178.

45 Bryan et al., *The Heart of the Race.*

46 Bhabha, *The Location of Culture*, 122, original emphasis.

47 Bill Ashcroft, Gareth Griffiths, and Helen Tiffin, *Post-Colonial Studies: Key Concepts* (New York: Routledge, 2000), 13.

48 Bhabha, *The Location of Culture*, 86.

49 Ashcroft et al., *Post-Colonial Studies*, 13.

50 Ibid.

51 Ania Loomba, *Colonialism/Post Colonialism* (London: Routledge, 1998), 179.

52 Orphelia Bennett, interview, 14 Oct. 2000.

53 Ibid. Caribbean nursing scholar Hermi Hyacinth Hewitt stated that the '109 students sitting the January 1946 examination' were the result of 'the practice of training nurses in several rural hospitals.' See *Trailblazers in Nursing Education Education*, 64.

54 Jennette Prince, interview, 8 Oct. 1999.

55 Ibid.

56 Nuffield Provincial Hospitals Trust, *The Work of Nurses in Hospital Wards: Report of Job-Analysis* (London: Nuffield Provincial Hospitals Trust, 1953), 28, original emphasis.

57 Dorothy Jones, interview, 29 Feb. 2000.

58 Ibid.

59 Jennette Prince, interview, 8 Oct. 1999.

60 Monica Mitchell, interview, 7 April 2000.

61 Hallam, *Nursing the Image*, 51.

62 Ann Bradshaw, 'The Virtue of Nursing: The Covenant of Care,' *Journal of Medical Ethics* 25 (Dec. 1999): 477.

63 Muriel Knight, interview, 9 Sept. 2006.

64 Butler, *Undoing Gender*, 1.

65 Nuffield Trust, *The Work of Nurses in Hospital Wards*, 37.

66 Ibid., 39.

67 Ancilla Ho-Young, interview, 15 Aug. 2007.

68 Agnes (Scott) Ellesworth, interview, 5 June 2001.

69 Ema Gamarnikov, 'Sexual Division of Labour: The Case of the Nursing,' in Annette Kuhn and AnneMarie Wolpe, eds., *Feminism and Materialism: Women and Modes of Production* (Boston: Routledge, 1978), 96–123.

70 Laura Tynes, interview, 6 Dec. 1999.

71 Ibid.

72 Ibid.

73 Butler, *Gender Trouble*, 33.

74 V. Harwood and M.L. Rasmussen, 'Performativity, Youth, and Injurious Speech,' *Teaching Education* 14/1 (2003): 25–36.

75 Virginia Travis, interview, 5 June 2001.

76 Ibid.

77 Ibid.

78 Sherene H. Razack, *Looking White People in the Eye: Gender, Race and Culture in Courtrooms and Classrooms* (Toronto: University of Toronto Press, 1998), 8.

79 Ibid.

80 Dorothy (Richards) Campbell, interview, 27 Oct. 2006.

81 'The Welfare of the Coloured People,' *Nursing Times* (5 Dec. 1958): 1426.

82 Ibid.

83 'Frustrated,' *Nursing Times* (5 Dec. 1958): 1426.

84 Daphne Veronica Clarke, interview, 27 April 2006.

85 Muriel Knight, interview, 12 Sept. 2006.

86 Carmencita Gomez, interview, 14 Oct. 1999

87 Elaine McLeod, interview, 5 May 1995.

88 Dorothy Jones, interview, 29 Feb. 2000.

89 Ibid.

90 Ancilla Ho-Young, interview, 15 Aug. 2007.

91 Ibid.

92 Jean Harry, 9 Aug. 2000.

93 Lillie Johnson, interview, 9 Aug. 1999.

94 Ibid.

95 Inez Mackenzie, interview, 13 Oct. 1999.

96 Hay Ho Sang, 'The Development of Nursing Education in Jamaica,' 386.

97 Hallam, *Nursing the Image*, 124.

98 Carol Baxter, quoted in ibid., 123.

99 Darlene Barnes, interview, 22 Oct. 1999.

100 Carol Boyce Davies and Molara Ogundipe-Leslie, *Moving beyond Boundaries: International Dimensions of Black Women's Writing*, vol. 1 (New York: New York University Press, 1995), 5.

101 Ibid.

102 Betsy Lucal, 'What It Means to Be Gendered Me: Life on the Boundaries of a Dichotomous Gendered System,' *Gender and Society* 13 (Dec. 1999): 784.

103 University of Toronto Archives, A79-001/001 (Certificate in Public Health Nursing).

104 Ibid.

105 Ibid.

106 Ibid.

107 Ibid.

108 Ibid.

109 'What Is a Student Nurse?' *The Pulse* (Atkinson School of Nursing, Toronto Western Hospital, 1967), 23.

110 Dianne Dodd, 'Commemorating Canadian Nursing.' Retrieved 15 April 2008 from http://crm.cr.nps.gov/archive/24-02/24-02-14.pdf.

111 Beverly Salmon, interview, 8 Aug. 2007.

112 Laura Tynes, interview, 6 Dec. 1999.

113 See Flynn, 'Beyond the Glass Wall,' 147.

114 Agnes Ellesworth, interview, 5 June 2001.

115 Cathy Williams, interview, 19 Nov. 2007.

116 The two-student policy has some merit. Ruth Bailey and Gwennyth Barton were admitted together at the Halifax Children's Hospital. Beginning in 1948, up until 1961, Hôtel Dieu in Windsor, Ontario, admitted two Black students per year.

117 Daphne Bailey, interview, 9 May 1995.

118 Joan Virtue, interview, 12 Sept. 2006.

119 Barbara Melosh, *The Physician's Hand: Work, Culture and Conflict in American Nursing* (Philadelphia: Temple University Press, 1982).

120 Cathy Williams, interview, 19 Nov. 2007.

121 Eleanor Shreve, interview, 29 April 2006.

122 Inez Mackenzie, 13 Oct. 1999.

123 Ancilla Ho-Young, interview, 15 Aug. 2007.

124 Ibid.

5 'I've always Wanted to Work': Black Women and Professionalism

1 In the United States, see e.g., James S. Cunningham and Nadja Zalokar, 'The Economic Progress of Black Women, 1940–1980: Occupational

Distribution and Relative Wages,' *Industrial and Labour Relations Review* 45/3 (1992): 540–55. In the case of Britain, see Lewis, 'Black Women's Employment and the British Economy'; Baxter, *The Black Nurse*, 16; Bryan et al., *The Heart of the Race*. For Canada, see Brand, 'Black Women and Work; Calliste, 'Women of "Exceptional Merit."'

2 Patricia Hill Collins, *Black Feminist Thought: Knowledge, Consciousness, and the Politics of Empowerment*, rev. ed. (New York: Routledge, 2000), 45.

3 Ibid.

4 All, except one of the Caribbean nurses who trained outside of Canada, whether through upgrading or writing the licensing exams, met the requirements for RN status.

5 Victor Turner, 'Betwixt and Between: The Liminal Period in *Rites de Passage*,' in *The Forest of Symbols: Aspects of Ndembu Ritual* (New York: Cornell University Press, 1967), 95.

6 Whether nursing is a profession has been the focus of numerous scholarly debates. Using the physician's model, some scholars maintain that based on nursing engagement with professionalization initiatives, such as improved education, credentials, registration, and autonomy that the occupation satisfies the requirements that constitute a profession. See, e.g., Kinnear, *In Subordination*; Celia Davies, *Gender and the Professional Predicament in Nursing* (Buckingham: Open University Press, 1995).

7 Darlene Clark Hine, *Black Women in White: Racial Conflict and Cooperation in the Nursing Profession, 1890–1950* (Bloomington: Indiana University Press, 1989), 10.

8 Eleanor Shreve, interview, 29 April 2006.

9 Beverly Salmon, interview, 8 Aug. 2007.

10 Ibid.

11 Agnes (Scott) Ellesworth, interview, 5 June 2001.

12 Kellogg African American Health Care Project: Black-owned and -operated Hospitals in the Detroit Metropolitan Area during the 20th Century. Retrieved 3 July 2008 from http://www.med.umich.edu/haahc/Hospitals/hospital1.htm.

13 Agnes Ellesworth, interview, 5 June 2001.

14 George Yancey, 'Introduction: Situated Black Women's Voices in/on the Profession of Philosophy,' *Hypatia* 23/2 (2008): 156.

15 Ibid.

16 Dorothy (Richards) Campbell, interview, 27 April 2006.

17 Ibid.

18 Gloria D. Bigham, 'To Communicate with Negro Patients,' *American Journal of Nursing* 64/9 (1964): 113–15. The author makes a similar argument

admonishing supervisors for being complicit in segregating patients, by not orienting their nurses, and being silent when discriminatory policies were being formulated about Black patients.

19 Dorothy Campbell, interview, 27 April 2006.

20 Ibid.

21 In-depth oral interviews about African-American health care from 1940 to 1960 included several men and women who acted individually to end segregation in Detroit hospitals. See Kellogg African American Health Care Project Oral Histories. Retrieved 4 July 2008 from http://www.med.umich. edu/haahc/theoral.htm. See also, Rhoda L. Goldstein, 'Negro Nurses in Hospitals,' *American Journal of Nursing* 60/2 (1960): 215–17. Goldstein maintained that in her study of African Americans in white hospitals, 'the strongest weapon of the Negro nurse is her professional status,' and that Black nurses were willing to point out to the 'hospital personnel that discriminatory acts threatened the hospital occupational system.'

22 Janette C. Allotey, 'Writing Midwives' History: Problems and Pitfalls' (*Midwifery* 2009); retrieved 24 Sept. 2009 from doi:10.1016/j.midw.2009.03.003. For a history of midwifery primary in Britain, see e.g., Susan Pitt, 'Midwifery and Medicine: Gendered Knowledge in the Practice of Delivery,' in Hilary Marland and Anne Marie Rafferty, eds., *Midwives, Society, and Childbirth: Debates and Controversies in the Modern Period* (London: Routledge, 1997), 218–32; Anne Witz, 'Medical Men and Midwives,' in Anne Witz, *Professions and Patriarchy* (New York: Routledge, 1992), chapter 4; Robert Dingwall, Anne Marie Rafferty, and Charles Webster, *An Introduction to the Social History of Nursing* (London: Routledge, 1988), chapter 8; Ann Oakley, *Essays on Women, Medicine and Health* (Edinburgh: Edinburgh University Press, 1993), chapters 10 and 11.

23 Monica F. Baly, *Nursing and Social Change* (New York: Routledge, 1995), 209.

24 Marland and Rafferty, *Midwives, Society, and Childbirth*, 6.

25 Baly, *Nursing and Social Change*, 209.

26 Daphne Veronica Clarke, interview, 27 April 2006.

27 Ibid.

28 Winston James, 'The Black Experience in Twentieth-Century Britain,' in Phillip D. Morgan and Sean Hawkins, eds., *Black Experience and the Empire* (London: Oxford University Press, 2004), 374.

29 Lillie Johnson, interview, 9 Aug. 1999.

30 Ibid.

31 Daphne Veronica Clarke, interview, 27 April 2006.

32 Anne Thompson, 'Establishing the Scope of Practice: Organizing European Midwifery in the Inter-war Years, 1919–1938,' in Marland and Rafferty, eds., *Midwives, Society, and Childbirth*, 20.

33 Lillie Johnson, interview, 9 Aug. 1999.

34 Ibid.

35 Peggy Levitt, 'Social Remittances: A Local-Level, Migration-Driven Form of Cultural Diffusion.' *International Migration Review* 32/124 (1999): 926–49.

36 Muriel Knight, interview, 12 Sept. 2006.

37 Vera Cudjoe, interview, 5 Jan. 1995.

38 Jennette Prince, interview, 8 Oct. 1999.

39 Pauline Leonard, 'Playing Doctors and Nurses: Competing Discourses of Gender, Power and Identity in the British National Health Service,' *Sociological Review* 51/2 (2003): 219.

40 Dorothy Jones, interview, 29 Feb. 2000.

41 Stuart Hall, 'Negotiating Caribbean Identities,' *New Left Review* 209 (1995): 3–14.

42 Victor Turner, 'Social Dramas and Stories about Them,' in W.J.T. Mitchell, ed., *On Narrative* (Chicago: University of Chicago Press, 1981), 137–64.

43 McPherson, *Bedside Matters*, 223.

44 Ibid.

45 Monica Mitchell, interview, 7 April 2000. Cynthia Toman pointed out that the issue of delegating certain tasks that were once the purview of physicians was a contested issue as nurse leaders grappled with the legal ramifications. In some hospitals nurses did assume certain tasks while in others it took longer. This might explain the reaction of nurses such as Monica. See, e.g., Cynthia Toman, '"Body Work": Nurses and the Delegation of Medical Technology at the Ottawa Civic Hospital, 1947–1972,' *Scientia Canadensis* 29/2 (2006): 155–75.

46 Muriel Knight, interview, 12 Sept. 2006.

47 For a discussion on how medical men in the United States in the twentieth century took control, authority, and ability to earn a living away from midwives to ensure the institutionalization of scientific medicine and that the medical field would be male dominated, see Judy Barrett Litoff, 'Midwifery and History,' in Rima Apple, ed., *Women, Health, and Medicine in America: A Historical Handbook* (New York: Garland, 1990), 443–58.

48 Dianne Dodd, 'Helen MacMurchy, Popular Midwifery and Maternity Services for Canadian Pioneer Women,' in Dianne Dodd and Deborah Gorman, eds., *Caring and Curing: Historical Perspectives on Women and Healing in Canada* (Ottawa: University of Ottawa Press, 1994), 135.

49 For a provocative discussion on race and midfery, see Sheryl Nestel, *Obstructed Labour: Race and Gender in the Re-emergence of Midwifery* (Vancouver: UBC Press, 2006).

50 Lillie Johnson, interview, 9 Aug. 1999.

51 Daphne Bailey, interview, 5 May 1995.
52 Ibid.
53 Daphne Clarke, interview, 27 April 2006.
54 Jennette Prince, interview, 8 Oct. 1999.
55 Daphne Clarke, interview, 27 April 2006.
56 Dorothy Jones, interview, 29 Feb. 2000.
57 Sarah Jane Growe, *Who Cares? The Crisis in Canadian Nursing* (Toronto: Canadian Publishers, 1991), 157.
58 Dorothy Jones, interview, 29 Feb. 2000.
59 Jennette Prince, interview, 8 Oct. 1999.
60 University of Toronto Archives, A1973-0053/012 (Obstetrical Record Book).
61 Jennette Prince, interview, 8 Oct. 1999.
62 Monica Mitchell, interview, 7 April 2000.
63 Dorothy Jones, interview, 29 Feb. 2000.
64 Gail Lewis, 'Situated Voices: "Black Women's Experience" and Social Work,' *Feminist Review* 53 (Summer 1996): 29.
65 Virginia Travis, interview, 5 June 2001.
66 Ibid.
67 Cathy Williams, interview, 12 Aug. 2007.
68 Ibid.
69 Charmaine Crawford, 'Black Women, Racing and Gendering the Canadian Nation,' in Notisha Massaquoi and Njoki Nathani Wane, eds., *Theorizing Empowerment: Canadian Perspectives on Black Feminist Thought* (Toronto: Inanna, 2007), 119.
70 Dorette Thompson, interview, 17 Aug. 1999.
71 Ibid.
72 Ibid.
73 Philippians 4:13.
74 Monica Mitchell, interview, 7 April 2000.
75 See Russell, 'The Glass Wall'; also see chapter 4.
76 Monica Mitchell, interview, 7 April 2000.
77 Carmelita Gomez, interview, 14 Oct. 1999.
78 June Heaven, interview, 11 Nov. 1999.
79 Ibid.
80 Frances Henry et al., *The Colour of Democracy: Racism in Canadian Society*, 2nd ed. (Toronto: Harcourt Brace, 2000), 55.
81 Philomena Essed, *Everyday Racism: Reports from Women of Two Cultures* (Alameda, CA: Hunter House, 1990) 3.
82 Karen Flynn, 'Nurses in Resistance,' in Sophie G. Harding, *Surviving the*

Hour of Darkness: The Health and Wellness of Women of Colour and Indigenous Women (Calgary: University of Calgary Press, 2005), 3–12.

83 See, e.g., Evelyn L. Barbee, 'Racism in Nursing,' *Medical Anthropology Quarterly* 74 (1993): 346.

84 Dorothy Jones, 29 Feb. 2000.

85 Ibid.

86 Ibid.

87 Interviewee did not want to be identified.

88 Janet Barrett, interview, 5 June 2000.

89 Luke 6:31. See Wanda Thomas Bernard, ed., *Fighting for Change: Black Social Workers in Nova Scotia* (Halifax: Nimbus, 2006) for a brief discussion of Black female professionals who are guided by their religious beliefs.

90 Marlene Watson, interview, 18 Jan. 2000.

91 Ibid.

92 Nancy Fraser, 'Rethinking Recognition,' *New Left Review* 3 (May–June 2000): 113.

93 Frieda M. (Parker) Steele, interview, 9 June 2001.

94 Ibid.

95 Dorette Thompson, interview, 17 Aug. 1999.

96 Ibid.

97 Muriel Knight, interview, 12 Sept. 2006.

98 Ibid.

99 Julie Fairman, 'Not All Nurses Are Good, Not All Doctors Are Bad ...,' *Bulletin of the History of Medicine* 78/2 (2004): 451–60 (Review).

100 Eleanor (Vincent) Shreve, interview, 29 April 2006.

101 See, e.g., Melosh, '*The Physician's Hand.*'

102 For a discussion on the transformations nursing underwent, see Alice J. Baumgart and Jenniece Larsen, eds., *Canadian Nurses Face the Future*, 2nd ed. (Toronto: Mosby Year Book, 1992); Pat Armstrong, Jacqueline Choiniere, and Elaine Day, eds., *Vital Signs* (Toronto: Garamond, 1993).

103 Brenda Lewis, interview, 24 Feb. 2000.

104 Marlene Watson, interview, 18 Jan. 2000.

105 Nancy Ward, interview, 5 Jan. 2000.

106 Ibid.

107 Interviewee did not want to be identified.

108 Ibid.

109 Cathy Williams, interview, 12 Aug. 2007.

110 Ibid.

111 Laura Tynes, interview, 6 Dec. 1999.

112 Ibid.

113 Jean Harry, interview, 8 Aug. 2000.
114 Ibid.

6 Combining Work, Family, and Community

1 *Nursing Times* (12 Feb. 1960): 175.
2 Daphne Bailey, interview, 5 May 1995.
3 Hill Collins, *Black Feminist Thought*, 47.
4 Chamberlain, *Family Love in the Diaspora*, 5. See also, Carby, 'White Woman Listen! 46.
5 See, e.g., Tracey Reynolds, 'Black Mothering, Paid Work and Identity,' *Ethnic and Racial Studies* 24/6 (2001): 1046–64.
6 For a discussion on how nurses in the United States manage their multiple roles, see, Patricia D'Antonio, *American Nursing: A History of Knowledge, Authority and the Meaning of Work* (Baltimore: Johns Hopkins University Press, 2010).
7 Daphne Bailey, interview, 5 May, 1995.
8 Changes in women's work continuity. Retrieved 13 July 2008 from http://www.statcan.ca/english/kits/pdf/social/women3.pdf.
9 Ontario Federation of Labour and the Workers Arts and Heritage Centre, 'A History of Women and Work.' Retrieved 7 Aug. 2009 from http://www.ofl.ca/uploads/misc/womenandwork/A_HISTORY_OF_WOMEN_AND_WORK_amended_Jan_11_(2).pdf.
10 Laura Tynes, interview, 6 Dec. 1999.
11 Dorothy (Richards) Campbell, interview, 27 April 2006.
12 Ibid.
13 Agnes (Scott) Ellesworth, interview, 5 June 2001.
14 Ibid.
15 Eleanor (Vincent) Shreve, interview, 29 April 2006.
16 Beverly Salmon, interview, 8 Aug. 2007.
17 Although 'maternal guilt' is a recent term used to describe the ambivalence that working mothers with children experience, it can be equally applied to earlier periods, exemplified in Dorothy R's feelings when she returned to work in the mid-1950s. See, e.g., Gale L. Cassidy and Lorraine Davies, 'Explaining Gender Differences in Mastery among Married Parents,' *Social Psychology Quarterly* 66 (2003): 48–61.
18 Janet Barrett, interview, 5 June 2000.
19 Nancy Zukewich Ghalam, 'Attitudes towards Women, Work and Family,' *Canadian Social Trends* 46 (Autumn 1997): 13.
20 Betty Clarke, interview, 19 Nov. 2007.

21 Arlie Hochschild, with Annie Machung, *The Second Shift: Working Parents and the Revolution at Home* (New York: Viking Penguin, 1989).

22 Michelene Ridley Malson, 'Black Women's Sex Roles: The Social Context for a New Ideology,' *Journal of Social Issues* 39/3 (1983): 103.

23 Virginia Travis, interview, 5 June 2001.

24 Agnes Ellesworth, interview, 5 June 2001.

25 Ibid.

26 Migration scholars often focus on the children left in the Caribbean with relatives by parents. For studies that focus on female migrants (mothers), in particular see, e.g., N. Foner, 'Women, Work and Migration: Jamaicans in London,' *Urban Anthropology* 4/3 (1975): 229–49; M. Byron, 'Migration, Work and Gender: The Case of Post-War Labour Migration from the Caribbean to Britain,' in M. Chamberlain, ed., *Caribbean Migration: Globalised Identities* (London: Routledge, 1998), 217–31; K.F. Olwig, 'The Migration Experience: Nevisian Women at Home and Abroad,' in J. Momsen, ed., *Women and Change in the Caribbean* (London: James Curry, 1993), 159–66.

27 June Heaven, interview, 11 Nov. 1999.

28 Ibid.

29 Joan Virtue, interview, 12 Sept. 2006.

30 Ibid.

31 Janet Barrett, interview, 5 June 2000.

32 Dorothy Jones, interview, 29 Feb. 2000.

33 Inez Mackenzie, interview, 13 Oct. 1999.

34 Ibid.

35 Elaine McLeod, interview, May 1995.

36 Ibid.

37 Ibid.

38 Carmencita Gomez, interview, 14 Oct. 1999.

39 Ibid.

40 Claire Robertson, 'Africa in the Americas?' in David Barry Gasper and Darlene Clarke Hine, eds., *More than Chattel: Black Women and Slavery in the Americas* (Bloomington: Indiana University Press, 1996), 10. Some scholars prefer the term *matrifocality*, which privileges the role of women as mothers. See, e.g., R.T Smith, 'The Matrifocal Family,' in J. Goody, *The Character of Kinship* (Cambridge: Cambridge University Press, 1973), 121–44.

41 Dorothy Campbell, interview, 27 Oct. 2006.

42 Frieda (Parker) Steele, interview, 9 June 2001.

43 Ibid.

44 Patricia Hill Collins, *From Black Power to Hip-Hop: Racism, Nationalism, and Feminism* (Philadelphia: Temple University Press, 2006), 131.

45 Monica Mitchell, interview, 7 April 2000.
46 R.J. Taylor et al., 'Development of Research on Black Families: A Decade Review,' *Journal of Marriage and the Family* 52 (1990): 993–1014, as quoted in Shirley A. Hill, 'Class, Race and Gender: Dimensions of Childrearing in African-American Families,' *Journal of Black Studies* 31/5 (2001): 498.
47 Monica Mitchell, interview, 7 April 2000.
48 See Acts 10:34–35.
49 June Heaven, interview, 11 Nov. 1999.
50 Ibid.
51 Brenda Lewis, interview, 8 Oct. 1999.
52 Ibid. Camille Hernandez-Ramdwar raises some of the issues of belonging and displacement of growing up in Winnipeg; see 'The Elusive and Illusionary: Identifying of Me, Not by Me,' in Carl E. James and Adrienne Shadd, eds., *Talking about Identity: Encounters in Race, Ethnicity and Language* (Toronto: Between the Lines, 2001), 115–21.
53 Beverly Salmon, interview, 8 Aug. 2007.
54 Ibid.
55 Virginia Travis, interview, 5 June 2001.
56 Naomi Banks, interview, 26 April 2006.
57 Joan Virtue, interview, 12 Sept. 2006.
58 Ibid.
59 Betty Clarke, interview, 19 Nov. 2006.
60 Ancilla Ho-Young, interview, 15 Aug. 2007.
61 Ibid.
62 See, e.g., Josephine Etowa et al., 'Depression: The "Invisible Grey Fog" Influencing the Midlife Health of African Canadian Women,' *International Journal of Mental Health Nursing* 16/3 (2007): 203–13; Tamara Beauboeuf-Lafontant, *Behind the Mask of the Strong Black Woman: Voice and the Embodiment of a Costly Performance* (Philadelphia: Temple University Press, 2009).
63 Daphne Clarke, interview, 26 April 2006.
64 Ibid.
65 Virginia Travis, interview, 5 June 2001.
66 Laura Tynes, interview, 6 Dec. 1999.
67 Cathy Williams, interview, 12 Aug. 2007.
68 Betty Clarke, interview, 19 Nov. 2007.
69 Frieda (Parker) Steele, interview, 9 June 2001.
70 Ibid.
71 Ibid.
72 June Heaven, interview, 11 Nov. 1999.
73 Frieda (Parker) Steele, interview, 9 June 2001.

74 'Hopes Race Bylaw Is Enforced,' *Dawn of Tomorrow* (Sept. 1944): 2.
75 Jean Daniels, 'The Woman's Window,' *Canadian Negro* 3 (Oct. 1955): 3.
76 "Churches Rapped!!! Grizzle, Moore Speak Out against Minstrel Shows,'. 1.
77 *Contrast* started in 1969; *Share* newspaper began in April 1978.
78 Frieda (Parker) Steele, interview, 9 June 2001.
79 Ibid.
80 Retrieved 19 Nov. 2007 from http://www.reuther.wayne.edu/collections/hefa_660.htm.
81 Ibid.
82 Dorothy (Richards) Campbell, interview, 27 April 2006.
83 Ibid.
84 Daphne Veronica Clarke, interview, 27 April 2006.
85 Ibid.
86 Retrieved 22 Nov. 2007 from http://gg.ca/honours/medals/hon04-qegj_e.asp.
87 Daphne Veronica Clarke, interview, 27 April 2006.
88 Beverly Salmon, interview, 5 May 1995. Black women in the Black British diaspora have had a history of challenging racial inequality in the education system; see, e.g., A. Phoenix, 'Theories of Gender and Black families,' in Gaby Weiner and Madeleine Arnot, eds., *Gender under Scrutiny: New Enquiries in Education* (London: Hutchison, 1987), 50–61.
89 Beverly Salmon, interview, 8 Aug. 2007.
90 Ibid.
91 Betty Clarke, interview, 19 Nov. 2007.
92 Ibid.
93 Virginia Travis, interview, 5 June 2001.
94 Inez Mackenzie, interview, 13 Oct. 1999.
95 Naomi Banks, interview, 26 April 2006.
96 Shreve, *The AfriCanadian Church*, 96.
97 Frieda (Parker) Steele, interview, 9 June 2001.
98 Evelyn Brooks Higginbotham, *Righteous Discontent: The Women's Movement in the Black Baptist Church, 1880–1920* (Cambridge: Harvard University Press, 1993), 187.

7 Nation, Home, and Belonging

1 Muriel Knight, interview, 12 Sept. 2006.
2 Vera Cudjoe, interview, 5 Jan. 1995.
3 Ibid. For a discussion of Toronto in the 1960s, see Althea Prince, *Being Black: Essays by Althea Prince* (Toronto: Insomniac Press, 2001), 27–35.

4 Daphne Bailey, interview, 29 May 1995.

5 Vera Cudjoe, interview, 5 Jan. 1995.

6 Davies, *Black Women Writing and Identity*, 4.

7 See, e.g., Alan B. Simmons and Dwaine E. Plaza, 'The Caribbean Community in Canada: Transnational Connections and Transformations,' in Lloyd Wong and Vic Satzewich, eds., *Transnational Identities and Practices in Canada* (Vancouver: UBC Press, 2006), 130–49.

8 Vera Cudjoe, interview, 5 Jan. 1995.

9 Eileen Jacobson, interview, 6. Jan. 1995.

10 Ibid.

11 Colin A. Palmer, 'Defining and Studying the Modern African Diaspora,' *Journal of Negro History* 85/1–2 (2000): 29.

12 Ibid.

13 James, 'Migration, Racism and Identity Formation,' 240.

14 Myrna Blackman, interview, 29 May 1995.

15 James, 'Migration, Racism and Identity Formation,' 243.

16 Ibid.

17 Myrna Blackman, interview, 29 May 1995.

18 Stuart Hall, 'Thinking the Diaspora: Home-Thoughts from Abroad,' *Small Axe* 3/6 (1999): 1. Retrieved 12 Oct. 2008 from http://www.questia.com/read/96537857?title=Thinking%20the%20Diaspora%3a%20Home-Thoughts%20from%20Abroad.

19 Jennette Prince, interview, 8 Oct. 1999.

20 Carmencita Gomez, interview, 14 Oct. 1999.

21 Ibid.

22 Frieda (Parker) Steele, interview, 9 June 2001.

23 Edna (Bailey) Black Searles, interview, 4 Sept. 1999. For a discussion on Blacks organizing in Toronto, see Amoaba Gooden, 'Community Organizing by African Caribbean People in Toronto, Ontario,' *Journal of Black Studies* 38/3 (2008): 413–26.

24 Eileen Jacobson, interview, 6 Jan. 1995.

25 Jennette Prince, interview, 8 Oct. 1999.

26 Toulis, *Believing Identity*, 271.

27 Edna Searles, interview, 4 Sept. 1999.

28 Lillie Johnson, interview, 21 May 2000.

29 Ancilla Ho-Young, interview, 15 Aug. 2007.

30 Virginia Travis, interview, 5 June 2001.

31 Genesis 4:9.

32 Beverly Salmon, interview, 8 Aug. 2007.

33 Betty Clarke, interview, 19 Nov. 2007.

34 Ancilla Ho-Young, interview, 15 Aug. 2007.

35 Monica Mitchell, interview, 7 April 2000.

36 Vera Cudjoe, interview, 5 Jan. 1995.

37 African Canadian online, http://www.yorku.ca/aconline/film/theatre/history.html; The Canadian encyclopedia. Retrieved 3 Dec. 2007 from http://www.thecanadianencyclopedia.com/index.cfm?PgNm=TCE&Params=A1S EC886006.

38 Claire Dwyer, 'Negotiating Diasporic Identities: Youth South Asian Muslim Women,' *Women's Studies International Forum* 23/4 (2000): 477.

39 Evelyn Brooks Higginbotham, 'African-Americans and the the Metalanguage of Race,' *Signs* 14/4 (1992): 266.

40 Ibid.

41 Beverly Salmon, interview, 8 Aug. 2007.

42 Dorothy (Richards) Campbell, interview, 27 April 2006.

43 Beverly Salmon, interview, 8 Aug. 2007.

44 Ibid.

45 Cathy Williams, interview, 19 Nov. 2007.

46 Ibid.

47 Walcott, *Black Like Who?*, 42; Eva Mackey *The House of Difference: Cultural Politics and National Identity in Canada* (New York: Routledge, 1999).

48 Anderson, *Imagined Communities*, 16.

49 Barbara Smith, ed., *Home Girls: A Black Feminist Anthology* (New York: Kitchen Table Press, 1983), li.

50 Ibid., liv.

51 Madeline Ang-Lygate, 'Everywhere to Go but Home: On (Re)(Dis)(Un) location,' *Journal of Gender Studies* 5/3 (1996): 378.

52 Walcott, *Black Like Who?*, 42.

53 June Heaven, interview, 11 Nov. 1999.

54 James Clifford, *Routes: Travel and Translation in the Late Twentieth Century* (Cambridge: Harvard University Press, 1999), 254.

55 June Heaven, interview, 11 Nov. 1999.

56 Brenda Lewis, interview, 24 Feb. 2000.

57 Inez Mackenzie, interview, 13 Oct. 1999.

58 Naz Rassool, 'Fractured or Flexible Identities? Life Histories of "Black" Diasporic Women in Britain,' in Heidi Safia Mirza, ed., *Black British Feminism: A Reader* (London: Routledge, 1997), 197.

59 Ancilla Ho-Young, interview, 15 Aug. 2007.

60 Ibid.

61 Ibid.

62 Jennette Prince, interview, 8 Oct. 1999.

63 Vera Cudjoe, interview, 5 Jan. 1995.

64 Linda Basch, Nina Glick Schiller, and Cristina Blanc-Szanton, *Nations Unbound: Transnational Projects, Postcolonial Predicaments, and Deterritorialized Nation-States* (Langhorne: Gordon and Breach, 1994), 7.

65 Eileen Jacobson, interview, 6. Jan. 1995.

66 Muriel Knight, interview, 12 Sept. 2006.

67 Jennette Prince, interview, 8 Oct. 1999.

68 Muriel Knight, interview, 12 Sept. 2006.

69 Ibid.

70 Joan Virtue, interview, 12 Sept. 2006.

71 Wong and Satzewich, *Transnational Identities*, 1.

72 Jonathon Rutherford, 'A Place Called Home: Identity and the Cultural Politics of Difference,' in Jonathon Rutherford, ed., *Identity, Community, Culture and Difference* (London: Lawrence and Wishart, 1990), 25.

73 Kezia Page, '"What If He Did Not Have a Sister [Who Lived in the United States]?" Jamaica Kincaid's *My Brother* as Remittance Text,' *Small Axe* (2006): 21, 39.

74 Clifford, *Routes*, 256, quoted in Page, '"What If He Did Not Have a Sister,"' 39.

75 Daphne Bailey, interview, 5 May 1995.

76 Ancilla Ho-Young, interview, 15 Aug. 2007.

77 Carmelita Gomez, interview, 14 Oct. 1999.

78 Ibid.

79 Naomi Banks, interview, 26 April 2006.

80 Jacqueline Nassy Brown, 'Black Liverpool, Black America, and the Gendering of Diasporic Space,' *Cultural Anthropology* 13/3 (1998): 298.

81 Cathy Williams, interview, 12 Aug. 2007.

82 Virginia Travis, interview, 5 June 2001.

83 Edna (Bailey) Black Searles, interview, 4 Sept. 1999. See also 'Barred [missing word] Hospitals Negro Girls [missing word] Nursing Ambition,' *Toronto Daily Star* (15 Oct. 1947).

84 Dorothy Campbell, interview, 27 April 2006.

85 Ibid.

86 'A Colored Veteran Registers Protest,' *Windsor Star* (ca. 1940). (In author's possession.).

87 Saud Joseph, 'Women, Nation, State in Lebanon,' in Caren Kaplan, Norma Alarcón, and Minoo Moallem, eds., *Between Women and Nation: Nationalisms, Transnational Feminisms, and the State* (Durham: Duke University Press, 1999), 162.

88 Dorothy Campbell, interview, 27 April 2006.

89 Bristow, 'A Duty to the Past.'
90 Frieda (Parker) Steele, interview, 9 June 2001. For an excellent discussion of the CCA, see Bristow, 'A Duty to the Past.'
91 The City of Windsor, Ontario, Canada. Retrieved 5 Nov. 2008 from http://www.citywindsor.ca/000350.asp?parks=alton.
92 Scholars Rinaldo Walcott, in *Black Like Who?*, and Katherine McKittrick, in *Demonic Grounds: Black Women and the Cartographies of Struggle* (Minneapolis: University of Minnesota Press, 2006), have commented on these sites as examples of denying Black Canadians legacy and history.
93 Agnes Ellesworth, interview, 5 June 2001.
94 Mary Chamberlain, ed., *Caribbean Migration: Globalized Identities* (New York: Routledge, 1998), 8.

Conclusion

1 Davies, *Black Women Writing and Identity*, 3.
2 Jean Peneff, 'Myths in Life Stories,' in Raphael Samuel and Paul Thompson eds., *The Myths We Live By* (London and New York: Routledge, 1990), 36–7. Steedman, *Past Tenses*.
3 Lillie Johnson, interview, 21 May 2000.
4 Ibid.
5 Ibid.
6 Psalm 30:5.
7 Lillie Johnson, interview, 21 May 2000.

Bibliography

Interviews (Tape-recorded by Author)

Bailey, Daphne. Toronto, Ont., 29 May 1995.

Banks, Naomi. Windsor, Ont., 26 April 2006.

Barnes, Darlene. Toronto, Ont., 22 Oct. 1999.

Barrett, Janet (pseudonym). Toronto. Ont., 5 June 2000.

Bennett, Orphelia (pseudonym). Scarborough, Ont., 14 Oct. 2000.

Blackman, Myrna. Brampton, Ont., 29 May 1995.

Campbell, Dorothy (Richards). Toronto, Ont., 27 April 2006.

Clarke, Betty. Toronto, Ont., 19 Nov. 2007.

Clarke, Daphne Veronica. Windsor, Ont., 27 April 2006.

Cudjoe, Vera. Toronto, Ont. 5 Jan. 1995.

Ellesworth, Agnes (Scott). Windsor, Ont., 5 June 2001.

Gomez, Carmencita. (pseudonym). North York, Ont., 14 Oct. 1999.

Harry, Jean. Scarborough, Ont., 9 Aug. 2000.

Heaven, June. North York, Ont., 11 Nov. 1999.

Ho-Young, Ancilla. Burlington, Ont., 15 Aug. 2007.

Jacobson, Eileen. Toronto, Ont., 6 Jan. 1995.

Johnson, Lillie. Toronto, Ont., 9 Aug. 1999.

Jones, Dorothy. (pseudonym). Rexdale, Ont., 29 Feb. 2000.

Knight, Muriel. Scarborough, Ont., 12 Sept. 2006.

Lewis, Brenda. Toronto, Ont., 24 Feb. 2000.

Mackenzie, Inez. Markham, Ont., 13 Oct. 1999.

McLeod, Elaine. Markham, Ont., 5 May 1995.

Mitchell, Monica. Toronto, Ont., 7 April 2000.

Prince, Jennette. North York, Ont., 8 Oct. 1999.

Salmon, Beverly. Toronto, Ont., 8 Aug. 2007.

Searles, Edna (Bailey) Black. Scarborough, Ont., 4 Sept. 1999.
Shreve, Eleanor (Vincent). Windsor, Ont., 29 April 2006.
Steele, Frieda (Parker). Windsor, Ont., 9 June 2001.
Thompson, Dorette. (pseudonym). Mississauga, Ont., 17 Aug. 1999.
Travis, Virginia. Windsor, Ont., 5 June 2001.
Tynes, Laura. Mississauga, Ont., 6 Dec. 1999.
Virtue, Joan. Scarborough, Ont., 12 Sept. 2006.
Ward, Nancy. (pseudonym). Toronto, Ont., 5 Jan. 2000.
Watson, Marlene. North York, Ont., 18 Jan. 2000.
Williams, Cathy. Toronto, Ont., 12 Aug. 2007.

Organizations and Archives

Caribbean Nurses Organisation, University of the West Indies, St Augustine
    Campus, Trinidad and Tobago, 1959.
Kellogg African American Health Care Project. Oral Histories. Retrieved 25
    Jan. 2010 from http://www.med.umich.edu/haahc/theoral.htm.
– Black-owned and -operated Hospitals in the Detroit Metropolitan Area dur-
    ing the 20th Century. Retrieved 3 July 2008 from http://www.med.umich.
    edu/haahc/Hospitals/hospital1.htm.
'New Detroit, Inc. Collection, 1967–1975.' Walter P. Reuther Library of Labor
    and Urban Affairs, Wayne State University. Retrieved 8 Oct. 2009 from
    http://www.reuther.wayne.edu/collections/hefa_660.htm.
'Owen Sound Negro Girl Leads Her Nursing Class,' PF 49, Owen Sound
    Historical Society Collection, Box 24: Izetta Fraser Collection, vol. 1, 'Black
    History.'
The Pulse. Atkinson School of Nursing Yearbook, Toronto Western Hospital,
    1967.
The Torgen. Toronto General Hospital Yearbook, 1966.
University of Toronto Archives
    A1973-0053/012 (Obstetrical Record Book).
    A79-001/001 (Certificate in Public Health Nursing).
Windsor Interracial Council (WIC) Records. Council Meeting Minutes, 30
    Jan.–21 June 1948. University of Windsor Archives-05-002, Box 1, File 1.

Newspapers and Periodicals

Canadian Negro
Contrast
Dawn of Tomorrow
Evening Telegram

Nursing Times
Share
Toronto Daily Star
Toronto Star
Windsor Star

Other Published Sources

Alexander, Ken, and Avis Glaze. *Towards Freedom: The African Canadian Experience.* Toronto: Umbrella Press, 1996.

Allotey, Janette C. 'Writing Midwives' History: Problems and Pitfalls.' *Midwifery* (2009). Retrieved 24 Sept. 2009 from doi:10.1016/j.midw.2009.03.003.

Althusser, L. 'Ideology and Ideological State Apparatuses' in L. Althusser, *Lenin and Philosophy and Other Essays.* London: New Left Books, 1971, 121-76.

'And A Child Shall Lead Them.' *Dawn of Tomorrow* (Jan. 1947): 4.

Anderson, Benedict. *Imagined Communities: Reflections on the Origin and Spread of Nationalism,* rev. ed. New York: Verso, 1991.

Ang-Lygate, Madeline. 'Everywhere to Go but Home: On (Re)(Dis)(Un)location.' *Journal of Gender Studies* 5/3 (1996): 375–89.

Apple, Michael W. *Ideology and Curriculum.* New York: Routledge, 2004.

Archibald, Washington. *Reflections on an Epic Journey.* Saddlers Village, St Kitts: G.W. Archibald, 1993.

Armstrong, Pat, Jacqueline Choiniere, and Elaine Day, eds. *Vital Signs.* Toronto: Garamond, 1993.

Arthurs, H.W. 'Civil Liberties – Public Schools – Segregation of Negro Students.' *Canadian Bar Review* 41 (Sept. 1963): 453–7.

Ashcroft, Bill, Gareth Griffiths, and Helen Tiffin. *Post-Colonial Studies: Key Concepts.* New York: Routledge, 2000.

Austin-Broos, Diane J. *Jamaica Genesis: Religion and the Politics of Moral Orders.* Chicago: University of Chicago Press, 1997.

Avery, Roberta. 'Rejection Still Troubles Nurse.' *Toronto Star* (6 Aug. 2001).

Backhouse, Constance. *Colour-Coded: A Legal History of Racism in Canada, 1900–1950.* Toronto: University of Toronto Press, 1999.

– "'I Was Unable to Identify with Topsy': Carrie M. Best's Struggle against Racial Segregation in Nova Scotia, 1942.' *Atlantis* 22 (1998): 16–26.

Baillargeon, Denyse. *Making Do: Women, Family, and Home in Montreal during the Great Depression.* Translated by Yvonne Klein. Waterloo: Wilfrid Laurier University Press, 1999.

Baly, Monica F. *Nursing and Social Change.* New York: Routledge, 1995.

Barbee, Evelyn L. 'Racism in Nursing.' *Medical Anthropology Quarterly* 7/4 (1993): 346–62.

Barrow, Christine, ed. *Family in the Caribbean: Themes and Perspectives*. Kingston, Jamaica: Ian Randle, 1996.

Basch, Linda, Nina Glick Schiller, and Cristina Blanc-Szanton. *Nations Unbound: Transnational Projects, Postcolonial Predicaments, and Deterritorialized Nation-States*. Langhorne, PA: Gordon and Breach, 1994.

Bauer, Elaine, and Paul Thompson. '"She's Always the Person with a Very Global Vision": The Gender Dynamics of Migration, Narrative, Interpretation and the Case of Jamaican Transnational Families.' *Gender and History* 16/2 (2004): 334–75.

Baumgart, Alice J., and Jenniece Larsen, eds. *Canadian Nurses Face the Future*, 2nd ed. Toronto: Mosby Year Book, 1992.

Baxter, Carol. *The Black Nurse: An Endangered Species – A Case for Equal Opportunities in Nursing*. Cambridge: National Extension College, 1988.

Beauboeuf-Lafontant, Tamara. *Behind the Mask of the Strong Black Woman: Voice and the Embodiment of a Costly Performance*. Philadelphia: Temple University Press, 2009.

Beckles, Hilary McD. 'Nursing Colonial Wounds: Nita Barrow and Public Health Reform after the 1930s Workers' Revolution,' in Eudine Barriteau and Alan Cobley, eds., *Stronger, Surer, Bolder: Ruth Nita Barrow – Social Change and International Development*. Kingston: University of the West Indies Press, 2001, 26–45.

Bernard, Wanda Thomas, ed. *Fighting for Change: Black Social Workers in Nova Scotia* Halifax: Nimbus Publishing, 2006.

Besson, Jean. 'Reputation and Respectability Reconsidered: A New Perspective on Afro-Caribbean Peasant Women,' in Christine Barrow and Rhoda Reddock, eds., *Caribbean Sociology: Introductory Reading*. Kingston, Jamaica: Ian Randle, 2001, 350–70.

Bhabha, Homi K. *The Location of Culture*. New York: Routledge, 1994.

Bigham, Gloria D. 'To Communicate with Negro Patients.' *American Journal of Nursing* 64/9 (1964): 113–15.

Binnie, Ruth. 'Home Economics and Supervision, 1940–1956.' *Journal of Education* 6/1 (1956): 48.

Black History Canada. 'Timeline: 1900–Present.' Retrieved 10 Sept. 2009 from http://blackhistorycanada.ca/timeline.php?id=1900.

'Black Theatre in Toronto, 1973–1988.' African Canadian Online. Retrieved 30 Jan. 2010 from http://www.yorku.ca/aconline/film/theatre/history.html.

Bobb-Smith, Yvonne. *I Know Who I Am: A Caribbean Women's Identity in Canada*. Toronto: Women's Press, 2003.

Bolles, A. Lynn. *We Paid Our Dues: Women Trade Union Leaders of the Caribbean*. Washington, DC: Howard University Press, 1996.

Bradbury, Bettina. 'Women's History and Working-Class History.' *Labour/LeTravail* no. 19 (Spring 1987): 23–43.

Bradshaw, Ann. 'The Virtue of Nursing: The Covenant of Care.' *Journal of Medical Ethics* 25 (Dec. 1999): 477–81.

Brand, Dionne. 'Black Women and Work: The Impact of the Racially Constructed Roles on the Sexual Division of Labour,' in Enakshi Dua and Angela Robertson, eds., *Scratching the Surface: Canadian Anti-Racist Feminist Thought.* Toronto: Women's Press, 1999, 83–96.

– *No Burden to Carry: Narratives of Black Working Women in Ontario, 1920s–1950s.* Toronto: Women's Press, 1991.

Brereton, Bridget. 'Society and Culture in the Caribbean, the British and French West Indies, 1870–1980,' in Franklin W. Knight and Colin A. Palmer, eds., *The Modern Caribbean.* Chapel Hill: University of North Carolina Press, 1989, 85–110.

Bristow, Peggy. 'A Duty to the Past, a Promise to the Future: Black Organizing in Windsor – The Depression, World War II, and the Post War Years.' *New Dawn: Journal of Black Canadian Studies* 2/1 (2007): 15–59.

– 'The Hour-a-Day Study Club,' in Linda Carty, ed., *And Still We Rise: Feminist Political Mobilizing in Contemporary Canada.* Toronto: Women's Press, 1993, 145–72.

– 'Whatever You Raise in the Ground, You Can Sell It in Chatham,' in Peggy Bristow et al., *'We're Rooted Here and They Can't Pull Us Up': Essays in African Canadian Women's History.* Toronto: University of Toronto Press, 1994, 67–142.

Brown, Jacqueline Nassy. 'Black Liverpool, Black America, and the Gendering of Diasporic Space.' *Cultural Anthropology* 13/3 (1998): 291–325.

Bryan, Beverley, Stella Dadzie, and Suzanne Scafe. *The Heart of the Race: Black Women's Lives in Britain.* London: Virago, 1985.

Bryce-Boodoo, M. 'A Fresh Look at Nursing Education in Trinidad and Tobago,' in *The Nursing Council of Trinidad and Tobago.* Port of Spain, 1976.

Burton, Antoinette, ed. *Archive Stories: Facts, Fictions, and the Writing of History.* Durham: Duke University Press, 2005.

Butler, Judith. *Undoing Gender.* New York: Routledge, 2004.

– *Gender Trouble: Feminism and the Subversion of Identity.* New York: Routledge, 1999.

Byron, Margaret. 'Migration, Work and Gender: The Case of Post-War Labour Migration from the Caribbean to Britain,' in M. Chamberlain, ed., *Caribbean Migration: Globalised Identities.* London: Routledge, 1998, 217–31.

Calliste, Agnes. 'Women of "Exceptional Merit": Immigration of Caribbean Nurses to Canada.' *Canadian Journal of Women and the Law* 6/1 (1993): 85–103.

Campbell, Carl C. *Endless Education: Main Currents in the Education System of Modern Trinidad and Tobago, 1939–1986.* Barbados: University of the West Indies Press, 1997.

– *The Young Colonials: A Social History of Education in Trinidad and Tobago, 1834–1939.* Barbados: University of the West Indies Press, 1996.

Carby, Hazel V. 'White Woman Listen! Black Feminism and the Boundaries of Sisterhood,' in Heidi Safia Mirza, ed., *Black British Feminism: A Reader.* New York: Routledge, 1997, 45–53. Originally published in Centre for Contemporary Cultural Studies, ed., *The Empire Strikes Back: Race and Racism in 70s Britain.* London: Routledge, 1983, 212–35.

Carter, Bob, Clive Harris, and Shirley Joshi. 'The 1951–1955 Conservative Government and the Racialization of Black Migration,' in Winston James and Clive Harris, eds., *Inside Babylon: The Caribbean Diaspora in Britain.* New York: Verso, 1993, 55–72.

Carty, Linda. 'African Canadian Women and the State: "Labour Only, Please,"' in Peggy Bristow et al., *'We're Rooted Here and They Can't Pull Us Up': Essays in African Canadian Women's History.* Toronto: University of Toronto Press, 1994, 193–229.

Cashmore, E. Ellis. *United Kingdom? Class, Race and Gender since the War.* London: Unwin Hyman, 1989.

Cassidy, Gale L., and Lorraine Davies. 'Explaining Gender Differences in Mastery among Married Parents.' *Social Psychology Quarterly* 66/1 (2003): 48–61.

Cassidy, Rosalind. 'Careers for Women.' *Journal of Educational Sociology* 17/8 (1944): 479–91.

Chamberlain, Mary. *Family Love in the Diaspora: Migration and the Anglo-Caribbean Experience.* New Brunswick, NJ: Transaction Publishers, 2006.

– 'The Family as Model and Metaphor in Caribbean Migration to Britain.' *Journal of Ethnic and Migration Studies* 25/2 (1999): 251–66.

– 'I Belong to Whoever Wants Me,' in B. Schwarz and P. Cohen, eds., 'Frontlines-Backyards,' special issue, *New Formations* 33 (1998): 47–58.

– *Narratives of Exile and Return.* London: Macmillan, 1997.

– ed. *Caribbean Migration: Globalized Identities.* New York: Routledge, 1998.

Chambers-Gordon, Sharon. '"Liberated in the Spirit": Telling the Lives of Jamaican Women in a Pentecostal/Revivalist Church.' *Women and Language* 24/2 (2001): 52–8.

'Changes in Women's Work Continuity.' *Canadian Social Trends.* (Autumn 1997). Statistics Canada Catalogue 11-008-XPE. Retrieved 13 July from 2008. http://www.statcan.ca/english/kits/pdf/social/women3.pdf.

Chevannes, Barry. *Rastafari: Roots and Ideology (Utopianism and Communitarians).* New York: Syracuse University Press, 1994.

Choy, Catherine Cenzia. *Empire of Care: Nursing and Migration in Filipino History.* Durham: Duke University Press, 2003.

'Churches Rapped!!! Grizzle, Moore Speak Out against Minstrel Shows.' *Canadian Negro* (1956): 1.

'City Parks: Alton Parker Park.' City of Windsor, Ontario, Canada. Retrieved 5 Nov. 2008 from http://www.citywindsor.ca/000350.asp?parks=alton.

Clark Hine, Darlene. *Black Women in White: Racial Conflict and Cooperation in the Nursing Profession, 1890–1950.* Bloomington: Indiana University Press, 1989.

– 'Rape and the Inner Lives of Black Women in the Middle West.' *Signs* 14 (Summer 1989): 912–20.

Clarke, Edith. *My Mother Who Fathered Me: A Study of the Families in Three Selected Communities in Jamaica.* Kingston, Jamaica: University of the West Indies Press, 1999.

Clarke, George Elliot, ed. *Eyeing the North Star: Directions in African-Canadian Literature.* Toronto: McClelland and Stewart, 1997.

Cliff, Michelle. *Abeng.* New York: Penguin, 1984.

Clifford, James. *Routes: Travel and Translation in the Late Twentieth Century.* Boston: Harvard University Press, 1999.

Conway, Martin A. 'Autobiographical Knowledge and Autobiographical Memories,' in David C. Rubin, ed., *Remembering Our Past: Studies in Autobiographical Memory.* Cambridge: Cambridge University Press, 1996, 67–93.

– *Autobiographical Memory: An Introduction.* Milton Keynes, UK: Open University Press, 1990.

Crawford, Charmaine. 'Black Women, Racing and Gendering the Canadian Nation,' in Notisha Massaquoi and Njoki Nathani Wane, eds., *Theorizing Empowerment: Canadian Perspectives on Black Feminist Thought.* Toronto: Inanna, 2007, 119–28.

Cunningham, James S., and Nadja Zalokar. 'The Economic Progress of Black Women, 1940–1980: Occupational Distribution and Relative Wages.' *Industrial and Labour Relations Review* 45/3 (1992): 540–55.

Daniels, Jean. 'The Woman's Window.' *Canadian Negro* (1956): 3.

D'Antonio, Patricia. *American Nursing: A History of Knowledge, Authority and the Meaning of Work.* Baltimore: Johns Hopkins University Press, 2010.

Davies, Carole Boyce. *Black Women Writing and Identity: Migrations of the Subject.* New York: Routledge, 1994.

Davies, Carol Boyce and Molara Ogundipe-Leslie. *Moving Beyond Boundaries: International Dimensions of Black Women's Writing,* vol. 1, New York: New York University Press, 1999.

Davies, Celia. *Gender and the Professional Predicament in Nursing.* London: Open University Press, 1995.

Dingwall, Robert, Anne Marie Rafferty, and Charles Webster. *An Introduction to the Social History of Nursing.* London: Routledge, 1988.

Dodd, Dianne. 'Commemorating Canadian Nursing.' Retrieved 15 April 2008 from http://crm.cr.nps.gov/archive/24-02/24-02-14.pdf

– 'Helen MacMurchy, Popular Midwifery and Maternity Services for Canadian Pioneer Women,' in Dianne Dodd and Deborah Gorman, eds., *Caring and Curing: Historical Perspectives on Women and Healing in Canada.* Ottawa: University of Ottawa Press, 1994, 135–62.

Dominion Bureau of Statistics, Education Statistics Branch, Education Bulletin no. 3, 'The Size Factor in One-Room Schools.' Ottawa: King's Printer. 1938.

Duncan, Carol B. '"Dey Give Me a House to Gather in di Chil'ren": Mothers and Daughters in the Spiritual Baptist Church.' *Canadian Woman Studies* 18/2–3 (1998): 126–31.

Dwyer, Claire. 'Negotiating Diasporic Identities: Youth South Asian Muslim Women.' *Women's Studies International Forum* 23/4 (2000): 475–86.

Ehrenreich, Barbara, and Dierdre English. 'Science and the Ascent of the Experts (Exorcising the Midwives),' in Barbara Ehrenreich and Dierdre English, eds., *For Her Own Good: 150 Years of the Experts' Advice to Women.* New York: Anchor, 1978, 69–100.

Elder, Glen H., Jr, John Modell, and Ross D. Parke, eds. *Children in Time and Place: Development and Historical Insights.* New York: Cambridge University Press, 1994.

Erskine, Noel Leo. *From Garvey to Marley: Rastafari Theology.* Gainesville: University Press of Florida, 2005.

Essed, Philomena. *Everyday Racism: Reports from Women of Two Cultures.* Alameda, CA: Hunter House, 1990.

Etowa, Josephine, et al. 'Depression: The "Invisible Grey Fog" Influencing the Midlife Health of African Canadian *Women.' International Journal of Mental Health Nursing* 16/3 (2007): 203–13.

Fairman, Julie. 'Not All Nurses Are Good, Not All Doctors Are Bad …' *Bulletin of the History of Medicine* 78/2 (2004): 451–60 (Review).

Fergus, Howard A. *A History of Education in the British Leeward Islands, 1838–1945.* Kingston, Jamaica: University of the West Indies Press, 2003.

Ferguson, Jeffrey. 'Race and the Rhetoric of Resistance.' *Raritan* 28 (2008): 4–32.

Flynn, Karen. 'Beyond the Glass Wall: Black Canadian Nurses, 1940–1970.' *Nursing History Review* 17 (2009): 129–52.

– 'Experience and Identity: Black Immigrant Nurses to Canada, 1950–1980,' in Marlene Epp, Franca Iacovetta, and Frances Swyripa, eds., *Sisters or Strangers: Immigrant, Ethnic, and Racialized Women in Canadian History.* Toronto: University of Toronto Press, 2004, 381–98.

– '"I'm Glad that Someone Is Telling the Nursing Story": Writing Black Cana-
   dian Women's History.' *Journal of Black Canadian Studies* 38/3 (2008): 443–60.
– 'Nurses in Resistance,' in Sophie G. Harding, ed., *Surviving the Hour of Darkness: The Health and Wellness of Women of Colour and Indigenous Women*. Calgary:
   University of Calgary Press, 2005, 3–12.
Foner, Nancy. 'Male and Female: Jamaican Migrants in London.' In 'Women
   and Migration,' special issue, *Anthropological Quarterly* (1976): 32–3.
– 'Women, Work and Migration: Jamaicans in London.' *Urban Anthropology* 4/3
   (1975): 229–49.
Forcey, Linda Rennie. 'Feminist Perspectives on Mothering and Peace,' in Eve-
   lyn Nakano Glenn, Grace Change, and Linda Rennie Forcey, eds., *Mothering:
   Ideology, Experience, and Agency*. New York: Routledge, 1994, 355–76.
Foucault, Michel. *Power/Knowledge*. London: Macmillan, 1980.
Fraser, Carey. *Ambivalent Anti-Colonialism: The United States and the Genesis of West
   Indian Independence, 1940–1964*. Westport, CT: Greenwood, 1994.
Fraser, Nancy. 'Rethinking Recognition.' *New Left Review* 3 (May–June 2000):
   107–20.
'Frustrated.' *Nursing Times* (5 Dec. 1958): 1426.
Gamarnikov, Ema. 'Sexual Division of Labour: The Case of the Nursing,' in
   Annette Kuhn and AnneMarie Wolpe, eds., *Feminism and Materialism: Women
   and Modes of Production*. Boston: Routledge, 1978., 96–123.
Gill, Margaret D. 'Nursing Politics and Social Change in the Caribbean: The
   Nita Barrow Years,' in Ruth Nita Barrow, Eudine Barriteau, and Alan Cobley,
   eds., *Stronger, Surer, Bolder: Social Change and International Development*. King-
   ston, Jamaica: University of the West Indies Press, 2001, 49–76.
Gillborn, D. 'Education Policy as an Act of White Supremacy: Whiteness, Critical Race Theory and Eucation.' Retrieved 4 Nov. 2010 from http://eprints.
   ioe.ac.uk/1654/1/gillborn2005education485text.pdf.
Gluck, Sherna Berger. 'What's So Special about Women? Women's Oral His-
   tory,' in Susan H. Armitage, Patricia Hart, and Karen Weathermon, eds.,
   Women's Oral History: The Frontiers Reader. Lincoln: University of Nebraska
   Press, 2002, 3–20.
Golding, John S.R. *Ascent to Mona as Illustrated by a Short History of Jamaican Medi-
   cal Care with an Account of the Beginning of the Faculty of Medicine, University of the
   West Indies*. Kingston, Jamaica: University of the West Indies Press, 1994.
Goldstein, Rhoda L. 'Negro Nurses in Hospitals.' *American Journal of Nursing*
   60/2 (1960): 215–17.
Gooden, Amoaba. 'Community Organizing by African Caribbean People in
   Toronto, Ontario.' *Journal of Black Studies* 38/3 (2008), 413–26.
Governor General of Canada. 'Queen Elizabeth II Golden Jubilee Medal.' Re-
   trieved 22 Nov. 2007 from http://gg.ca/honours/medals/hon04-qegj_e.asp.

Grizzel, Stanley. *My Name Is Not George: The Story of the Brotherhood of Sleeping Car Porters in Canada*. Toronto: Umbrella Press, 1998.

Growe, Sarah Jane. *Who Cares? The Crisis in Canadian Nursing*. Toronto: Canadian Publishers, 1991, 157.

Gupta, Tania Das. *Racism and Paid Work*. Toronto: Garamond, 1996.

Hagey, Rebecca, et al. 'Immigrant Nurses' Experience of Racism.' *Journal of Nursing Scholarship* 33/4 (2001): 389–94.

Haight, Wendy L. *African-American Children at Church: A Socio-Cultural Perspective*. Cambridge: Cambridge University Press, 2002.

Hall, Stuart. 'Negotiating Caribbean Identities.' *New Left Review* 209 (1995): 3–14.

– 'Old and New Identities, Old and New Ethnicities,' in Les Back and John Solomos, eds., *Theories of Race and Racism: A Reader*. New York: Routledge, 2000, 144–53.

– 'Thinking the Diaspora: Home-Thoughts from Abroad.' *Small Axe* 6 (1999): 1–19.

Hallam, Julia. *Nursing the Image: Media, Culture and Professional Identity*. London: Routledge, 2000.

Hamilton, Sylvia. *The Little Black School House*. Maroon Films, 2007.

– 'The Women at the Well: African Baptist Women Organize,' in Linda Carty, ed., *And Still We Rise: Feminist Political Mobilizing in Contemporary Canada*. Toronto: Women's Press, 1993, 189–203.

Harrigan, Patrick J. 'The Schooling of Boys and Girls in Canada.' *Journal of Social History* 23/4 (1990): 803–16.

Harris, Clive. 'Post War Migration and Industrial Reserve Army,' in Winston James and Clive Harris, eds., *Inside Babylon: The Caribbean Diaspora in Britain*. New York: Verso, 1993, 9–54.

Harwood, V., and M.L. Rasmussen. 'Performativity, Youth, and Injurious Speech.' *Teaching Education* 14/1 (2003): 25–36.

Hay Ho Sang, Pamela Elizabeth. 'The Development of Nursing Education in Jamaica, West Indies, 1900–1975.' Ed.D. dissertation, Columbia University Teachers College, 1985.

Henry, Frances. *Reclaiming African Religions in Trinidad: The Socio-Political Legitimation of the Orisha and Spiritual Baptist Faiths*. Trinidad and Tobago: University of the West Indies Press, 2003.

– et al. *The Colour of Democracy: Racism in Canadian Society*, 2nd ed. Toronto: Harcourt Brace, 2000.

Herbert, Joanna. *Negotiating Boundaries in the City: Migration, Ethnicity, and Gender in Britain*. Aldershot: Ashgate, UK, 2008.

Hernandez-Ramdwar, Camille. 'The Elusive and Illusionary: Identifying of Me,

Not by Me,' in Carl E. James and Adrienne Shadd, eds., *Talking about Identity: Encounters in Race, Ethnicity and Language.* Toronto: Between the Lines, 2001, 115–21.

Hewitt, Hermi Hyacinth. *Trailblazers in Nursing: A Caribbean Perspective, 1946–1986.* Barbados: Canoe Press, 2002.

Hezekiah, Jocelyn. *Breaking the Glass Ceiling: The Stories of Three Caribbean Nurses.* Kingston, Jamaica: University of the West Indies Press, 2001.

Higginbotham, Evelyn Brooks. *Righteous Discontent: The Women's Movement in the Black Baptist Church, 1880–1920.* Cambridge: Harvard University Press, 1993.

– 'African-Americans and the Metalanguage of Race.' *Signs* 17/2 (1992): 251–74.

Hill, Clifford. *West Indian Migrants and the London Churches* London: Oxford University Press, 1963.

Hill, Clifford. 'From Church to Sect: West Indian Religious Sect Development in Britain.' *Journal for the Scientific Study of Religion,* 10/ 2 (1971): 114–12.

Hill Collins, Patricia. *From Black Power to Hip-Hop: Racism, Nationalism, and Feminism.* Philadelphia: Temple University Press, 2006.

– *Black Feminist Thought: Knowledge, Consciousness, and the Politics of Empowerment,* rev. ed. New York: Routledge, 2000.

Hill, Daniel G. 'Negroes in Toronto: A Sociological Study of a Minority Group.' Doctoral dissertation, University of Toronto, 1960.

Hill, Lawrence. *Trails and Triumphs of African-Canadians.* Toronto: Umbrella Press, 1996.

Hill, Shirley A. 'Class, Race and Gender: Dimensions of Childrearing in African-American Families.' *Journal of Black Studies* 31/4 (2001): 494–508.

Hochschild, Arlie, with Annie Machung. *The Second Shift: Working Parents and the Revolution at Home.* New York: Viking Penguin, 1989.

Hodge, Merle. 'We Kind of Family,' in Patricia Mohammed, ed., *Gendered Realities: Essays in Caribbean Feminist Thought.* Kingston, Jamaica: University of the West Indies Press, 2002, 474–85.

– 'Young Women and the Development of a Stable Family Life in the Caribbean,' in L. Mathurin, ed., *Savacou* 13/11 (Gemini 1977), 39–44.

Hope, E.M. '"Island Systems and the Paradox of Freedom": Migration in the Post-Emancipation Leeward Islands,' in K.F. Olwig, ed., *Small Islands, Large Questions: Society, Culture and Resistance in the Post-Emancipation Caribbean Society.* Ilford, UK: Frank Cass, 1995, 161–78.

'Hopes Race Bylaw Is Enforced.' *Dawn of Tomorrow* (Sept. 1944): 2.

'Hotel London Discharges Colored Help and Replaces Them with White Ex-Service Men.' *Dawn of Tomorrow* 6 (April 1934): 2.

Hucks, Tracey E., and Dianne M. Stewart. 'Authenticity and Authority in the

Shaping of the Trinidad Orisha Identity: Toward an African-Derived Religious Theory.' *Western Journal of Black Studies* 27 (2003): 176–85.

Iacovetta, Franca. 'Manly Militants, Cohesive Communities, and Defiant Domestics: Writing about Immigrants in Canadian Historical Scholarship.' *Labour/
Le Travail* no. 36 (1995): 227–34.

James, Winston. 'The Black Experience in Twentieth-Century Britain,' in
Phillip D. Morgan and Sean Hawkins, eds., *Black Experience and the Empire.*
London: Oxford University Press, 2004, 347–86.

– 'Migration, Racism and Identity Formation: The Caribbean Experience in
Britain,' in Winston James and Clive Harris, eds., *Inside Babylon: The Caribbean
Diaspora in Britain.* New York: Verso, 1993, 231–88.

Jones, Claudia. 'The Caribbean Community in Britain,' in Winston James and
Clive Harris, eds., *Inside Babylon: The Caribbean Diaspora in Britain.* New York:
Verso, 1993, 49–57.

Joseph, Suad. 'Women, Nation, State in Lebanon,' in Caren Kaplan, Norma
Alarcón, and Minoo Moallem, eds., *Between Women and Nation: Nationalisms,
Transnational Feminisms, and the State.* Durham: Duke University Press, 1999,
162–81.

Kempadoo, Kamala. *Sexing the Caribbean: Gender, Race, and Sexual Labor.* New
York: Routledge, 2004.

Kennedy, David. *The Well of Being: Childhood, Subjectivity, and Education.* New
York: State University of New York Press, 2006.

King, Ruby V. Grannum, "The Importance of Post Graduate Education for Graduate Nurses," Caribbean Nurses Organisation, Conference, Barbados, 1959.

Kinnear, Mary. *In Subordination: Professional Women, 1870–1970.* Montreal and
Kingston: McGill-Queen's University Press, 1995.

Kramer, Ann. *Many Rivers to Cross: The History of the Caribbean Contribution to the
NHS.* London: Sugar Media, 2006.

Kyte, Jack, et al. *Native Born: A Brief History of the Black Presence in Pictou County:
The World Wars.* Retrieved 25 April 2010 from http://www.parl.ns.ca/native-
born/wars.htm.

Lamberston, Ross. '"The Dresden Story": Racism, Human Rights and the Jewish
Labour Committee of Canada.' *Labour/Le Travail* no. 47 (2001): 1–36.

Lemke-Santangelo, Gretchen. *Abiding Courage: African-American Migrant Women
and the East Bay Community.* Chapel Hill: University of North Carolina Press,
1996.

Leonard, Pauline. 'Migrating Identities: Gender, Whiteness, and Britishness in
Post-Colonial Hong Kong.' *Gender Place and Culture* 15/1 (2008): 45–60.

– 'Playing Doctors and Nurses: Competing Discourses of Gender, Power and
Identity in the British National Health Service.' *Sociological Review* 51/2
(2003): 218–37.

Levitt, Peggy. 'Social Remittances: A Local-Level, Migration-Driven Form of Cultural Diffusion.' *International Migration Review* 32/124 (1999): 926–49.

Levy, Andrea. *Small Island*. London: Headline, 2004.

Lewis, Gail. 'Situated Voices: "Black Women's Experience" and Social Work.' *Feminist Review* 53 (Summer 1996): 24–56.

– 'Black Women's Employment and the British Economy,' in Winston James and Clive Harris, eds., *Inside Babylon: The Caribbean Diaspora in Britain*. New York: Verso, 1993, 73–96.

Lewis, Norah L., ed. *Freedom to Play: We Made Our Own Fun*. Waterloo: Wilfrid Laurier University Press, 2002.

Litoff, Judy Barrett. 'Midwifery and History,' in Rima Apple, ed., *Women, Health, and Medicine in America: A Historical Handbook*. New York: Garland, 1990, 443–58.

Loomba, Ania. *Colonialism/Post Colonialism*. London: Routledge, 1998.

Lorde, Audre. *Zami: A New Spelling of My Name*. Watertown, MA: Persephone, 1982.

Lucal, Betsy. 'What It Means to Be Gendered Me: Life on the Boundaries of a Dichotomous Gendered System.' *Gender and Society* 13/6 (Dec. 1999): 781–97.

Mackey, Eva. *The House of Difference: Cultural Politics and National Identity in Canada*. New York: Routledge, 1999.

Mama, Amina. *Beyond Masks: Race, Gender and Subjectivity*. New York: Routledge, 1995.

Manley, Beverley. *The Manley Memoirs*. Kingston, Jamaica: Ian Randle, 2008.

Marland, Hilary, and Anne Marie Rafferty, eds. *Midwives, Society, and Childbirth: Debates and Controversies in the Modern Period*. London: Routledge, 1997.

Marshall, Paule. *Brown Girl, Brownstones*. New York: Feminist Press, 1996.

Mason, Karen M., and Tanya Zanish-Belcher. 'Raising the Archival Consciousness: How Women's Archives Challenge Traditional Approaches to Collecting and Use, or What's in a Name?' *Library Trends* 56/2 (2007): 344–59.

Massaquoi, Notisha, and Njoki Nathani Wane, eds. *Theorizing Empowerment: Canadian Perspectives on Black Feminist Thought*. Toronto: Inanna, 2007.

Mayers, Janice. 'Access to Secondary Education for Girls in Barbados, 1907–1943: A Preliminary Analysis,' in Verene Shepherd, Bridget Brereton, Barbara Bailey, eds., *Engendering History: Caribbean Women in Historical Perspective*. New York: St Martin's Press, 1995, 258–78.

McKittrick, Katherine. *Demonic Grounds: Black Women and the Cartographies of Struggle*. Minneapolis: University of Minnesota Press, 2006.

McLean-Wilson, Clare. 'A Triumph of Will.' *Northern Terminus: The African Canadian History Journal* 3/7 (2006): 7–8.

McPherson, Kathryn. *Bedside Matters: The Transformation of Canadian Nursing, 1900–1990*. Toronto: Oxford University Press, 1996.

– '"The Case of the Kissing Nurse": Femininity, Sexuality, and Canadian Nursing, 1900–1970,' in Kathryn McPherson, Cecilia Morgan, and Nancy M. Forestell, eds., *Gendered Pasts: Historical Essays in Femininity and Masculinity in Canada.* London: Oxford University Press, 1999, 179–98.

Melosh, Barbara. *'The Physician's Hand': Work, Culture and Conflict in American Nursing.* Philadelphia: Temple University Press, 1982.

Mignon, Duffy. 'Reproducing Labor Inequalities: Challenges for Feminists Conceptualizing Care at the Intersections of Gender, Race, and Class.' *Gender and Society* 19/1 (2005): 66–82.

Modibo, Najja Nwofia. 'The Shattered Dreams of African-Canadian Nurses.' *Canadian Woman Studies* 23/2 (2004): 111–17.

Morrissey, Marietta. 'Explaining the Caribbean Family,' in Christine Barrow, ed., *Caribbean Portraits: Essays on Gender Ideologies and Identities.* Kingston, Jamaica: Ian Randle, 1998, 79–90.

Morton, Desmond. 'When Canada Won the War.' *Canadian Historical Association Historical Booklet* no. 54 (1995): 1–34.

'Multicultural Theatre.' *The Canadian Encyclopedia: The Encyclopedia of Music in Canada.* Retrieved 3 Dec. 2007 from http://www.thecanadianencyclopedia.com/index.cfm?PgNm=TCE&Params=A1SEC886006.

Murrell, Nathaniel Samuel, William David Spencer, and Adrian Anthony McFarlane, eds. *Chanting Down Babylon: The Rastafaria Reader.* Philadelphia: Temple University Press, 1998.

Mussaleem, Helen. 'Manpower Problem in Nursing.' *Canadian Nurse* 63/8 (1967): 25–8.

Nakano Glenn, Evelyn. *Issei, Nisei, War Bride: Three Generations of Japanese American Women in Domestic Service.* Philadelphia: Temple University Press, 1986.

'Negro Girl Popular Nurse, Guelph.' *Toronto Evening Telegram* (28 Feb. 1950): 10.

Nestel, Sheryl. *Obstructed Labour: Race and Gender in the Re-emergence of Midwifery.* Vancouver: UBC Press, 2006.

Nova Scotia. *Annual Report of the Superintendent of Education for Nova Scotia.* 1 July 1933, 176.

Nuffield Provincial Hospitals Trust. *The Work of Nurses in Hospital Wards: Report of Job-Analysis.* London: Nuffield Provincial Hospitals Trust, 1953.

Oakley, Ann. *Essays on Women, Medicine and Health.* Edinburgh: Edinburgh University Press, 1993.

Oliver, Reverend W.P. 'The Negro in Nova Scotia.' *Nova Scotia Journal of Education* 13 (Feb. 1964): 18–21.

Olwig, K.F. 'The Migration Experience: Nevisian Women at Home and Abroad,' in J. Momsen, ed., *Women and Change in the Caribbean.* London: James Curry, 1993, 159–66.

– ed. *Small Islands, Large Questions: Society, Culture and Resistance in the Post-Emancipation Caribbean Society*. Ilford, UK: Frank Cass, 1995.

Ontario Federation of Labour and the Workers Arts and Heritage Centre. 'A History of Women and Work.' Retrieved 7 Aug. 2009 from http://www.ofl.ca/uploads/misc/womenandwork/A_HISTORY_OF_WOMEN_AND_WORK_amended_Jan_11_(2).pdf.

Pachai, Bridglal and Henry Bishop. *Images of Our Past: Historic Black Nova Scotia*. Halifax: Nimbus, 2006.

Page, Kezia. '"What If He Did Not Have a Sister [Who Lived in the United States]?" Jamaica Kincaid's *My Brother* as Remittance Text.' *Small Axe: A Caribbean Journal of Criticism* 10/3 (2006): 37–53.

Palmer, Colin A. 'Defining and Studying the Modern African Diaspora.' *Journal of Negro History* 85/1–2 (2000): 27–52.

Palmer, Ransford, ed. *In Search of a Better Life: Perspectives on Migration from the Caribbean*. New York: Praeger, 1990.

Peach, Ceri. *West Indian Migration to Britain: A Social Geography*. London: Oxford University Press, 1968.

Peach, G.C.K. 'West Indian Migration to Britain.' *International Migration Review* 1/2 (Spring 1967): 34–45.

– 'Factors Affecting the Distribution of West Indians in Great Britain.' *Transactions of the Institute of British Geographers* 38 (June 1966): 151–63.

Pearson, David G. 'Race, Religiosity and Political Activism: Some Observations on West Indian Participation in Britain.' *British Journal of Sociology* 29/ 3 (1978): 340–57.

Peneff, Jean. 'Myths in Life Stories,' in Raphael Samuel and Paul Thompson, eds., *The Myths We Live By*. London: Routledge, 1990, 36–48.

Peters, Marie Ferguson. 'Parenting of Young Black Children in Black Families: A Historical Note,' in Harriette Pipes McAdoo, ed., *Black Families*, 4th ed. Twin Oaks, CA: Sage, 2007, 203–14.

Philips, Deborah, and Alan Tomlinson. 'Homeward-Bound Leisure, Popular Culture and Consumer Capitalism,' in Dominic Strinati and Stephen Wagg, eds., *Come on Down: Popular Media Culture in Post-War Britain*. New York: Routledge, 1992, 9–45.

Phoenix, A. 'Theories of Gender and Black Families,' in Gaby Weiner and Madeleine Arnot, eds., *Gender under Scrutiny: New Enquiries in Education*. London: Hutchison, 1987, 50–61.

Pierson, Ruth Roach. *They're Still Women after All: The Second World War and Canadian Womanhood*. Toronto: McClelland and Stewart, 1986.

Pilkington, Andre. *Racial Disadvantage and Ethnic Diversity in Britain*. Basingstoke, UK: Palgrave Macmillan, 2003.

Pilkington, Edward. *Beyond the Mother Country: West Indians and the Notting Hill White Riots.* London: I.B. Tauris, 1988.

Pitt, Susan. 'Midwifery and Medicine: Gendered Knowledge in the Practice of Delivery,' in Hilary Marland and Anne Marie Rafferty, eds., *Midwives, Society and Childbirth: Debates and Controversies in the Modern Period.* London: Routledge, 1997, 218–32.

Polletta, Francesca, and James M. Jasper. 'Collective Identity and Social Movements.' *Annual Review of Sociology* 27 (2001): 283–305.

Ponzanesi, Sandra, and Daniela Merolla, eds. *Migrant Cartographies: New Cultural and Literary Spaces in Post Colonial Europe.* Lanham, MD: Lexington Books, 2005.

Prince, Althea. *Being Black: Essays by Althea Prince.* Toronto: Insomniac Press, 2001

Purdy, Sean. '"It Was Tough on Everybody": Low-Income Families and Housing Hardship in Post–World War II Toronto.' *Journal of Social History* 37/2 (2003): 457–82.

Rassool, Naz. 'Fractured or Flexible Identities? Life Histories of "Black" Diasporic Women in Britain,' in Heidi Safia Mirza, ed., *Black British Feminism: A Reader.* London: Routledge, 1997, 187–204.

Razack, Sherene H. *Looking White People in the Eye: Gender, Race and Culture in Courtrooms and Classrooms.* Toronto: University of Toronto Press, 1998.

Reynolds, Tracey. 'Black Mothering, Paid Work and Identity.' *Ethnic and Racial Studies* 24/6 (2001): 1046–64.

Richmond, Anthony H. *Colour Prejudice in Britain: A Study of West Indian Workers in Liverpool, 1941–1951.* London: Routledge and Kegan Paul, 1954.

Ridgeway, Cecilia L., and Shelley J. Correll. 'Unpacking the Gender System: A Theoretical Perspective on Gender Beliefs and Social Relations.' *Gender and Society* 18/4 (2004): 510–31.

Ridley Malson, Michelene. 'Black Women's Sex Roles: The Social Context for a New Ideology.' *Journal of Social Issues* 39/3 (1983): 101–13.

Robertson, Claire. 'Africa in the Americas?' in David Barry Gasper and Darlene Clarke Hine, eds., *More than Chattel: Black Women and Slavery in the Americas.* Bloomington: Indiana University Press, 1996, 3–40.

Robinson, John A. 'Perspective, Meaning and Remembering,' in David C. Rubin, ed., *Remembering Our Past: Studies in Autobiographical Memory.* Cambridge: Cambridge University Press, 1996, 199–217.

Romain, Gemma. *Connecting Histories: A Comparative Exploration of African-Caribbean and Jewish History and Memory in Modern Britain.* London: Kegan Paul, 2006.

Rose, E.J.B., et al. *Colour and Citizenship: A Report on British Race Relations.* London: Oxford University Press, 1969.

Russell, Sheila Mackay. '"The Glass Wall": A New Chapter in the Human Drama in a Hospital.' *Chatelaine* (Oct. 1964): 27, 67–73.

Rutherford, Jonathon. 'A Place Called Home: Identity and the Cultural Politics of Difference,' in Jonathon Rutherford, ed., *Identity, Community, Culture and Difference.* London: Lawrence and Wishart, 1990, 9–27.

Sangster, Joan. *Earning Respect: The Lives of Working Women in Small Town Ontario, 1920–1960.* Toronto: University of Toronto Press, 1995.

Schneider, Wolfgang, and Michael Pressley. *Memory Development between Two and Twenty.* New Brunswick, NJ: Lawrence Erlbaum, 1997.

Senior, Olive. *Working Miracles: Women's Lives in the English-Speaking Caribbean.* Bloomington: Indiana University Press, 1991.

Shadd-Evelyn, Karen. *I'd Rather Live in Buxton.* Toronto: Simone and Pierre, 1996.

Shand, Gwendolyn V. 'Adult Education among the Negroes in Nova Scotia.' *Nova Scotia Journal of Education* 5/10 (1961): 3–13.

Shkimba, Margaret, and Karen Flynn. 'In England We Did Nursing: Caribbean and British Nurses in Great Britain and Canada, 1950–1970,' in Susan McGann and Barbara Mortimer, eds., *New Directions in Nursing History: International Perspectives.* New York: Routledge, 2004, 141–57.

Shreve, Dorothy Shadd. *The AfriCanadian Church: A Stabilizer.* Grand Rapids, MI: Paideia Books, 1983.

Silvera, Makeda. *Silenced: Talks with Working-Class Caribbean Women about Their Lives and Struggles as Domestic Workers in Canada.* Toronto: Sister Vision Press, 1983.

Simmons, Alan B., and Dwaine E. Plaza. 'The Caribbean Community in Canada: Transnational Connections and Transformations,' in Lloyd Wong and Vic Satzewich, eds., *Transnational Identities and Practices in Canada.* Vancouver: UBC Press, 2006, 130–49.

Singer, Jefferson A., and Martin A. Conway, 'Should We Forget Forgetting?' *Memory Studies* 1/3 (2008): 279–85.

Slevin, Kathleen F. 'Intergenerational and Community Responsibility: Race Uplift Work in the Retirement Activities of Professional African American Women.' *Journal of Aging Studies* 19/3 (2005): 309–26.

Smith, Barbara, ed. *Home Girls: A Black Feminist Anthology.* New York: Kitchen Table Press, 1983.

Smith, M.G. *West Indian Family Structure.* Seattle: University of Washington Press, 1962.

Smith, R.T. 'The Matrifocal Family,' in Jack Goody, ed., *The Character of Kinship.* Cambridge: Cambridge University Press, 1973, 121–44.

Smith, Raymond T. *The Negro Family in British Guiana: Family Structure and Social*

Status in the Villages. London: Routledge and Kegan Paul, in association with the Institute of Social and Economic Research, University College of the West Indies, Jamaica, 1956.

Smith, Zadie. *White Teeth.* New York: Random House, 2000.

Solomos, John. *Race and Racism in Britain.* 2nd ed. New York: St Martin's Press, 1993.

Spencer, R.G. *British Immigration Policy since 1939: The Making of Multi-Racial Britain.* New York: Routledge, 1997.

Srigley, Katrina. '"In Case You Hadn't Noticed!" Race, Ethnicity, and Women's Wage-Earning in a Depression-Era City.' *Labour/LeTravail* no. 55 (2005): 69–105.

Steedman, Carolyn. *Past Tenses: Essays on Writing, Autobiography and History.* London: Rivers Osram Press, 1992.

Strinati, Dominic, and Stephen Wagg. *Come on Down: Popular Media Culture in Post-War Britain.* Routledge: New York, 1992.

Sugiman, Pamela. 'Passing Time, Moving Memories: Interpreting Wartime Narratives of Japanese Canadian Women.' *Histoire sociale/Social History* 36/73 (2004): 51–79.

– 'Privilege and Oppression: The Configuration of Race, Gender, and Class in Southern Ontario Auto Plants, 1939 to 1949.' *Labour/Le Travail* no. 47 (2001): 83–114.

Sutherland, Neil. *Growing Up: Childhood in English Canada from the Great War to the Age of Television.* Toronto: University of Toronto Press, 1997.

Sutton, Constance, and Susan Makiesky-Barrow. 'Social Inequality and Sexual Status in Barbados,' in Christine Barrow and Rhoda Reddock, eds., *Caribbean Sociology: Introductory Readings.* Kingston, Jamaica: Ian Randle, 2001, 371–88.

'Take Action.' *Clarion* 1/1 (1946).

Talbot, Carol. *Growing Up Black in Canada.* Toronto: Williams-Wallace, 1984.

Tatum, Beverly. *'Why Are All the Black Kids Sitting Together in the Cafeteria?' and Other Conversations about Race.* New York: Basic Books, 1999.

Taylor, R.J., et al. 'Development of Research on Black Families: A Decade Review.' *Journal of Marriage and the Family* 52 (1990): 993–1014.

Taylor, Ula Y. *The Veiled Garvey: The Life and Times of Amy Jacques Garvey.* Chapel Hill: University of North Carolina Press, 2002.

'The Welfare of the Coloured People.' *Nursing Times* (5 Dec. 1958): 1426.

Theobald, Robin. 'The Politicization of a Religious Movement: British Adventism under the Impact of West Indian Immigration.' *British Journal of Sociology* 32/2 (1981): 202–23.

Thomas-Hope, Elizabeth. *Caribbean Migration.* Kingston, Jamaica: University of the West Indies Press, 2002.

Thompson, Anne. 'Establishing the Scope of Practice: Organizing European Midwifery in the Inter-War Years 1919–1938,' in Hilary Marland and Anne Marie Rafferty, eds., *Midwives, Society, and Childbirth: Debates and Controversies in the Modern Period.* London: Routledge, 1997, 14–37.

Thompson, Becky, and Sangeeta Tyagi. *Names We Call Home: Autobiography on Racial Identity.* New York: Routledge, 1996.

Toman, Cynthia. '"Body Work": Nurses and the Delegation of Medical Technology at the Ottawa Civic Hospital, 1947–1972.' *Scientia Canadensis* 29/2 (2006): 155–75.

Toulis, Nicole Rodriguez. *Believing Identity: Pentecostalism and the Mediation of Jamaican Ethnicity and Gender in England.* Oxford: Berg, 1997.

Turner, Victor. 'Social Dramas and Stories about Them,' in W.J.T. Mitchell, ed., *On Narrative.* Chicago: University of Chicago Press, 1981, 137–64.

– 'Betwixt and Between: The Liminal Period in *Rites de Passage*,' in *The Forest of Symbols: Aspects of Ndembu Ritual.* New York: Cornell University Press, 1967, 93–111.

Vickerman, Milton. *Cross Currents: West Indian Immigrants and Race.* New York: Oxford University Press, 1999.

Walcott, Remaldo. *Black Like Who? Writing Black Canada.* Toronto: Insomniac Press, 1997.

Walker, James. *Racial Discrimination in Canada: The Black Experience.* Ottawa: Canadian Historical Association, 1985.

Waters, Chris. '"Dark Strangers" in Our Midst: Discourses of Race and Nation in Britain, 1947–1963.' *Journal of British Studies* 36 (April 1997): 207–38.

Webster, Charles. *National Health Care Service: A Political History.* Oxford: Oxford University Press, 1997.

Webster, Wendy. *Imagining Home: Gender, Race and National Identity, 1945–64.* London: UCL Press, 1998.

Weedon, Chris. *Feminist Practice and Poststructuralist Theory.* Oxford: Basil Blackwell, 1989.

– *Identity and Culture: Narratives of Difference and Belonging.* London: Open University Press, 2004.

West India Royal Commission Report. Cmd. 6607 (June 1945), as quoted in Hermi Hyacinth Hewitt, *Trailblazers in Nursing Education: A Caribbean Perspective, 1946–1986.* Barbados: Canoe Press, 2002.

Windsor Mosaic. 'The Hour-a-Day Study Club.' Retrieved 21 June 2010 from http://www.windsor-communities.com/african-organ-studyclub.php.

Winks, Robin W. *The Blacks in Canada: A History.* 2nd ed. Montreal: McGill-Queen's University Press, 1997.

Witz, Anne. 'Medical Men and Midwives,' in Anne Witz, *Professions and Patriar-chy*. New York: Routledge, 1992, chapter 4.

Wong, Lloyd, and Vic Satzewich, eds. *Transnational Identities and Practices in Canada*. Vancouver: UBC Press, 2006.

Woods, H.D., and Sylvia Ostry. *Labour Policy and Labour Economics in Canada*. Toronto: Macmillan, 1962.

Woodward, Kath. *Questioning Identity: Gender, Class, Ethnicity*. New York: Routledge, 2004.

Wortham, Robert A. 'W.E.B. Dubois, the Black Church and the Sociological Study of Religion.' *Sociological Spectrum* 29/2 (2009): 144–72.

Yancey, George. 'Introduction: Situated Black Women's Voices in/on the Pro-fession of Philosophy.' *Hypatia* 23/2 (2008): 155–9.

Zanish-Belcher, Tanya, and Karen M. Mason. 'Raising the Archival Conscious-ness: How Women's Archives Challenge Traditional Approaches to Collecting and Use, or What's in a Name?' *Library Trends* 56/2 (2007): 344–59.

Zukewich Ghalam, Nancy. 'Attitudes towards Women, Work and Family.' *Canadian Social Trends* 46 (Autumn 1997): 13–18.

Index

abuse: in the family, 4–5; from patients, 154. *See also* punishment

activism, 4, 38, 133, 185–6, 204, 211–13, 220, 225, 227, 256n60

Africa, 153; in diaspora, 7–8, 164, 225. *See also* African Americans; African descent; African traditions; Black Atlantic; Black Canadians; Black Church; diaspora

African Americans, 64, 129, 131, 148, 186, 217, 223, 243n20; and health care, 131, 264n12, 265n21

African descent, 10, 60, 198, 204

African traditions, 193, 242n19

agency, 12, 42, 46, 125, 166, 173, 207, 219

Antigua, 13, 32, 39, 51, 68, 74, 76–7, 96, 127, 139, 195, 206–7

apprenticeship, 13, 94, 105, 107–8, 123, 159

Baptist Church, 60–1, 66, 69, 170, 178, 187, 242n19, 252nn73, 74. *See also* Black Church; Christianity; religion

Barbados, 13, 18, 57, 62, 73, 79, 96, 98, 101–2, 123, 138, 193, 205–7

Bhabha, Homi, 10, 83, 104

Black Atlantic, 6

Black Canadians, 6, 20–1, 24, 47, 55, 62, 129, 150, 177, 190, 194, 199, 201, 209–10, 213–14, 216–17, 221, 225, 276n92

Black Church, 8, 60–1, 70, 243n20, 252nn70, 73, 74

Black Power, 118, 183

Boyce Davies, Carol, 85

Bristow, Peggy, 22, 242n14, 246n17, 249n73, 258n4, 276n89

Butler, Judith, 10, 95, 103–4, 108, 111, 261n43. *See also* gender performance

Caribbean: culture, 19, 53, 83, 208, 214; diaspora, 8, 246n13; identity, 192–3; region, 9–11; studies, 7. *See also* diaspora

Catholicism, 8–9, 36, 60, 69, 76, 178, 195. *See also* Christianity; religion

child care, 16, 18–19, 30, 165–72. *See also* children

childhood, 4, 6, 14, 17–18, 20–1, 24, 28, 35, 40–1, 98, 134, 148–9, 153, 163, 176, 199–200, 215–16, 218–19,

STUDIES IN GENDER AND HISTORY

General editors: Franca Iacovetta and Karen Dubinsky